MW00581486

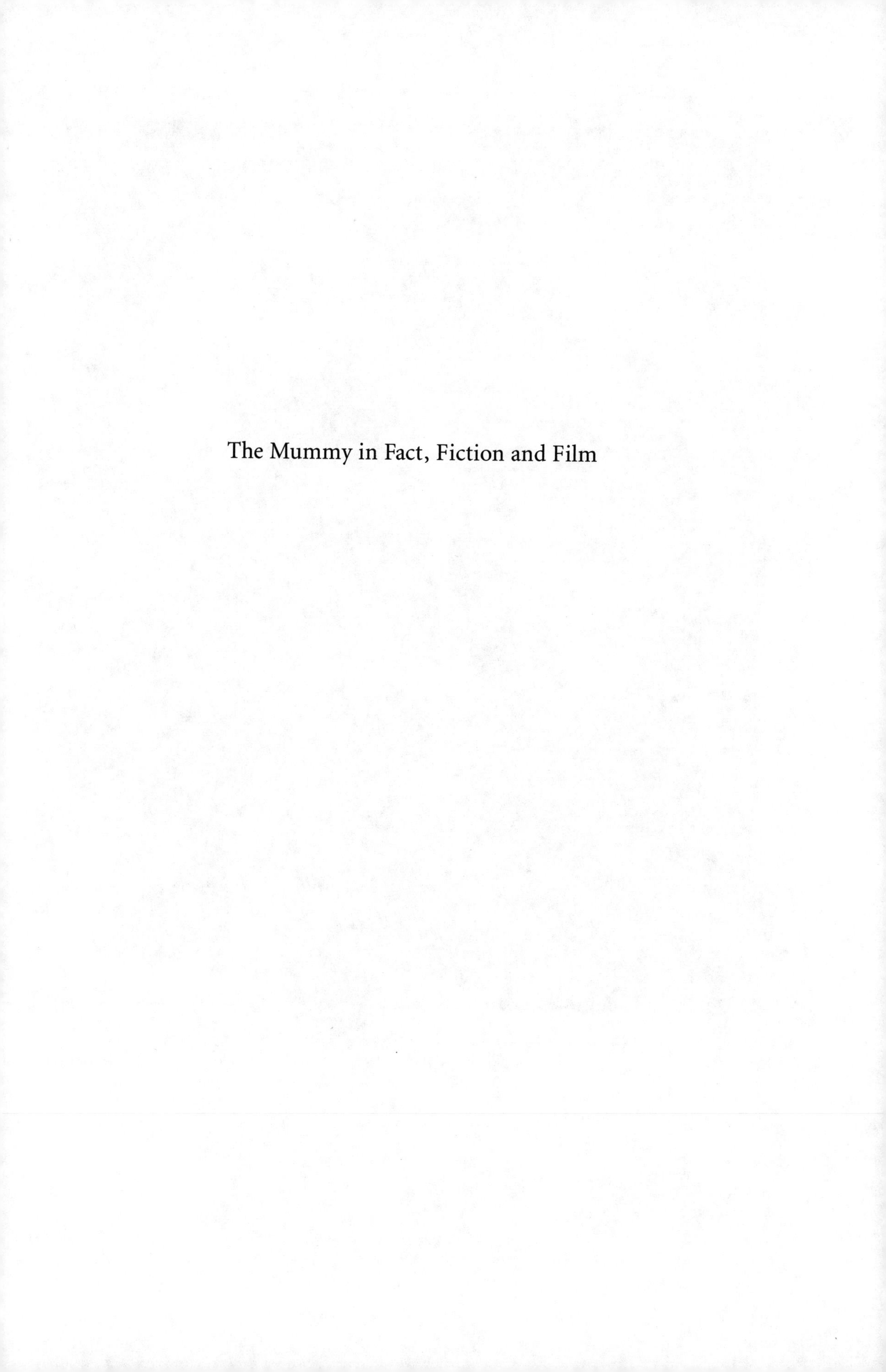

The Mummy in Fact, Fiction and Film

COLIN '96
COWIE

The Mummy in Fact, Fiction and Film

SUSAN D. COWIE *and* TOM JOHNSON

foreword by GEORGE HART

McFarland & Company, Inc., Publishers

Jefferson, North Carolina, and London

ALSO BY TOM JOHNSON

Censored Screams:
The British Ban on Hollywood Horror in the Thirties
(McFarland, 1997)

Hammer Films:
An Exhaustive Filmography
(McFarland, 1996)

Frontispiece: Boris Karloff, Dickie Owen, and Christopher Lee
in a drawing by Colin Cowie

Library of Congress Cataloguing-in-Publication Data

Cowie, Susan D.
The mummy in fact, fiction and film / Susan D. Cowie and
Tom Johnson ; foreword by George Hart.
p. cm.
"Chronological list of mummy films": p.
Includes bibliographical references (p.) and index.
ISBN 0-7864-1083-3 (illustrated case binding : 50# alkaline paper) ∞
1. Mummies in motion pictures. 2. Mummies in literature.
3. Mummies. I. Johnson, Tom, 1947– II. Title.
PN1995.9.M83C68 2002
791.43'675—dc21 2001044508

British Library cataloguing data are available

Manufactured in the United States of America

On the cover: Lon Chaney, Jr., portrays a mummy in the 1959 film *Castle of Terror*

McFarland & Company, Inc., Publishers
Box 611, Jefferson, North Carolina 28640
www.mcfarlandpub.com

Contents

Foreword

The ancient Egyptians believed in what we might call "magic" and the efficacy of curses and spells, and they were also very fond of stories involving the miraculous and supernatural; but I am not sure what they would make of the malignant curses and lumbering bandaged "undead" corpses of the "mummy" genre of gothic fiction and films. There is a popular image of the Egyptians as being obsessed with death, due in part to modern reactions to the spectacular nature of the royal tombs— the Pyramids and the marvelously decorated tombs in the Valley of the Kings. The truth is exactly the opposite. They enjoyed this life so much that they wanted it to go on forever. Their view of the "afterlife" was basically an idealized version of their life on earth. Because of this they took the things they needed and used in life with them into their tombs, which they termed houses or mansions of eternity. Although they were very literal in some of their beliefs, they did not expect their corpses to actually walk upon the earth after they were mummified. In most instances the legs were bound tightly together and would be a serious impediment to mobility!

Thanks to the spectacular preservative qualities of the Egyptian climate and landscape (which may have inspired the ancient belief in the continuance of life beyond death), great numbers of funerary artifacts have survived to the present day and can be seen in museums throughout the world, particularly in Europe and the United States. I hope that this book will encourage those of you not already interested in Egyptology to visit museums— or Egypt itself— and see the furniture, clothes, jewelry and spectacular sculpture and painting of this vibrant and fascinating ancient civilization. In many museums you will also be able to see actual mummies, which are generally of individuals of considerably less stature than the actors swathed in bandages in films. The great care they took to preserve their bodies (which they believed their spirits still needed) means that today we can learn a great deal about how they lived, what they ate, their state of health and the diseases that afflicted and in some cases killed them.

I am closely involved with two museums in London: the British Museum and the Petrie Museum of Egyptian Archaeology at University College London. The British Museum, whose extensive collections cover the entire history of world civilization, has one of the premier collections of Egyptian art and artifacts in the world. The galleries of Egyptian funerary archaeology provide a spectacular survey of ancient Egyptian burial customs and material, including animal and human mummies. The specially designed exhibition structure aims to explain the Egyptian attitude to life and death. The Petrie Museum of Egyptian Archaeology is situated close by. This is the world's largest university teaching collection ands open to the general public. It was founded by Sir William Flinders Petrie, a pioneer of scientific excavation techniques in archaeology, whose work still forms the foundation of modern Egyptology. In a comparatively small space its displays offer a concise but thorough survey of Egyptian civilization.

I would strongly urge all visitors to London to make time to visit both of the museums and take the opportunity to see something of the real ancient Egypt.

George Hart,
British Museum Education Service
Chairman, Friends of the Petrie Museum

Preface

It was the ancient Persians who gave Egypt's preserved dead their name — mummies— but real interest in these artifacts outside Egypt began with gossipy ancient Greek Herodotus, the archetypal tourist guide author, who wrote compellingly of Egypt in his monumental history of the Greco-Persian wars.

More than two thousand years later, Napoleon Bonaparte arrived in Egypt with not only an army of soldiers, but a greater army of scholars, engineers, philologists, botanists, entomologists, artists and historians. He did not succeed in his vision of conquering Egypt, but his report on the expedition published as *Descripition de l'Egypte* is still one of the great works on the glories of Egypt. He lost the war, and along with it, one of the greatest treasures of all time — the Rosetta Stone, the key which unlocked the long lost language of Ancient Egypt.

The rich collectors now become part of the story, launching expeditions to acquire *objets d'art*, colossal statuary, burial goods and other materials. These expeditions proliferated together with a hardy tourist trade. Authors of curious tales begin to play with strange Egyptian characters and themes.

Then come scholars who invent the science of Egyptology — those who work with delicate trowels and brushes, rather than crowbars and dynamite, meticulously recording their discoveries and publishing them for a curious world. Great museums become greater still, graced with Egypt's past.

And then, Howard Carter finds a staircase, hidden for thirty centuries under rubble; he calls his Patron, Lord Carnarvon, to be present as they open an almost perfect time capsule. Tutankhamun is found. It is the first worldwide media event of Egyptology, capturing the attention of not just the scholars, the gifted amateurs with bottomless pockets, and the rich dilettantes, but the ordinary folk reading their newspapers over breakfast, safe at home. It is also possibly the first example of checkbook journalism — the *Times* of London wins exclusive rights to the discovery and every other newspaperman is left floundering until someone reports ... a Curse!

Since then, mummies have become part of all our lives— in print (in scores of publications from the academic to pulp fiction), on film (both as documentary and creepy thriller), and on television, too.

Our hope, in this book, is to share with you the tale of the mummy in fact, film and fiction. Each aspect could no doubt command its own volume — indeed *fact* alone fills many a library shelf and now even CD-ROMs— so you will pardon any omission, as we have been selective to give you a flavor of each aspect and send you looking for more.

We should like to thank The Lincoln Center, New York, The British Film Institute, London, Mark A. Miller, Tom Weaver, Randy Vest, Elaine Hahn, Greg Mank, Mike and John Brunas, George Hart and Tania Watkins at the British Museum, Trevor Wayne for his suggestions to the factual script and for sharing his and his wife Dr. Anne Wayne's personal photographs of Egypt, Fred Humphreys, Dr. Wayne Kinsey and Ton Paans.

To all our readers, in the words of the ancient Egyptians— Life, Health and Prosperity!

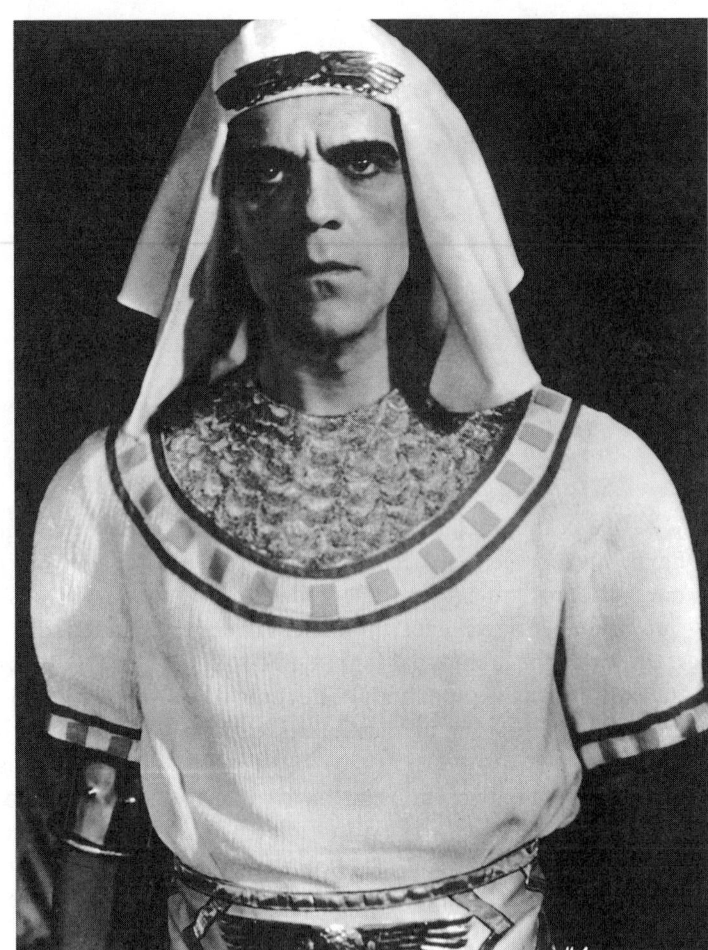

Right: **Boris Karloff as Imhotep in Universal's *The Mummy*, 1932.**

I

The Mummy in Fact

A Brief Outline

There is no precise record of when mankind first thirsted after immortality in whatever form was possible — for what could be more awful than black nothingness?

There is no precise record of when mankind first sought connection with a divine power — for what could be more awful than to be alone and defenseless in eternity?

In Egypt, way before recorded history, and in other ancient civilizations around the world too, these two great human desires began to bear fruit. Of all the civilizations that discovered and used the process of mummification — at first just naturally and later through scientific contrivance — the Egyptians were arguably the greatest. Since the authors intend in this volume to concentrate largely on Egyptian mummies in the Fact section, it would be remiss not to consider, however briefly, other important mummies.

A mummy, by definition, is the preserved body of a human being or an animal. Preservation may be by any means, either deliberate or natural. Mummies survive to the present day from many ancient cultures, and the means of their preservation can be wet, dry, cold, or heat processes.

The bog-bodies of Northern Europe — like the 2000 year old Lindow Man, found in 1984 in Cheshire, England — are an example of wet mummies. The preserved people had either fallen accidentally or been deliberately sunk into wet, marshy places. The acidity of the bog and the exclusion of oxygen by total submersion preserved the bodies by preventing bacterial dissolution of the remains, leaving us with startlingly vibrant visitors from our past. So well does a bog preserve remains that discovery of a bog-body always involves the police, as radiocarbon dating has to be used to determine the age of the body.

Denmark has the best bog-bodies, dating from 500 B.C. to the Roman Period and up to A.D. 400. The well-preserved corpses have a number of common features. They appear to have been killed on dry land and cast into the bog; they may have been human sacrifices or possibly executed criminals. Many have injuries suggesting ritual killing, and forensic evidence suggests a common death date in mild mid-winter, suggestive of a festival celebration like our modern Christmas. Most bodies are naked, but Huldre Fen bog-woman, who died in A.D. 95, was wearing a lambskin cape, a checked skirt and headscarf, and she had a string of two amber beads and a beautiful horn comb with her, all suggestive of an important place in society. Grauballe Man, who died between 1,540 and 1,740 years ago, had most of his internal organs intact, and his fingerprints were studied in great detail. We are told that his last meal consisted of vegetable soup containing barley and a kind of muesli of sixty kinds of plant seeds. Thereafter he died from many injuries including a slashed throat. Many bog-mummies show this kind of overkill; necks knotted with cords to strangle, throats cut and skulls caved by multiple blows all on the same bodies are not uncommon and suggest a ceremonial death.

In Chile and Peru the earliest mummies were those of fishing peoples living along the coasts. These were probably natural mummies, preserved by the desiccating action of the sands in which they were interred. By 3000 B.C. the mourners were removing internal organs and sun-drying the bodies before burial.

Mummies from later cultures have been found in Colombia, Peru, Ecuador, and Chile from the coastal plains to the mountain heights. There is evidence that many of these cultures treated the mummies of their forebears as sacred objects. In A.D. 1532 when the Europeans arrived in the Andes, the Incas worshipped the mummy of their dead king, believing him to be a god. They believed their worship would keep his soul alive; his mummy was enthroned, fed and clothed by attendant priests who carried him through the streets of the capital, Cuzco, on holy holidays.

Mummies of the Chancay people (A.D. 100–1470) were wrapped in many layers of cloth purposely woven for the burial. The Chancay were gifted weavers and embroiderers, using cloth as a form of currency, so the burials were very important to them. Fine quality clothing and textiles indicated a person's importance, and years of work must have gone into the making of the fabrics for the most important mummies. Some Chancay burials include cloth-making implements like looms, thread, and spindles. Ordinary Chancas were wrapped in cloth and buried in pits with a few goods. Rich Chancas were buried in large tombs, some with stairs leading down to the many rooms full of beautiful grave gifts. Chimu mummies were those of a highly developed farming people, contemporary with the Chancay, whose mummies were provided with false heads atop the mummy bundle. X-rays of one Chimu mummy revealed a crouching body covered in layers of fine cotton and wool cloths with plates of metal believed to be gold covering the eyes, a bracelet on one wrist, and shells round the heels. The mummy also wore a pouch containing avocado pits, raw cotton and coca leaves, which the Chimu chewed to relax, coca being a raw form of cocaine.

On the Peruvian coast a vast cemetery was found at Ancon; the high levels of natural salts in the soil seemed to have aided the preservation of the bodies, which were interred with their pet dogs. Some Peruvian mummies had more assistance in survival by a careful mummification process—removal of internal organs, smoke-drying the shell and rubbing it with oils, resins and herbs—but most were achieved naturally by the hot, dry climate of the coast or the freezing cold of the mountains. The drying process was facilitated by the layers of fabric that swathed the body, drawing off the body fluids. The dead were usually placed in a sitting position with their knees drawn up to the chest; hands were flattened against the face and arms and legs bound tightly in place. In Bogota, Colombia, fourteen mummies were found in a cave in the Colombian Andes. The mummies were wearing necklaces of animal teeth and carved seashells. The bodies had had their internal organs removed through incisions at the base of the spine; they were subsequently bound in the usual position and possibly smoke-dried to aid preservation.

The Incas practiced human sacrifice, and during droughts or times of other crises children were selected with their parents' approval for mummification as an offering to the gods. Earlier archaeologists believed that these children were drugged, killed quickly and prepared as gifts with the finest grave-gifts possible, but recent work on the some of the mummies indicates that the children were aware and terrified at the moment of their deaths, though drugged enough to be unable to resist or cry out, thereby dishonoring their parents and priests. When the Inca king died some of his favorite wives and servants were killed to accompany him on his journey to the next world.

Mummies have been found in the Americas from Argentina to Alaska. Most mummies have been found in caves, like those of the Navaho in Arizona. In Alaska, the freezing cold preserved the bodies so well that the tattooed bodies of the Inuit are still vibrant in their designs. In the nearby Aleutian Islands, the population buried their dead in volcanic caves; some of these bodies had had their insides removed and the space was filled with dry grass.

Occasional accidental mummification takes place, as with the celebrated Iceman found 10,000 feet up the Alps on the Austro-Italian border by two German climbers on September 19, 1991. About 5,300 years previously he had been overwhelmed by a sudden snowstorm and killed by exposure and cold; glaciers covered his body until freak weather once more revealed his presence. He is the oldest well-preserved mummy in the world, and the seventy-odd objects found with him have caused early historians to rethink many long-held beliefs about the communications and interactions of early peoples, their level of technological sophistication, and their way of life. His blood, bones, organs and DNA will increase our knowledge of the history of illnesses and the development of humankind. On a wry note, we must add that this mummy was in such a superb state of preservation that, on first discovery, he was thought to be the victim of foul play, and so the police had first crack at the scene — much to the ire of forensic archaeologists! — hacking it out of the ice and helicoptering it back to the police labs at Innsbruck. He then generated an international diplomatic incident as both Austria and Italy laid claim to the remains. Though he was later proved to have been found in Italy, it was agreed that he should be returned there only when the Austrians have finished their research, which will be many years in the future.

In 1770, on Tenerife in the Canary Islands around a thousand mummies were found in a volcanic cave. They were identified as the Guanche people, who had practiced preserving their dead over many centuries. Their methods were remarkably similar to the Egyptian method: bodies were dried and stuffed with plants after the removal of the internal organs. Sadly, few Guanche mummies survived, as they were ground up to make medicines.

The Scythian peoples were nomadic and ruled central Asia from the seventh to the third century B.C. They carefully mummified dead chiefs and nobles, removing internal organs and stuffing the body shell with frankincense, parsley, and hair. The beautiful textiles buried with their chiefs depict their way of life as horsemen. Chiefs were buried with their mummified horses, and warriors had tattoos which recorded their exploits. Their burial mounds are found in Siberia where the freezing cold has helped to preserve the mummies.

In China, too, the desire for immortality led to the important dead being preserved. A second century B.C. princess believed that being buried in a jade suit of 2160 pieces of jade linked with gold wire would preserve her body, but under the jade, she decayed away. More successful was Lady Dai of the Han Dynasty around 168 B.C. Her mummy was discovered in Hunan Province in 1972 in a deep tomb. She was wrapped in twenty layers of silk in a nest of six wooden coffins, all wonderfully painted. The coffins were covered in multiple layers of bamboo matting and about five tons of charcoal whose purpose was to soak up any water and keep the mummy perfectly dry. Her tomb was then sealed with clay and dirt to keep it airtight. Forensic pathology showed that her body had been preserved by soaking in a bath of mercury salts.

Australian aborigines, native South and North Americans all used natural drying methods to preserve bodies. In New Guinea, mummified ancestors are still revered and part of everyday life. Bodies are tied to a bamboo stretcher and smoke-dried, then painted with red ochre. In Buddhist temples and some Christian churches holy people are sometimes mummified and displayed. In Palermo, Sicily, there are six thousand mummies in the catacomb. The oldest mummies are the monks who lived and worshipped there, and who preserved their dead with a year long process. The custom then spread to the wealthier families. The oldest mummy is that of Father Silvestro da Gubbio, who died in A.D. 1599. His body was left in a special cellar on earthenware pipes for a year until all the body fluids had drained away: then it was taken upstairs and left to dry in the sunshine. Before he was reclothed in his robes he was washed in vinegar and wrapped in straw and perfumed herbs. In the nineteenth century, the monks invented another method, where the bodies were soaked in arsenic or milk-of-magnesia which resulted in softer, more lifelike skin. The Capuchin monks are the guardians of the catacombs and cemeteries and keep the records. Once a year they gently clean the six thousand mummies. The last Sicilian to be mummified was the Sleeping Beauty, Rosali Lombardo, aged two, who died in 1920. Her father, a doctor, developed a unique process and the little girl, with her pink hair ribbon, looks peacefully asleep. Like the ancient Egyptians, Sicilians do not find mummies disturbing but view the bodies as a direct link with their dead forebears. Children were often taken to visit great-great-grandparents, and families would share picnics while keeping the mummies up to date with family gossip! Visitors would also pray for the mummies, and the coffins the mummies lie in are hinged, so that the relatives might hold hands with the dead during prayers.

American Revolutionary John Paul Jones died in France in 1792; since he was an American, rather than a French hero, his grave was neglected and forgotten. More than a century later it was discovered by General Horace Porter, U.S. Ambassador to France. He reported finding Jones after a five year search and the body was exhumed, being "marvelously well preserved, all the flesh remaining intact but slightly shrunken and of a grayish-brown or tan color.... The face presented a natural appearance" (*Encyclopedia of Mummies*, 1998, Facts on File Inc., p. 87). The ambassador arranged an autopsy at the Paris School of Medicine where a quantity of alcohol ran out of an opening in the back during an examination of the thoracic cavity. It was discovered that Jones had been mummified in whiskey. The body was subsequently returned to the United States and was buried in the U.S. Naval Academy Chapel in 1913.

In London, medical students pay their respects to the English philosopher Jeremy Bentham who died in 1832. According to his instructions his friend, the surgeon to whom he left his body, had Bentham's head mummified and had his skeleton dressed in everyday clothes surmounted by a wax head. The whole recreation, plus head, was encased in glass and placed in University College. Bentham referred to his bequest as his Auto Icon (self image).

In the twentieth century, people have begun mummifying famous politicians and celebrities rather than royalty or saints. In Salt Lake City, Utah, U.S., one can even pay to have a dead relative or pet embalmed and wrapped in the Egyptian manner following archaeologists' attempts to recreate mummies by the old methods. In Moscow, Vladimir Lenin was preserved using a secret process with paraffin wax, though the future of this Communist icon is debatable as the current leaders of Russia decide whether to bury him in his home town in deference to his own — long ignored — wish. Thousands of visitors came to gaze on him each year and a visit to his mausoleum is an integral part

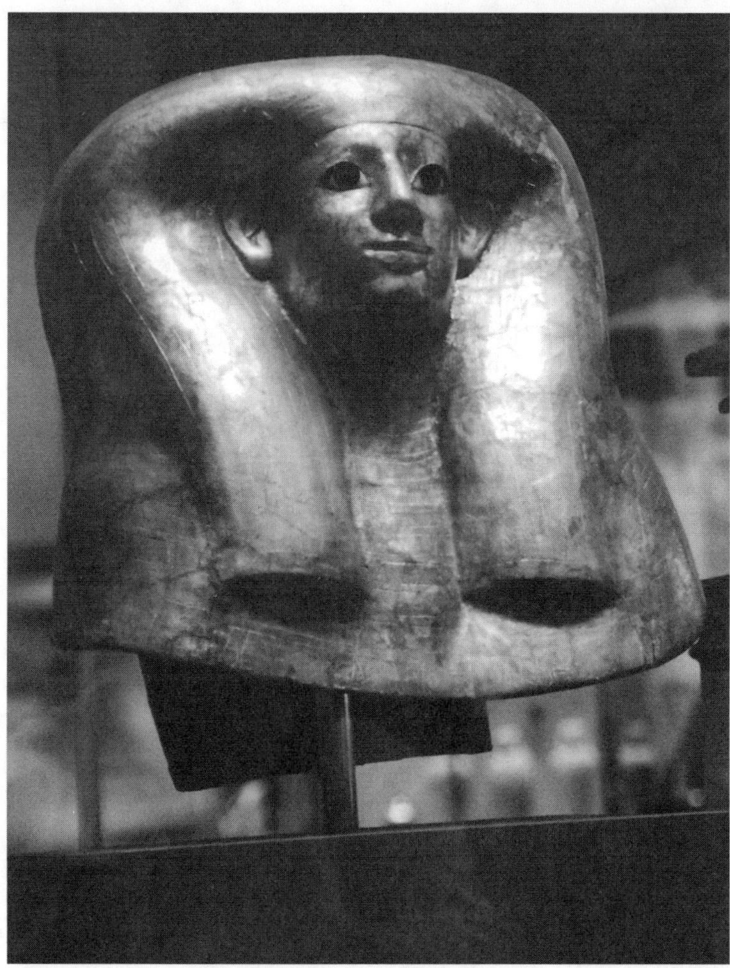

Hatnofer's funeral mask, gilded cartonage. (Courtesy Colin Cowie 1998.)

of a visit to Moscow. Indeed, the shape of the mausoleum is based on the Step Pyramid! The embalmers of Lenin improved their skills and passed them on to the morticians who worked on Eva Peron in 1952. By then, the technique was so good that her body stayed soft and supple, perfectly preserved — so perfect that the poor dead woman suffered the fate of many an Egyptian maiden thousands of years before at the hands of those who were supposed to revere and protect them.

All the mummies in our museums are carefully monitored; the work of the mortuary priests of old delays rather than stops the processes of death. Precisely controlled temperature and humidity are necessary to keep the mummies in their present state so that we can pass them on to our descendants in the hope that they will learn even more about the lives of these special visitors from our past.

As techniques improve for the study of mummies, and make study without destruction possible, we can only thank the foresight of generations of archaeologists who cherished the mummies and cared for them so that future archaeologists might learn from them. We can enjoy the work of Egyptologists such as Dr. Rosalie David, head of the Manchester Mummy Project, whose work with her colleagues has unlocked many details of the lives of the ordinary folk who were mummified, and who retested mummies in the interesting sequence of events that showed both nicotine and cocaine present in some early mummies. There is Professor Bob Brier whose team recreated a mummy, with the help of an anonymous donor who left his body to science, to check on the data from the old texts; and Professor Denis van Gerver of the University of Colorado, who recently rescued many Nubian mummies and kept them safely stored until they could be studied in Boulder, Colorado. His team found evidence of a tetracycline-type antibiotic in the mummies and theorized that it could have come from eating moldy wheat as a medicine. As he so wryly put it when explaining a scientist's excitement at such new discoveries," It's like opening the tomb of a queen and finding she's wearing panty hose!"

The Chronology of Egypt— The King Lists with Existing Mummies

The long span of Egyptian history from the unification of the two kingdoms in 3100 B.C. is divided into three major time periods; the Old, Middle and New kingdoms which are separated by intermediate periods and finish with a late period. Within this framework rulers are grouped chronologically into dynasties generally comprising successive members of the same family.

This division into dynasties and their numbering, 1 to 31, is derived from the work of an Egyptian priest named Manetho who lived during the reign of Ptolemy II Philadelphus in the middle of the third century B.C. Manetho drew on previously compiled records and king lists to draw up a comprehensive listing. However, his sources (some of which survive on temple walls in Egypt) were not without omissions of subsequently unpopular rulers. Even at the dawn of recorded history men were rewriting it!

The omissions—most famously of the female "king" Hatshepsut, and the Kings Amenhotep IV (Akhenaten, sometimes called the heretic), Smenkhare, Tutankhamun, and Ay—added to the custom of restarting the calendar at year 1, following each king's coronation, have caused some problems in assigning dates to the reigns and known events. This uncertainty has bred a considerable number of theories and controversies about the chronology of Ancient Egypt and its relationship with other contemporary cultures.

Another potentially confusing area is the rendering of the names of ancient Egyptian kings in modern languages. Some writers prefer to use names based on those recorded by Manetho, whose work only comes to us via quotations and synopses in Greek and later in Roman times, whilst others transliterate the hieroglyphs into modern phonetic equivalents. This latter course is made difficult by the fact that the ancient Egyptian script does not record vowels. These modern versions are also subject to amendment as philologists continue their studies of the language. In a note to the authors, Trevor Wayne, who is studying hieroglyphs, comments wryly,

> The problem with names is that every Egyptologist seems to have their favorite versions! Some of the younger generation still favor the Manetho inspired Sesostris, Amenophis, Sethos, etc. Others go with the flow moving from Amenophis to Amunhotep to Amenhotpe (yeuk!) [sic]. Others like Sir Alan Gardiner made up their mind and stick to it rigidly (His most 'famous' name was 'Hatshepsowe' who sent an expedition to a land called 'Pwene'). And then there are confusing 'conventions'—the god is Amun—the king Tutankhamun but Horemheb/Haremhab/Horemhab's first wife is the lady Amenia! The god is Toth—the king Tuthmosis/Tuthmose/Dhutmose—but private individuals are now rendered Djehutimes!

In the list below we have therefore used the names that are the most popularly used, in general.

Early Dynastic Period: 3100–2650 B.C.
(Also called the Archaic Period)

First Dynasty Narmer—Menes—Aha (possibly another name for Menes)—Djer—Djet—Adjib—Semerkhe—Qaa

Second Dynasty Hotepsekhemwy—Raneb—Ninetjer—Peribsen—Khasekhem

Old Kingdom: 2650–2150 B.C.

Third Dynasty Sanakht—Netcherikhe-Djoser—Sekhemkhe—Khaba—Huni

Fourth Dynasty Snofru—Cheops—Radjedef—Chephren—Mycerinus—Shepseskaf

Fifth Dynasty Userkaf—Sahure—Neferirkare—Shepseskare—Raneferef—Niuserre—Menkauhor—Isesi—Unas

Sixth Dynasty Teti — Pepi I — Merenre — Pepi II

Seventh and Eighth Dynasties Ephemeral kings of whom very little evidence has been found

First Intermediate Period: 2134–2040 B.C.

Ninth and Tenth Dynasties Kings who ruled from Herakleopolis and partly contemporary with the Eleventh Dynasty kings who ruled from Luxor (Thebes)

Eleventh Dynasty Intef I — Intef II — Intef III — Nebhepetre Mentuhotep (often listed as I and II)

The First Intermediate Period ended with Mentuhotep's defeat of the Herakleoplolitan kings.

Middle Kingdom: 2040–1640 B.C.

Eleventh Dynasty Nebhepetre Mentuhotep — Mentuhotep III — Mentuhotep IV

Twelfth Dynasty Amenemhet I — Sesostris I — Amenhemhet II — Sesostris II — Sesostris III — Amenemhet III — Amenemhet IV — Sobeknofru

Thirteenth Dynasty Wegef I — Amenemhet V — Sobekhotep I — Hor — Amenemhet VI — Sobekhotep II — Sobekhotep III — Sobekhotep IV — Sobekhotep V

This Dynasty collapsed after a succession of short-lived, little known kings.

Fourteenth Dynasty A little known group of kings contemporaneous with the end of the Thirteenth Dynasty

Second Intermediate Period: 1640–1550 B.C.

Fifteenth and Sixteenth Dynasties The Hyksos kings, who were not native Egyptians, ruled from the delta.

These dynasties were contemporary with each other and included kings such as Salitis, Khyan and Apophis.

*[From this point on, * by a name denotes an existing mummy.]*

Seventeenth Dynasty A number of native kings who ruled from Luxor were contemporary with the previous two and ended with the expulsion of the Hyksos rulers from the North. Noted kings were: Intef V — Sobekemsaf — Seqenenre — Seqenenre Tao I — Seqenenre Tao II* — Kamose

New Kingdom: 1550–1070 B.C.

Eighteenth Dynasty Ahmose I* — Amenhotep I* — Tuthmosis I* — Tuthmosis II* — Hatshepsut — Tuthmosis III* — Amenhotep II* — Tuthmosis IV* — Amenhotep III* — Amenhotep IV (Akhenaten or Smenkhare)* — Tutankhamun* — Ay — Horemheb

Nineteenth Dynasty Ramesses I — Seti I* — Ramesses II* — Merenptah* — Seti II* — Amenmesses — Siptah* — Tawosre

Twentieth Dynasty Setnakht — Ramesses III* IV* V* VI* to Ramesses XI

Third Intermediate Period: 1070–712 B.C.

Twenty-first Dynasty Smendes — Amenemnisu — Psusennes I* — Amenemope* — Osorkon I — Siamun — Psusennes II — PinudjemI — Masaharta* — Menkheperre — Smendes — PinudjemII*

Twenty-second Dynasty Sheshonk I — Osorkon II — Takeloth I — Sheshonk II — Osorkon III — Takeloth II — Sheshonk III — Sheshonk IV — Sheshonk V — Osorkon IV — Osorkon V

Twenty-third and Twenty-fourth Dynasties Ephemeral kings of whom little is known; the Twenty-fourth Dynasty appears to have only two kings.

Bakenre (Bocchoris) — Piankhy (Piye)

Late Period: 712–332 B.C.

Twenty-fifth Dynasty Shabaka — Shebitku — Taharka — Tantamani

Twenty-sixth Dynasty Necho I — Psammetichus I — Necho II — Psammetichus II — Apries — Amasis — Psammetichus III

Twenty-seventh Dynasty Persian rulers: Cambyses — Darius I — Xerxes I — Artaxerxes — Darius II

Twenty-eighth Dynasty Amyrtaeus

Twenty-ninth Dynasty Neferites — Psammutis — Neferites II

Thirtieth Dynasty Nectanebo I — Nectanebo II

A second group of Persian rulers including: Artaxerxes III — Arses — Darius III

Graeco-Roman Period: 332 B.C.–A.D. 295

Thirty-first Dynasty Macedonian: Alexander the Great — Philip Arridaeus — Alexander IV

Thirty-second Dynasty Ptolemaic: Ptolemy I to Ptolemy XV, including Queens Cleopatra I to Cleopatra VII

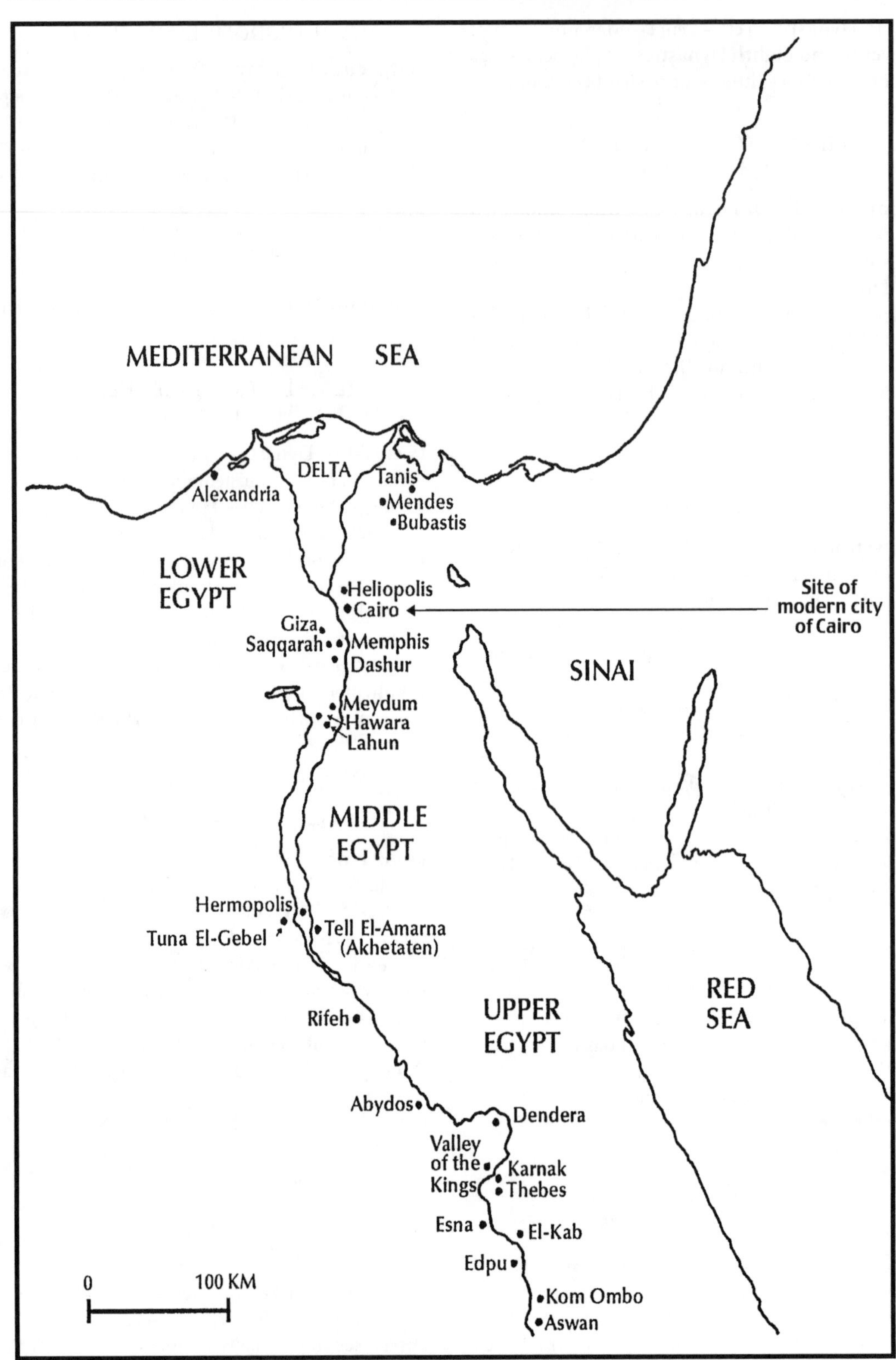
MEDITERRANEAN SEA
DELTA
Alexandria
Tanis
Mendes
Bubastis
LOWER EGYPT
Heliopolis
Cairo
Site of modern city of Cairo
Giza
Saqqarah
Memphis
Dashur
SINAI
Meydum
Hawara
Lahun
MIDDLE EGYPT
Hermopolis
Tuna El-Gebel
Tell El-Amarna (Akhetaten)
Rifeh
UPPER EGYPT
RED SEA
Abydos
Dendera
Valley of the Kings
Karnak
Thebes
Esna
El-Kab
Edpu
Kom Ombo
Aswan
0
100 KM

Ancient Egypt. (Sue Cowie)

After the death of the last Cleopatra, in 30 B.C., Egypt became a Roman province and no longer a nation in its own right. When the Empire was divided in A.D. 395, Egypt was administered from Byzantium until the Arab conquest in A.D. 641.

In the Beginning...

The people of Egypt have a great love of life; it has always been so. Such a love of life and an appreciation of the world lends itself to the creation of a concept of life continuing after death in a similar, if improved and glamorized, manner.

If a scientist were to create an environment to nurture life, he would find the perfect "petri dish" in the Egypt of prehistory. Egypt has been described as "the gift of the Nile" so many times that one is apt to forget just what a truth it is. Before our technological age made the creation of the High Dam at Aswan possible, Egypt relied on the annual Nile flood for the gift of wonderful, rich black mud and abundant moisture at just the right time in which to plant, germinate, and irrigate the crops. At that time geography and natural forces presented the early peoples who wandered into the Nile valley with a set of absolute parameters that offered the chance for the growth of civilization.

The Nile Valley nestles between cliffs at the edge of deserts which provide natural protection from raiding foreigners. The river, with its annual flood, renewed the fertility of the land and made further roaming unnecessary so that settled farming communities could evolve. And with the development of agriculture came the possibilities of surpluses which enabled communities to support craftworks, the need for some sort of recording system for land and produce, an officialdom of some kind to coordinate planning and to operate relief during bad times, and some kind of military system.

These systems were evolved over generations of prehistoric Nile peoples. Gradually the small family groups combined into confederations of towns and villages, through loose alliances of several of these confederations into two kingdoms and one based in the delta and the other in the upper river valley. During this time the absolutes remained — the daily rising of the sun without whose heat and light nothing would live, the river providing water and food, and the annual gift of fertile soil binding the once wandering people to its banks. Added to this was the proliferation of local deities being molded into local pantheons as civilization progressed, and the growth of powerful families taking the lead in planning and caring for their particular areas whilst acquiring wealth and position for themselves.

And always there existed a stark contrast between life and death — the red, harsh sand of the desert, never far away, and the thick, black fertile living earth from the river flood. Even now the contrast is noted by tourists who can stand with feet slightly apart — one in dead desert, one in fertile farmland where the two parts of Egypt meet. It is no wonder, then, that a concept of life as a duality emerged from these people or that they saw nothing strange in their multiplicity of gods and goddesses. As a simple expedient, no man could afford to waste the soil deposits from the flood and so the desert sands were the practical place to bury the dead.

It is often believed that the first Egyptian mummies, naturally dried by the hot sands, were observed by their descendants as sand blew away or as wild animals foraged in the ground. However the concept first impinged on them, they began to view continuing life after death as a fact, witnessed by the survival of these bodies. Therefore they began to bury "necessities" with the bodies— food, water, favorite possessions, and so on. The mummy displayed in the British Museum of the man affectionately known as Ginger was a product of this time. Found at Gebelein in the desert, Ginger died around 3200 B.C. and was placed in the hot, dry sand. His nails and skin are well preserved, as is the integrity of his body. The drying action of the sand and heat have kept his body intact, although he was buried with all internal organs in place. The gap of five thousand years seems very small to observers who come to study him, and in many ways he is immortal by his own beliefs.

Sir William M. Flinders Petrie — one of the founders of the modern science of archaeology — excavated cemeteries of these early people and created a dating system using the development of their pots and jars. The Arabs working on his digs named him "Father of Pots" as a result, and the system with minor amendments remains remarkably accurate to this day. Flinders Petrie evolved an excavating technique that set the pattern for future Egyptologists and ended the grab-it-and-go method of study that had preceded him. His meticulous care and detailed recording system set the gold standard for proper study of a site.

It was a perplexing time for Egyptology; many people could not see a link between the people of the pit burials and the mummies swathed in linen, and thought them entirely unrelated. As a science and an intellectual discipline, Egyptology had grown out

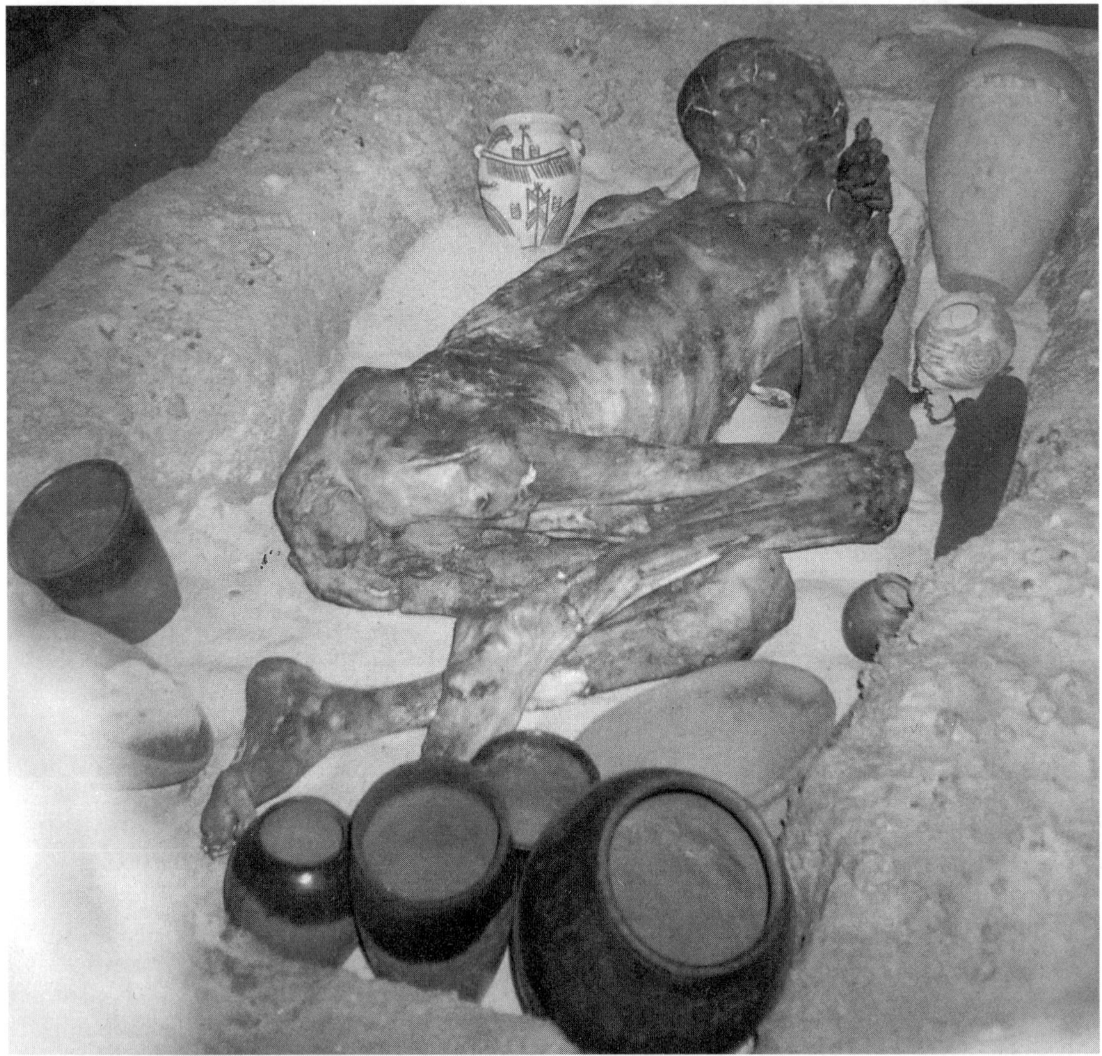

Predynastic sand burial. "Ginger" in the British Museum, circa 3200 B.C. (Courtesy Colin Cowie 1998.)

of a passion for collecting rare and beautiful — and sometimes bizarre — objects and an Imperial dogfight, mainly between the French and English. There was no process for back-tracking the civilization to its roots, and many of the early Egyptologists, as devout men and women, were also hampered by the desire to find evidence of the Old Testament stories and a validation for the Judeo-Christian framework of their own lives. That they achieved so much from the days of Napoleon to the present day tells us what exceptional human beings they were — and are. For Egyptology does not stop, and is not important only to the past. Modern Egyptology bridges the millennia, using its findings to relate to the modern world, preserving the great finds of the past for us and our descendants, and finds ever more exact, non-invasive, and nondestructive ways to learn from our ancestors. And through them and the interest their work inspires in specialist and rabid amateur alike, those ancient souls have achieved their goal — they are remembered and they do live — forever.

Predynastic

The origin of Egyptian civilization and the inspiration for their religious iconography and their singular writing lies somewhere in remote prehistory during the thousands of years known today as the Predynastic Period. Archaeologists have discovered burials from these earliest times in which the presence of grave goods suggests a belief in an after life. This belief remained a central tenet of the religious beliefs of the people of the Nile Valley as they developed their single, unified kingdom with its central organization during periods of decline and foreign occupations, through periods of glorious high civilization and status as a world power, to an eventual decline and annexation to the empires of succeeding great powers. Today the difficulties of sorting out the development of the beliefs of these people is linguistic. Many philologists argue that our ability to develop concepts comes from our ability to articulate ideas and that our forbears often did not have the language that would enable certain concepts to develop. Similarly today, writers often sprinkle texts with words and phrases from other languages because the precision of those words perfectly express the ideas, whereas a translation cannot but blur the meaning. When translating the texts of Ancient Egypt, then, how much more difficult must it be? These people were, in effect, alien to us. They had a sense of corporateness that we have lost. John Romer, the famous Egyptologist with a genius for communication, explains that the Western world has lost that corporateness that, for example, built Notre Dame de Paris or Canterbury Cathedral where the craftsmen of Egypt, in tomb or on great monuments, worked as a whole team, able to carve the powerfully graceful arm of Ramesses II — the statue that inspired Shelley to pen Osymandias without the modern eye seeing where one man's work ceased and another began.

Ancient Egyptians had an appreciation of the power of words. An Egyptian's greatest wish was to have his or her name remembered, because if it was remembered and spoken, that person would have life in the other world and would continue to work, play and worship as on earth. The writing on stela or the wall of a tomb or on a roll of papyrus would make the idea a reality: so one could insure against the provision for one's mummy failing in times to come by writing the foods and beverages and other requisites together with their quantities alongside the frequency of their provision and it would become real for the owner of the mummy. The same belief is reflected in the Bible in Genesis— when God articulates a thought it becomes reality: "Let there be..." and it is so. The Memphite theology uses very similar language and it has been suggested by some scholars as an influence or inspiration for Genesis— bearing in mind that Moses was

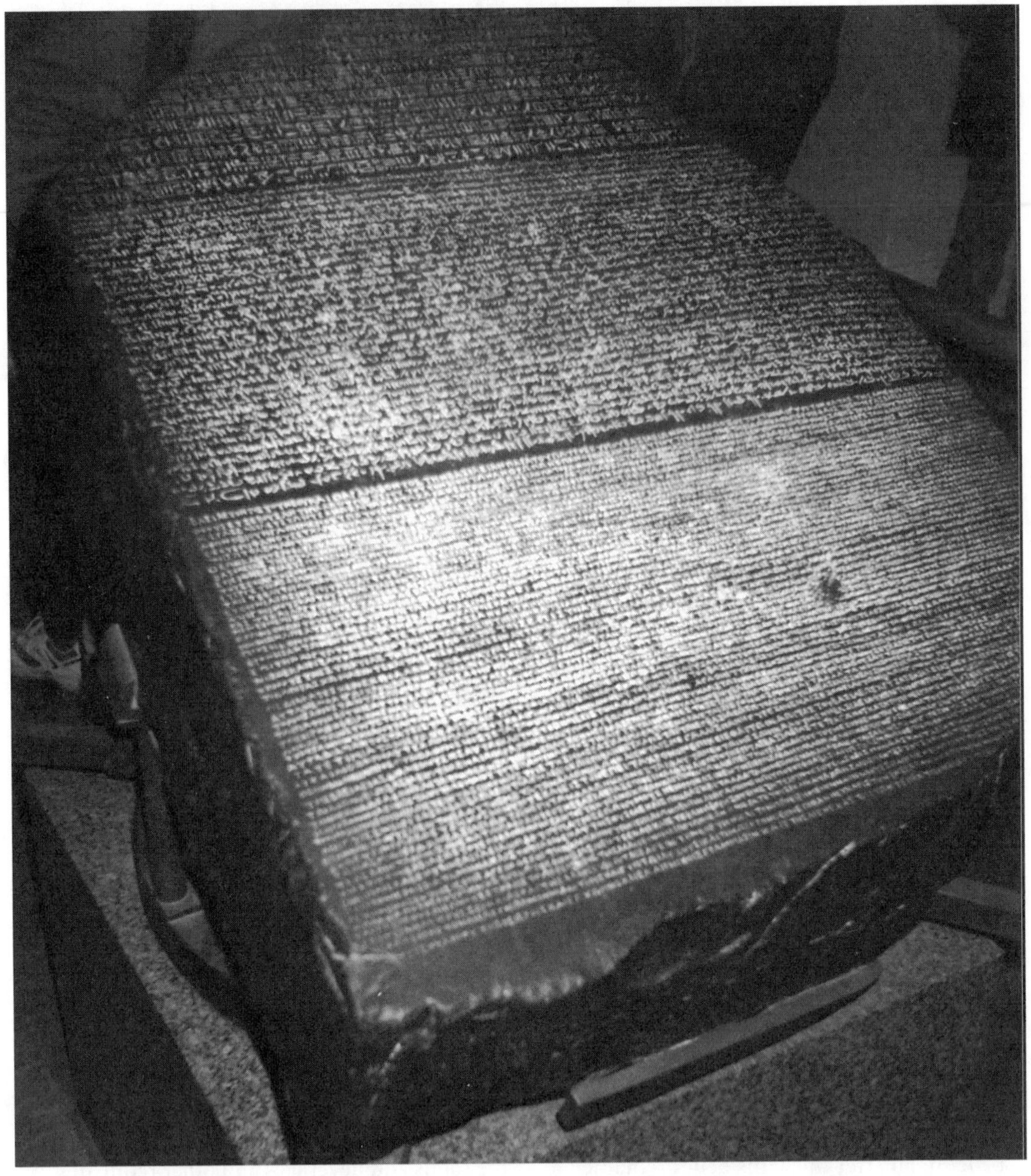

The Rosetta Stone — key to the code of hieroglyphs. (Courtesy Colin Cowie 1998.)

born in Egypt! When the kings of old spoke, the words became law irrespective of which country one speaks. Little wonder that scribes were held in such high esteem, for they had the ability to write these powerful words and to read them back, which few other people, however powerful, could do.

So if you then take a language which no one has heard articulated for thousands of years, written in a form which records no vowels, able to be read in many directions, it must be evident that a great deal is still to be learned about Egypt despite the work of Champollion and his intellectual descendants! But for the arrogance — or was it respect for history?—that inspired Ptolemy to commemorate an event with what equates to a commemorative plaque today in the Greek he himself spoke at court, in Demotic, the common tongue and hieroglyphs, the sacred writing of the gods, we who come after would have no clues to *begin* making sense of their conceptual world. And but for the collector's passion, the French officer whose soldiers dug up the Rosetta Stone whilst making defenses may well have battered it into more usefully sized fragments.

Therefore when we read of "spells" the mental image we get is of panto-magicians, not devout priests. Spells seemed an apt term to those early translators, for were these words not dedicated to a plethora of gods who, in the main, had animal heads on human bodies? They could not call them prayers in all conscience. And yet can we really believe that those people were any less devout than the people of our own time? The gods of Egypt were worshipped with piety and devotion for nearly six thousand years—three times as long as Christianity has yet held sway. Fortunately in our age we are free not to judge the merits of another's worship. For all our scholarship these days philologists still have to resort to the "best educated guess" when trying to untangle the theology of Ancient Egypt.

Niche statue, Old Kingdom, 4th or 5th Dynasty. (Courtesy Colin Cowie 1998.)

Early Mummies

However it came about, the time came when the early Egyptians, amid their growing civilization, believed passionately that life after earthly death existed. The survival of the bodies in the pit burials seemed impiric evidence of this and therefore right-thinking people must provide for the needs of the dead person.

Originally grave gifts were every day items and possible favorite possessions; food, water, ornaments, toys for children, possibly an artifact that one had used in life as a mark of one's profession and status. Eventually the powerful and wealthy expected better gravesites and more protection from the depredations of weather and wild animals. The constant concept was bodily integrity. Pit burials were no longer just holes in the sand. Small rooms were created in the ground, lined with mud brick to stop the sand shifting about and if one was wealthy enough, roofed with wood or even encoffined with wood. Stones and earth piled above made a bench-shaped marker for the burial. The ancients called them "houses of eternity." Those who came after noted their similarity to the benches outside Arab homes and called them *mastaba* tombs, adopting the Arabic word for bench. For the more important, the tomb also required a chapel where offerings and prayers could be left and extra rooms for the storage of grave goods if the deceased was to continue to enjoy the earthly life style just left.

Sadly, in some cases, these new houses of eternity defeated their purpose. The body, no longer in contact with the hot, dry sand and wrapped in rushes and wood, putrefied as natural bacteria, supplied once again with oxygen and humidity, multiplied and broke down the body. A *process* to prepare the body for eternity was necessary and the search for such a process and its evolution took many centuries beginning at the end of the First Dynasty (2920–2770 B.C.) and coming to its peak in the Twenty-first Dynasty. The process of mummification finally died out in the early days of the Christian church in the first century A.D.

The Development of Mummification

The belief was held by the Egyptians that as well as a body, each person had a soul or spirit that would live on after death. A person's spirit could eat, drink, move about, make love, work, and so on, but in order to do these things it had to have a recognizable body to live in. If the body was destroyed, the spirit might not survive after death, so preservation was very important. The ancient Egyptians believed in many aspects of a person's soul but the most common were the *ka* and *ba*.

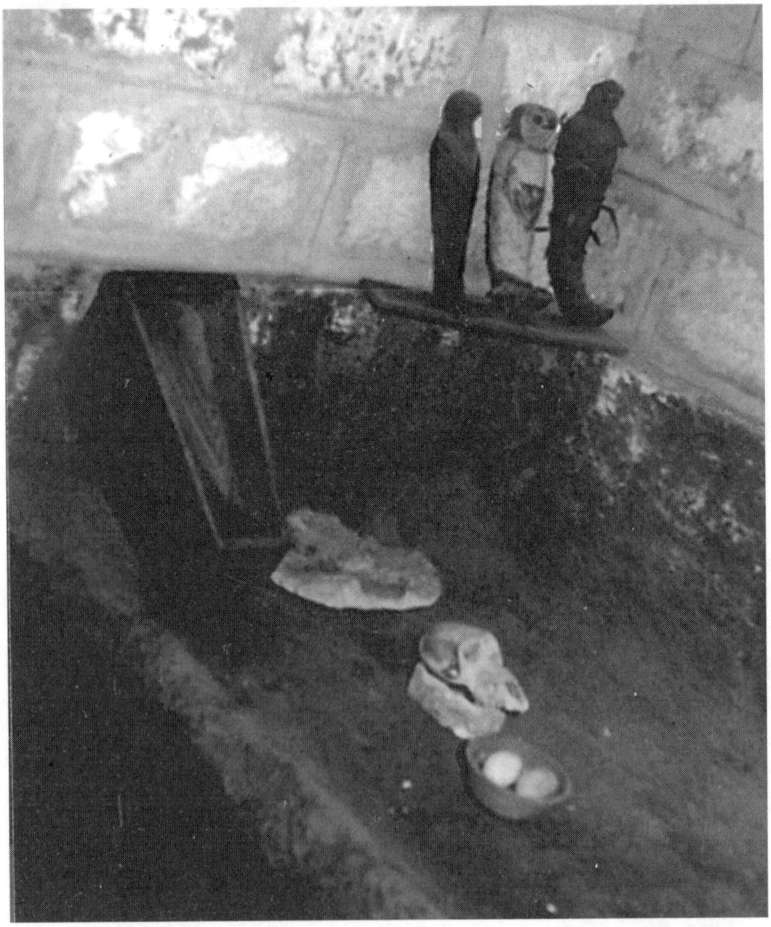

A person's *ka* was his unseen twin, his double. Egyptians believed that all people and their kas were created by the god Khnum, the ram-headed god, on a potter's wheel from clay. The ka lived in the body until death, but once death occurred the ka, too, would die unless it was provided with the exact image of the deceased. In extremis a statue would substitute as a home, but a lifelike mummy was the best possible provision. The ka also required food to survive.

The mummification room at Hermopolis. Mummified hawks are propped against the wall. A mummified ibis rests in a wooden coffin and a baboon's skull can be seen in the foreground. The latter two species were sacred to Thoth the Egyptian god of wisdom. (Courtesy Trevor Wayne 1974.)

A person's *ba* was another form of his spirit, but unlike the ka which stayed in the tomb within the mummy, the ba was able to leave and travel. It is usually illustrated as a small bird with a human head resembling the deceased, but it was said to be able to assume any form it liked. The ba could fly through any material, so solid rock or filled burial shafts were no obstacle. However, it always returned to the tomb at night and like the ka it needed to be able to find and recognize its mummy. Without a mummy there could be no ka and ba and therefore no afterlife; death would be final and complete — a horrendous prospect to any Egyptian. Therefore the most pressing need was a process for creating a recognizable mummy.

In the earliest times, the king alone was thought to be able to attain immortality. As a living god on earth, he kept the balance of the world in his person; he mediated with the gods for his land and peoples, and after death it was believed that he became an immortal god who could still help his people by being their advocate in the heavenly courts. His people equated him with Osiris, who they believed had ruled Egypt in the distant past and who had been slain by his brother Set who had hacked his body to pieces and scattered them all over the land. Osiris's wife Isis had searched and retrieved the pieces, bound them together and revived him so that they could conceive a son, Horus. Osiris subsequently became the god of the underworld and the judge of the dead in whose court each heart was weighed against the feather of Ma'at, goddess of truth and justice. Thereafter he was depicted as wrapped like a mummy, with a green-blue face denoting resurrection. A dead person had the term Osiris added to the front of his name, showing that he had passed from this life to the next.

During these early days the king could confer great honor on any of his favorites by allowing them to be buried alongside his tomb, so that they could partake of his new existence. Later still the idea of afterlife for nobles and then for anyone who could afford it meant that the embalmers had a great many more subjects to practice their arts

The ceremony of "Opening the Mouth," usually performed by the heir. (Courtesy Colin Cowie 1998.)

upon. But in all this time, the poor continued to be buried in pits on the desert rim. Mummies of this period were buried in a flexed or fetal position.

The amounts of grave goods that accompanied the king and his nobles was a temptation for other less fortunate mortals. The great edifices of the pyramids having been plundered, later kings sought eternal refuge in an isolated valley but they, too, were disturbed — fortunately for the Egyptologists perhaps— and reinterred in old tombs in secret to preserve their eternal rest. These mummy caches, as they have become known, contained some of the greatest monarchs of Egypt and added tremendously to what we know of mummification. But more of them later.

One early idea was to wrap the body in cloth to protect it from the atmosphere and to coat the cloth with resin, which had two functions: as it dried it stiffened around the body, preserving its shape, and it also became airtight, like a shell.

One of the earliest attempts at mummification discovered to date was a First Dynasty king, discovered by Flinders Petrie at Abydos, some 150 kilometers north of Thebes. Abydos was a sacred city, especially dedicated to the cult of Osiris. Early French archaeologists Auguste Mariette and Emile Amelineau had already worked at Abydos, and many believed the site to be played out, but Flinders Petrie recognized how important it was in the understanding of the First Dynasty and began to reexcavate in 1899. Arthur Mace, later to work with Carter on the tomb of Tutankhamun, came to Abydos to work with Petrie on the tomb of King Zer. Four workmen found a wrapped arm upon which they could see a gold bead, and because Petrie had a well-trained and disciplined workforce, they sent for Mace at once without disturbing the relic. Mace brought the arm to Petrie and when they unwrapped it they found four bracelets of gold and faience. Mace and Lady Petrie set about restringing the beads, under the watchful eye of one of Petrie's workmen and when it was done, Petrie weighed the bracelets, using English gold sovereigns as weights. When the balance was made, Petrie gave the sovereigns to the delighted workman. As to the arm and the bracelets, he recorded many years later in *Seventy Years In Archaeology*: "When Quibell came over on behalf of the Museum, I sent up the bracelets by him. The arm — the oldest mummified piece known — and its marvelously fine tissue of linen were also delivered to the Museum. Brugsch only cared for display; so from one bracelet he cut away the

"The Sheik" cult statue in wood circa 2490 B.C. Lecture slide c. 1890, printed direct from glass slide. (Sue Cowie Collection.)

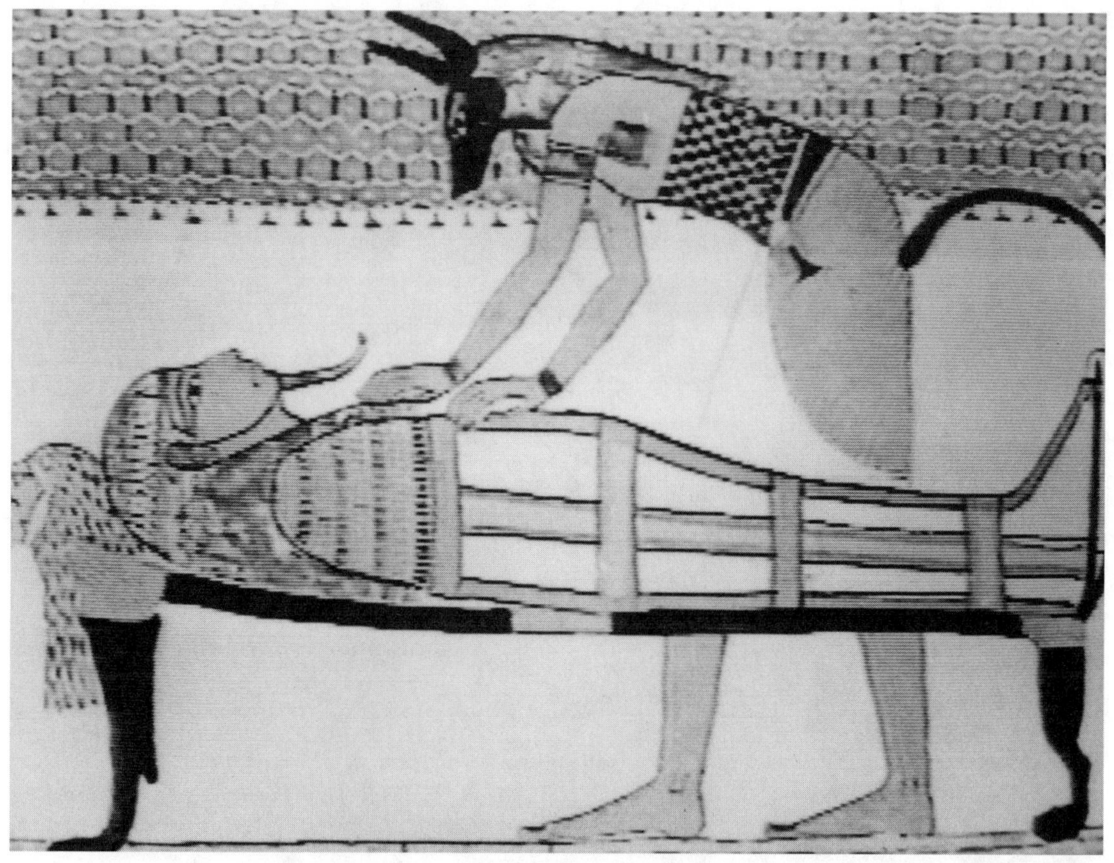

Anubis placing the mask on a mummy. (Colin Cowie 1998.)

half that was of plaited gold wire, and he also threw away the arm and the linen. A museum is a dangerous place."

When Petrie found the body of a Fourth Dynasty noblemen called Nefermaat at Meidum, he was convinced that the flesh had been stripped off before bandaging; he had not realized that the soft tissue could disintegrate so totally that the linen would touch the bone. Dr. Douglas Derry later proved this to be so in his work on Old Kingdom mummies.

During the Fourth Dynasty embalmers began to remove the internal organs to prevent putrefaction. However, they were part of the mummy and so needed to be preserved too. At first organs were just packed separately, but later special urns called canopic jars were made to protect the viscera, so named for the shrine of Osiris at Canopus where the god was worshipped in the form of a pot topped with his head. The stomach, liver, intestines and lungs were all dried out and packed into the containers, each guarded by a son of Horus, who was in turn guarded by goddesses. As in the legend of Osiris, it was believed that the body parts would be magically reassembled in the afterlife. During the Middle Kingdom the urns were made with the head of the guardian god as a stopper for each one. Jackal-headed Duamutef protected the stomach; falcon-headed Qebsenuef was in charge of the intestines; human-headed Imseti watched the liver, and baboon-headed Hapi took care of the lungs. Isis, Nephthys, Selket, and Neith protected the guardians.

Champollion, code breaker of the Rosetta Stone, was the first person to perceive the purpose of canopic jars. His notes on them read, "Fibrous tissue ... Animal smell / Object impregnated and covered in a

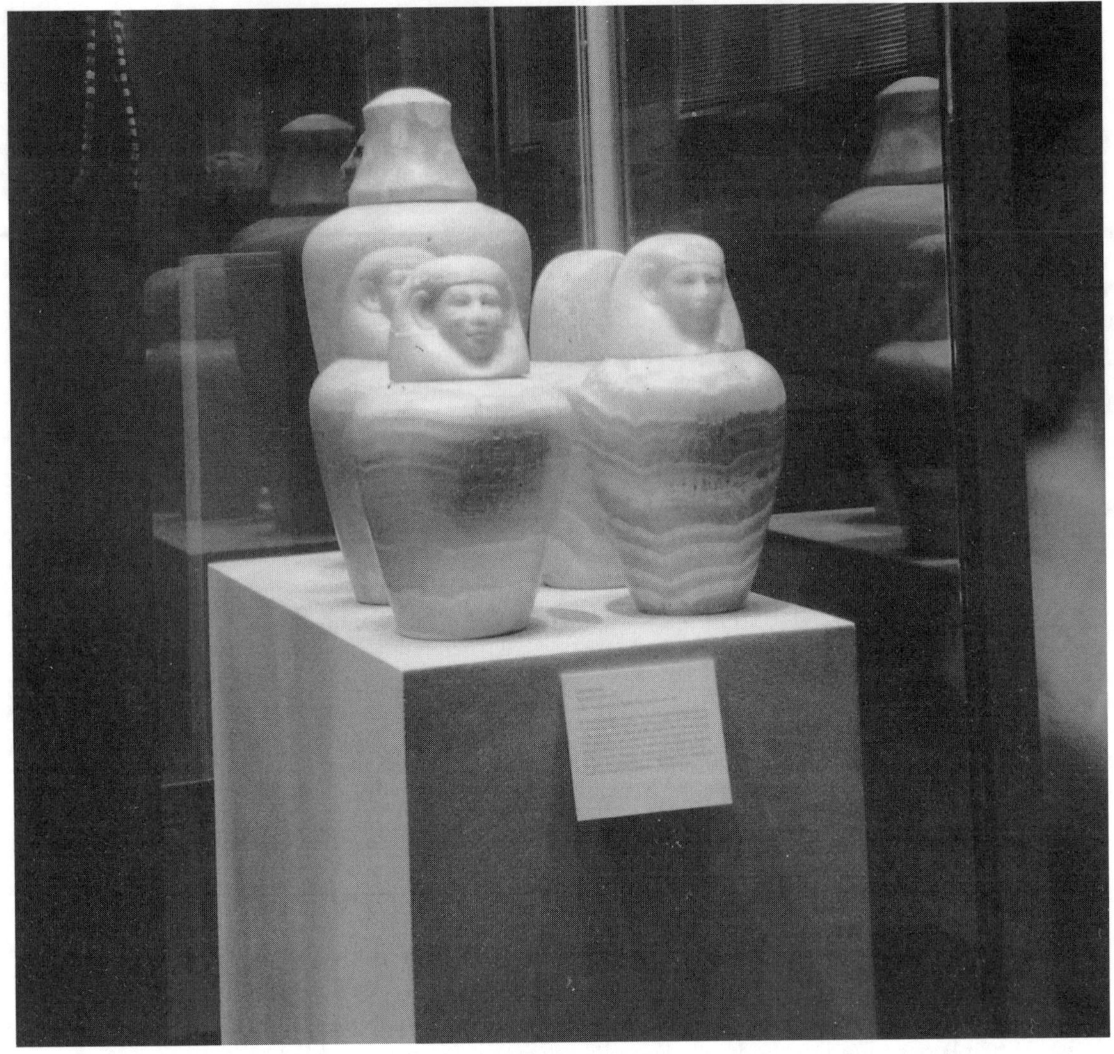

Canopic jars with portrait heads. (Courtesy Colin Cowie 1998.)

thick layer of balm / Found at the bottom of the vase / Just wrapped in cloth … / Liver and brain or cerebellum."

In some early mummies, the brain was left in situ and shrank as it dried. There are reports of the sound of brains rattling about inside mummies' skulls! There seems to be no evidence of the preservation of the womb from female mummies although great care was taken to preserve male reproductive organs, even to the extent of presenting the penis erect so that it could function sexually in the afterlife. Oddly, the ancients generally did not remove the kidneys and never purposely disturbed the heart, which to them was the center of being controlling intelligence, thought, and memory.

In most New Kingdom burials, the heart is protected by a scarab beetle in the wrappings over the heart on the chest. The scarab was a common insect who laid its eggs in cattle dung which it balled up to protect the eggs. The beetle would then push the ball along in front of it until it found a safe place to store it. Later, new beetles could be seen emerging from the ball, and the Egyptians equated this with the concept of immortality and resurrection. They identified the

Seti I and Osiris at Abydos. Seti I was murdered at the beginning of Universal's 98 *The Mummy*. (Sue Cowie Collection.)

wavy ridges on the beetle's back with the sun's rays and imagined the ball to be the sun disk itself. They envisaged a cosmic beetle-shaped god pushing the sun disk across the sky each day. The Heart Scarab was very important because one's heart was central to the invitation to eternal life. After death, the journey to the afterlife culminated in the judgment Hall of Osiris where the deceased recited a negative confession where 42 sins are denied—including those forbidden in the Ten Commandments—to prove his worth to enter the afterlife. His heart was then taken and laid on a set of scales. On the balancing side the feather from the headdress of the goddess Ma'at was used as a weight. On earth Pharaoh was her representative and embodied the balance that kept the world safe. A heart that weighed more than the feather was thrown to the Devourer of Souls and the deceased ceased to exist. The ibis-headed god, Thoth, recorded the outcome of each judgment and those whose hearts were righteous entered the afterlife.

Around the time that embalmers were beginning to remove organs, they also realized the desiccant power of a naturally occurring salt called *natron*. A compound of sodium bicarbonate and sodium chloride, it drew moisture from the body most efficiently. The organs of Queen Hetepheres, wife of Snofru, first king of the Fourth Dynasty, were found coated in natron in an alabaster box divided into four compartments. Generally, though, results were not good, although the bandaging of

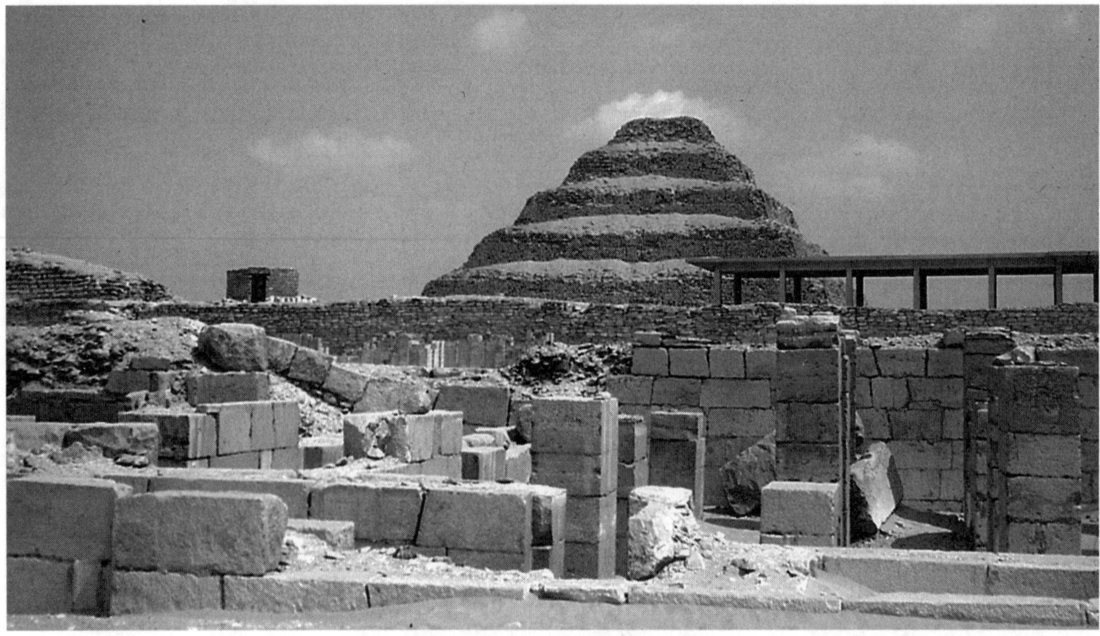

The Step Pyramid at Saqqara. The first pyramid, devised and constructed by the architect Imhotep (who was deified by later generations) for his King Djoser (Dynasty III). The remains of some of the buildings that made up the extensive surrounding complex can be seen in the foreground. (Courtesy Anne Wayne 1983.)

mummies achieved a sophistication. In some cases the bandages were arranged to imitate the hang of clothing. The person's portrait was painted on the top layer of the shroud and briefly the technique of thinly plastering the wrapped body to preserve its shape was tried but abandoned as ineffective. Old Kingdom mummies (2650–2150 B.C.) were on the whole unsatisfactory.

With practice and experimentation however, the processes improved. Dehydration with natron and the removal of abdominal organs became widespread practices during the Middle Kingdom (2040–1640 B.C.) and many mummies from this period survive intact. Some, like Wah, an official under Mentuhotep III (Eleventh Dynasty) were wrapped in vast amounts of cloth. Wah had 375 square yards of material around his body. However, cheap burials also continued—Mentuhotep's soldiers interred at Deir el-Bahari were mummified by the sand as in olden times.

It is from this period that the oldest known instruments and materials used in embalming originate, belonging to a man called Ipy. The wastage from his embalming was buried nearby, as it was thought to contain fragments of the dead man. There were sixty-seven sealed jars containing soiled rags, packets of natron, sawdust, oils and broken jars. There was also an embalmer's wooden platform, roughly five feet wide and seven feet long, with its twelve inch blocks for raising the corpse to let body fluids drain away. Some while later Winlock found a similar cache of embalming equipment used at the ceremonies of Lady Henettowey. While a thousand years had passed since Ipy's funeral, the only apparent change in equipment seemed to be the substitution of a wicker bed and mat for the board.

As the Eighteenth Dynasty began, embalmers made important advances and the mummies that have survived from this period are numerous. Much of what Egyptologists have learned first hand about mummification from this period comes from working with Royal mummies that had obviously received the best care. By now the various grades of the embalmer's art were in place and remained unchanged until after Herodotus had faithfully recorded them in his *History.* When first translated from the Greek they were held to be pretty fanciful and he was thought to be a gullible recorder of tourist gossip. However, modern science has found his lists to be accurate indeed, and restored his reputation just a little! As a tourist of course, he would not have been allowed to witness the processes of the embalmer's art, but he had evidently interviewed the priests at some length, and they had been open to his questions. After all, the Greeks who cremated their dead thought the Egyptians were most odd anyway to want to preserve dead bodies intact.

> Mummification is a distinct profession. The embalmers, when a body is brought to them, bring out sample statues in wood, painted to resemble nature, and ordered as to quality.
>
> The best and most expensive is said to resemble a being whose name I cannot mention in this connection. The second best is somewhat inferior and less expensive, and the third is the least costly of all. After pointing to these differences in quality, they ask which of the three is desired, and the relatives of the dead man, having agreed on a price, depart and leave the embalmers to their work.
>
> The most perfect procedure is as follows: As much of the brain as it is possible is extracted through the nostrils with an iron hook, and what the hook cannot reach is dissolved with drugs. Next, the flank is slit open with a sharp Ethiopian stone and the entire contents of the abdomen removed. The cavity is then thoroughly cleansed and washed out, first with palm wine and again with a solution of pounded spices. Then it is filled with pure crushed myrrh, cassia, and all other aromatic substances except frankincense. (The incision) is sewn up, and then the body is placed in natron, covered

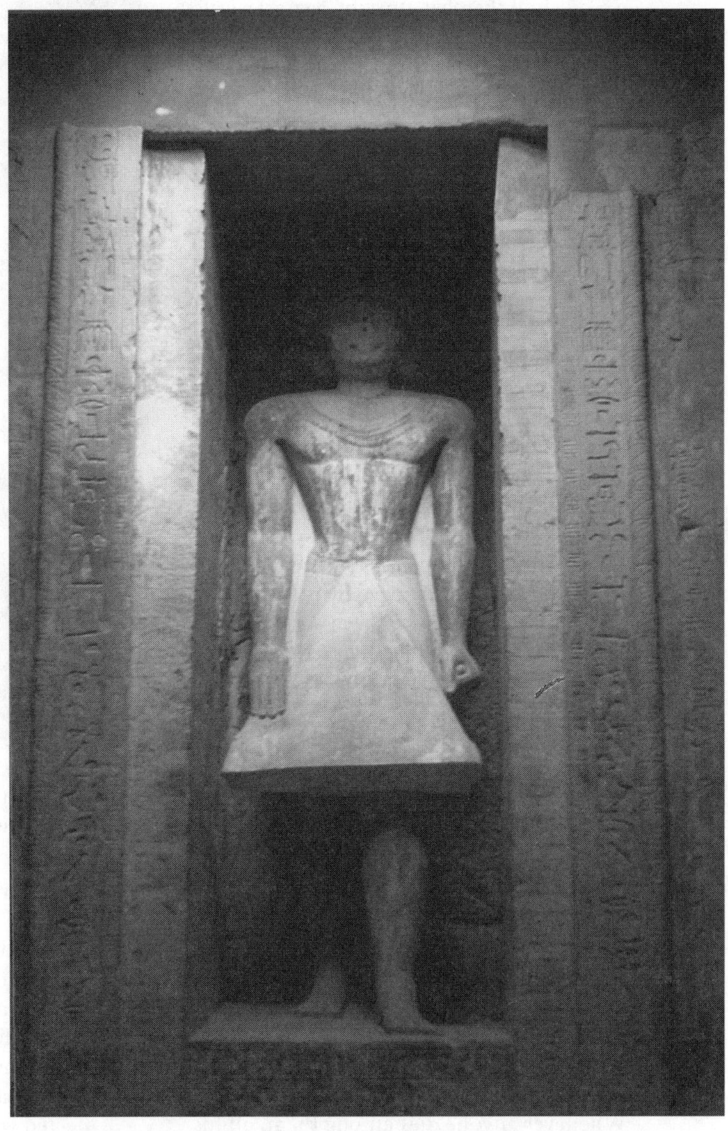

The ka statue of Mereruka (vizier Dynasty VI) in his tomb at Saqqara stands in a niche above an altar to receive offerings. The niche is a "false door" allowing the ka of the deceased to pass back into his world from beyond. Robbers have gouged out the eyes and metal overlay of the eyebrows. (Courtesy Trevor Wayne 1974.)

entirely for seventy days, never longer. When this period, which may not be longer, is ended, the body is washed and then wrapped from the head to the feet in linen which has been cut into strips and smeared on the underside with gum which is commonly used by the Egyptians in place of glue. In this condition the body is given back to the family, who have a case of wood made, which is shaped like a human figure, into which it is placed. The case is then sealed and stored in a sepulchral chamber, upright, against a wall.

When for reasons of expense, the second quality is required, the procedure is different. No cut is made and the intestines are not removed, but oil of cedar is injected with a syringe into the body via the anus, which is then stopped up to prevent the liquid running out. The body is then immersed in natron for the proscribed number of days, on the last of which the oil is drained out. The effect is so strong that as it leaves the body it takes with it the stomach and intestines in a liquid form. And because the flesh is too dissolved by the natron, nothing is left of the body but the bones and the skin. After this it is returned to the family with no further treatment.

The third method used for embalming the bodies of the poor is merely to evacuate the intestines with a purge, and keep the body in natron for seventy days. It is then given back to the family to be taken away [Translation; Aubrey de Selincourt, *Herodotus: The Histories*; Penguin Classics, 1954].

Ritual statue, 12th Dynasty. Amenemhat II or Senwosret II. (Courtesy Colin Cowie 1998.)

Four hundred years later, Diodorus Siculus, another Greek, born in Sicily, wrote a forty volume history of which fifteen survive including a text on Egypt and embalming. Diodorus visited Egypt in 59 B.C. when it was part of the Roman empire; so the process he records is a late form of mummification. The three classes of embalming are still listed, but he adds some interesting notes on the craft:

Whenever anyone dies among them, all his relatives and friends, plastering their heads with mud, roam about the city lamenting until the body received burial. Nay more, during that time they indulge in neither baths, nor wine, nor in any other food worth mentioning, nor do they put on bright clothing. There are three classes of burial, the most expensive, the medium, and the most humble.... Now the men who treat the bodies are skilled artisans who have received this professional knowledge as a family tradition; and these lay before the relatives of the deceased a price-list of every item connected with the burial and ask then in what manner they wish the body to be treated. When an agreement has been reached on every detail and they have taken the body, they turn it over to the men who have been assigned to the service and have become

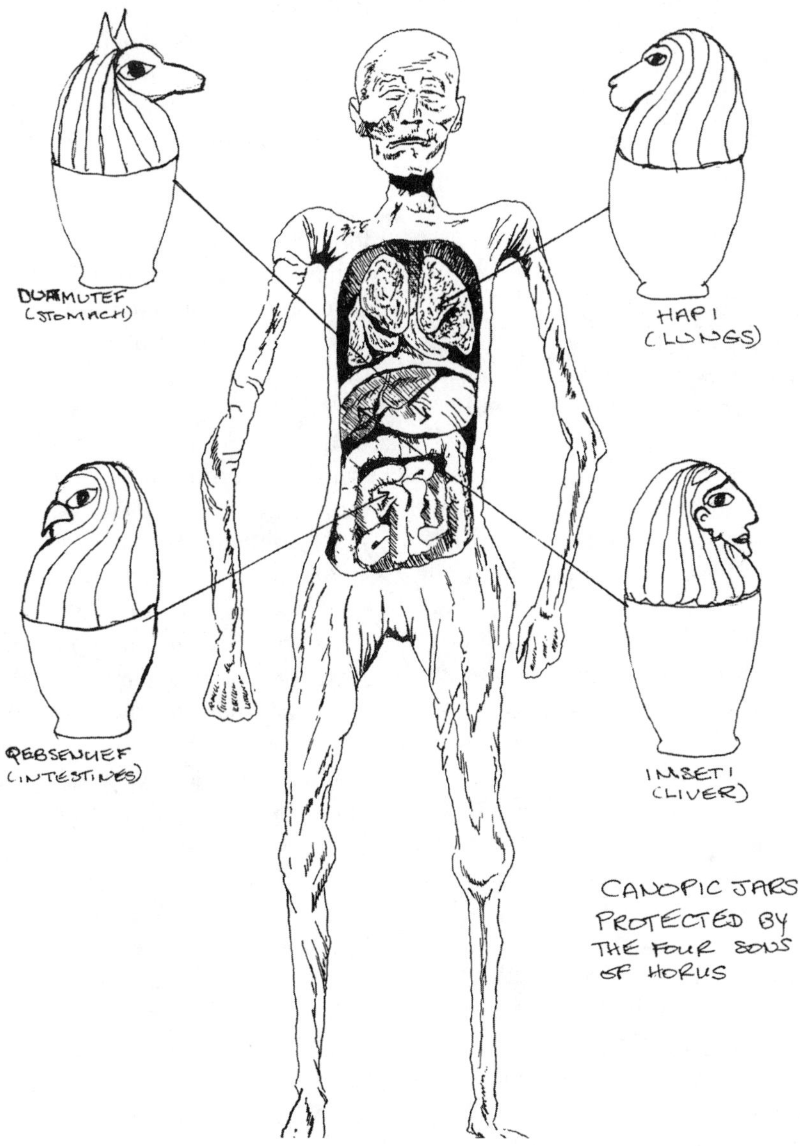

Drawing showing the distribution of viscera into canopic jars. (Courtesy Wayne Kinsey.)

inured to it. The first is the scribe, as he is called, who, when the body has been laid on the ground, circumscribes on the left flank the extent of the incision; then the one called the slitter cuts the flesh, as the law commands, with an Ethiopian stone and at once takes to flight on the run, while those present set out after him, pelting him with stones, heaping curses on him, and trying, as it were, to turn the profanation on his head; for in their eyes everyone is an object of general hatred who applies violence to the body of the same tribe or wounds him or, in general terms does him any harm.

The men called embalmers, however, are considered worthy of every honor and consideration, associating with the priests and even coming and going in the temples without hindrance, as being undefiled. When they have gathered to treat the body

> after it has been slit open, one of them thrusts his hands through the opening in the corpse into the trunk and extracts everything but the kidneys and heart, and another one cleanses each of the viscera, washing them in palm wine and spices. And in general, they carefully dress the whole body for over thirty days, first with cedar oil and certain other preparations, and then with myrrh, cinnamon, and such spices as have the faculty not only of preserving it for a long time but also of giving it a fragrant odor. And after treating the body they return it to the relatives [Selima Ikram and Aidan Dodson, *The Mummy in Ancient Egypt*: *Equipping the Dead for Eternity*; Thames on Hudson, 1998].

Diodorus supports Herodotus's claim that embalming was a family profession, which explains why so few references to the process can be found in the papyri that have been discovered in Egypt. One of the few references that springs to mind also supports Herodotus's assertion that frankincense was not used on the body, as the precious spice was reserved for anointing the head during part of the ritual. While Herodotus is vague about costings, Diodorus gives a detailed list of the charges. Many of these lists exist from the Greek occupation of Egypt. H. I. Bell translated one in the 1920s; the most expensive item being the linen, followed by the Anubis mask for the priest/embalmer to wear during the ceremony. Since only one such mask has survived, it seems sensible to assume that it was destroyed at some later part of the ritual. The costing for a "dog" probably refers to an Anubis statue to guard the tomb. These three items alone account for 208 drachmae out of a cost of 440 drachmae and 16 obols for the complete package, including professional mourners as were recorded on earlier tomb paintings. Indeed, by Diodorus's time the ritual was so set as a custom that the embalmers were still using Volcanic glass—the "Ethiopian stone"—for incising the corpse when perfectly fine, sharp scalpels were available. In the early days of the process, only sharpened copper had been available, and it did not satisfactorily cut flesh, so the glass shards had been adopted. In the same way, professional scribes were selling "Book of the Dead" papyri which were prewritten with spaces for the deceased's name to be added more often than creating a personal copy for the deceased, and copying texts whose meaning and significance had long since been lost but whose presence was believed to be imperative for the deceased to enter the afterlife. This process continued in Egypt up to the introduction to Christianity in the first century A.D. when the practice declined, violating the tenets of the new faith as it did. The Early Church Fathers wrote against mummification and the dying St. Anthony is reported to have urged his followers not to return his body to Egypt in case he should be mummified.

With such care taken of the rest of the body, it seems incongruous that the brain should be cast away during mummification. It seems apparent that the Egyptian physicians, while aware of the brain's existence, attributed no importance to it; there are few references to it in medical papyri. The Edwin Smith Surgical Papyrus noted three specific brain injuries—all results of trauma so extensive that the brain was exposed. The text also notes that severe blows to the head can affect the functioning of the limbs. Had the Egyptians realized the importance of the brain to life, it is highly unlikely that they would have thrown it away. In some early mummies the brain was removed through a hole in the back of the skull but this practice was abandoned for a far easier one of breaking the ethmoid bone which is located at the front part of the skull base; the bone is a delicate honeycomb and easily breached. Any small probe can then be used to scoop out the contents of the skull. In the freshly deceased, the viscous remains of the brain clings to the probe, and corpses that have been left for a couple of days before delivery to the embalmers—a common practice for those with pretty wives or daughters whose bodies needed protecting from the occasional necrophiliac on the embalming

Funerary equipment. (Courtesy Colin Cowie 1998.)

team — would have brains that, in the words of pathologist Dr. Wayne Kinsey M BChb, MRCPATH, "would be like runny porridge in that heat. You would only need to stir it with a probe and turn the body over ... the liquefied brain would drain out through the nostrils."

While Diodorus tells us that the men responsible for mummification were well respected, the materials of their trade and the stench it must have engendered cannot have made them popular in society. Perhaps another reason for the profession being passed down family lines was that outsiders would not be eager to join such a family. A busy mortuary would have dozens of bodies in various stages of the process around at any one time — as witnessed by the wooden toe tags displayed in several museums, ensuring that families got the correct body back! — and would of necessity have to be a good way away from the rest of the population. Professor Bob Brier came up against a similar problem when his team set about re-creating a mummification; he got academic approval to go ahead with his experiments and was then refused permission to use his university's campus! In an internal memorandum dated November 14,1993 from Dr. Walter S. Jones of Long Island University he is told.

> During a meeting last Friday, the University Officers reviewed your memorandum regarding your proposal to mummify an unembalmed human cadaver on University property during the summer of 1994. Consideration was given to all the issues you raised in your recent memorandum as well as to others such as public relations, health and security, external approval processes etc.
>
> The unanimous judgment of the group was that the project ought not to take place on University property. Perhaps a site in Egypt would be more appropriate. In your continuing conversations with the National Geographic Society please exclude the possibility of using a University site. Thank you very much" [Brier, 1996].

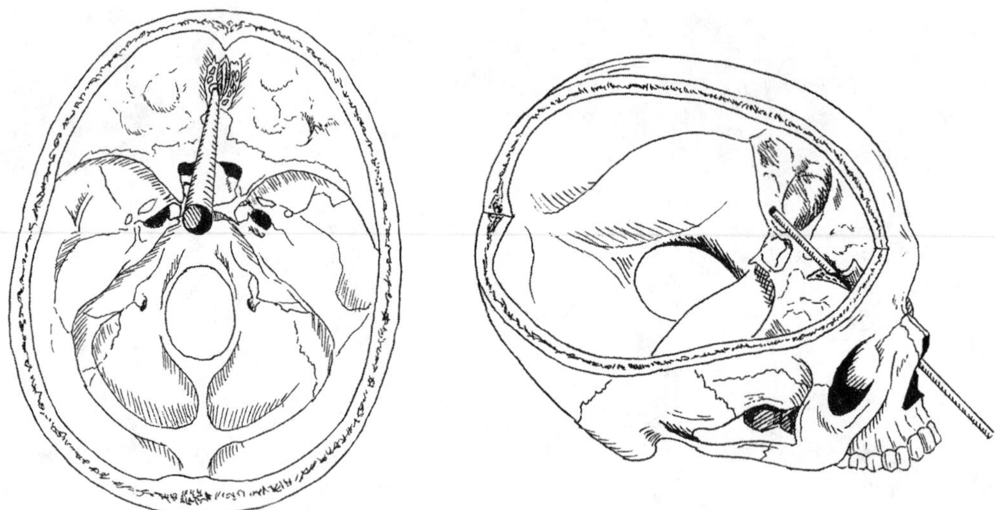

Left: **View through top of skull. Probe into brain to remove matter via broken ethmoid bone .** ***Right:*** **To remove brain from skull, probe through nostril, breaking ethmoid bone. (Both illustrations courtesy of Wayne Kinsey.)**

Eventually, Brier was invited to perform the mummification at the University of Maryland's School of Medicine, and after traveling to Egypt to collect natron and spices, he and his team were filmed carrying out the process. The film is a fascinating record and reports of the project have had TV airings all over the world.

The Middle Kingdom and Onwards

The Middle Kingdom was an interesting time in Egypt — a period of stability and consolidation after an occupation by the foreign Asiatics. While there are no truly famous kings, to the layperson at least, the reemergence of the country and the resumption of the customs speaks volumes about the native people and their determination that Egypt should be great again. For three hundred years before the Hyksos returned for a second occupation, Egypt returned to its old ways and old gods.

The pharaoh who built the original complex at Deir el Bahri, which later inspired Hatshepsut's architect Sennenmut to build his monarch's glorious mortuary temple nearby, was called Neb-Hepet-Re Montuhotep, where he had six pit tombs dug for his wives in the foot of the cliffs nearby. Edouard Naville, a Swiss archaeologist, found three of the queens' tombs— Henenit, Kemsit and Kauit, and Herbert Winlock found the remaining three — Mayet, Ashayet, and Sadeh. Henenit's tomb contained her almost complete mummy, whilst fragments of the two other queens were found on Naville's dig. Winlock found intact the bodies of Mayet and Ashayet. Neither archaeologist being particularly interested in mummies (!) it was left to Derry to examine them. An attempt had been made to preserve the bodies, as they were found with bags of natron and stained bandages, although no incisions were found. It appears that the royal ladies had been laid to rest without the removal of their organs. This is a much earlier form of mummification and shows perhaps that skills had been lost during the interregnum of the foreign kings. Derry noted with interest that the bodies had dehydrated after burial — the plethora of insect eggs in the mummies were ample

Cartonage coffin. Intermediate Period, 25th Dynasty. (Courtesy Colin Cowie 1988.)

evidence for this assumption. He also noted marks on the skin of jewelry that had been wrapped in bandages while the soft tissue remained on the limbs.

A few Middle Kingdom mummies had their organs removed, and in such cases the cavity is filled with straw, sawdust or linen to preserve the lifelike appearance. Middle Kingdom embalmers laid mummies prone with their hands stretched out alongside or covering the pubic region.

With the second expulsion of the foreigners, Egypt entered a golden age. In five hundred years three dynasties ruled — the eighteenth to the twentieth. It was a period of stability at home, growth of empire outside the country's borders, and prosperity. The wealth generated from foreign conquest enabled the pharaohs to build as not seen since the Pyramid age, and to prepare their Houses of Eternity with the finest materials and artists ever. The New Kingdom has bequeathed us a large collection of mummies— both royal and common — due in some part to the exceptional low humidity of the valley that was chosen to protect their tombs, as well as to the skills of the embalmers, and to the now common practice of removing the brain and internal organs along with more generous coats of resin that dried to make the mummy firmer. Mummies from this period often had false eyes to enhance their appearance and were buried stretched out with hands at the sides. Pharaohs' mummies had their hands crossed over the breast, while queens had only one arm across the torso.

The Eighteenth Dynasty includes two of the most controversial

Pharaohs. The first was Hatshepsut, the widowed queen of Tuthmose II, who, whilst acting as the regent for her husband's son, born of a minor wife, assumed the full titulary and ruled as Pharaoh herself. Then there was Amenhotep IV, son of Amenhotep III, who changed his name to Akhenaten and built a new capital on a virgin site in middle Egypt. He attempted to replace the myriad gods and goddesses with a monotheistic cult of the sun's disk, which he termed the Aten.

Bob Brier speculates that the dearth of mummies from the Armarnan period, so named after Armar, the modern name for the site of Akhenaten's new capital, might be the result of the monotheistic nature of Aten worship; for if there is only one god, the Osiris cult and its ramifications were probably not recognized. Possibly, says Brier, mum-mification was only minimally practiced. Both of these controversial figures are today the subject of intense debate and speculation, both scholarly and in more popular works, and in historical fiction. However, both seem to have made minimal lasting impact on Egyptian civilization, which simply reverted to the traditional path on their deaths.

Hatshepsut was succeeded by the prince for whom she had been regent. He became the famous warrior Pharaoh Tuthmose III, whose armies swept across the Middle East almost into what is now modern Southeast Turkey. This king is often referred to as "the Napoleon of Ancient Egypt" not only for his military prowess but also for his apparent lack of height. However, estimates of the king's height in life, based upon measurements taken from his mummy, have recently been shown to be in error. The lack of stature is actually due to the fact that mummy is missing both feet!

Akhenaten was succeeded by a nine year old prince, Tutankhaten, who very quickly changed his name to Tutankhamun and set about the restoration of the traditional religion.

Within a generation the throne had passed to another family, known today as the Nineteenth Dynasty, whose early rulers Seti I and Ramesses II — known as the Great due to his long reign and prodigious building program — set about destroying all traces of Akhenaten.

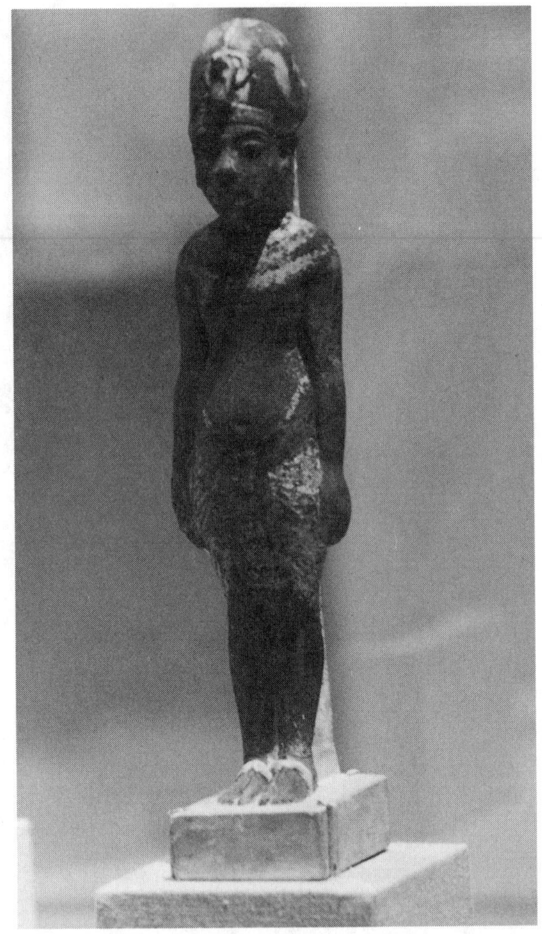

Armarnan king, complete but unnamed. Restored. (Courtesy Colin Cowie 1998.)

Tutankhamun shared the fate of Akhenaten — like Hatshepsut before them — of having his name removed from the official king lists, despite his strongly orthodox views. However, the discovery of his virtually intact tomb in 1922 ensured that he has become the best known of all pharaohs, eclipsing both his mighty warrior ancestor and his powerful long-lived successor. Towards the end of the Twentieth Dynasty the pharaohs, nearly all named Ramesses, died quickly after one another. The power of the

The mortuary temple of Hatshepsut. This temple was built for the female pharaoh Hatshepsut (Dynasty XVIII). A famous cache of royal mummies was found in 1881 in a tomb at the foot of the cliffs. The Valley of the Kings lies beyond the cliffs. (Courtesy Trevor Wayne, 1974.)

Pharaoh was diminishing as the power of the priests of Amun grew. One high priest, Herihor, had his name inscribed in a cartouch as Pharaoh. Priest-kings became the power in southern Egypt, but did not rule Lower Egypt. The erosion of central power put the royal burials at risk and a series of tomb robberies occurred. Several papyri exist that document the trials and punishments of the criminals who ransacked the tombs for portable treasure, destroying mummies to snatch amulets, and breaking and burning mummy cases to recover gold from the decorations.

Inspections were made of all the tombs, and two benefits came from these terrible events. Firstly, careful examination of the mummies enabled the embalmers to improve their skills to emulate their ancestors. From now on, internal organs would be packed inside the body cavity after treatment and no longer in canopic jars, since these objects were smashed by the tomb robbers in search of treasure. Placement in the body cavity seemed safer. Secondly, a decision was made to hide the royal mummies after repairs so that their rest would not be disturbed again, which kept them safe for three thousand years.

The Twenty-first Dynasty has left us more than forty mummies, examples of the zenith of the embalmer's art. Embalmers sought to reduce the emaciated appearance of mummies by packing bodies before wrapping. Herihor's wife, Nozme, had her cheeks rounded with packing and human hair glued on to her eyebrows. She had false eyes modeled in black and white stone to show a pupil. Queen Ka-Maat-Re had packing slipped between her skin and muscles to recreate her living form, and poor Queen Henettowey was so generously stuffed that her chin, cheeks, and neck burst. A new part of the mummification ritual is added at this time as male faces are painted red and female faces yellow, to reflect the paintings on the tomb walls and the statues in the mortuary temples.

12th Dynasty wooden coffin. Note the eyes, so the deceased can stay in touch with the world. (Courtesy Colin Cowie 1998.)

This wonderful attention to detail—both of preserving the body by careful removal of perishable matter and by the enhancement of the appearance of the mummies—was continued into the Twenty-second Dynasty. The skills then began to decline so far that in the Late Period embalmers were creating so-called "fake mummies."

The embalmers seem to have become very slapdash in their methods, and parts of bodies which became detached during the ritual were not carefully restored to their rightful owner. The yards of bandages used to finish a corpse before handing it back to the relatives could hide a multitude of errors. Some have had limbs shortened or sawn off to fit mummy cases and many have missing limbs replaced with sticks or mud and straw. In one case, Lady Teshat, whose mummy currently resides in the Minneapolis Institute of Art, has an extra skull bandaged between her thighs! It is believed that careless embalmers chose to dispose of a "spare" head this way to avoid a problem!

One oddity from the Persian Period is recorded by Bob Brier in his book *Egyptian Mummies* where the deceased nobleman Amentefnakht was mummified in his own sarcophagus. "When the lid was opened, an unwrapped mummy was found lying on its back in an inch of brown liquid covering the bottom of the sarcophagus ... a bed of natron had been made in the bottom of the sarcophagus, Amentefnakht placed upon it and then the sarcophagus sealed. As bodily fluids seeped out ... the bottom of the mummy came in contact with the natron, now in solution, which perpetrated the wrappings. The top of the mummy would be the last to come into contact with the natron; thus it was exposed to bacteria longest. Because the sarcophagus had been sealed with plaster, the brown liquid, a combination of natron and body fluids, could not escape." And so Dr. Zaky Saad had found him at Saqqara, better preserved on the bottom than the top. Brier suggests that either the embalmers were performing a ritual whose practical basis had been lost or that no one cared that much about the poor man. Either way, as the practical skills of mummification were lost, the art of bandaging the remains became a high art form.

Late Mummies

When Alexander the Great conquered Egypt, his first act was to visit the oracle of Amun at Siwa where he was declared the son of the sun, thereby making it possible for him to be declared pharaoh. On his death in 323 B.C., one of his generals, Ptolemy, seized control of Egypt and founded the Greek Ptolemaic Dynasty that held Egypt for nearly three hundred years.

History tells us that Alexander was mummified and a dedicated band of archaeologists periodically announce the discovery of his tomb. Supposedly buried with golden armor and his conquering sword in a crystal sarcophagus, the world awaits his reemergence from his long sleep. Legend has it that Cleopatra VII, known to us from rather biased Roman histories, showed Mark Anthony Alexander's mummy when they were deciding how to conquer the world.

It strikes one as odd that the Greeks should have had such a fascination with the Egyptian practice of mummification, since their custom dictated cremation and utterly forbade any cutting of the human body. Records exist of Greek physicians grumbling that they should have liked to study at the Alexandrian school of medicine, since only there was dissection permitted, which resulted in the experts on anatomy all being graduates of Alexandria.

The Greeks in Egypt adopted the local practices and their mummy cases are a charming blend of adopted — though usually misunderstood — religious symbolism and Greek art. Because of the essentially foreign occupation, the number of scribes and priests who could write and read hieroglyphs plummeted. Greek became the official state language, although the population's indigenous language continued to be spoken and written. It is at this time that the Rosetta Stone, the modern key to the ancient sacred language, was made, serving as an official record in two languages — Egyptian, rendered in both Hieroglyphs and Demotic, and Greek.

Funeral mask on coffin, Ptolemaic period. (Courtesy Colin Cowie 1998.)

When the Romans annexed Egypt after the naval defeat of Cleopatra VII and Mark Anthony at Actium, they continued the process of mummification with as much enthusiasm as they adopted the religious practices, although the outward appearance of the finished mummy seems to have been more important than the intricacies of the internal process. Elaborate bandaging and delightful portrait masks made from painted and gilded papyrus

Erotic musicians, Ptolemaic period. (Courtesy Colin Cowie 1998.)

tied to the head of the mummy bundle are the Roman addition to the art of mummification. They replaced the stylized cartonnage masks of earlier times and are regarded by many as the world's first true portraits. They are a fascinating record of the fashions of the day, and it is believed that they were commissioned and painted long before death, and enjoyed as works of art in the home. Most of the portraits have been found in the Fayoum area and come from the first two centuries A.D. Flinders Petrie, excavating in Hawara in 1888, was one of the first to study and appreciate these beautiful articles.

Bandaging techniques reached new heights with elaborate patterns, often underlaid with slivers of gold sheeting so that it gleamed through the spaces, suggesting the entire gilding of the body without the resulting expense. Sometimes yellow plaster buttons replaced the gold leaf as an added saving on the mummification costs.

The practice of mummification continued on pagan and Christian alike until banned by Theodosius II in A.D. 392. For over a thousand years, most mummies rested peacefully, but eternal rest was not to be their destiny—at least, not in the way they hoped.

Mummies Rediscovered

As the mummies rested, empires rose and fell. Egypt continued to have invaders and visitors alike. When the Persians annexed Egypt as part of their Empire, they noted with interest that well preserved mummies were blackened, seemingly painted with a substance that reminded them of the bitumen they knew from their own lands. Indeed, the word the world uses today to describe these preserved dead—*mummy*—comes from the Persian word "mum" and the Arabic "mumiyah," both of which mean bitumen.

Around a thousand years ago, people in Europe believed that dried mummies had healing powers—the result no doubt of wild travelers' tales. They previously had a cure-all restorative made from bitumen, which was a natural substance found in the Persian mountains, but prohibitively expensive. Mummies appeared to be of the same substance, and so they were ground up in vast quantities as a cheaper method of obtaining the cure-all powder! A lucrative trade developed where the common cemeteries were dug up and shipped off. As an internal medicine, mummy was held to cure concussion, epilepsy, paralysis, coughs, ulcers, poisoning, and headaches. It could be applied to bruises and broken bones alike and was said to prevent infection and stop bleeding. Many important people, like Francis I of France, A.D. 1515–47, a contemporary of Henry VIII of England, would not go anywhere without their bag of ground mummy as an essential first aid kit. But by the A.D. 1600s, the common mummy pits were all but bare.

Not to be deprived of the trade, the Egyptians used their entrepreneurial skills to create new mummies with the castoffs of society by dunking them in pitch or asphalt and sun-drying the bodies, creating "instant mummy." By A.D. 1700, word of the deception spread to Europe and personal consumption of ground mummy dropped. The businessmen merely found another outlet and sold mummies for fertilizer instead. Mummy was also added to paints as an artist's mixing medium and the wrappings were recycled. In the 1800s, paper mills in the United States were using mummy wrappings as rags in papermaking. When they hit a hitch in being able to bleach the resin-soaked bandages to a proper white, they solved the problem by making brown paper instead! The wrappings were also a good, cheap source of fuel back in their native land

Wall painting in Tomb of Nacht, Luxor. Ladies at a banquet. (Sue Cowie Collection.)

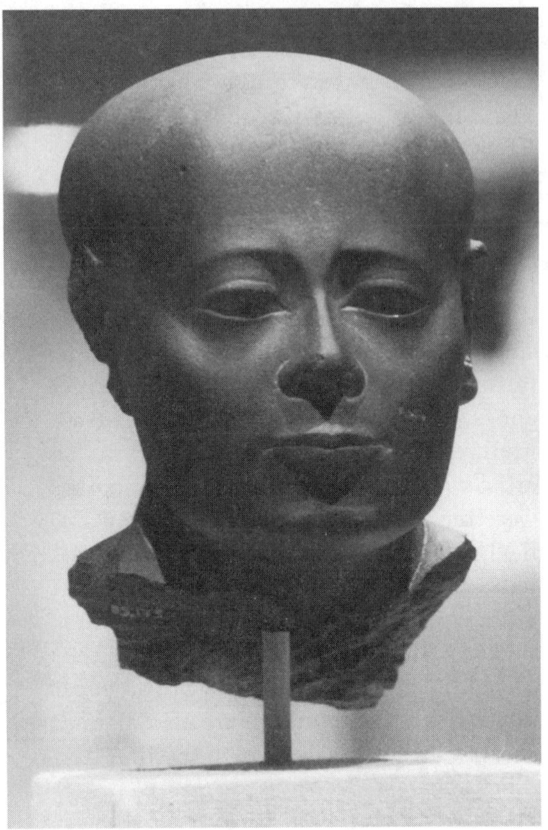

Wesinwer, Priest of Montu. Portrait head of cult statue, Ptolemaic period. (Courtesy Colin Cowie 1998.)

because the resin in them burned so well. One cannot imagine the vast numbers of mummies that were lost to these practices; the surviving mummies are therefore all the more precious.

When Napoleon took his army and his scholars to Egypt, he sparked a growing appreciation of the history of that beautiful land. It did not stop him from bringing back the odd souvenir, of course, such as a mummy head for his wife, Josephine. Odd limbs, and particularly heads, seem to have been first choice for the returning soldier or tourist from this time onward. The acquisition of mummies, their cases, and their grave goods also became a burning passion. Once the military troubles had settled, the rich and famous set about collecting with a zeal that is almost terrifying, but a zeal that has graced our greatest museums with their most breathtaking treasures, preserving these fragile visitors from the past for future generations.

Early Explorers and Egyptologists

Christian occupants of the Valley of Kings simply used it as acceptable shelter and took little or no interest in the dead. Even though the location of Thebes was delineated on Abraham Ortelius's map of Egypt, dated 1595, few were curious. In 1668 Father Charles François notes that he visited "the place of the mummies called Biban el Melouc" but records nothing further. Traveling the country between 1714 and 1726, Father Claude Sicard, head of the Jesuit Mission in Cairo, visited the Valley and appreciated its significance, and located several tombs.

Richard Pococke followed on, publishing his account of the journey in *Observations on Egypt* in 1743. His principal claim to "fame" is that he emulated the Greeks and Romans and wrote his name on the monuments he visited!

James Bruce in 1768 published highly romantic Hellenized versions of the wall paintings he saw on his visit. The year 1798 brought Bonaparte and his troops and the interest in Egypt blossomed suddenly. Scholars like Baron Vivant Denon accompanied Napoleon and helped to make the study of Egypt highly fashionable back home in Europe.

The stories of the field agents for the rich collectors that now make up the next phase in the story of mummies reads like something out of *Boys' Own Paper*. The extraordinary men who traveled Egypt, searching for, negotiating for, acquiring, and devising safe methods of transportation for their treasures, fill several volumes.

What overwhelmingly confident creatures they were — going about a foreign land, generally without speaking the native language, risking entanglements with bandits or paid ruffians of rival collectors, and negotiating with local officials who made money by playing one faction off against another, driven by the need to acquire ever more interesting, beautiful, and rare objects.

The first who springs to mind is Giovanni Belzoni (1778–1823). Born the son of a barber in Padua, Italy, he spent his early life in Rome preparing to be a monk; but the entry of the French into Rome sent him wandering about Europe. Arriving in England, which was the one western European country not under Napoleon's sway in 1803, he spent the next ten years in theaters and fairgrounds, weightlifting and doing feats of strength. The introduction of fountains and waterfalls into his act made him study hydraulics and became a skill he could call upon. He met the new pasha of Egypt in Malta in 1814 and persuaded Mohammed Ali to let him help with the modernization of his land.

Belzoni arrived in Alexandria leaving an England panting for more treasures like the Rosetta Stone, key to hieroglyphs, and war booty from the French, on show in the British Museum. The project for which Belzoni and his wife had traveled to Egypt was a disaster and they had to find other means of making a living. At Thebes on the Nile's west bank lay a superb head, called at that time Young Memnon, described by Sir William Hamilton, husband of Lord Nelson's mistress Lady Emma, as "*the most beautiful and perfect piece of Egyptian sculpture that can be seen throughout the whole country.*" At eight tons, the French had failed to carry it away; but Henry Salt, the newly appointed His Britannic Majesty's Consul, was prompted to acquire it.

Salt had been asked by Sir Joseph Banks, Trustee of the British Museum, to be on the lookout for additions to the national collection. Salt commissioned Belzoni to safely deliver the head. A competitor, Bernadino Drovetti was so sure that Belzoni would fail that he made him a gift of a magnificent granite sarcophagus lid found in a tomb to add to the statue. Belzoni, all the while, was learning about Egypt and its monuments as the country wove its spell on him.

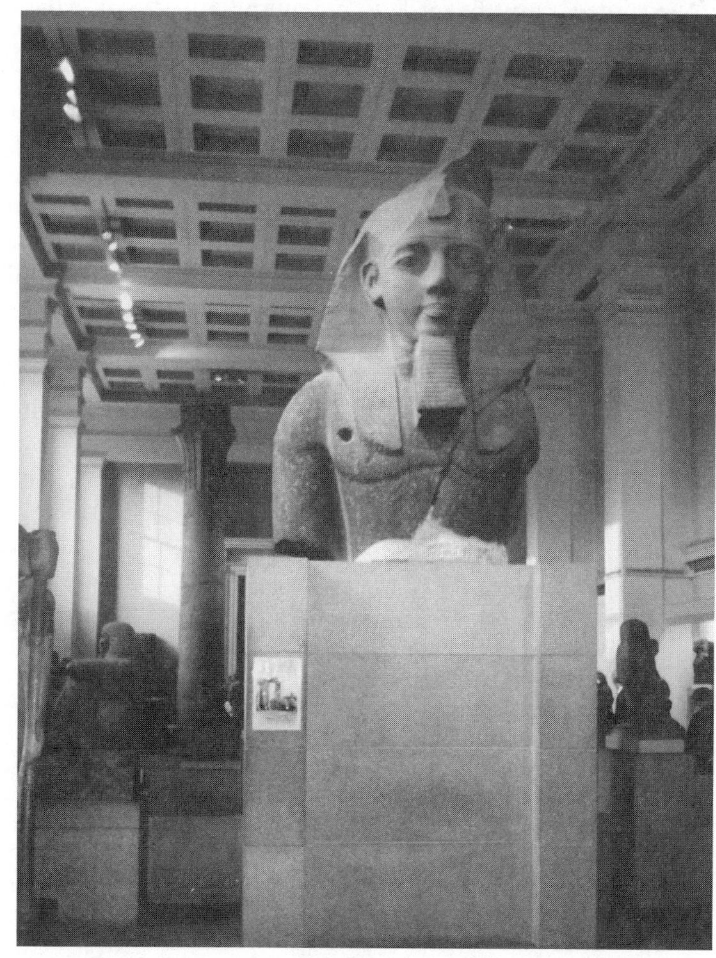

"Young Memnon"—rescued from the sands by Giovanni Belzoni in 1816. The statue of Rameses II was one of the first major Egyptian works acquired for the British Museum. (Courtesy Colin Cowie 1998.)

The Belzonis set up home in the Ramasseum while Giovanni made his preparations. While he waited to fulfill his mission, he saw the wonders of Aswan, collected stelae and obelisks, and discovered a tomb now known to be that of Ay, the man who usurped the throne on the death of Tutankhamun. The head and Belzoni's treasures from Karnak were safely transported to Cairo, on their way at last to England. Salt then agreed to finance Belzoni's explorations round Abu Simbel. Just as the European armies had fought for colonies, now archaeologists were fighting for sites. Whilst engaged in this tussle, Belzoni recorded a visit he made to a mummy pit. It reads like part of an action-packed film script:

> Of some of these tombs many persons could not withstand the suffocating air, which often causes fainting. A vast quantity of dust rises, so fine that it enters into the throat and nostrils, and chokes the nose and mouth to such a degree that it requires great power of lungs to resist it and the strong effluvia of mummies. This is not all; the entry or passage where the bodies are is roughly cut in the rocks, and the falling of the sand from the upper part or ceiling of the passage causes it to be nearly filled up. In some places there is not more than a vacancy of a foot left, which you must contrive to pass through in a creeping posture like a snail, on pointed and keen stones that cut like glass. After getting through these passages, some of them two or three hundred yards long, you generally find a more commodius place perhaps high enough to sit.... But when my weight bore on the body of an Egyptian, it crushed it like a bandbox. I naturally had recourse to my hands to sustain my weight, but they found no better support; so that I sunk altogether among the broken mummies, with a crash of bones, rags and wooden cases, which raised such a dust as kept me motionless for a quarter of an hour, waiting till it subsided again. I could not move from the place, however, without increasing it, and every step I took crushed a mummy in some part or other.

Belzoni had a magic touch when it came to discovering tombs. Finding four mummies, he noted with keen observation, "Among the others I found one that had new linen, apparently, put over the old rags; which proves that the Egyptians took great care of their dead, even for many years after their decease." He also found the magnificent tomb of Seti I, father of Ramesses the Great. He would never know the king's name though, for the secret of hieroglyphs had not yet been broken.

In a week's stay in the Valley of Kings, Belzoni increased the known number of royal tombs by half. His return to Cairo did not bring him pleasure though; his discoveries were all being credited to other people, principally Henry Salt, and the return on the pieces he was able to sell was inadequate. During his wife's absence, he found a way into the Great Pyramid and became the first Westerner to lay eyes on the burial chamber and to scratch his name upon the wall where one can still see it to this day.

Back in London in March 1820, he found himself something of a celebrity. *The Times* wrote about his work and discoveries. A book of his adventures was published and an exhibition of the wax impressions, 182 life-size drawings, the 800 small ones, and 500 hieroglyphs from Seti I's tomb opened in Piccadilly on May 1, 1821. The book and the exhibition engendered interest in each other, Belzoni's showmanship skills reigned supreme, and the arrival of Seti's sarcophagus and a splendid obelisk from Philae, all stimulated interest in the first burst of Egyptomania England had ever seen. One of the mummies he had found had a public unrolling — another first in satisfying the public's interest.

He died of dysentery pursuing another historical site on the coast of Africa in 1823. Bruce Norman, in his book *Footsteps: Nine Archaeological Journeys of Romance and Discovery* (BBC Books, 1987), describes Belzoni as "Unwittingly ... the first of a new generation of Egyptologists who, instead of

Egyptian Hall, Piccadilly, London. Site of Belzoni's exhibition of Seti's tomb. Steel engraving, 1830. (Sue Cowie Collection.)

making a detailed study of classical authors, emphasized first-hand, on-site observations and excavation."

The Next Generation

Scholars and antiquarians such as John Gardner Wilkinson, James Burton, and Robert Hay, all added to the growing science of Egyptology. Thomas Young, William Bankes, and Jean-François Champollion had provided a beginning to the understanding of the language of the ancients. Carl Richard Lepsius arrived to work on behalf of the Prussians, sending home 15,000 antiquities in three years, and making some of the most complete surveys to date.

Around 1844 archaeology came of age in that it developed a conscience and wholesale plundering — however enthusiastic and well-intentioned — was not so readily tolerated. We must thank such farseeing men as Auguste Mariette, who was one of the instigators of a national Egyptian Museum and a Government Antiquities Service. An importance was attached to context, too. Like a police investigation, the site of a mummy find and its environs are of equal importance as the mummy itself. Our museums are littered with mummies which have no provenance to speak of, such as the mummy of Lady Ta-Kesh, in the Museum in Chiddingstone Manor, belonging to the Maidstone Borough Council in Kent, England. The authors, when inquiring about documents relating to the acquisition of the mummy, were told sadly by the current curator," We have no documents about her. In fact, the first three curators kept no notes or documents at all, except in their own memoirs, as the museum was a private collection. We would love to have contemporary documents about the development of the collection." Lady Ta-Kesh lived in the Twenty-fifth or Twenty-sixth Dynasty, around 700–650 B.C., and was the daughter of the Doorkeeper of Osiris Pa-Muta. She was brought to England in the 1820s and purchased at a customs house sale by Sir William Geary, who resided in the village of Hadlow, Kent. He donated it to the local philosophical society in about 1835. Samuel Birch of the British Museum unwrapped the mummy in 1843 assisted by local physician H. W. Diamond, who made incisions in the abdomen and skull to examine the mummification process. The mummy was subsequently presented to the Thomas Charles Museum housed in Chiddingstone Manor and was bequeathed to the town of Maidstone with the rest of his collection in 1855. But of her life, where and when her mummy was found and anything more about her ... we know nothing. Local school children come to see her as part of the Museum's excellent educational provision, and in saying her name, the curator and the authors agree, they give her the eternal life for which she longed.

Mariette, sent to acquire papyri for the Louvre used his funds to clear part of the desert and discovered the Serapeum — the burial place of the sacred Apis bulls. He remained to do fieldwork and by 1858 Mariette had been appointed the Khedive's Director Of Egyptian Monuments, setting up the first Egyptian Museum at Bulaq in 1863. One of his many successes was the recovery of the coffin and jewels of Queen Ahhotpe, a Seventeenth Dynasty queen whose intact mummy came into the hands of the Governor of Qena in 1860. The mummy itself was not seen again, but alerted the interested parties to the possibility of other mummies awaiting discovery. His successor, Gaston Maspero, was to have an even greater triumph.

One of the greatest discoveries came about when a stray goat stumbled down a partially concealed tomb shaft. At least, that's how one of the versions goes. In truth, the collection of royal mummies— or *cache* as it was called — at Deir el-Bahari had been found earlier by an enterprising family named Abd el-Rassul, who used it as a private savings account, carefully picking choice pieces of grave goods and papyri to finance their family needs. But by the mid 1870s too many important papyri and other artifacts were reaching the west with no apparent source. A terrifying official investigation was ordered by Maspero. "Despite brutal interrogation by the feared mudir of Qena, Duad Pasha, the two held their tongues and after some months Ahmed was released from custody; of Hussein, perhaps ominously, we hear no more. Mohammed Ahmed Abd el-Rassul, an elder brother and head of the clan, was intelligent enough to realize that the chances of successfully exploiting the tomb further were slim. Against his brothers' wishes, he decided to cut the family's losses and claim the baksheesh on offer for the information of the find" (Reeves, 1996). Maspero was away, having left his assistant Emile Brugsch in charge when the site of the cache became known. Brugsch set off straightaway, and although he had been told about the cache, he could not believe his eyes when he finally arrived.

> Soon we came upon cases of porcelain funerary offerings, metal and alabaster vessels, draperies and trinkets, until, reaching the turn in the passage, a cluster of mummy cases came into view in such number as to stagger me. Collecting my senses, I made the best examination of them I could by the light of my torch, and at once saw that they contained the mummies of royal personages of both sexes; and yet that was not all. Plunging on ahead of my guide, I came to the (end) chamber ... and there standing against the walls or here lying on the floor, I found even a greater number of mummy cases of stupendous size and weight. Their gold coverings and their polished surfaces so plainly reflected my own excited visage that it seemed as though I was looking into the faces of my own ancestors.

The Egyptian Museum in Cairo, home of the royal mummies and a fabulous collection of antiquities including the treasures from Tutankhamun's tomb. A stock shot of the exterior was used in Boris Karloff's *The Mummy*. (Courtesy Trevor Wayne 1974.)

Balancing the need to record the find in detail with the very real fear of attack by the locals fired with stories of a stupendous treasure, Brugsch cleared the cache as fast as possible and sent the mummies downriver to Bulaq under guard. The find had brought to light forty royal or noble mummies with their coffins and five thousand nine hundred odd smaller objects. At first, they could not comprehend why a single tomb could contain so many kings, queens and nobles, many of the greatest of whom were in dreadful condition. They also wondered where the grave goods of all these mummies were. But they soon discovered that the Abd el-Rassuls had found one of the ancient hiding places that was the ancient priest-kings' answer to disturbed earlier burials.

It has taken a century of work to determine what happened between the original tomb robberies and the recovery of the cache. Experts seem to agree on the following scenario as the most likely run of events. Previously buried in the as yet unconfirmed cliff tomb of Queen Ahmose-Inhapi, the mummies of Ramesses I, Sethos I, and Ramesses II had notes on their coffin dockets about their removal to a new hiding place. The family vault of the high priest Pinudjem II had been chosen to receive the royal visitors after year 11 of Shoshenq I of the Twenty-second Dynasty.

A second royal cache came to light in 1898 in the tomb of Amenophis II. Like Brugsch before him French archaeologist Victor Loret could hardly believe his eyes. On the right hand side of the burial chamber in the first side room he found three stripped corpses minus their coffins. The first, dubbed Elder Lady by Elliot Smith, had long, flowing hair, "a thick veil (covering) her forehead and left eye." The second was a young boy with the youth lock they recognized from statues and wall paintings, "a magnificent tress of black hair." The third, disturbingly, was a young woman with a dislocated jaw. All had pierced skulls and the breast of each was opened. With no identity apparent, Loret assumed they were close family members of Amenophis II. Nine more reasonably intact mummies, along with some coffins, were in the other side room. Again, Loret assumed a family link, until he studied them closer. "The coffin and mummies were a uniform grey color. I leaned over the nearest coffin and blew on it so as to read the name. The grey tint was a layer of dust which flew away and allowed me to read the nomen and prenomen of Ramesses IV. Was I in a cache of royal coffins? I blew away the dust of the second coffin, and a cartouche revealed itself, illegible for an instant, painted in matt black on a shiny black background. I went over to the other coffins ... everywhere cartouches!"

And the names were no less awesome than the Deir el-Bahari cache — Tuthmosis IV, Amenophis III (in a coffin inscribed for Ramesses III, covered with a lid inscribed for Seti II), Merenptah (in the lower part of Sethnakhte's coffin), Seti II, Siptah, Ramesses IV, Ramesses V, Ramesses VI, and an unknown female, possibly Tawosret, in the upturned lid of Sethnakhte's coffin. A further mummy on a wooden boat in the tomb's antechamber suggests it to be Sethnakhte himself.

The two caches give us, in the words of Francis Llewellyn Griffith "The mummies of the hero kings and builders of the empire in the XVIIIth, XIXth and XXth Dynasties at Deir el-Bahari; in the tomb of Amenophis II lay the bodies of sovereigns of the same dynasties who enjoyed to the full the fruits of their predecessors' conquests, and of those who reigned feebly. Altogether we now have in the flesh the series of the Theban monarchs of the New Kingdom almost complete."

The mummies in the second cache were believed to have been collected from various tombs and earlier caches and reinterred in a single occasion, Amenophis II being rewrapped on the same date. Dockets on the

Funerary figurine, Rameses II, 19th dynasty. (Courtesy Colin Cowie 1998.)

mummies indicate that this was done in year 12 or 13 (i.e., 1058 B.C.) of Smendes of the 21st Dynasty. Grafton Elliott Smith who examined the mummies noted, "On the back of the head of the mummy of Siptah there is a hole ... in the right parietal bone ... deliberately made by means of blows from some sharp instrument and similar to openings that I found in the mummies of Seti II, Ramesses IV, Ramesses VI (and possibly that of Rameses V also).... I was inclined to look upon them as wounds ... made by plunderers, who ... chopped through the bandages and so damaged the cranium." The three mummies found in the antechamber were thought to have been in the same room as the large cache initially, as a toe was found in the floor debris belonging to one; they appear to have been moved during a subsequent rifling of the tomb when the other mummies were plundered and finally left where Loret found them at some later undetermined date.

We shall leave aside the controversies evoked by the royal mummies being restored and recoffined — not always in the right containers— which has led some Egyptologists to doubt the names the ancient restorers put on their handiwork, preferring to agree with Herbert Winlock, who noted somewhat drily in 1932, "The docket written by the ancient officials must be accepted unless there is very strong evidence against it." And since we know that names in Ancient Egypt are never taken lightly and that several unidentified bodies are found alongside their named tombmates in these caches, it is safe to assume that the priests who performed the restorations only tagged those bodies that they were assured owned the names given them.

The two great treasures that the caches had presented to the modern world also begged the question of the existence of other caches. Where, for example, were Horemheb, Ay, and Tuthmosis I? Alan Gardiner noted some faint graffiti at the entrance to Horemheb's tomb referring to an unspecified command for works ordered by Herihor, the then High Priest of Amun. Certain scribes, including Butehamun and Djehutymose, carried out the work thought to be either the removal of the king for reburial, or, more probably, an official investigation into the condition and safety of the tomb. Some scholars believe this "work" was in fact the recycling of buried wealth to prop up the claims of various high priests of Amun to the crown, and refer to the 4000-odd markings left by the scribes, 130 by Butehamun alone around the Theban hills, pointing out tombs which could be cleared. Perhaps the restorations were not wholly done out of piety, but they bequeathed us a wonderful treasure.

Other Discoveries

After the magnificent discoveries in the late 1800s, many scholars felt that Egypt had given up her greatest treasures and secrets and that little more of any consequence remained to be discovered. It was the age of the rich patron, financing digs with employed experts. Men like the fabled Theodore Davis, the wealthy American who for many years held the concession — official permission — to dig in the Valley of the Kings. Davis, though not a specialist, was passionate about Egyptology, and his generosity and sense of national pride benefited The Metropolitan Museum of Art in New York and other fortunate institutions. Davis's friend, Mrs. Andrews, wrote about his approval of an antiquities inspector named Howard Carter, who used his not inconsiderable artistic talents to supplement his meager salary. Carter assiduously followed up clues about blackmarket antiquities by constant dialogue with the locals, antique dealers, and buyers— like Davis himself— to track down stolen objects and bring the thieves to book. Interestingly, we can find little evidence of the *buyers* being punished! Carter was described as "a most efficient officer — is absolutely fearless—carries no arms— and rides about quite unattended at all hours of the night." Carter and his backer, Lord Carnarvon, dug in Egypt for many years before their greatest find. The discovery of the virtually intact tomb of the Pharaoh Tutankhamun in 1922 is so well known and commented upon that it is not necessary to go into it in great detail here. When Carter finally came to look on the face of the pharaoh, the very fact that he had not been disturbed had contributed to the deterioration of his mummy. The remains were all but carbonized by the chemical interactions of the preserving agents and the almost hermetic sealing of the coffins.

Tutankhamun's tomb, while hastily put together, nevertheless gives a clear picture of the preparations made for the eternal home of the mummy—furniture, food, amusements, weapons, gifts from family and close friends, souvenirs of the early years of his life, wine from the best vintages of his

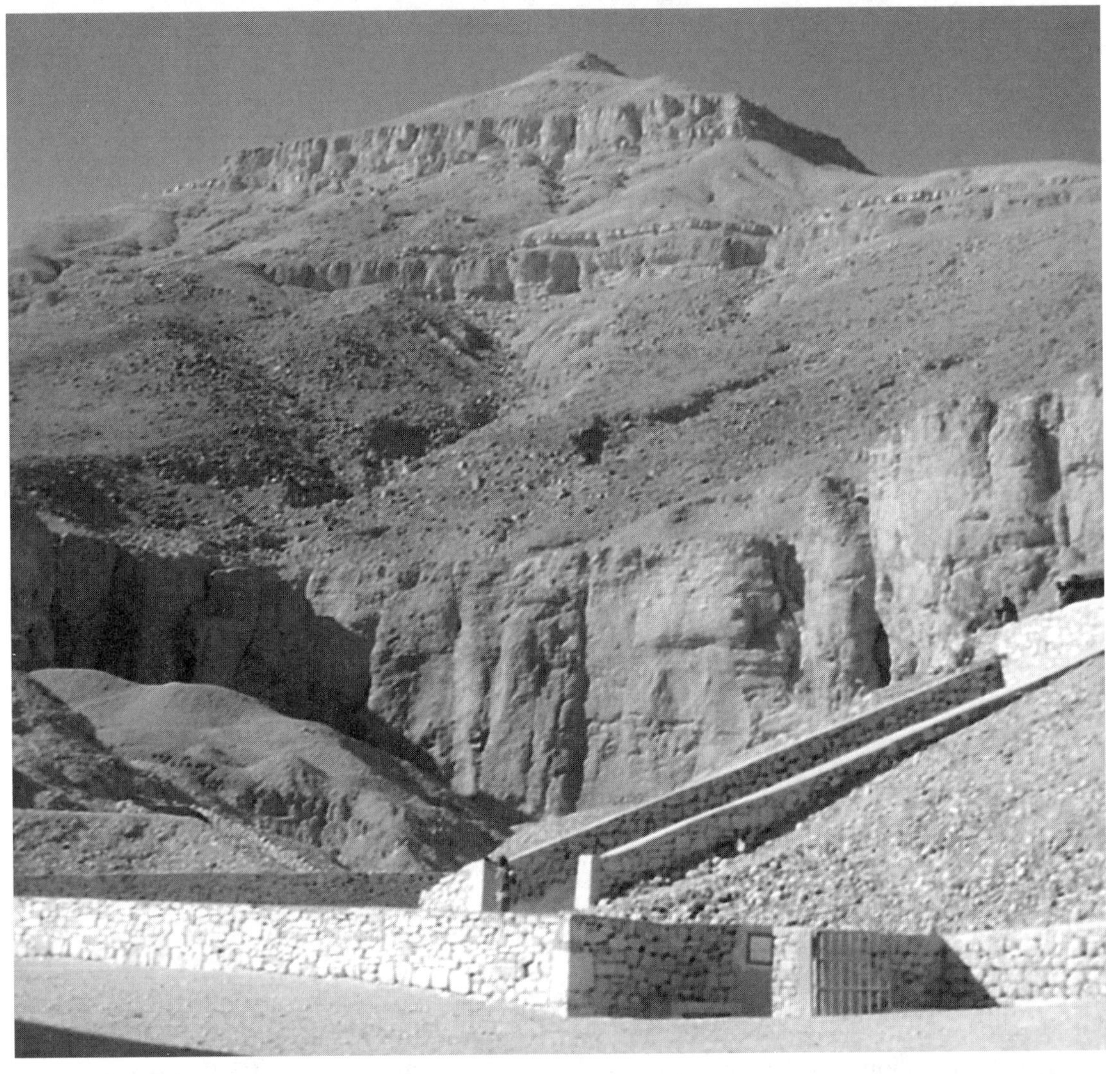

The Valley of the Kings. Tutankhamun's tomb (Dynasty XVIII) lies below the floor of the valley behind the wall in the foreground. The king still rests in his tomb. The sloping entrance above is to the later tomb of Rameses VI (Dynasty XX). The construction of this later tomb helped ensure that Tutankhamun would remain undisturbed down to modern times. The natural pyramidal peak at the head of the valley was sacred to the Cobra goddess Meretseger. (Courtesy Trevor Wayne 1974.)

vineyards, transport—all bringing in sharp relief the everyday life of the young king; and sacred objects too, to ensure that the life and status did not change. Surprisingly, and to many scholars disappointingly, there were no documents in the tomb. No Book of the Dead specifically created for him. No records of his life and achievements. But by the tenets of his faith, he lives forever, his name known and spoken frequently, his mummy still nestling in its tomb—to date, the only known monarch still to rest in the Valley. Certain archaeologists hope this will not always be so, and some return as often as possible to continue the search.

The discovery of pharaonic burials in the Delta during World War II did not receive much publicity although, the objects found were equally as beautiful and as important as Tutankhamun's.

So much of Egypt is still to be explored and excavated. So much remains to be discovered. Some scholars believe that 90 percent of the ancient Egyptian legacy is as yet untouched. Museums and universities continue to dig, record, and evaluate their work and take part in the conservation of what we already have to study. It would take several pharaonic fortunes to foot the bill of doing the job properly. But one of the joys of Egyptology is that it links us to our distant past with such startling clarity, marking our differences and similarities, and helps towards completing the picture about the development of the human race.

The Curse of the Pharaohs?

Since the discovery of Tutankhamun's tomb, the everyday world has been conscious of a so-called Curse on those who disturb the rest of the long dead. That the Curse should have evolved by way of "beating" a news embargo instigated by the Earl of Carnarvon, and that many famous archaeologists have dug their way happily into retirement or even more happily died whilst still actively digging at venerable ages, seems to do nothing to lessen the hold the notion of the Curse has on otherwise sentient and sane human beings. We should consider soberly how we would feel if some millennia from now other humans—or other thinking beings?—wanted to study *us* in the way we have studied the ancients. Would we mind our remains being thoroughly investigated by every resource known to science? Our writings scanned for evidence of our thought processes and spiritual development? (God forbid anyone leaves a National Enquirer lying around!) Our belongings carbon-dated, their materials identified, our level of civilization and culture judged by what we left behind? Many things made our forbears less than careful in the early days of the science of Egyptology. Agents for the wealthy and powerful, whose only criterion was enhancing the prestige of their patrons by acquiring the grandest works of Egyptian art, did as much damage, if not more, than the hungry fellahin who systematically robbed ancient sites to feed their families. The imperial *anima*, too, was responsible for an assurance that we find breathtakingly arrogant nowadays; because of a conviction that white European ethics were superior and that the "natives" were decadent and past redemption, the natives were treated badly—albeit that *their* ancestors had a highly sophisticated, spiritual, and cultured civilization while *ours* were wearing skins, painting themselves blue, and dancing round bonfires.

Fortunately, for the science of Egyptology and our salvation, a group of more enlightened scholars came hot on their heels, anxious to examine in minute detail the debris left by the treasure hunters and to rescue from it great areas of knowledge and understanding.

As far as anyone can tell with any degree of assurance, there is no such thing as a Pharaonic Curse. There are some references to the safety of tombs, and condemnation of any who think to disturb the rest of the dead,

Ptolemaic figures of Osiris. (Courtesy Colin Cowie 1998.)

although they mostly refer to the possible embezzlement of funds left for mortuary temples and offerings. But the purpose of a tomb with its mummy and grave goods was very different from the Gothic-horrors of our own Christian catacombs. Herbert Winlock took exception to the silly stories that followed the death of Carnarvon, a man who had come to Egypt because his health was poor and who was quite frail, and the growing "roll of the dead," who supposedly had succumbed to the curse. These include an elderly Egyptologist from the Louvre who died in his bed, and a friend of a tourist, who had entered the Tomb, and was subsequently run over by a taxi! Mace, suffering occasional bouts of pleurisy contracted long before Tutankhamun was discovered, was reported as dying of a "mystery illness." In an effort to return some sanity to the question, Winlock kept his own "death roll"; he made a point of writing to correct any daft stories that appeared in the press and his notes are most interesting: "George J. Gould; Friend of Lord Carnarvon's, tourist in Egypt, traveling for his health. Was ill before he ever came to Egypt.... Arthur E. P. Weigall, who was not allowed in the tomb except with the public. Had no part in any way with the tomb.... "Prince" Ali Fahmy Bey, murdered in the Savoy Hotel in London by his French wife. If he was ever in the tomb it was as a tourist.... The workman in the British Museum, London, said to have fallen dead while labeling objects from the tomb. But there are no objects from the tomb in the British Museum and never have been.... If tourists are subject to the curse it should be remembered that a large number of them are elderly people traveling in Egypt for their health."

Howard Carter was more blunt and concise — when asked about the Curse, especially later in his life — his favorite reply was "*The answer is spherical and in the plural....*"

The Paleopathologists

The study of mummies has grown over the decades from small groups of interested collectors to the current burgeoning science of paleopathology. The importance of this new discipline is outlined by one of its most gifted practitioners, Dr. Rosalie David, head of the Manchester Mummy Project since 1973, and Keeper of Egyptology, with the status of Senior Lecturer at Manchester University Museum, England. In her book *The Mummy's Tale*, Davis writes:

> Multidisciplinary scientific studies can give a picture of daily existence in ancient Egypt which is more realistic, though often less glamorous, than the view provided by art or literature.... The study of ancient Egyptian remains holds out unique opportunities. Relatively large numbers of mummified remains still survive, partly because the near-ideal environmental conditions have preserved the bodies, and partly because the ancient Egyptian religious beliefs prompted the development of mummification and its continuation over a period of some three thousand years. Egypt also has a relatively unbroken population sequence, particularly in the more remote regions of the Nile Valley which remained isolated to some extent from the later arrivals who settled mainly in the Delta. Thus, Egypt provides an unequaled opportunity to study disease in a society which has remained fairly constant and has survived in a virtually unchanged environment for thousands of years.

The first studies of mummies were, in an artistic sense, part of the preparations for the *Description de l'Egypte*, commissioned by Napoleon Bonaparte. Following the explosion of interest and the wholesale shipping of mummies to Europe for sale as collectors' items, a fashion for what was believed to be more scientific study arose. In truth, the planned outcome of many of these "studies" was the recovery of jewelry and sacred amulets from amid the wrappings, and detailed notes were not kept. Once "scientific" study became fashionable, dealers scoured Egypt for quantities of them. Giovanni Belzoni paid regular wages plus bonuses to acquire as many mummies in the shortest available time, often working with his collectors himself. He noted in 1821, "But what a place of rest: surrounded by bodies, by heaps of mummies in all directions, which, previous to my being accustomed to the sight, impressed me with horror ... though, fortunately, I am destitute of the sense of smelling, I could taste that the mummies were rather unpleasant to swallow."

During his exhibition of some of his discoveries in the Egyptian Hall, Piccadilly, London, the mummy of a young man was unwrapped before an invited audience of the most eminent doctors of the day. Bringing a mummy back from a visit to Egypt became a necessity as recorded by Father Geramb in 1833, who told the ruler Mohammed Ali Pasha, "It would be hardly respectable, on one's return from Egypt, to present oneself in Europe without a mummy in one hand and a crocodile in the other." Amelia B. Edwards, founder of the Egypt Exploration Fund (later Society), also noted in her book *A Thousand Miles Up the Nile* that "there is in fact a growing passion for mummies among the Nile travelers." The demand became so great that the price rose until a mummy was a costly luxury souvenir within a short space of time.

Mummy unrolling became social events—possibly the highlight of an at home, or the culmination of a dinner or supper party. One of the few serious investigations at this time was at Leeds, England, in 1828. The Leeds Philosophical and Literary Society made one of the earliest recorded scientific investigations of a mummy from Egypt. A special team was created including a surgeon, a physician, and a chemist, together with the Society's secretary. They partially unwrapped and dissected a mummy. They chemically analyzed parts of the body, made an anatomical study, and translated and interpreted the texts. They recorded details of the man's physical condition and the techniques of mummification used, naming him as Natsef-Amun who served in the great temple complex at Thebes.

This same subject was later investigated by Dr. David's team and she commented, "Natsef-Amun, well placed in society and with a successful career, participated in the sacred rituals offered to Egypt's greatest deities, but the investigation shows that he suffered sickness and disease and possibly endured a violent death." In 1989, the science had come a long way from Natsef-Amun's first encounter.

Thomas John Pettigrew (1791–1865), son of a naval surgeon and trained as a surgeon himself, had a wide range of interests that encompassed the literary and archaeological developments of his day. An acquaintance of Belzoni, with his doctor's training it was understandable that Pettigrew's contribution related to mummification techniques and diseases of the ancient Egyptians. He unrolled and gave demonstrations on large numbers of mummies, some of which he purchased for his own collection and others that were given to him so that the donors could be present at the autopsies. The procedure he followed during his unwrappings was detailed; he used a multidisciplinary approach, consulting experts on textiles, fiber, insects and so on. His contemporary, Augustus Bozzi Granville (1783–1872), published the findings of his own investigation into an Egyptian mummy of the Persian Period, exhibiting evidence of ovarian disease. These early studies laid the groundwork for future research, but the fashion for less scientific unrollings changed to disapproval of interfering with the long dead, and died out.

The serious interest was revived in 1908 when Dr. Margaret Murray, working in Manchester, England, unwrapped and autopsied two brothers using the same multidisciplinary approach. Dr. Murray felt that she had to justify the opening of tombs and examination of bodies in the light of new knowledge. She insisted that the study be detailed, careful, without sentimentality, and above all, without "fear of the outcry of the ignorant." Nor was she the only expert working in the field. In Cairo, Grafton Elliot Smith held the Chair of Anatomy at the Government School of Medicine. His early work in paleopathology was done in 1901 on a group of bodies found in Upper Egypt. He recorded bone measurements and mummification processes. Another project — saving mummies from the 1900 alterations on the dam at Aswan — brought six thousand mummies into his care. With W. R. Dawson and F. W. Jones, both of whom came from England specifically to join him, he revealed for the first time many of the diseases the ancient suffered from.

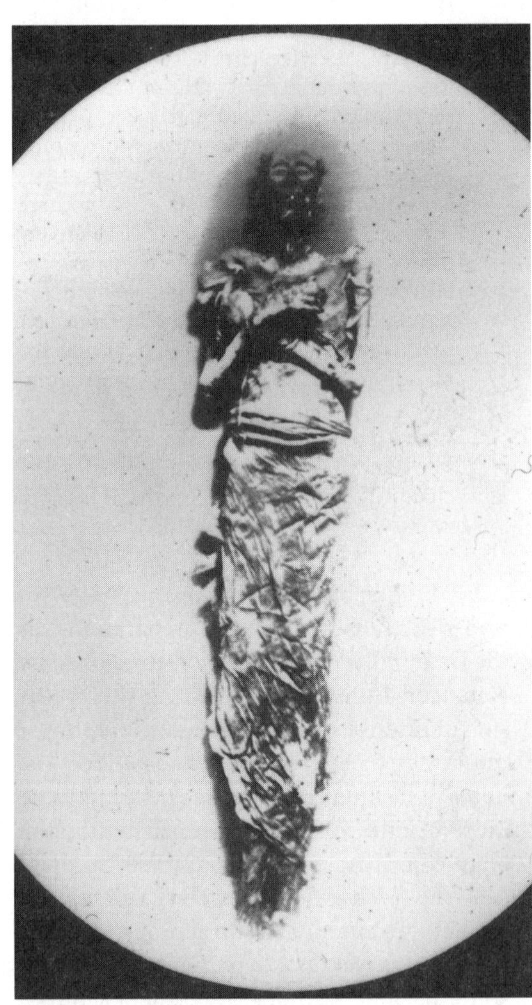

Mummy of Rameses II. Unwrapped June 1, 1886. Lecture slide, circa 1890, printed direct from glass slide. (Sue Cowie Collection.)

The discovery of the royal mummy caches enabled Elliot Smith to compile a history of the development of mummification techniques. He also had the honor of performing the private detailed examination of the Eighteenth Dynasty pharaoh, Tuthmosis IV, after its public unwrapping. He instituted another aspect of paleopathology by using radiography for the first time in the study of a royal mummy.

The early years of the twentieth century brought new insights. Armand Ruffer, Professor of Bacteriology at Cairo's Government School of Medicine, began the study of histopathology in relation to Egyptian mummy remains, investigating traces of diseases in both skeletons and mummies. He also developed methods of rehydrating ancient tissue to give it a semblance of its former condition. The rehydrated tissue was them examined histologically to determine evidence of disease.

The third great contributor, also based in Cairo, was Alfred Lucas. Lucas initially went to Egypt for his health, as his lungs were not good. He stayed to become Chemist to the Antiquities Service from 1923 to 1932. He analyzed many ancient materials and substances, and advised on conservation and restoration techniques, especially during the Tutankhamun dig and at the discovery of the royal tombs at Tanis. His book *Ancient Egyptian Materials and Industries*, published in 1926, remains a benchmark and his experiments were the first to validate Herodotus's account of mummification. He also noted for the first time that natron was used as a salt and not a solution in mummification rituals.

Over the past twenty-five years, the science of paleopathology has grown almost geometrically. The introduction of nearly nondestructive techniques have allowed the study of mummies to gather maximum information with minimal damage. The results have added immeasurably to our understanding of life in ancient Egypt. Flinders Petrie, the "Father of British Egyptology" was particularly farsighted when he wrote in 1904, "To raid the whole of past ages, and to put all that we think effective into museums is only to ensure that such things will perish in the course of time. A museum is only a temporary place. There is not one storehouse in the world that has lasted a couple of thousand years.... It is then to the written record and published illustrations that the future will mainly have to look." Little could he have guessed what other magic the science of our day could effect — or can we imagine what future students of ancient Egypt will be able to do? Nowadays the study of a mummy can involve conventional radiography, computer tomography (CT) scans, endoscopy, histology, serology, dental studies, and scientific facial reconstruction — all of them telling us more about these visitors from the past.

In a contemporary investigation, the mummy will be slowly and carefully unwrapped. Textiles, materials, and fibers will be examined by various experts, including those who can translate any texts found on the wrappings. The layers and the pattern of mummy wrappings will be carefully recorded for comparison with others and as a way of fixing dates. The composition and methods of weaving the textiles will receive attention too.

The mummy will have a radiological examination — in whole and in close-up of specific areas. An X-ray will have been taken prior to the unwrapping to fix the location of objects within the wrappings. The "reading" of such X-rays is a developing skill and matching the fact to the picture is a helpful guide to the study of those mummies as yet undisturbed by Egyptologists.

The remains are then subjected to a range of pathological techniques from which much medical evidence can be obtained. The dental health of the mummy is examined with care too, for a great deal can be learned from the state of the mouth. Diseases are tracked through the traces they have left on the remains being examined. Any insects or seeds that have become trapped during or after the mummification process are then examined. Sometimes they can narrow down the time of year when death occurred, just as in a police investigation today.

The fingerprints can often be studied, either from the mummy itself or rehydrated tissue from the fingers and toes. And most magically of all, the face of the deceased can be re-created using set, scientific parameters so that he or she can "live again," as the Book of the Dead puts it.

Often these wonderful techniques can raise as many questions as they answer. Take, for example, "1770," the only "name" of a mummy in the Manchester collection, and star of the BBC video that was prepared alongside the investigation for the layman to be able to follow and enjoy the team's work. Poor 1770 was not in good condition; it had been chosen for the study because it could never be put on show. All the disciplines were carried out and some odd anomalies began to present themselves. 1770 appeared to have been prepared for burial both as a woman and a man — a fake phallus being found in the groin region, contrasting with the golden nipple shields that the mummy also had. The legs were in dreadful condition and led the team to speculate, along with the virtual absence of any body skin, whether 1770 had been in water for a long period prior to mummification. There appeared to be evidence of the legs being chewed off below the knees. False limbs and a beautifully modeled foot showed the detailed care of the embalmer in "restoring" the body prior to wrapping. The body also had a beautiful pair of sandals under the soles of the feet within the wrappings. As most people went barefoot, could 1770 have been noble, they conjectured? Certainly, anyone coming to their death because of crocodile attack would have been treated with reverence by the Egyptians and prepared for burial with piety and care, for the crocodile was a sacred animal.

X-rays showed that 1770's skull was badly damaged and had to be pieced together so that a mold could be made for facial reconstruction. Thirty separate pieces of skull encrusted with mud and bandages were reassembled, but fortunately, the most important areas still existed and most of the teeth were present. Casts were made of each fragment and a 3-D jigsaw created so that a mold could be made. There was a very obvious defect of the bone to the left of the nose, and scientists felt certain that 1770 suffered from considerable nasal congestion. Next, small pegs were fitted at specific points on the newly created skull, and cut to precise lengths to enable the soft tissue to be built up with soft clay. The face began to take shape, with the sculptor bearing in mind that other disciplines had confirmed that 1770 was a teenager. The mouth was left slightly open to reflect a person suffering breathing problems, stressing the adenoidal appearance. A classic Egyptian face, bearing a marked resemblance to modern Egyptians, began to take shape. The head was then painted and fitted with glass eyes, which brought it vibrantly to life. Hair and eyelashes were added; possibly a more accurate hairdo will follow at a later date, but 1770 already had fans who wanted to see the finished article. Additional coloring and makeup were minimal since everyone agreed that the care with which the face was reconstructed did not demand extra cosmetics.

The mummy called 1770 was thought to have been found by Flinders Petrie at Hawara in the 1890s. Its exact date was unknown but it was thought to be from the Graeco-Roman period. The carbondating of the bones and bandages showed some surprising and exciting results. It was also around this time that the team decided, on a balance of probability, that 1770 was female, and began to refer to "her" as such.

Carbon 14 tests showed that 1770's bones were a thousand years older than her bandages. The wrappings dated from the later period of Roman occupation but the bones were from a period between the Second Intermediate period, when Egypt was occupied by foreign invaders for the second time, and the Nineteenth Dynasty. The wrappings, cartonnage mask, sandals and nipple shields are all of the late date but there was no evidence of what must have been the original wrappings and amulets. The original state of the teenage mummy upon unwrapping was now much more understandable; much of the original tissue must have been lost during rewrapping.

Damage to the skeleton also could have taken place during rewrapping; evidence of an attempt at rehydration prior to rewrapping was evident by the insects in the bandages. These answers, however, brought about other questions.

The careful restoration and rewrapping of the teenager in late Roman times, including costly decorations and materials, as well as the evidence of the reinterring royal mummies in caches by priests of later generations, suggests that the embalmers knew that 1770 was a person of considerable importance. Since provision for both sexes was made, and no name was added to the new wrappings, they did not know *who* the mummy was. Who 1770 really is could forever remain a mystery.

The study of the development of diseases has been greatly enhanced by work done on mummies. A reasonably fixed population, over a long, stable period of time, provides a good way of tracking the development of illnesses across the ages.

The teeth of mummies have provided some interesting insights into the diet and health of the ancient population as well. Whatever the social class of the mummy, teeth are usually in bad condition due to sand grinding down the surfaces of the tooth enamel. Sand got everywhere, and despite careful preparation, the daily bread of Egypt was contaminated with sand. In many instances, the teeth laid down natural dentine over the exposed pulp, effectively healing themselves, but the evidence of ulcers, so severe as to eat away the bones of jaw and skull, are horrendous. A vast amount of Egyptians must have been used to excruciating toothache on a regular basis. Teeth can also determine the age of a mummy; whether or not wisdom teeth are present aids the archaeologist in narrowing the age of the body. Sand, too, has been found in many of the lungs examined; the winds of the desert blew fine sand into the respiratory tracts of the population and caused several illnesses, including psittacosis.

A large number of mummies examined have evidence of parasites— the most common being the bilharzia worm that causes schistosomiasis. The worm is found in stagnant water, and since many of the population were barefoot — and indeed, still are — the infective cycle is easily set up. The worms invade the body through the skin, and attach themselves to blood vessel walls where they release their eggs into the bloodstream. Eggs enter the bladder and intestines and eventually pass out of the body. If the eggs should enter fresh water they hatch into larvae, which enter the bodies of certain types of water snails. After a period of development they move back into human hosts, penetrating the skin and entering the blood vessels. Here they become mature bilharzia worms and reattach themselves to the blood vessels— and the cycle begins again and can result in death for the host. The Ebers Papyrus, which specializes in medical matters, describes various cures for blood in the urine, which is one symptom of the disease. Remains of calcified eggs have been found in preserved livers and kidneys of mummies, and calcification of the bladder can be detected by radiology. Other conditions noted in paleopathology include osteoarthritis, degenerative spondylosis, calcified cartilage, lithiasis of the bladder, and scoliosis.

The discipline of paleopathology runs across all strata of ancient Egyptian society. Let us note just two of the many interesting, documented instances.

In the village of Duch, in the extreme south of the Kharga Oasis, Serge Sauneron, Director of the Institut Français d'Archeologie Orientale in Cairo, obtained a concession to carry out excavations. Although the site had been known for over a century, it had never been investigated in detail. The evidence pointed to a population of around 5,000 at its height, and there was a vast necropolis. The site was known to have been occupied between the first century B.C. until the fifth century A.D.— roughly the Roman occupation; although late in the stream of Egyptian history the site was isolated for much of its existence, and burial customs had been continued through the centuries. The site, which contained seven hundred bodies, many mummified, some skeletal, was in poor condition due to pillage and flooding from the irrigation canals close to the necropolis. This was the first time a large number of mummies had been studied in situ as a homogenous series, making it possible to identify a cross-section of the population, both in time, and by social class. Classic osteometric methods and radiology were used; mummies were cleaned, photographed, measured, and X-rayed. Samples were taken of hair, nails, skin, resin, and embalming materials— all were analyzed. The mummies were then restored to selected tombs.

Dunand and Lichtenberg reported,

> At Duch we are dealing with a population of Mediterranean type, of slim build and average height (men 1.65 m, women 1.55 m), pale skinned ... almost identical in feature to the populations of the Nile Valley.... In several cases there is evidence of a fatal fracture resulting from trauma: in one case, for example, an old woman died from a fracture to the thighbone; in another, a child died as a result of a fractured skull.... 74% were suffering from osteoarthritis of the spinal column — an unusually high percentage probably attributable to manual labor — and a further 84% were suffering from scoliosis. Striae relating to arrested growth ... indicating fairly frequent periods of food shortage. Parasitic illnesses ... such as filariasis and in particular bilharzia were also identified ... despite the overall health of the population which can only be described as poor the average lifespan (not taking into account perinatal mortality which must have been very high) was 38. Mummification appears to have been virtually universal.... Although abdominal evisceration was rare, removal of the brain was very common ... in 65% of cases. Differences in the construction of the mummies show that Herodotus's description of the different categories of treatment ... hold good even at this late date. The most elaborate treatment involved gilding the body and in particular the face.

The other example comes from the opposite end of the social scale — Pharaoh Ramesses II, the Great, who caused great concern. When his mummy was X-rayed by G. Elliot Smith in 1912, it was already showing signs of deterioration, kept as it was in a glass case. By 1975, Ramesses was in dire straits, and a rescue package for him was negotiated between the French and Egyptian Governments. The Pharaoh went by air to Paris, was met by a guard of honor to note his status as a head of state, and was feted by all France. The work done on him in France represents the high point of the study of museum-based mummies. Today's methods give a vast amount of new information about the mummy without damaging it in any way.

Finding the cause of the deterioration and arresting it were imperatives in the study. From among the wrappings, minute samples of the mummy's chest and hair were taken for analysis. Dr. Jean Mouchacca succeeded in identifying the destructive organism — a fungus with the splendid name *Daedalea biennis Fries!*

In-depth studies were made of the Pharaoh's skeleton: walls of his femoral arteries, teeth, and the whole mummy. Evidence showed that he limped slightly and suffered from a stiffening of the spine; also his head was inclined too far forward in relation to the spine. To "rectify" this, his embalmers fractured the front and back of his neck so they could lay him straight after he had dried in the natron. Like most Egyptians his teeth were in a bad state with numerous abscesses. The evidence suggests that he died from a general infection, and at a great age.

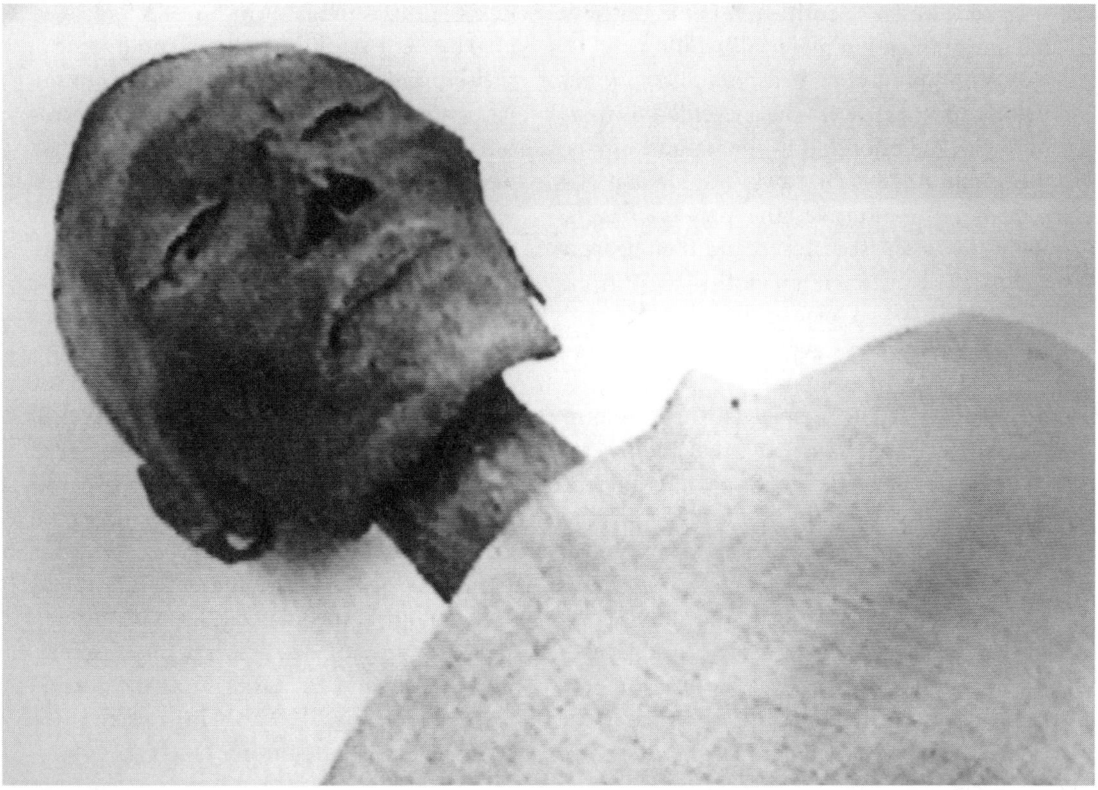

Top: **Rameses II, covered in a shroud given to him by the Louvre Museum. (Courtesy Colin Cowie 1998.)**
Bottom: **Facade of the British Museum circa 1930. (Sue Cowie Collection.)**

Because the scientists did not know how the mummification materials would react to treatment involving heat or cold, Lionel Balout and Colette Roubert decided to treat him with radiation to kill the fungus. Under the watchful eye of Dr. Sawki Nakhla, Egypt's official representative, the process began. Ramesses was first restored and then draped in a piece of ancient linen cloth — a gift from the Louvre — and placed in a cedarwood coffin to return to Egypt. "He had been reborn a second time and recovered all his former radiance. The doctors who tended him merely played the same part that the priests had played before them. Respecting ancient tradition, they had given Ramesses's spirit the dwelling it desired: a perfect body" (Sygma).

Ramesses returned to his home and a special case, temperature and humidity controlled, with an antibacterial gas in the case. And many of his equals are in similar new cases. The work continues ... and who knows what news will come out of Egypt next? Perhaps the labyrinth of KV5, discovered by Kent Weeks's team, will hold some of the mummies of Rameses the Great's sons in its depths. Or a donkey will stumble into a burial chamber, as has happened more than once in the past — in fact, as recently as 1996, when a donkey's uncertain footing led the way to a cemetery of some ten thousand Graeco-Roman mummies of the first and second centuries A.D. These mummies, lying beneath Egypt's Bahariya Oasis, are completely untouched and in need of at least ten years' concentrated work and study to clear and conserve them. Dubbed the Valley of the Golden Mummies, this find will add immeasurably to our understanding of the past. Or perhaps the Nubian digs will unearth mummies of the black pharaohs that many archaeologists speculate about. One thing is sure — Egyptology is a vibrant and fascinating science, and Egypt itself, as the current travel ads tell us, is awaiting the celebration of its seventh millennium!

II

The Mummy in Film, Television and Stage Production

A century of mummy stories— and the occasional play — precede the arrival of the Mummy on film. Before the discovery of Tutankhamun's tomb in the 1920s sparked off mummy hysteria and the genesis of "the mummy's curse," only a handful of films had used the mummy as a player. Early filmmakers Georges Méliès and Walter Booth produced prototypes: Méliès, with *Cleopatra* in 1899, where an evil old man had hacked a mummy to pieces and subsequently used fire to resuscitate the living woman, and Booth, with *The Haunted Curiosity Shop* in 1901, where a living mummy appears before the eyes of a scholar to have its wrappings fall away and its flesh melt until only the skeleton remained.

Further examples include *The Vengeance of Egypt* (1912), where Napoleon himself superintends the digging up of a mummy case, and the theft of a scarab ring by one of his officers brings death to the soldier's sweetheart. In *The Avenging Hand* (1915), an Egyptian princess goes to London looking for the hand cut off by marauding archaeologists. Both are listed in film histories but are now lost.

Die Augen der Mumie Ma (1918) with Pola Negri and Emil Jannings still exists. Jannings was later to be one of the screen's greatest stars and recipient of one of the original Academy Awards. He played the title role, and frightened the wits out of Pola Negri. In this film, a young English painter is taken to a "haunted tomb" and shown a mummy's blinking eyes. In reality, the eyes are those of a young girl who is forced to play her part by her mad guardian; inquisitive visitors are scared away by this subterfuge and the guardian can continue the (to him) romantic idyll with his ward. Love conquers temporarily, and she elopes with the painter. Her guardian pursues them relentlessly, and finally, she drops dead from his harassment. In grief and madness, he stabs himself.

Cinema-going audiences were not spellbound by these forays into mummy lore. Most of the films were regarded as kiddie chillers or a family outing on public holidays. And then Howard Carter unearthed the steps which led to the door of Tutankhamun's tomb — and mummy mania broke loose. As part of this madness the Earl

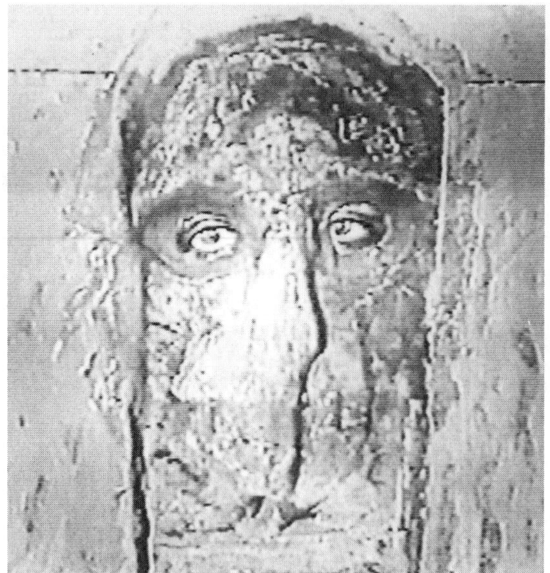

Die Augen der Mumie Ma **(1918).**

of Carnarvon planned a film of the discovery to recoup some of his money.

The spell of Ancient Egypt had been cast over the Western world before, but never as such a blanket media event. Everywhere people were discussing the find and "the curse" (and not quite finding a good explanation as to why the chief desecrator, Howard Carter, survived, remained healthy, and died a normal death aged 66!). The boy-king's discovery generated as much, if not more, excitement than all the major blockbuster movies of the present day put together. Papers ran stories on every aspect of the dig, the treasures, the wall paintings, the people involved; newsreels reported the progress of the clearing, redolent with twenties "bright young things" rubbernecking as part of the social season. In London and elsewhere, fashion, furniture, fine arts, and anyone who could get in on the act went Egypt crazy. "Even the new model Singer sewing machine of that year went Pharaonic, and it was seriously proposed that the new underground extension from Morden to Edgware, then under construction, should be called Tootancamden because it passed through Tooting Common and Camden Town" (Graves).

An elegant young lady named Lady Elizabeth Bowes-Lyon (now Her Majesty Queen Elizabeth the Queen Mother) simply had to have lingerie in her trousseau that reflected the styles of the tomb paintings. A replica of the tomb went on show in the amusement park of the British Empire Exhibition at Wembley. Dancers did the "Anubis Trot."

On the death of Carnarvon — a not uncommon death in those pre-antibiotic days— folk began remembering other strange tales they had heard, like the experiences of Joseph Lindon Smith and his young wife, and their friends Mr. and Mrs. Arthur Weigall. Lindon Smith and his friends had set up home in a tomb to prepare a drama which told the tale of the heretic Pharaoh Akhnaton doomed to wander in limbo as a punishment of Amen-Ra, to entertain the glitterati of Luxor on an "auspicious date." Both the young wives had identical dreams of being struck by the flail of one of the colossal pharaonic statues in the Temple at Karnak — one across the belly and one across the eyes. Shortly thereafter, one had a miscarriage and the other almost went blind with trachoma, necessitating both families' immediate withdrawal from Luxor to Cairo and the cancellation of the play.

Unnoticed at the time, the reminder of these tales, along with a newspaper serialization of Burton Stevenson's 1917 novel *A King in Babylon*, made the public clamor for more mummy excitement. *A King in Babylon* concerned a film company making a movie about two ancient lovers, mummified and interred in a tomb near the film location, who prove to be previous incarnations of the hero and heroine of the film. It is perhaps surprising that no major film company satisfied this avid market. One thinks of Lon Chaney, Sr., in particular, as born to add this character to his roll call of the macabre, but only pulp magazines and comics preserved interest in the subject ... until Universal tapped into ready-made movie queues by commissioning a new project for one of their most popular stars. But before that, we must examine *The Film That Never Was.*

In 1922 the Earl of Carnarvon was sitting on a gold mine — both literally and figuratively — with the discovery of King Tutankhamun's tomb; as the concession holder, it lay in his power to agree to the sale of all the rights to the discovery. And the Earl was a thoroughly modern chap, interested in publishing and the movies, as well as the more academic recordings of his triumphs.

Having sold the rights to reports on the dig itself to *The Times* in London, Carnarvon turned his thoughts to other enterprises, and in a long, excited letter to Carter from England he detailed his plans. Carter was urged to carefully scan the photographs that emerged daily from the seconded Harry Burton's darkroom; they were to be divided into groups: 1) "free prints for the press," 2) "prints for the press on payment," and 3) "prints which we reserve — the best" (definitely the aristocratic "we" and not collective, although in another part of the letter Carnarvon assures Carter that his own rights to the discovery would be fully protected along with those of his benefactor). These last prints were to grace the book that would record their discovery, although the Earl had already suggested to Carter that the archaeologist actually write it with Sir Alan Gardiner. As he so artlessly put it, "The two of you can muddle it out." Carter had wryly discussed the matter of rights with *The Times*' Cairo correspondent, Arthur Merton; Merton assumed their contract was to protect the scholarly and scientific use of the material, and Carter agreed, in a way, for "the scientific requirements swelled the cinematographic rights."

The Earl was looking to the cinema to increase his profit margin on the discovery. He was in discussions with Pathé and many others, including the Hollywood Goldwyn Picture Company, but actual sums had not been discussed. The Earl had, however, sketched out a treatment for the movie, and he included it for Carter's interest. There were to be seven sections to the film:

Section One — the approach to the Valley of the Kings or Biban el-Muluk and its elaborate necropolis, crossing the Nile and passing the Colossi of Memnon and Hatshepsut's magnificent mortuary temple, over the Theban cliffs, and into the Valley itself.

Section Two — The history of the excavation and earlier explorations from 1907 onwards. This film footage ("which we can get up," the Earl noted) would be followed by the discovery of the tomb itself, just 13 feet below that well-known tourist attraction, the entrance to Rameses VI's tomb, and the uncovering of the steps and two sealed doorways.

Section Three — The contents of the corridor and first chamber, with the two life-sized sentinel figures bathed in electric lights.

Section Four — The official opening of the tomb, restaged for film. All the notables were expected to reprise their roles.

Section Five — A look at the treasures found to date, including the three golden couches, the sentinels, four dismantled chariots, fabrics, the golden throne, and any other delights which might have been found before the film crew arrived.

Section Six — the unveiling of the mummy, which it was assumed, would be found in its sarcophagus and coffins.

Section Seven — "A strong and uplifting ending...."

A copy of this treatment was obviously sent to the various bidders. Goldwyn proposed to add sequences showing "the essence and idea of Ancient Egypt, including the Pyramid and the Sphinx," and dramatized versions of "the wonderful ceremonies attendant upon the interment of a dead Pharaoh, with living people chosen from living Egyptians looking like those from Tutankhamen's [*sic*] time." Who would know that they would have to wait until 1999 for *National Geographic* to make part of the film for the wondrous Imax system as part of the millennium celebrations? Goldwyn's representative enthused that the film could become "one of the biggest and most profitable events in film history." Although unshot, one can imagine the impact such a film would have had. The letters between the Earl and Goldwyn reveal how remarkably aware the Earl was of the wider cultural implications of the discovery beyond academia; a vast public awaited, hungry for images, styles, and artifacts from Ancient Egypt.

On February 13, 1923, the *New York Times* reported that a film company—not American!—had tried to take unauthorized pictures with the aid of a telescope. Carter had apparently hotly pursued them, but finally negotiated peace. Three days later the London *Times* reported that "definite arrangements for the official film of the excavation are not yet completed. The matter is receiving Lord Carnarvon's close attention." Finally, the rights were kept by the archaeologists, using equipment said to have been provided by Sam Goldwyn. All this when the priority was the charting, cataloguing, and clearing of the first rooms of the tomb. The death of the Earl brought an end to the film that never was.

....

The Mummy (U.S., 1932, Universal) Released December 1932; 72 minutes; black and white

Credits: Director: Karl Freund; Producer: Carl Laemmle, Jr.; Associate Producer: Stanley Bergerman; Screenplay: John L. Balderston (from Nina Wilcox Putnam's and Richard Schayer's story); Director of Photography: Charles Stumar; Art Director: Willie Pogany; Music: James Dietrich; Editor: Milton Carruth; Special Effects: John P. Fulton

Cast: Boris Karloff (Imhotep/Ardath Bey), Zita Johann (Helen Grosvenor/Anck-es-en-Amon), David Manners (Frank), Edward Van Sloan (Dr. Muller), Arthur Byron (Sir Joseph), Bramwell Fletcher (Norton), Nobel Johnson (The Nubian), Kathryn Byron (Frau Muller), Leonard Mudie (Prof. Pearson), James Crane (King Amenophis), Eddie Kane (Dr. LeBarron), Tony Marlow (Inspector), Pat Somerset (dancer), C. Montague Shaw, Leland Hodgson (small talkers)

It was 1932, and horror in Hollywood was hot. After the twin successes of *Dracula* and *Frankenstein*, each of which were released in 1931, studios were looking for both scripts and stars that could match what Universal Pictures had achieved with Bela Lugosi and Boris Karloff. Universal, too, was looking for properties to keep its new stars busy.

Karloff had proven himself to be the more versatile actor of the two, and Universal was scrambling to find a blockbuster title for its star while horror movies were still popular. The fledgling genre was already in trouble. *Frankenstein* had encountered severe censorial problems, mostly in England, but plenty in America, too. After Lugosi's *Murders in the Rue Morgue* (1932), with its thinly veiled mating of women with an ape raising both eyebrows and protests, Universal began toning down its horrors. Karloff was then featured in *The Old Dark House* (1932), which had as much comedy as horror. But what to do next?

The discovery of King Tutankamun's tomb was only ten years past, and was still in the public consciousness, due to the legendary "curse" that supposedly befell the expedition, as much as ongoing reports of the finds as the tomb was cleared, season by season. Carl Laemmle, Jr., producer of the earlier horrors, felt that there might be additional gold to be taken from King Tut by adapting the "curse" into a movie. Chosen to write a treatment were Nina Wilcox Putnam and Richard Schayer.

Their story concerned Cagliostro, a magician in Ancient Egypt, who lived for over 3,000 years by injecting himself with nitrates. Most of this time was spent hunting and killing women who resembled the one who discarded him centuries before. Settling in modern San Francisco with his Nubian slave, the grudge-holding magician sets his sights on one Helen Dorrington, a dead ringer for his lost love. After creating a crime wave by using radio waves, the villain is waylaid by Professor Whemple and Helen's lover.

Even Boris Karloff would have had trouble with *this* version, but Laemmle, Jr., was impressed; in March he announced the production of *Cagliostro*. After several months, writer John L. Balderston was brought in.

Balderston had been a correspondent during World War I, and later the London correspondent for the New York *World* magazine. After seeing the London production of Bram Stoker's *Dracula*, adapted from the novel by Hamilton Deane, Broadway producer Horace Liveright bought the rights and engaged Balderston to "Americanize" the play. After the success of the Universal film version in 1931, Balderston was chosen to adapt Peggy Webling's stage version of Mary Shelley's *Frankenstein* for the screen. *The Mummy* was Balderston's first original screenplay credit; the picture has little to do with the Putnam/Schayer concept.

Universal accepted Balderston's script on September 12, 1932. Wisely jettisoned from the earlier scenario was the pseudoscientific mumbo jumbo, which was replaced by the supernatural. Balderston returned to Universal's initial point of interest and wrote in a mummified alter ego for the main character. Imhotep is seen only briefly as an actual mummy; after being revived, he appears as the more human-looking Ardath Bey. This character is all that is left of the "Cagliostro" treatment, and in physical appearance only. Bey's motivations, while hardly admirable, are at least on a higher plane than Cagliostro's.

Like John L. Balderston, first time director Karl Freund was no stranger to fantasy films. He was the cinematographer on *The Golem* (1921), *Metropolis* (1927), *Dracula* (1931), and *Murders in the Rue Morgue* (1932). Born in Bohemia, Freund was a cinema innovator; he is credited with making the camera a mobile instrument that changed the "look" of movies. After arriving in Hollywood he became associated with Universal, and in addition to photographing the abovementioned horrors, supposedly wrote the final scene for *All Quiet On The Western Front* (1930).

Karl Freund's career as a director spanned three years and eight pictures, culminating in Peter Lorre's *Mad Love* (1935). Freund continued his career as a top cinematographer throughout the forties (*Tortilla Flat* 1942, *Key Largo* 1948) then turned to television in the fifties. He pioneered the use of multiple cameras while associated with *I Love Lucy*.

After several title changes (*Cagliostro*, *King of the Dead*), Universal temporarily settled on *Im ho tep*. There actually *was* an Im-Ho-Tep; he was something of a Renaissance man of the Third Dynasty, serving Pharaoh Djoser as a scientist, physician, architect, scribe, and inventor of the first stone pyramid. The name of the fictional character's long-lost love also belonged to a historical figure; Anck-es-en-Amon was the wife of Tutankhamun. The picture was eventually retitled while in production.

The Mummy began filming in late September 1932 and concluded a month later. Location work was done in the Mojave Desert's Red Rock Canyon. Art Director

Willy Pogany designed authentic-looking sets and artifacts, setting a standard for Mummy movies that went unmatched until Hammer's version twenty-seven years later.

Considering John L. Balderston's association with *Dracula*, its not surprising that *The Mummy* resembles it in some key ways. Both pictures take place, to American eyes, in distant and exotic lands; both Dracula and Imhotep are cultured, ageless beings who desire a young, modern woman; each has a human helper; both use supernatural powers rather than brute strength, and both can only be destroyed by supernatural, pseudoreligious means. Their main difference is that Imhotep is motivated by love; Dracula is merely satisfying his bloodlust.

Imhotep's love for Anck-es-en-Amon has endured for 4,000 years, and the original screenplay had her soul inhabiting many bodies. Scenes were shot of these reincarnations including an early Christian martyr, a barbarian, and a French aristocrat. Incredibly, these elaborately staged scenes were not included in the release print. As released, *The Mummy* ran only 72 minutes, compared to 75 for *Dracula* and 71 for *Frankenstein*, so it is odd that *none* of the reincarnation scenes were used; they must have been fascinating. But what is left was certainly enough to captivate an audience.

Archaeologist Sir Joseph Whemple (Arthur Byron), head of the 1921 British Museum Field Expedition, has unearthed the mummy of Imhotep, a High Priest of Karnak … and a deadly curse on anyone who disturbs his rest. Dr. Muller (Edward Van Sloan) is against defying the curse, but young Norton (Bramwell Fletcher) has no fear; the Mummy returns to life as he reads from the Scroll of Thoth. Whemple and Muller find Norton a raving madman, and Imhotep gone.

Bramwell Fletcher, Boris Karloff, Edward Van Sloan, Arthur Byron in *The Mummy* (Universal, 1932).

A decade later, Frank (David Manners), Sir Joseph's son, who has followed in his father's footsteps, meets a mysterious Egyptian, Ardath Bey (Karloff), while on a dig. He leads the team to the tomb of Princess Anck-es-en-Amon. Ardath Bey, in fact the living mummy of Imhotep, plans to revive the Princess, his forbidden love of centuries ago, and the cause of his mummification when he attempted to restore her to life after she died from a sudden illness. Her soul now inhabits the body of Helen Grosvenor (Zita Johann), and Ardath Bey, by supernatural means, takes control of the young woman.

Bey attempts to eliminate all that stands between him and Anck-es-en-Amon, first by inducing Sir Joseph to suffer a heart attack. When he begins the ancient process to transform Helen into a creature like himself, Anck-es-en-Amon's soul speaks out, refusing to be part of the blasphemy. Frank and Muller arrive as Helen prays to the goddess Isis, whose statue incinerates both the Mummy and the Scroll.

Due to Universal's pains to avoid the excesses of *Frankenstein* and *Murders in the Rue Morgue*, *The Mummy* barely qualifies as a horror movie. The picture avoids blatant visual shocks; its terrors are quiet and subtle. Imhotep appears as an actual mummy only briefly, but the scene is among the most memorable in film history.

After Whemple and Muller have left him alone with the Mummy, Norton is consumed with curiosity. Disregarding the fears of the older men, he opens a small box inscribed "Death — Eternal punishment for anyone who opens this casket. In the name

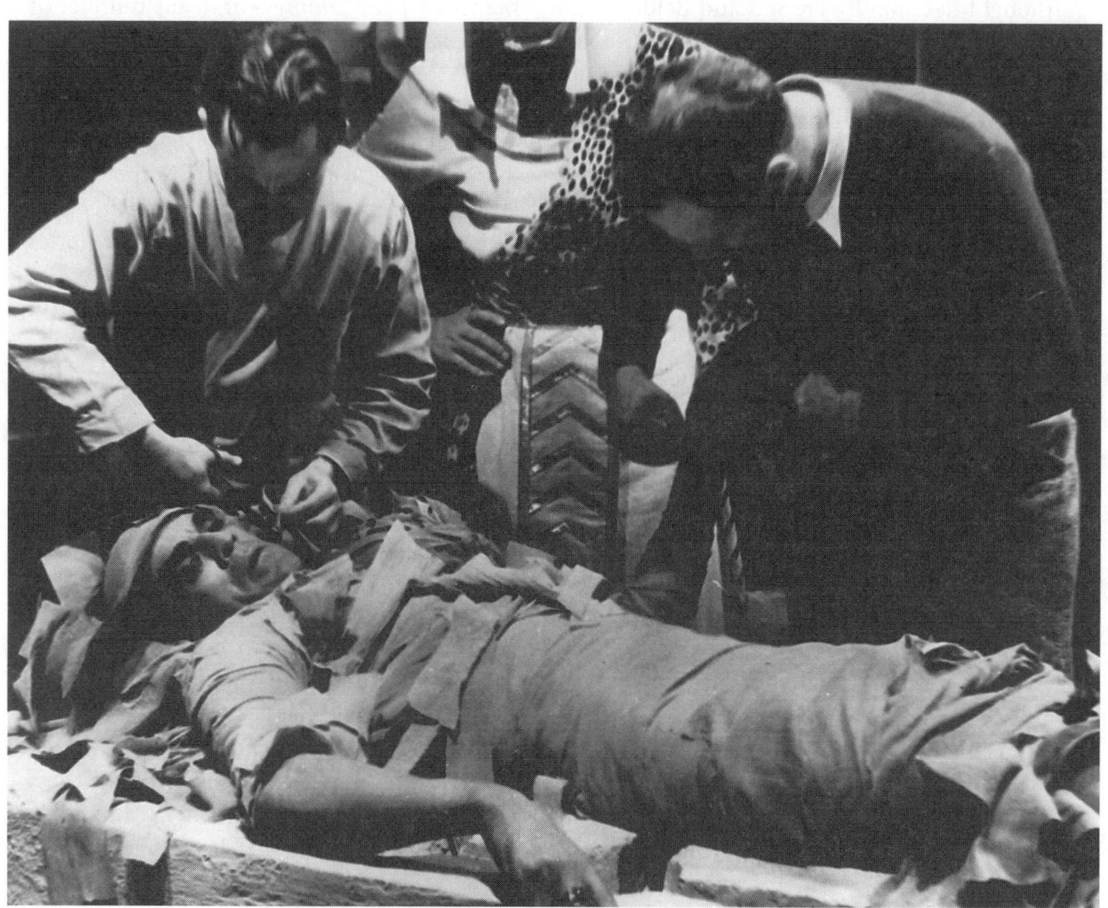

Boris Karloff undergoing makeup, apparently unconfortably for Universal's *The Mummy* (1932).

of Amon-Ra, the King of the Gods." With sweating hands, he gingerly removes the crumbling Scroll of Thoth that has the power to restore the dead to life. Outside the tomb his companions argue over whether their find should be abandoned; inside Norton whispers as he reads the Scroll.

Behind him, the Mummy opens his left eye with agonized slowness; a pinpoint of light on the pupil announces his return to life. His right arm lowers from his shoulder through rotting bandages, then his left. As Norton continues to read, a withered hand snakes out for the Scroll. Norton turns his head, sees, screams and laughs hysterically. "He went for a little walk!" he babbles to Whemple. "You should have seen his face!"

The scene is played without music, in the deathly silence of the tomb — a well-thought decision by Freund and Balderston. No "acting" was needed by Karloff; that would come later. What really made the scene work was the Mummy's incredible makeup.

Much of *The Mummy*'s success can be attributed to Jack P. Pierce, who also devised Karloff's makeup for *Frankenstein*. From *Dracula* to *House of Dracula* (1945), Pierce was Universal's makeup master, and he created more monsters than Baron Frankenstein! Born Janus Piccoulas in Greece in 1889, Pierce emigrated to America around 1900 and had settled in Los Angeles by 1906. He entered show business on the ground floor as a projectionist, moved up to stunting, and from 1915 to 1925 did some minor acting and directing.

His big break came in 1926 when he created the ape makeup for Jacques Lernier in *The Monkey Talks*. Universal head, Carl Laemmle, quickly snatched up Pierce as a full-time makeup man, and the rest, as they say, is history.

Boris Karloff arrived in Pierce's makeup room around 11 A.M. and left the chair eight hours later. During this period Karloff suffered almost as much as Imhotep must have while being mummified. The procedure went as follows: Karloff's ears were flattened to his head, and his entire face covered with cotton strips. On top of the cotton was placed collodion. His hair was then caked with "beauty clay," then his body wrapped with 150 yards of rotting bandages, then dusted down with Fuller's earth.

The resurrection scene was shot until 2:00 the following morning, and Karloff returned home at dawn after an equally uncomfortable removal of the makeup. It's easily said, but the results were worth the ordeal and have never been surpassed. His makeup as Ardath Bey was equally magnificent but less arduously applied.

Much has been written about Karloff's talents as an actor, his warm personality, and his humble acceptance of his success. Let's just say that it's doubtful that any other actor from any period could better his performance in *The Mummy*— or in any number of his best pictures.

After his sudden success at age 44 (with over 60 films dating from 1919), Karloff became a major star in *Frankenstein*, and after *The Mummy* was identified by most with "monsters." Actually, these were the only monsters he ever played (unless one includes *Die! Monster! Die!* 1968). He brought to *The Mummy*, as he did to so many roles, an odd combination of revulsion and sadness, making Imhotep among his most memorable characters in a most memorable career.

Born in England on November 23rd 1887, he came to Canada in 1909 to seek his fortune, and found it twenty-two years later in Hollywood. After a spotty career on stage, often playing minor roles in forgotten productions, he appeared on-screen in *His Majesty The American* in 1919. He made his last picture almost half a century later. In between were some classics (*Bride of Frankenstein* 1935, *The Body Snatcher* 1945), many entertaining programs (*The Walking Dead* 1936, *House of Frankenstein* 1945) and a few bombs. Through them all he seemed to keep his career and profession in perspective; and over thirty years after his death (February 2, 1969), he remains as popular as ever.

"*The Mummy* beggars description," enthused the *Los Angeles Times*, (January 21, 1933). "It is one of the most unusual talkies ever produced. Eerie, mystifying, surely the mantle of the late Lon Chaney will eventually fall upon the actor Karloff, here established as a finished character star." Few could disagree, and few did. "For purposes of terror, there are two scenes in *The Mummy* that are weird enough in all conscience" (*New York Times*, January 7, 1933). "Chances are it will be a big hit."

Unlike most of its descendants, *The Mummy*, in addition to its expected thrills, gives the viewer an unexpected sense of Egyptian history and religion. It would be interesting to find out how many future Egyptologists saw *The Mummy* as children. Although no other Mummy picture would approach the character and subject in so subtle a fashion, every future excursion, for better or worse, owes *The Mummy* a debt.

Mummy's Boys (U.S., 1936, RKO) Released October 2, 1936; 68 minutes; black and white

Credits: Director: Fred Guiel; Producer: Lee Marcus; Screenplay: Jack Townley, Phillip G. Epstein, Charles Roberts (from Townley's and Lew Lipton's story); Art Director: Van Nest Polgase, Feild Gray; Costumes: Edward M. Stevenson; Photography: Jack Mackenzie; Music: Roy Webb; Sound: James G. Stewart; Editor: John Lockert

Cast: Bert Wheeler (Stanley), Robert Woolsey (Aloysius), Barbara Pepper (Mary Browning), Moroni Olsen (Dr. Sterling), Frank M. Thomas (Dr. Browning), Willie Best (Catfish), Francis McDonald (Haschid Bey), Charles Coleman (Kendall), Frank Lackteen (Haschid's assistant), Mitchell Lewis (Sheik Haroun Pasha), Tiny Stanford (construction foreman), Frederick Burton (Prof. Edwards), Gerals Rogers (sailor), Dewey Robinson (hotel manager), Frank Moran (Larson), Ethan Laidlaw (Peters), Edward Keane (captain), Jack Rice (second officer), George Lollier (third officer). Rita Rozelle (telephone operator), Donald Kerr (steward), Edith Craig (Sheik's wife), Nobel Johnson (tattoo artist), Pedro Rigas, Nick Shaid (fakirs), John Davidson (cafe manager), Pat Somerset (English officer), Gil Perkins, Al Haskell (cops)

Bert Wheeler and Bob Woolsey, while hardly household names today, had a successful run as a comedy team appearing in twenty-one feature films spanning many years. *Mummy's Boys*, however, was not one of their best, although the basic idea of mixing knuckleheads and monsters wasn't a bad one, as Abbott and Costello proved in 1948 when they met Frankenstein. One problem here was that the Mummy lacks the charisma necessary to stand up to the fooling around; in fact, the character is often funny in *straight* horror pictures. Another problem is that the Mummy was not really a Mummy.

Archaeologist Phillip Browning (Frank M. Thomas) is terrified by a deadly curse; nine of the thirteen members of his party who entered the tomb of King Pharantine several months earlier are dead. Browning decides to return the King's artifacts to his tomb.

Browning's ad for excavators is answered by Stanley Wright (Wheeler) and Aloysius C. Whittaker (Woolsey), two Long Island ditchdiggers. They join Browning, his daughter Mary (Barbara Pepper); Haschid Bey (Francis McDonald), a slippery Egyptian; and Dr. Sterling (Moroni Olsen), a surviving member of the expedition; and set off for Cairo.

Sterling disappears from the Hotel D'Orient, and, fearing he is next, Browning gives the boys the map to the King's tomb. Aloysius, concerned that Stanley might lose the map, has it tattooed onto his partner's back. The tomb is eventually reached, but Browning has vanished. The boys, with Mary, enter the tomb and are soon trapped in a cave-in caused by Dr. Sterling.

Sterling admits to Browning, his prisoner, that he killed the other party members. He joins the others with a poison-filled needle, feigning confusion as to how he got into the tomb. Before he can strike, Sterling accidentally drops his incriminating diary, which is found by Stanley. Panic ensues; Sterling, dressed like a Mummy, is finally overpowered. Browning frees himself, and Haschid Bey, actually a policeman, arrives with a team to excavate the good guys.

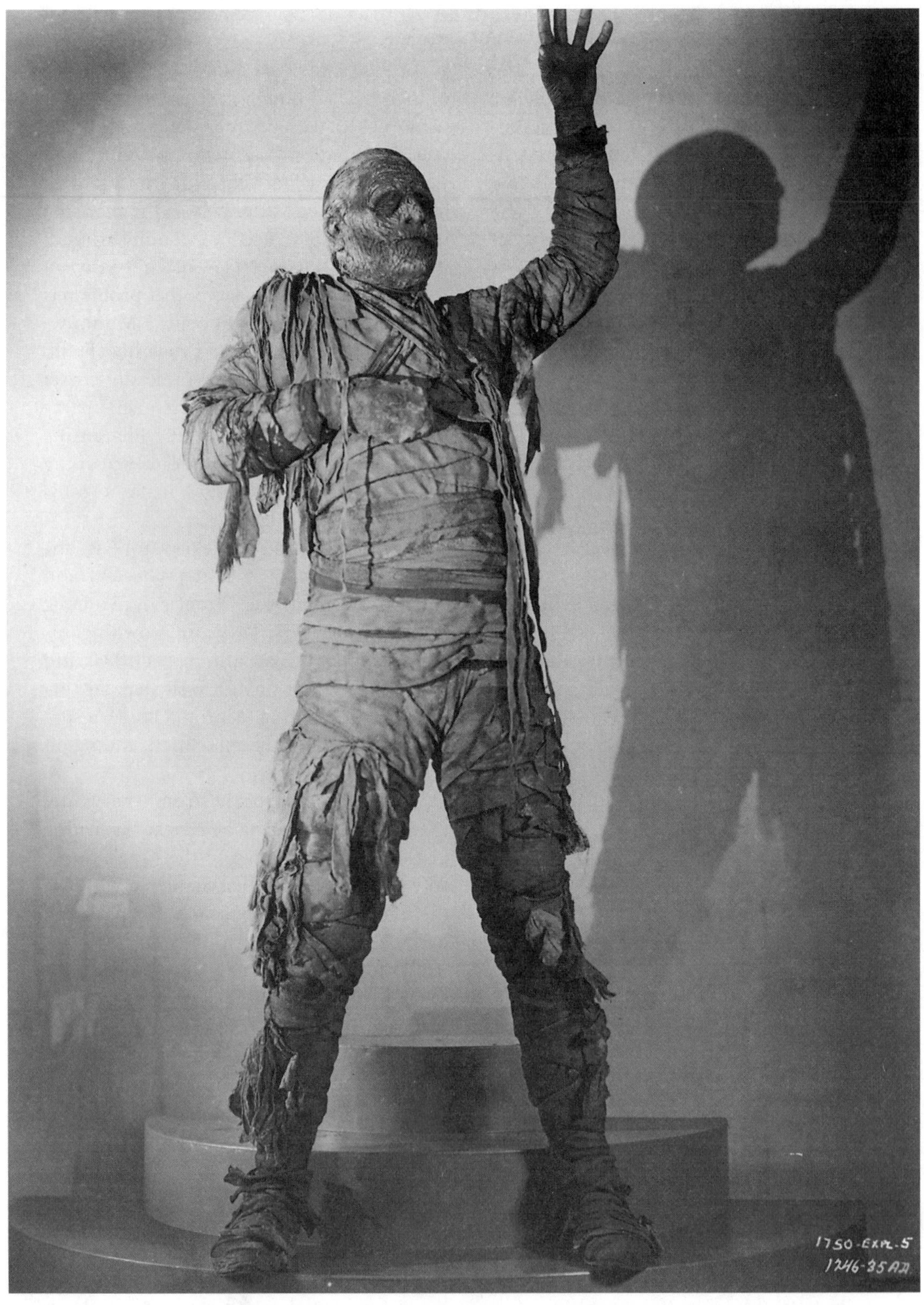

Lon Chaney, Jr., as Kharis in ***The Mummy's Tomb*** (Universal, 1942).

Although most of Wheeler and Woolsey's pictures would probably be considered less than hilarious by today's comedic standards, this one is particularly tough going. None of the sight gags or lines are especially funny, and none of the Mummy's few "scary" scenes are in any way frightening. The movie *might* have worked somewhat better with an established "villain" like Lionel Atwill in the cast, but not even Boris Karloff could have saved this one. The only connection between this and *The Mummy* was Nobel Johnson in a walk-on.

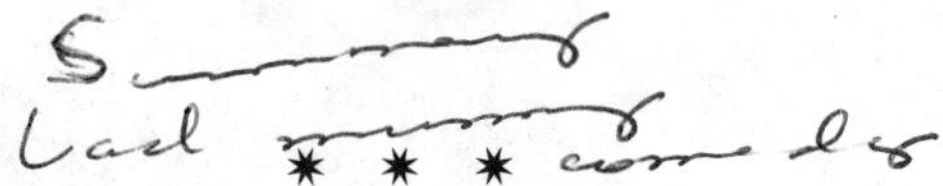

The Universal "Kharis" Series 1940–1945

The Mummy's Hand (1940), *The Mummy's Tomb* (1942), *The Mummy's Ghost* (1944), and *The Mummy's Curse* (1944) are as hard to dislike as they are to praise. They were strictly wartime "B" movies—nothing more, nothing less—ground out by the Universal horror factory as effortlessly and as cheaply as possible. No one—fans, critics, or producers—had any pretensions to the contrary.

Lon Chaney, Jr., who shuffled through the last three pictures, said—often—that Kharis was the least rewarding character he had ever played, which, considering his career, was quite an indictment. "The Mummy said he thought somebody was nuts," wrote Frederick C. Othmar in the *Philadelphia Inquirer*, September 14, 1943, "and he meant you." Chaney, Jr. said, "For absurd reasons known only to yourselves, you customers pay your hard-earned cash to see Mummy movies."

Chaney, Jr.'s point was well made. The Kharis pictures (and, let's face it, *most* Mummy films) are predictable and generally unimaginative when compared to other horror characters like Dracula and the Frankenstein monster. Kharis has no dialogue, moves too slowly to be much of a threat, and evokes little audience sympathy. Yet, these movies have that indefinable "something" that make them still watchable over fifty years later. What they lack in art, they make up for with entertainment.

Although *The Mummy* (1932) is one of the great horror-fantasy films, it is not part of the Kharis series and has little in common with *any* Mummy picture. Boris Karloff gave a one-of-a-kind performance in a one-of-a-kind movie that defied sequels and remakes. Karloff's graceful and cultured Imhotep was seen only briefly in bandages, and is *not* the image one conjures when picturing *The Mummy*. More easily seen is the shambling ragbag of Lon Chaney, Jr.—arm outstetched, eyes (or eye) glaring, as he slowly approaches his rapidly retreating victim.

Forgotten by all but the most studious of horror-Mummy fans is that Tom Tyler, not Lon Chaney, Jr., first played Kharis. Born Vincent Markowski on August 9, 1903 in Port Henry, New York, Tyler had the honor of being the screen's first "real" Mummy. He was an exceptional athlete, holding an American weightlifting title for fourteen consecutive years. Tyler broke three national records, most notably in the "clean and jerk," hefting all but 300 pounds. His athletic career peaked in 1928 when he appeared in the Olympics.

Like other Olympians, Tyler was called to Hollywood for his athletic build. His first role was as an extra in a howling mob, not unlike those that would later hound Kharis. Like many fledgling actors, Tyler was forced to supplement his meager income when between roles with "real" jobs that often called on his special physical prowess.

After a dearth of horror movies in 1937–38, due to several factors (including a British ban and public indifference), the once-popular genre returned to almost full strength in 1939 with Universal's *Son of Frankenstein*. This success was quickly followed by *Tower of London* (1939), *Black Friday* (1940), and *The Invisible Man Returns* (1940), and Universal next decided to dust off *The Mummy*.

Tom Tyler as Kharis in Universal's *The Mummy's Hand* (1940).

Tom Tyler had, by this time, found his niche starring in "B" Westerns and occasionally appeared in minor roles in major pictures like *Stagecoach* (1939). He was chosen to play Kharis in *The Mummy's Hand* due to a superficial resemblance to Boris Karloff, who also "appeared" in flashback scenes. Despite his good performance, there was little chance of Tyler becoming a "Universal horror star"—he was too popular in Westerns. *The Motion Picture Herald* named him 1942's top money making Western star, and Tyler had also made a name for himself with the serial crowd in *The Adventures of Captain Marvel* (1941). After playing *The Phantom* in a 1943 serial, Tyler contracted a crippling rheumatoid condition that more or less ended his career. He returned briefly to films in the early 1950s and died of a heart attack in Michigan on May 1,1954.

Tom Tyler passed his bandages, no doubt willingly, to Lon Chaney, Jr. in 1942. Chaney, Jr. had become Universal's answer to his own father, Karloff, and Bela Lugosi after his success as *The Wolfman* (1941) and was hustled into every Universal horror property imaginable, whether he was suitable for it or not. The son of the silent era's greatest character star was born Creighton Tull Chaney on February 10, 1906 in Oklahoma City. After being discouraged from entering pictures by Chaney, Sr., Creighton did just that after his father's death in 1930. Films like *Girl Crazy* (1932) did little to advance his career, but things picked up slightly after changing his name to Lon Chaney, Jr. "They starved me into it," he often said.

Chaney, Jr.'s career remained undistinguished until catching fire in *Of Mice and Men* (1939), in which he gave his best performance as the pathetic Lennie. Universal snatched him up; after scoring in *Man Made Monster!* (1941), *The Wolfman* (1941), and *The Ghost of Frankenstein* (1942), Chaney, Jr. found himself wrapped from head to toe in gauze.

One frequent and often justifiable rap against Chaney, Jr.'s acting was his "lack of charisma." If so, it never hurt him *less* than as Kharis; even Mick Jagger would have been blunted under those bandages. That said, Chaney, Jr. made the least of the acting opportunities given him, and proved that not only was he no Karloff, but that he couldn't fill Tom Tyler's wrappings either. Chaney, Jr.'s dislike of the role is well-documented elsewhere and his complaints *are* understandable—Kharis is hardly an actor's dream. On the other hand, it probably beat being a contractor (which is what he might have been if not for his surname).

It is easy to dismiss, as many have done, Chaney, Jr.'s three performances as the Mummy, but the truth is there is not much any actor could do with such a part. Christopher Lee (*The Mummy*, 1959) gave the only truly outstanding performance as the character (excluding Karloff's totally different Imhotep). If Chaney, Jr., falls short, so has everyone else. Chaney, Jr.'s career sagged after horror ran out of gas in the mid-forties, but he managed a few well-played supporting roles (*High Noon* 1952, *The Defiant Ones* 1958) in the following decade. He hit bottom in the sixties (*Dr. Terror's Gallery of Horrors* 1967) and died on July 12, 1973 after completing the horrendous *Dracula v. Frankenstein* (1973).

The Kharis series was grade "B" all the way, as a glance at its credits reveals. The first three were written by Griffin Jay, who,

Dick Foran feels ***The Mummy's Hand*** as wielded by Tom Tyler (Universal, 1940).

despite some twenty screenplays to his credit, fails to merit a mention in most film encyclopedias or a death notice in *Variety*. His other forties scripts included *The Devil Bat's Daughter* (1946), *Return of the Vampire* (1943), and *Cry of the Werewolf* (1944). The Mummy pictures may well have been his best work. His co-author on *The Mummy's Hand* was Maxwell Shane, who was more at home with comedy (such as Jack Benny's radio show and Art Linkletter on TV) than horror. He did, however, produce the Boris Karloff-hosted *Thriller* TV series in the sixties.

Kharis series directors were equally lacking in eye-catching credits. Christy Cabanne (*The Mummy's Hand*) directed Douglas Fairbanks in the twenties, but by the thirties he was reduced to programmers. Despite directing around 150 pictures, *The Mummy's Hand* was Cabanne's only brush with horror, and is probably the best remembered of his films.

Harold Young (*The Mummy's Tomb*), like many directors, began his career as an editor, working with Alexander Korda. He directed *The Scarlet Pimpernel* (1935) for Korda, but it was mostly downhill afterwards. Young reached his nadir in 1945 with Universal's *The Frozen Ghost* with Chaney, Jr., and *Jungle Captive*. His career ended in 1954.

Leslie Goodwins (*The Mummy's Curse*) may be best remembered for his *Mexican Spitfire* series for RKO with Lupe Velez, and that says it all. Only Reginald Le Borg (*The Mummy's Ghost*) showed any flair for, or interest in, horror pictures, directing ten genre entries including *Weird Women* (1944) and *The Black Sleep* (1956), both with Chaney, Jr.

While these were competent directors, they make no one forget Karl Freund or Terence Fisher; they were simply grinding out pictures for an easily pleased wartime audience. The real strength of the Kharis pictures lay in their interesting cast lists, populated by George Zucco, Eduardo Cianelli, Turhan Bey, John Carradine, and Martin Kosleck, in addition to Tyler and Chaney, Jr. Anyone who can't enjoy these actors shouldn't be watching horror movies in the first place.

Perhaps the most serious indictment against Kharis is that he was never invited to a Universal "monster rally" (*House of Frankenstein* 1944, *House of Dracula* 1945, *Abbott and Costello Meet Frankenstein* 1948), possibly because of his inappropriate attire. Although the Kharis pictures added little to art or Egyptology, they provided their war-weary audiences with pleasant escapist entertainment that can still be enjoyed today.

The Mummy's Hand (U.S., 1940, Universal) Released September 20, 1940; 67 minutes; black and white

Credits: Director: Christy Cabanne; Producer: Ben Pivar; Screenplay: Griffin Jay, Maxwell Shane (based on Jay's original story); Director of Photography: Elwood Bredell; Editor: Philip Cahn; Art Director: Jack Otterson; Associate Art Director: Ralph M. DeLacy; Music: Frank Skinner, Hans J. Balter; Musical Director: Charles Previn; Assistant Director: Vaughn Paul; Set Director: Russell A. Gausman; Sound: Bernard B. Brown; Technician: Charles Carroll; Makeup: Jack Pierce; Gowns: Vera West

Cast: Dick Foran (Steve Banning), Peggy Moran (Marta Solvani), Wallace Ford (Babe Jenson), Eduardo Cianelli (High Priest), George Zucco (Andoheb), Cecil Kellaway (The Great Solvani), Charles Trowbridge (Dr. Petrie), Tom Tyler (Kharis), Siegfried Arno (The Beggar), Eddie Foster (Egyptian), Harry Stubbs (Bartender), Michael Mark (Bazaar owner), Mara Tartar (girl), Leon Belasco (Ali), Frank Lackteen, Murdock MacQuarrie (Priests), Jerry Frank, Kenneth Terrell (Egyptian thugs)

An ancient high priest (Eduardo Cianelli), nearing death, sends for Andoheb (George Zucco), an Egyptologist and member of the Society of Karnak. When he arrives at the Hill of the Seven Jackals, Andoheb is told an ancient secret.

Thirty centuries into Egypt's past, the Royal Prince Kharis (Tom Tyler) loved Princess Ananka. After her untimely death, Kharis attempted to use sacred tana leaves to restore her to life, but his blasphemous act was discovered. He was sentenced to a living death as her mummified protector.

The high priest astonishes Andoheb with an unbelievable truth — Kharis still lives. He can be fully restored with the fluid of three tana leaves ... but nine would create an uncontrollable monster. The high priest dies, leaving Andoheb as the Mummy's master.

Steve Banning (Dick Foran) and Babe Jenson (Wallace Ford), two down-on-their-luck archaeologists, join forces with Dr. Petrie (Charles Trowbridge) of the Cairo Museum to authenticate an ancient vase. Petrie enlists the help of Andoheb, who brushes it off as a fake while realizing it could lead to the discovery of Ananka's tomb. Banning and Jenson receive backing from "The Great Salvani" (Cecil Kellaway), a stage magician, and, with Petrie and Salvani's daughter Marta (Peggy Moran), trek across the sands ... while Andoheb and his henchman (Siegfried Arno) await.

An accidental explosion opens an entrance to Ananka's tomb; inside they discover the princess and her guardian. As Petrie examines Kharis, Andoheb suddenly appears and revives Kharis, who strangles the doctor. By placing tana fluid in the tents of the remaining party members, Andoheb plans to eliminate the unbelievers— excepting the beautiful Marta. He plans to immortalize both her and himself in an action oddly similar to Kharis's centuries in the past. Babe prevents this new blasphemy while Steve sets Kharis ablaze with a burning brazier.

When it became evident that horror movies were again back in style, Universal, the company that started it all with *Dracula* (1931), led the pack once again with sequels to its earlier classics (*The Invisible Man Returns* 1940) and new properties (*Black Friday* 1940). *The Mummy* may have seemed like a natural to remake or make a sequel to, but its unique qualities made that difficult. The company wisely chose a completely different approach. Imhotep was only glimpsed briefly in his wrappings but Kharis, the new Mummy, who would spend most of the picture in them. This obviously called for an actor with greater physical gifts than thespic, making Tom Tyler the perfect choice.

In *The Mummy*, Imhotep, once revived, didn't require a keeper or protector; his plans and actions were of his own making. Kharis, however, needed both and got them in the form of Andoheb, in some ways the picture's *real* villain. Another new wrinkle was the wrinkled tana leaves, three of which — properly brewed during the full moon — kept Kharis more or less ambulatory with their fluid. The tana leaves *did* present a problem though. "Should Kharis obtain a large amount of the fluid," intoned the high priest," he will become an uncontrollable monster, a soulless demon with the desire to kill and kill."

The Mummy's Hand began production in May 1940 on a two-week schedule, typical of the Hollywood "B" production standards of the period. As cost-cutting measures, footage from *The Mummy*, an incredible set from James Whale's *Green Hell* (1940), and *Son of Frankenstein*'s musical score were incorporated, which brought in the picture for under $85,000.

The film premiered at New York's Rialto Theatre on September 20, a quick five months later, with the flashback sequence tinted green. Reviews, as they so often are with horror movies, were mixed: " ... a lot of mumbo-jumbo ... a second rate thriller" (*New York Daily News*, September 20). "Thrilling, chilling, grilling little movie nightmare" (*New York Post*, September 19). "Muddled in the writing and clumsy in production ... bush league ... formula stuff, it's all strictly for the lesser duals" (*Variety*, September 25). "Manages to raise a few more goose pimples than other recent horror movies.... Makes Frankenstein's creation look like a movie hero" (*Philadelphia Record*, October 21).

Speaking of heroes, they are a major weak point of *The Mummy's Hand*. Steve Banning and Babe Jenson, as played by Dick Foran and Wallace Ford, are less like archaeologists than two thirds of the Three Stooges.

Preventing them from being the worst part of the pictures was Cecil Kellaway's "comic" magician. This poorly conceived character almost destroys the movie. To see how Banning should have been played, see Peter Cushing in *The Mummy* (1959).

This aside, *The Mummy's Hand* contains several extremely well done and underrated horror sequences, chief among them Kharis' return to life. As Dr. Petrie putters near the supine Mummy he is startled by Andoheb, who had previously dismissed a vase as provenance of the tomb's existence and declined to join the expedition.

"Where did you come from?" asks Petrie.

"The important thing, doctor," smirks Andoheb," is that I'm here."

"Then you knew about the tomb. Yet you insisted the vase was an imitation."

"There are some things in science that should be brought to light ... and there are others, doctor, that should be left alone. Since you are here

I think it's fitting that you should learn what you've stumbled upon."

Andoheb leads Petrie to Kharis, placing the doctor's hand on the Mummy's wrist. "For a scientist you're very unobservant Dr. Petrie," he intones as Petrie stiffens ... he has felt Kharis' pulse!

"This is absurd," blurts Petrie. "Fantastic!"

Andoheb produces a small container. "In this vial there is a fluid from nine tana leaves ... *nine* tana leaves Dr. Petrie. That wouldn't mean anything to you ... but watch." He pours the liquid into Kharis' mouth. "Now Dr. Petrie."

The Mummy's pulse increases. "He's alive," Petrie gasps. The Mummy's hand snakes upward, grasping Petrie's throat, eyes black and inhuman.

"The destiny of the Priest of Karnak is fulfilled," says Andoheb," Not one of you who tried to enter the tomb of Ananka will leave the valley alive."

Due to its relative novelty, *The Mummy's Hand* was the best of the Kharis pictures, but this should not be taken as faint praise. Despite a few false steps, the picture is still frightening and looks much better than its meager budget would suggest. The three following movies would lift *The Mummy's Hand*'s best ideas and, while individually interesting, as a group were merely repetitive.

The Mummy's Tomb (U.S., 1942, Universal) Released October 23, 1942; 60 minutes; black and white

Credits: Director: Harold Young; Associate Producer: Ben Pivar; Screenplay: Griffin Jay, Henry Sucher (based on Neil P. Varnick's original story); Director of Photography: George Robinson; Art Director: Jack Otterson; Associate Art Director: Ralph M. DeLacy; Editor: Milton Carroth; Music: Hans J. Salter; Sound: Bernard B. Brown; Set Director: Russell A. Gausman; Associate Set Director: Andrew J. Gilmore; Assistant Director: Charles S. Gould; Makeup: Jack Pierce; Gowns: Vera West.

Cast: Lon Chaney (Kharis), Dick Foran (Stephen Banning), John Hubbard (John Banning), Elyse Knox (Isobel Evans), Wallace Ford (Babe), Turhan Bey (Mehemet Bey), George Zucco (Andoheb), Mary Gordon (Jane Banning), Cliff Clark (Sheriff), Virginia Brissac (Ella Evans), Paul E. Burns (Jim), Frank Reicher (Prof. Norman), Eddy C. Walker (Chemist), Frank Darien (Old Man), Harry Cording (Vic), Myra McKinney (Vic's Wife), John Ragers (Steward), Otto Hoffman (Caretaker), Emmett Vogan (Coroner), Fern Emmett (Laura), Janet Shaw (Girl), Dick Hogan (Boy), Bill Ruhl (Nick), Guy Usher (Doctor) Pat McVey (Jake), Jack Arnold (Reporter), Glenn Strange (Farmer), Rex Lease (Al), Grace Cunard (Farmer's Wife), Lew Kelly (Bartender), Charles Marsh (Man), Walter Byron (Searcher), Eddie Parker (Chaney's stunt double)

Andoheb (George Zucco), who has miraculously survived a shooting, recruits Mehemet Bey (Turhan Bey) to replace him as Kharis' keeper. Badly burned, missing an eye and several fingers, Kharis (Lon Chaney) is alive but in a comatose state. Before dying, Andoheb instructs Mehemet to take Kharis to Mapleton, Massachusetts, where the surviving members of the Banning Expedition now reside, years after their horrific experiences in Egypt.

Lon Chaney, Jr., in true monster fashion, carries off Elyse Knox in Universal's *The Mummy's Tomb* (1942).

Steve (Dick Foran), now an elderly yarn spinner, is Kharis's first target for revenge. Revived by the tana fluid, Kharis throttles Banning, leaving a mysterious mold on his throat. Babe (Wallace Ford), following the murder of Steve's sister (Mary Gordon), believes Kharis is responsible, but is dismissed as a lunatic by the Sheriff (Cliff Clark). After giving his theory to the local press, Babe joins his old partner at Kharis's hands.

One of the few who believe Babe is Steve's son, John (John Hubbard), who suspects that Mehemet, posing as a cemetery caretaker, is controlling Kharis. The Mummy abducts Isobel (Elyse Knox), John's fiancée, and is trailed by a posse to the Banning home. After Mehemet is gunned down, Isobel is rescued and Kharis set ablaze.

By 1942, Lon Chaney (minus the "Junior") had, by default, become the ranking horror star. After effective roles in *Man Made Monster* 1941, *The Wolfman* 1941, and *The Ghost of Frankenstein* 1942, Chaney was the obvious— and only—choice to play Kharis in *The Mummy's Hand* sequel. The question is, why did Universal choose to think a sequel was warranted?

Although following *The Mummy's Hand* by only two years, the events in *The Mummy's Tomb* take place at least thirty years later. In addition to Kharis there are three other characters present from *The Mummy's Hand*— and one of them is a real surprise. Andoheb, as played by George Zucco, was last seen bouncing down a huge flight of stairs with several pounds of lead in

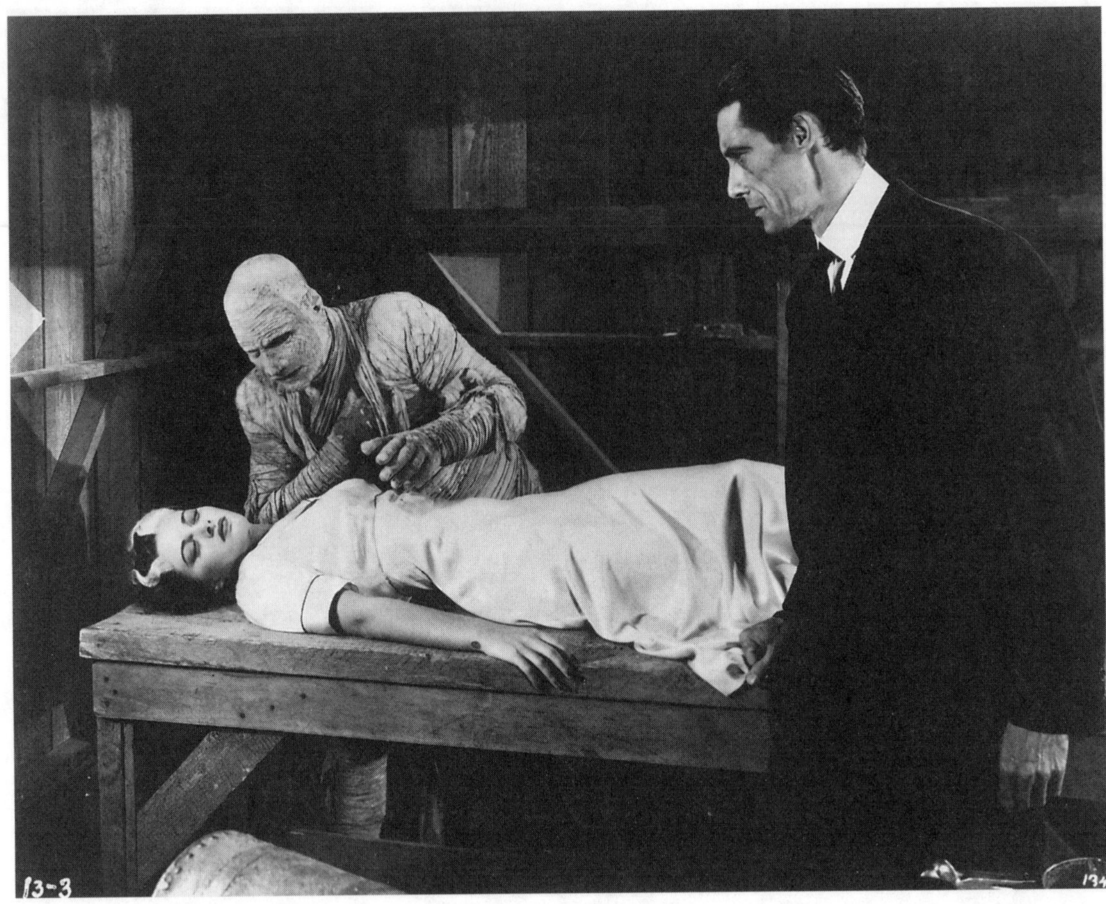

Ramsay Ames menaced by two who know how: Lon Chaney, Jr., and John Carradine. *The Mummy's Ghost* (Universal, 1949).

his body. He returns, however, relatively unscathed, to provide more problems for Steve and Babe. It seems that he merely suffered a "shattered arm." While one shouldn't expect much logic in a movie like *The Mummy's Tomb*, Andoheb's survival is only slightly less incredible than Kharis's.

The time frame is also difficult to swallow; although Steve and Babe have aged convincingly, technology appeared to have stood still the last three decades or so. Equally disturbing is the picture's setting of Mapleton, which is a long way from Egypt in more ways than one. Universal was clearly taking the easy (and cheap) way out. The studio seems to have had little real interest in the character — he was now just another monster in its stable. The monster-as-avenger plot was also distressingly similar to Universal's last two Frankenstein pictures.

The movie was released at the Rialto as the top half of a double feature on October 23, 1942, supported by the superior *Night Monster* (with Lionel Atwill and Bela Lugosi). Unlike its predecessor, *The Mummy's Tomb* did not split critics; most disliked it.

"There it was in black and white — the invasion of Mapleton, Mass. by an alive mummy, 3000 years old! This is no whodunit, but an old order meller which finally ends in destruction for the mummy ... unless there is a sequel" (*New York Post*, October 26). "The Rialto returns to its old love, horror films. *The Mummy's Tomb* is one of those would-be thrillers that could only scare a small child. The performance of Lon

Chaney, Jr. is simply that of a man completely smeared with a particularly revolting makeup. *The Mummy's Tomb* should disturb no one but those who made it" (*New York Sun*, October 26). "With no deviation from formula and obviously on a low budget, [the] pic will get by as [a] secondary dueller with audiences not too particular on credulity" (*Variety*, October 14). "I experienced the strange feeling ... that all this has happened before.... Lon Chaney has taken on the job of scaring audiences just as his father did before him, but in spite of a most horrendous mask, he is no more successful in projecting this kind of horror than Boris Karloff was ten years ago" (*New York Daily News*, October 25). One of the few voices of support came from *The Boston Herald* (October 22): "It is perfectly charming."

If *The Mummy's Tomb* had been the first such picture, it might not have been too bad. There's nothing particularly wrong with any aspect — we've just seen it all before.

The Mummy's Ghost (U.S., 1944, Universal) Released July 7, 1944; 60 minutes; black and white

Credits: Director: Reginald LeBorg; Associate Producer: Ben Pivar; Executive Producer: Joseph Gershenson; Screenplay: Griffin Jay, Henry Sucher, Brenda Weisberg (based on Jay's and Sucher's original story); Director of Photography: William Sickner; Art Directors: John B. Goodman, Abraham Grossman; Editor: Saul A. Goodkind; Musical Director: Hans J. Salter; Sound: Bernard B. Brown; Technician: Jess Moulin; Set Decorators: Russell A. Gausman, L. R. Smith; Assistant Director: Melville Shyer; Makeup: Jack P. Pierce; Gowns: Vera West

Cast: Lon Chaney (Kharis), John Carradine (Yousef Bey), Robert Lowery (Tom Hervey), Ramsay Ames (Amina), Barton MacLane (Inspector Walgreen), George Zucco (High Priest), Frank Reichner (Prof. Norman), Harry Shannon (Sheriff Elwood), Emmett Vogan (Coroner), Lester Sharpe (Dr. Ayad), Claire Whitney (Ella Norman), Oscar O'Shea (Night Watchman), Jack C. Smith, Jack Rockwell (Deputies), Carl Vernell, Martha MacVicar (Students), Stephen Barclay (Harrison), Dorothy Vaughan (Ada Blade), Mira McKinney (Martha Evans), Bess Flowers, Caroline Cooke (Townswomen), Eddy Waller (Ben Evans), Fay Holderness (Woman), Ivan Triesault (Guide), Anthony Warde (Detective), Peter Sosso (Priest), David Bruce (voice on radio)

The high priest (George Zucco) welcomes Yousef Bey (John Carradine) to the Temple of Arkham and relates the legend of Kharis, who supposedly perished in a fire in Mapleton, Massachusetts. In Mapleton, Prof. Norman (Frank Reicher) tells the same story to his Egyptology class. When students Tom Hervey (Robert Lowery) and Amina (Ramsay Ames) discuss the lecture, Amina — an Egyptian — is visibly disturbed.

Kharis (Lon Chaney), who survived the flames, is drawn to Norman's home as he brews tana fluid. Amina, in a trance, follows Kharis to Norman's home where, after strangling the professor, the Mummy drains the fluid.

The Sheriff (Harry Shannon) finds the telltale mold on Norman's throat and realizes that Kharis has returned. Amina, whose hair has mysteriously turned white, is also a suspect.

Yousef Bey, after arriving in Mapleton, contacts Kharis. He has come to unite Kharis with Princess Ananka, and man and mummy travel to the Scripps Museum in New York where her body is housed. When Kharis reaches into the mummy case, her bandaged form vanishes. Yousef Bey concludes that she has been reincarnated ... but into whose body has her soul entered?

They return to Mapleton, and to Amina. Kharis takes her to his lair in a mining shack, where Yousef Bey becomes obsessed with her beauty. Weakening, he tries to claim her for himself by giving her tana fluid, but Kharis throws him through a window to his death.

The Mummy carries Amina to a swamp, pursued by Tom and a posse. Caught in a quicksand bog, Kharis and Amina — now an aged horror — sink to the bottom.

Although basically the same old thing, *The Mummy's Ghost* is slightly better than its predecessor. Lon Chaney seems to be trying to elicit some sympathy for his character and almost succeeds in making us realize, briefly, that Kharis was once human. Director Reginald LeBorg no doubt deserves the credit for not permitting Chaney to simply shuffle through the part. John Carradine's lecherous turn as Yousef Bay is also a welcome addition, but George Zucco's return as the high priest is merely disconcerting.

Lon Chaney did quite a bit of crying to the press about the rigors of playing Kharis. "I sweat and I can't wipe it away," he moaned to a United Press scribe. "I itch and I can't scratch." Considering the enormously greater discomfort being suffered by those fighting World War II, his complaints probably generated little sympathy.

The script by Griffin Jay, Henry Sucher, and Brenda Weisberg makes little sense — even for a horror movie; there are more holes in the plot than in Kharis' bandages. No explanation is given for Ananka's disappearing mummy, Amina's rapid aging, Kharis' lack of burns, and who cared for him all these many years, and why. Again, one doesn't watch *The Mummy's Ghost* to study logic or learn Egyptology, but a little common sense would have been appropriate.

The Mummy's Ghost was released on July 7, 1944 to — you guessed it — condescending reviews. "The Mummy has always been the least impressive of movie monsters and he is doing nothing to enhance his reputation in his latest incarnation. Lon Chaney scares the people in the picture at a great rate, but he is not likely to have much effect on the blood pressure of the audience. Let's hope this time those Egyptians are satisfied and let their old Mummy stay dead" (*New York World Telegram*, June 30, 1944). "Hand tailored to the Rialto patronage. As a sop for logic, the movie falls back on gruesome makeup, stalking monstrosities, reincarnated spirits, and attendant hocus pocus" (*New York Daily News*, July 1, 1944). "More giggly than gruesome — a new dish of believe it or not horror fare. Only, you can't take it very seriously" (*New York Post*, July 1, 1944). "This is the fourth of Universal's Mummy series, but it's too much to hope it's the last" (*New York Daily Mirror*, July 1, 1944). "It's all very silly" (*New York Journal American*, July 1, 1944). And "Oh please Universal — do not disturb their rest" (*New York Herald Tribune*, July 1, 1944).

Although *The Mummy's Ghost* would seem to have shut the sarcophagus on the Kharis legend, decent box office takings induced Universal to take one more shot. Incredibly, *The Mummy's Curse* went into production less than a month after the premier of *The Mummy's Ghost*.

The Mummy's Curse (U.S., 1944, Universal) Released December 22, 1944; 62 minutes; black and white

Credits: Director: Leslie Goodwins; Associate Producer: Oliver Drake; Executive Producer: Ben Pivar; Screenplay: Bernard L. Schubert; Original Story: Leon Abrams, Dwight V. Babcock, Bernard L. Schubert and T. H. Richmond; Director of Photography: Virgil Miller; Camera: William Dodds; Special Effects: John P. Fulton; Editor: Fred R. Feitshans; Art Directors: John B. Goodman, Martin Obzina; Musical Director: Paul Sawtell; Music: Oliver Drake; Set Decorators: Russell A. Gausman, Victor A. Gangelin; Sound: Bernard B. Brown; Technician: Robert Pritchard; Properties: Ernie Smith, Eddie Case; Makeup: Jack P. Pierce; Gowns: Vera West; Assistant Director: Mack Wright

Cast: Lon Chaney (Kharis), Peter Coe (Dr. Ikor Zandaab), Virginia Christine (Princess Ananka), Kay Harding (Betty Walsh), Dennis Moore (Dr. James Halsey), Martin Kosleck (Ragheb), Kurt Katch (Cajun Joe), Addison Richards (Pat Walsh), Holmes Herbert (Dr. Cooper), Charles Stevens (Achilles), Wilham Farnum (Michael), Napoleon Simpson (Goobie), Ann Codee (Tante Berthe), Herbert Heywood (Hill), Nina Bara (Cajun girl), Eddie Abdo (Pierre), Tony Santoro (Ulysses), Eddie Perker, Bob Pepper (Chaney's doubles), Carey Loftin, Teddy Mangean (stuntmen)

Twenty five years have passed since Kharis (Lon Chaney) and Princess Ananka (Virginia Christine) sank into the swamp. They are accidentally unearthed by government workers draining the Louisiana marshes. Dr. Halsey (Dennis Moore) and Dr.

Virginia Christine, carried away by Lon Chaney, Jr., in Universal's ***The Mummy's Curse*** (1944).

Zandaab (Peter Coe) of the Scripps Museum are quickly on the scene but Zandaab has a secret motive — to return the mummies to Egypt. He recruits Ragheb (Martin Kosleck), one of the excavators; the pair revive Kharis with the sacred tana leaves to please the ancient god Amon-Ra. Ananka also returns to life, crawling out of the swamp and absorbing the recuperative rays of the sun. She is found walking, in a trance-like state, and is taken to Dr. Halsey, who is impressed with — and suspicious of — her familiarity with Egyptian lore. Zandaab believes her to be the reincarnation of Ananka and sends Kharis to claim her.

Kharis begins a reign of terror, killing Tante Berthe (Ann Codee), Cajun Joe (Kurt Katch) and Dr. Cooper (Holmes Herbert), in whom Ananka has confided her unnamed fears. Kharis finally finds Ananka and takes her to a monastery where Zandaab gives her the tana fluid. He is distracted from his goal when Ragheb abducts Betty (Kay Harding), breaking the sacred code of Amon-Ra. When Zandaab threatens Ragheb with Kharis' wrath he is stabbed. Kharis attacks Ragheb and buries them both as he brings down the monastery roof. Halsey arrives and finds the mummified body of Ananka.

Despite the negative criticism that could be (and was) leveled at the Kharis series, it did well where it counted — at the box office. Pictures like these defy reviews, and their greatest liability may also have been their greatest strength. Audiences knew exactly what to expect, and kept coming back for more.

More turned out to be less; *The Mummy's Curse* was an unimaginative rehash of the three previous pictures, with Lon Chaney returning to his nonacting style of *The Mummy's Tomb*. The time frame had become even more incomprehensible. *The Mummy's Curse* takes place twenty five years after the events of *The Mummy's Ghost*, which would place it in 1969. Either that, or *The Mummy's Hand* took place in the late 1800s; take your pick. Added to the confusion is the Louisiana bayou setting — when last seen Kharis had sunk into a Massachusetts marsh. While one can appreciate Universal's desire for a little variety in the series, it might have been better to think of a new plotline than to arbitrarily change the locale.

Production began on July 26, 1944, with twelve days scheduled; but as of August 8, Ananka's return from the swamp had yet to be shot, adding several extra shooting days. *The Mummy's Curse* was released on December 22, as the bottom half (in more ways than one) of a double bill with *House of Frankenstein*. Considering that *The Mummy's Curse* broke no new sand, it might have been better to give Kharis a walk on in the Frankenstein monster rally and get it over with.

Kharis had clearly run out of tana fluid, as noted by his reviewers, "OK as a dual support ... can't pass muster in standard fashion" (*Variety*, December 20, 1944). "A wretched little shocker. It is all very juvenile and silly. It's time to tell that Mummy he's a bore" (*New York Times*, March 31, 1945). "The plot follows the visual meller formula" (*Motion Picture Exhibitor*, December 27, 1944).

The Kharis series officially (and mercifully) ended with *The Mummy's Curse*, but Universal would bring the character back a decade later as "Klaris" to meet Abbott and Costello. This was perhaps the final indignity for a poor monster who had suffered much.

Lon Chaney was now released from the role, and would soon be released from his Universal contract. As his star sank in the fifties, he would be forced to accept another variation on the despised character in the Mexican *La Casa Del Terror* (1959). Chaney would play Kharis in more amenable surroundings on TV's *Route 66* in the 1963 Halloween episode "Lizard's Leg and Owlet's Wing," supported by Boris Karloff (as the Frankenstein monster) and Peter Lorre (as Peter Lorre). The Kharis pictures were among the weakest monster series of the forties and are beneath any discussion of cinematic artistry or Egyptian ambiance. They are plodding, unimaginative and repetitious, with any one picture's best moment a rip-off from a previous entry. Yet they continue to have interest, perhaps due more to the powerful concept of a living mummy than to any quality in the films themselves.

Here ended the Universal mummy series; resurrection awaited Kharis at Hammer.

* * *

The Tomb of King Tarus (U.S., 1952, TV)

Tales of Tomorrow, a live television production, broadcast *The Tomb of King Tarus* on October 31, 1952 from the ABC studio in New York. Directed by Don Medford, the small cast of Walter Able, Charles Nolde, and Richard Purdy performed on one *very* cheap looking set.

Three archaeologists, after searching for eight years, discover the elusive tomb of Tarus, but fall out due to their differing reactions to a forbidding curse. The King is found—mummified, but still alive. Quincy panics and shoots the mummy in its sarcophagus. When the body is examined a strange fluid is found to have been pumped into its mouth. This life-sustaining liquid has kept Tarus alive for centuries and is now dripping away. The men argue over who should have what little remains. Jay kills Quincy in a fight and is shot by Doc as he removes the fluid container. By lifting the bottle, the curse has been enacted; the door to the chamber lowers, trapping Doc with the three corpses.

Oddly, the most memorable moment of the series was courtesy of master mummy portrayer Lon Chaney, who played the Monster in an adaptation of *Frankenstein* in the series that same year. "Prior to the live telecast," reported Greg Mank in *It's Alive!*, "Chaney became inebriated, got confused, and played the televised performance believing it was the final dress rehearsal. As the director and crew battled hysteria, Chaney cursed under his breath and gingerly picked up and put down the breakable props which were supposed to crumble in his mighty grasp."

The Tomb of King Tarus is about what one would expect from a low budget live television show from 1952; it's a curiosity item and little more. It might have been more interesting if Lon Chaney had been involved.

Abbott and Costello Meet the Mummy (U.S., 1955, Universal) Black and white; 79 minutes

Credits: Director: Charles Lamont; Producer: Howard Christie; Screenplay: John Grant; Original Story: Lee Loeb; Director of Photography: George Robinson ASC; Art Directors: Alexander Golitzen, Bill Newberry; Set Decorations: Russell A. Gausman, James M. Walters; Sound: Leslie I. Carey, Robert Pritchard; Film Editor: Russell Schoengarth, ACE; Gowns: Rosemary Odell; Hair Stylist: Joan St. Oegger; Makeup: Bud Westmore; Special Photography: Clifford Stine, ASC; Assistant Director: Phil Bowles; Music Supervision: Joseph Gershenson; Script Supervisor: Betty Abbott; Dialogue Director: Milt Bronson

Cast: Bud Abbott (Peter Patterson), Lou Costello (Freddie Franklin), Marie Windsor (Madame Rontu), Michael Ansara (Charlie), Dan Seymour (Josef), Kurt Katch (Dr. Zoomer), Richard Karlan (Hetsut), Richard Deacon (Semu), Eddie Parker (Klaris), Chandra Kaly Dancers, Mazzone-Abbott Dancers (Dance Troupes), Mel Welles (Iben), George Khourly (Habid), Veola Vonn (Dancer), Jan Arvan, Jean Hartelle (Waiters), Kem Dibbs (First Policeman), Ted Hecht (Anzi), Michael Vallon (Dr. Azzui), Harry Mendoza (Magician), Mitchell Kowal (Second Policeman), Kam Tong (Chinese Busboy), Robin Morse (Waiter), Lee Sharon (Blonde Girl), Carole Costello (Cigarette Girl), Donald Kerr (Newspaper Man), John Powell (Bit), Peggy King (Vocalist)

Pete (Bud Abbott) and Freddie (Lou Costello) become involved with Dr. Zoomer (Kurt Katch), an Egyptologist who has uncovered the mummy of Klaris (Eddie Parker—and note the "l"), who guards the tomb of Princess Ara. Klaris also holds a gold medallion that, supposedly, tells the location

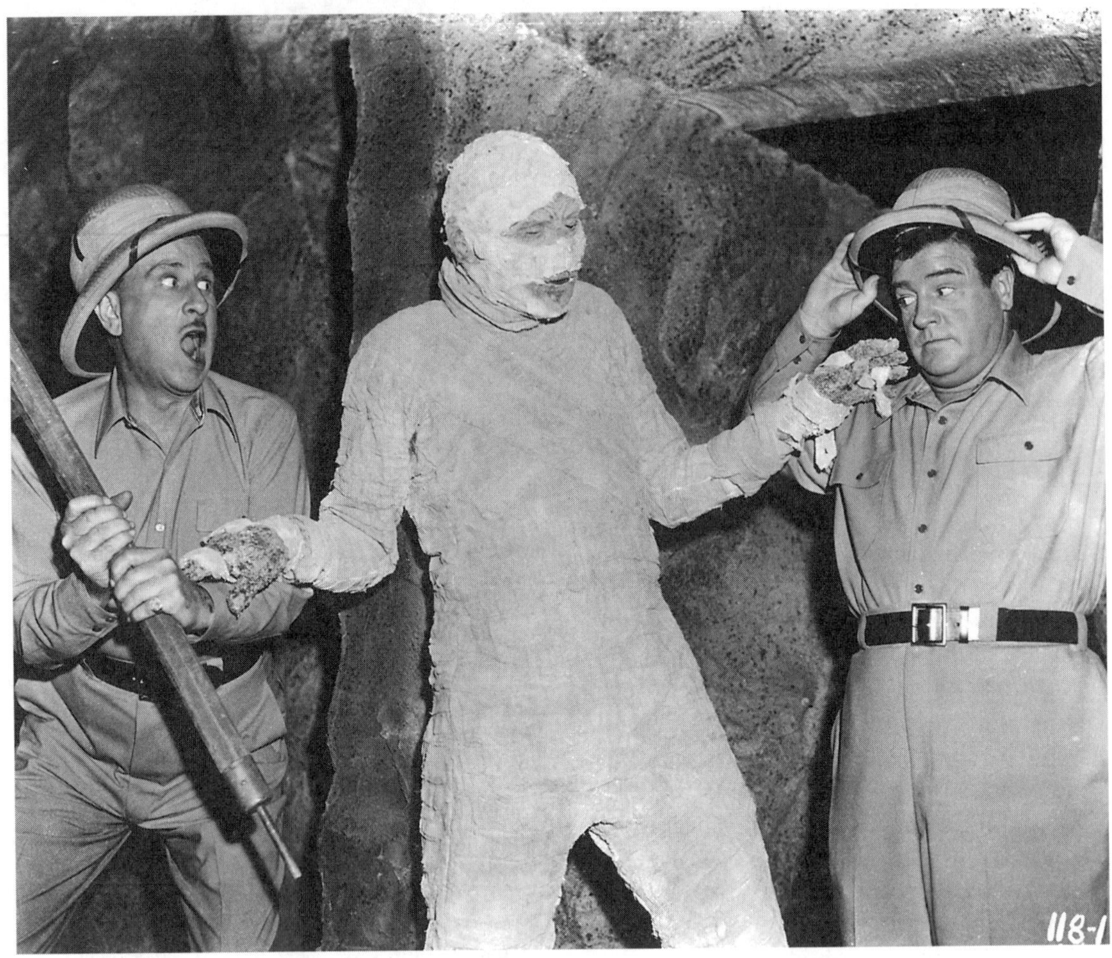

Bud Abbott and Lou Costello meet Eddie Parker (Universal, 1955).

of her treasure. This information soon becomes the property of the disreputable Semu (Dan Seymour), head of the followers of Klaris and the equally slippery Madame Rontu (Marie Windsor).

Dr. Zoomer is killed by Semu's thugs, leaving Pete and Freddie with the medallion. They learn of its true value when Madame Rontu offers too much money for it. Freddie manages to eat the thing as Pete had hidden it in a hamburger. An X-ray reveals the medallion in Freddie's stomach; the directions to the treasure are, not surprisingly, in hieroglyphs.

All of the concerned parties, including the revived Klaris, meet in the tomb. After the expected misadventures (Freddie disguised as the Mummy, an inopportune explosion, etc.), Klaris is destroyed and the treasure is found.

If nothing else, *Abbot and Costello Meet the Mummy*, finally gave Eddie Parker the opportunity to play a monster for real, after stunting for the Universal's stable of creatures. As Klaris, he was given little to do, but was no worse than Chaney (which is to say he was equal to the task). Bud Westmore's makeup was less effective than Jack Pierce's design, due to a disconcerting gap in the facial bandages.

As for the "stars," the comedy team's best picture *Abbott and Costello Meet Frankenstein* (1948, and not too bad as a horror movie either), was originally scheduled to feature Kharis along with Dracula (Bela Lugosi), the Wolfman (Lon Chaney) and, of course, the Monster (Glenn Strange). The mummy was mercifully dropped; enough is enough! Lon Chaney was well accounted for, and we couldn't give the Kharis role to, say, a stuntman, could we?

By 1954 the team careers of Abbott and Costello, and Lon Chaney and Kharis were on the way down. Since meeting Frankenstein, the boys encountered Boris Karloff in *Abbott and Costello Meet the Killer* (1949), then renewed their relationship with the original Mummy in *Abbott and Costello Meet Dr. Jekyll and Mr. Hyde* (1953). These were pretty pale when compared to the teams' early forties classics, and it seemed as though their fifteen year ride was over.

Lon Chaney was unceremoniously dropped by Universal in 1946. His last picture under contract was the miserable *Pillow of Death*, an "inner sanctum" mystery. Chaney returned for the one-shot. *Meet Frankenstein*, then was again shown the door. He was resilient enough to find a new career as a supporting actor in *High Noon* (1952), often showing more talent than he had as a star. At least he wasn't playing the Mummy any more.

Kharis fared even more poorly. After *The Mummy's Curse*, his name would not be evoked for over a decade.

Abbott and Costello Meet Dr. Jekyll and Mr. Hyde, while hardly classic cinema (or likely to have amused Robert Louis Stevenson), did well enough that Universal was

Lon Chaney, Jr., makes a comeback as his least favorite character in 1959's *Castle of Terror*.

willing to have the boys meet one more monster. Let's see ... what's left?

The production of *Abbott and Costello Meet the Mummy* began in November 1954 and was given a twenty-five day schedule. The picture came in five days early and several thousand under budget—and it shows. In addition to the boys' tired routines and predictable script, the whole thing simply looks like the end of the road. It was. Abbott and Costello officially split in May 1955, the same month as the picture opened. This last opus was not the best way for a wonderful collaboration to end, but then, these things seldom end well. It didn't do the Mummy much good either.

Leslie Halliwell, in *The Dead That Walk* (Grafton Books, 1986), describes the film as "a rather sad parody filled with reprises of half-baked vaudeville routines such as 'the disappearing body' and 'look out, he's behind you!' When the mummy finally makes his unfrightening appearance it is in perfunctory garb, a sort of turn-of-the-century one-piece bathing suit with facial wrappings amounting to little more than a yashmak, behind which the healthy features of stuntman Eddie Parker shine cheerfully. There is such a teddy bear aspect to this mummy that it seems a pity he has to be blown up in the finale ... the mummy comedy had been their last chance, and they (and their scriptwriters) muffed it" (1986, p. 231).

Alan Frank, in *Horror Movies* (Octopus, 1976), comments "*It was Universal's insistence upon flogging a dead mummy that had really brought about the temporary demise of this screen monster*" (1976, p. 82).

Pharaoh's Curse (U.S., 1957, United Artists/Bel-Air) Released February 1957; approx. 65 minutes; black and white

Credits: Original Story and Screenplay: Richard Landau; Music: Les Baxter; Producer: Howard W. Koch; Director: Lee Sholem; Photography: William Margulies; Supervising Editor: John F. Schreyer; Editor: George A. Gittens; Assistant Director: Paul Wurtzel; Set Designer: Bob Kinoshita; Set Decorator: Clarence Steenson; Sound Mixer: Joe Edmondson; Sound Editor: John Bushelman; Executive Producer: Aubrey Schenck; Makeup: Ted Coodley; Special Effects: Jack Rabin, Louis DeWitt

Cast: Mark Dana (Capt. Storm); Ziva Shapir [Rodann] (Simira); Diane Brewster (Sylvia Quentin); George Neise (Robert Quentin); Alvaro Guillot (Numar, The Mummy); Ben Wright (Andrews); Guy Prescott (Dr. Faraday); Kurt Katch (Brett); Terence De Marney; Richard Peel; Robert Fortin; Ralph Clanton

Pharaoh's Curse unwrapped the mummy legend to such an extent that our hero was not even wearing traditional bandages. The production company, Bel-Air, also made *Voodoo Island* with Boris Karloff, with which *Pharaoh's Curse* was released in February 1957 as the bottom half of a double feature.

Production began on *Curse of the Pharaohs*, as it was first titled, on March 30, 1957. Ziva Shapir (renamed Rodann), a former Miss Israel, had been signed by Universal International to a long term contract in September 1955. She was "loaned out"—an archaic studio policy almost as old as the pyramids—to Bel-Air to star as, of all things, an Egyptian.

The desert scenes were shot in Death Valley—incredibly in only one day. Director Lee ("Roll 'Em") Sholem told author Tom Weaver, "We flew out of Burbank early in the morning and landed in the desert just as the sun was coming up. The company and cameras and all the equipment were all on trucks; we started at one end of the canyon in Death Valley and worked all the way down to the other end. We moved with the sun. We shot all the desert exteriors, finished the day's work and came home. One day!"

That left five to go, as the production moved to American International Studios. "You would be amazed how little area we used," added Sholem, "We did that by constantly redressing the sets. We'd put a piece or a prop in front of the camera in the foreground. Then we'd move the pieces around and you'd think it was a whole different area!"

So ... what do we get for SIX days' work?

In 1902 a British patrol, led by Captain Storm (Mark Dana), is sent into the Egyptian desert to bring back an archaeological team due to growing political unrest. With them is Sylvia Quentin (Diane Brewster) whose husband Robert (George Neise) heads the dig. They are met in the desert by Simira (Ziva Rodann), a native girl looking for her brother, also on the team. When they arrive at the site, a tomb has been opened and Simira's brother Numar (Alvaro Guillot) is taken ill and metamorphosizes into a rapidly aging, blood-sucking corpse inhabited by the spirit of the high priest. The creature is destroyed and the tomb sealed with no record made of its discovery.

Although the plot isn't much, it *is* a bit different which, for a mummy movie, is saying quite a bit. The film is high on atmosphere, the acting is competent and in no way do we sense a rushed production. The creature, as adequately played by Alvaro Guillot, looks good in close-up but, viewed at full length, resembles a terminally ill man in pajamas on his way to a medical checkup. In many ways it's at least as good as any of the Lon Chaney pictures but lacking a horror star, has been dismissed — unfairly-by many fans.

Reviews were about what one would expect: "Lots of mumbo jumbo and sequences that should scare the kiddies ... the story is interesting and sort of confusing ... cast, direction and production are average"(*Motion Picture Exhibitor*). "Highly colored but cheaply cast and staged ... characters are taken from stock but not even dusted" (*Kinematograph Weekly*).

Pharaoh's Curse created a minor controversy when Los Angeles TV station KRCA refused to run spot ads for the double feature, deeming them to be too frightening. United Artists threatened a breach of contract suit; KRCA offered to play the spots after 11 p.m. so as to not frighten children. Producer Aubrey Schenck, apparently not sensing the PR coup, announced, "There is nothing frightening about these spots!"

Robot vs. The Aztec Mummy (1957)

Despite its initial lack of quality (which would be multiplied ten-fold when Jerry Warren got hold of it). *La Momia* inspired three sequels. One should remember though that there is often no direct correlation between quality and sequels. As with *La Momia*, there are several versions of this picture, none of which are very interesting.

The authors saw the American International release version of 1964, which is probably no better or worse than the others. The movie's original title was *Momia Contra el Robot Humano* (Mummy vs. the Human Robot). Other titles include *LaMomia Azteka Contra el Robot Humano*, *El Robot Humano*, and *The Aztec Mummy vs. the Human Robot.* As with *La Momia* it was misdirected by Rafael Lopez Portillo.

Psychiatrist Dr. Ramon, an outcast due to his theories on regression of the soul, uses his wife Flora as a guinea pig. He takes her back to the ancient Aztec Empire in which, as Zochi, she was the lover of Popoca, a fearsome warrior. Their relationship was forbidden by tribal priests due to Zochi's higher station and Popoca was buried alive. Zochi, after being given a golden breastplate and bracelet (on which were inscribed directions to an Aztec treasure), was murdered and the treasure went unclaimed. Flora's long repressed memories are overheard by the evil Dr. Kripp.

Dr. Ramon, Flora, and her father unearth Zochi's body and recover the golden breastplate; but the hieroglyphs are unfathomable without the missing bracelet. When they return to the tomb to recover it, the party is attacked by the mummified Popoca. They barely escape with their lives — and the bracelet.

Popoca later seizes both Flora and the treasure and takes them to his tomb where she is rescued by her father. But Dr. Kripp abducts Flora and uses her to force Dr. Ramon's cooperation. Popoca arrives to save his ancient lover and is attacked by Kripp's robot. In the ensuing battle Popoca triumphs; he is then given the golden artifacts by Dr. Ramon and returns to his tomb.

Words fails to convey the effect of this sleep-inducer. It may have been watchable in its original undubbed form, but somehow this is doubtful. The idea of replacing Egyptian mummy lore with Aztec isn't as interesting as one would hope, although the regression angle wasn't badly done. The picture (and the mummy) unravels when the robot comes on, thankfully, fairly late.

Proving that there is no accounting for taste, this debacle inspired *La Maldición de la Momia* (*The Curse of the Mummy*) two years later. Popoca returned in 1961 in *The Living Head* and in 1964 in Rene Cardona's *Wrestling Women vs. the Aztec Mummy*. The series gradually turned him from "baddie" to "almost goodie." In 1971 poor Popoca fared badly against Santo in both *Santo Against the Mummy* and *The Mummy's Revenge* when, according to John Martin in *The Dark Side*, "he appears to have retired gracefully back to his tomb. Bung him a few tana leaves, though (or bung some maniacal Mexican director or other a batch of coca leaves, perhaps!) and who knows!"

* * *

The Hammer Films Ltd. Mummies

Hammer seemed destined to revive all the classic horror characters following the success of their *The Curse of Frankenstein* and *Dracula*, both filmed in gorgeous color. This

Christopher Lee as the screen's first Technicolor *Mummy* (Hammer/Universal, 1959).

added a wonderful dimension to the genre and Hammer's Jack Asher was a master of lighting, making the sets glow.

Hammer only made four Mummy pictures; *The Mummy, The Curse of the Mummy's Tomb, The Mummy's Shroud* and *Blood from the Mummy's Tomb.** Unlike their other canons—Frankenstein and Dracula—there is no continuity (thank Heaven) in the story lines and the same mummy does not pop up with the boring regularity of slices of toast. As such, they are a collection of mummy tales rather than a series.

The Mummy, as the first, had the supreme team of technicians and artists you would expect from Hammer at that time. The roll of actors was splendid—the top earners, Christopher Lee and Peter Cushing, supported by the cream of English theater and television; an excellent director, Terence Fisher, whose economy of shooting and joy of the cinema medium brought art and finance together in a way that delighted the management; superb art direction under Bernard Robinson, aided by art historian Andrew Low, who had a special love for the period, reproducing the art works of the ancient world and making such a good job of it that they *still* pop up in films and TV shows today; majestic music by Franz Reizenstein; a splendid action packed script by Jimmy Sangster; excellent makeup by genius Roy Ashton, who almost *could* make a silk purse out of a sow's ear; and produced by Michael Carreras, son of one of the firm's founders, Sir James Carreras, and marketed with all that showman's energy and expertise. What a pedigree for a movie!

The Curse of the Mummy's Tomb was almost as well received, but not of the caliber of the first. Still it had a splendid team—though Michael Carreras had to write, produce, and direct, and did not get to make the film he really wanted to. Sir James had had his usual brainwave for the birth of the film. Title and poster first—rest later. "There's no holding Hammer," said James Carreras, "one of Hammer's most successful horrifics a few years ago was *The Mummy*. A sequel was almost inevitable. Now it's coming in *The Curse of the Mummy's Tomb*, the terrifying story of a gigantic mummy, 3000 years old which comes to life and terrorizes the Nile Valley."

A press release at the time developed his words: "Dabbling in things they don't understand, they bring to life a monstrous 20-foot giant which goes on a murder rampage in Cairo. When the gigantic creature escapes into the desert, aircraft and parachute troops go in pursuit. All hell breaks loose in a shattering climax" (Hammer Films Ltd.). The company then decided that the mummy film was to be the supporting half of a double bill with Fisher's *The Gorgon* as the main offering; the original concept of the film was no longer viable. Made at Elstree instead of the diminutive sets at Bray, would make one think that the usual size constraints that Bernard Robinson worked under would be history but it was just the opposite. As Fred Humphreys records in *Dark Terrors*, "Elstree's Stage 3 (150 feet by 100 feet) had to stretch to accommodate six sets; the Library and Garden, Desert Expedition Headquarters, Annette's Tent, King's Office, Embankment Alley and Stairs and the Cairo Restaurant. Bernard was forced to condense so many sets that magnificent desert vistas became cramped backdrops with potted palms and plaster rocks." A similar problem would be evident during the shooting of *The Mummy's Shroud*.

Although the production team was still top grade, the cast's star qualities had diminished. No major star was cast for *Curse*, although the actors produced an entertaining movie, somewhat reminiscent of a comic book retelling of a mummy tale. Roy Ashton,

**Note: In order to discuss the four Hammer films as a group and in sequence, there will be a change in the normally chronological arrangement of this section.* Jonny Quest—The Curse of Anubis, *a 1964 animated cartoon for television, will be presented* after *all Hammer films have been discussed, even though the last Hammer mummy film was released in 1971.*

Terence Morgan and Dickie Owen in *The Curse of the Mummy's Tomb* (Hammer/Columbia, 1964).

teaming up with the wardrobe department, tried to create a mummy costume that was less restrictive and uncomfortable than Christopher Lee's. The looser headpiece did not produce the half-bone, half-bandage of the promos, but a baggy blob with a forehead that Fred Humphreys compares with the Elephant Man! "We can only assume the mummy's asthmatic breathing was due to Jeanne Roland lying prostrate in her negligee at the top of the stairs," says Fred. He does, however, praise the use of the wide screen, and in particular the interdeck shots on the liner and the traveling shot through the tomb — shown under the credits as well as in the body of the movie — a two-minute, fifty-second single shot of the wonderful artifacts created by the art department, and two extras doubling as tomb statues covered in dust.

The Mummy's Shroud kept the technical team, joined by John Gilling to write and direct. The cast were again not crème de la crème, but competent. The last Hammer film to be shot at Bray, Bernard Robinson with Don Mingaye again worked wonders with the cramped surroundings, and Les Bowie produced the beautifully accurate sand-mummified body of Kah-to-Bey and created the best demise yet for a rampaging mummy. Hammer was sliding gently downhill in the mummy movie genre but still had more class than the B-picture Kharis movies of Universal in the forties. It was believed that a new screenplay, a new concept of mummy movie, was not viable and that the old themes had been worn out.

The decision to shoot *Blood From the Mummy's Tomb* was urged on the company by Howard Brandy, a peripheral associate of

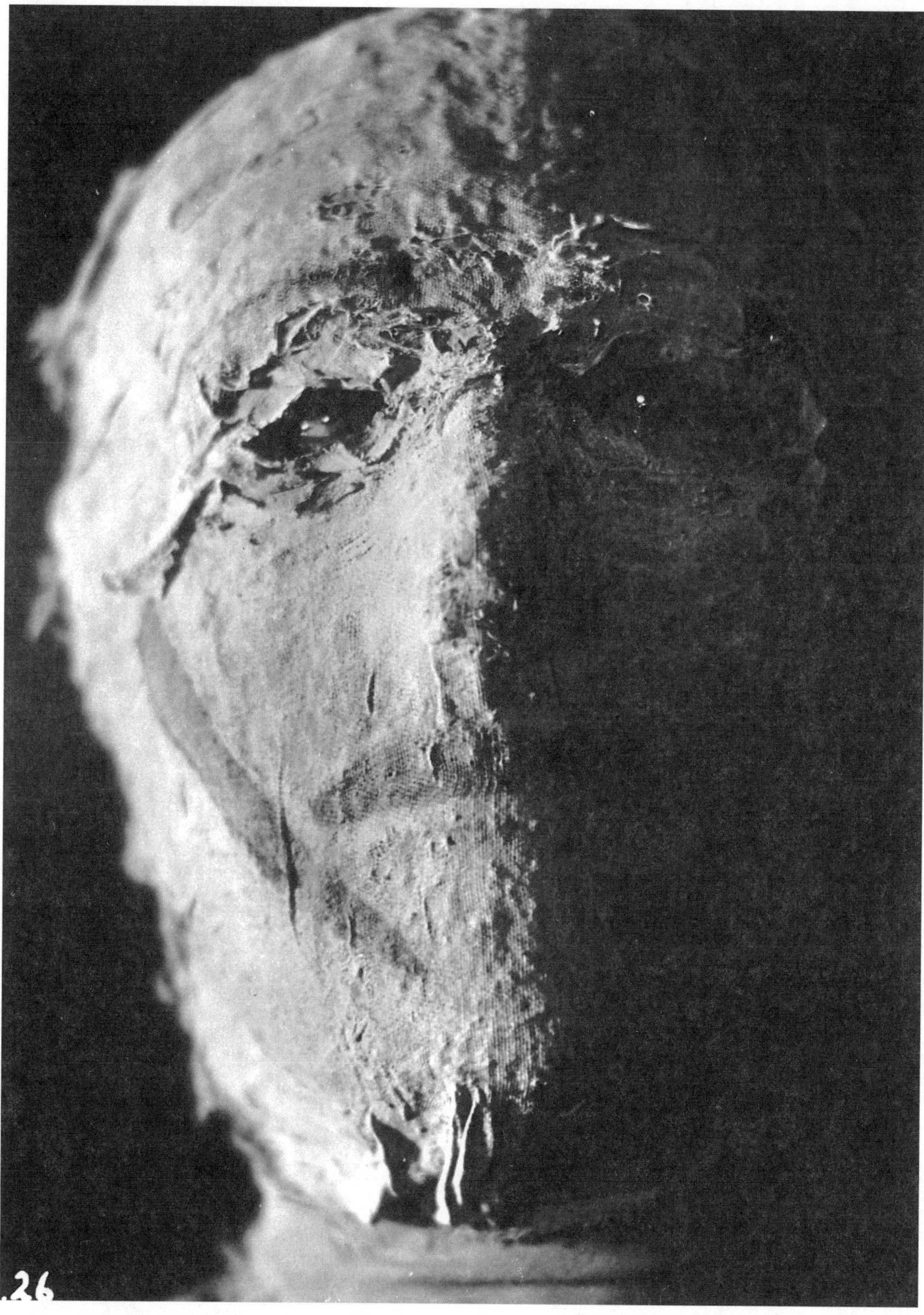

Eddie Powell in ***The Mummy's Shroud*** (Hammer/20th Century–Fox, 1967).

the company. Hammer was no more the "cinematic rep company" that had created its greatest films. Seth Holt in *auteur* mode, did not share his concept of the finished film with anyone and when he died, Michael Carreras, who had just rejoined the company, was forced to try and make sense of the existing film, like a pre-Champollion linguist trying to make sense of hieroglyphs. He then had to finish the film with one week of scheduled time to go.

The finished film was one of the best mummy films ever, and has an other-worldly sense that works, even if it is owed to the muddle to finish it.

Michael Carreras produced *all* the Hammer mummy movies—and reveled in the concept. He often remarked with wry amusement that Tony Hinds didn't like mummy movies because they were not truly horror classics—whereas *Frankenstein* and *Dracula* had literary antecedents that made them "art." But Michael liked the dynamism that he saw was possible in a mummy film with a decent script. All the films he produced for the genre are entertaining and good value for your ticket money—and some have truly wonderful, heartstopping moments.

The Mummy (1959) Produced February 1959; Released September (U.K.), December (U.S.); 88 minutes; Technicolor

Credits: Director: Terence Fisher; Producer: Anthony Hinds; Associate Producer: Anthony Nelson-Keys; Executive Producer: Michael Carreras; Screenplay: Jimmy Sangster (based on Nina Wilcox Putnam's screenplay); Director of Photography: Jack Asher; Music Composer: Frank Reizenstein; Music Director: John Hollingsworth; Supervising Editor: James Needs; Editor: Alfred Cox; Production Design: Bernard Robinson; Makeup: Roy Ashton; Camera: Len Harris; Production Manager: Don Weeks; Sound Recordist: Jock May; Hairstyles: Henry Montsash; Costumes: Molly Arbuthnot; Artifacts: Margaret Carter Robinson; Technical Advisor: Andrew Low; Assistant Director: John Peverall; Second Assistant: Tom Walls; Third Assistant: Hugh Harlow; Continuity: Marjorie Lavelly; Focus: Harry Oakes; Clapper: Alan McDonald; Boom: Jim Perry; Sound Camera Operator: Al Thorne; Sound Maintenance: Charles Bouvet; Assistant Art Director: Don Mingaye; Stills: Tom Edwards; Publicist: Colin Reid; Casting Director: Dorothy Holloway; Assistant Director: Chris Barnes; Special Effects: Bill Warington, Les Bowie

Cast: Peter Cushing (John Banning), Christopher Lee (Kharis), Yvonne Furneaux (Isobel/ Ananka), Eddie Byrne (Inspector Mulrooney), Felix Aylmer (Stephen Banning), Raymond Huntley (Joseph Whemple), George Pastell (Mehemet), Michael Ripper (Poacher), John Stuart (Coroner), Harold Goodwin (Pat), Dennis Shaw (Mike), Willoughby Gray (Dr. Reilly), Stanley Meadows (Attendant), Frank Singuineau (Head Porter), George Woodbridge (Constable), Frank Sieman (Bill), Gerald Lawson (Irish Customer), John Harrison, James Clarke (Priests), David Browning (Sergeant)

Egypt 1895; injured archaeologist, John Banning (Peter Cushing), is unable to join his father Stephen (Felix Aylmer) and Uncle Joe (Raymond Huntley) as they open the newly discovered tomb of Princess Ananka, having ignored warnings by Mehemet (George Pastell). Alone in the tomb, as Uncle Joe confirms the find to John, Stephen suffers a breakdown whilst reading the Scroll of Life. He returns to an English nursing home while John and his uncle clear and subsequently reseal the tomb.

England 1898; John is urgently summoned to Engerfield Nursing Home where his father has asked to see him, breaking a three-year silence. Stephen, though apparently lucid, is warning about "a living mummy" that will destroy them all. John assumes it is another phase of his father's breakdown and offends him by trying to reason the elder man from his fear. Close by, the mummy is resurrected by the magic words as read by Mehemet from the Scroll. The mummy emerges from a swamp-like bog into which the case carrying it, together with other artifacts, has been pitched by inept, inebriate porters. Mehemet, the current High Priest of Karnak, sends Kharis (Christopher Lee) to exact vengeance on the desecrators of the Princess's tomb.

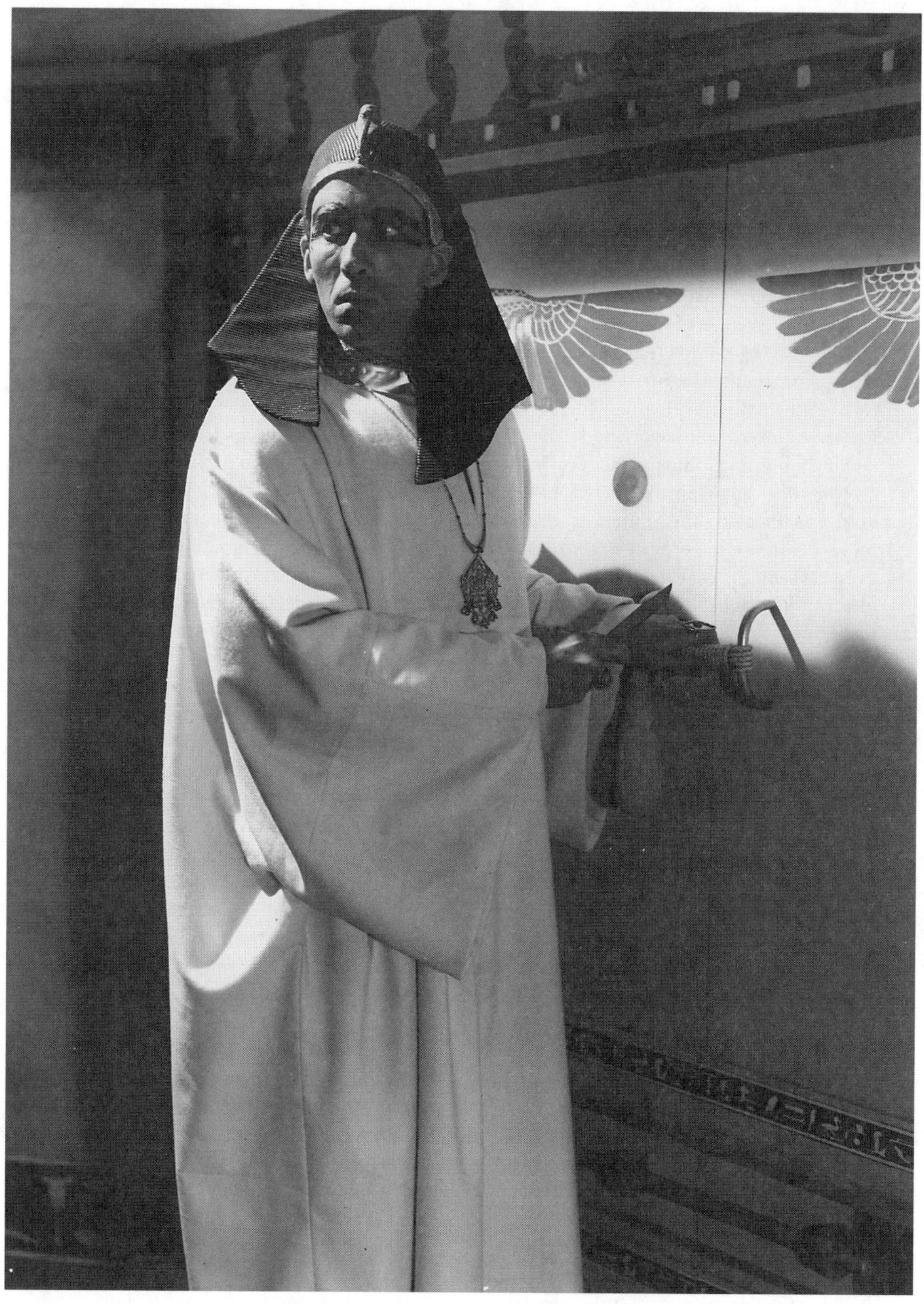

Christopher Lee prepares to commit a sacrilege in ***The Mummy*** (Hammer/Universal, 1959).

Kharis's first act of vengeance is on Stephen, now locked in a padded cell; he breaks in, an unstoppable nemesis, and chokes the old man. John and Uncle Joe decide to investigate possible suspects, and in reviewing the late archaeologist's papers, John recounts the legend of the living mummy. Kharis, once High Priest of Karnak, officiated over the funeral rites of his princess, whom he secretly loved, after she died on her pilgrimage to discover the birthplace of her god. At the closing of the ceremonies, having completed his duties to the dead princess and his god, Kharis felt free to try the ultimate blasphemy—to revive the woman he loved, whose vows to Karnak were no longer binding following her death. However, he was caught in the act before the revival was effected, and sentenced to living, mute death as a perpetual guard to the princess's mummy. Uncle Joe scoffs at the idea, but John is beginning to doubt his original refusal to believe his father.

"*...A fairy story— nothing more...*" asserts Uncle Joe, retiring for the night, only to be attacked and killed by Kharis in the hall of the Banning mansion, despite John's impotent intrusion and the emptying of a revolver into his bandages at close range. A skeptical Inspector Mulrooney (Eddie Byrne) listens to John's account of the night's events, and his suspicions of the perpetrator, and he is unable to prevent the mummy's attack on John shortly thereafter. John is only saved by the intervention of his wife Isobel (Yvonne Furneaux) who is dressed in flowing nightclothes, with her hair spilling across her shoulders. In this fashion she resembles Ananka so uncannily that the mummy stumbles away in confusion.

Despite Mulrooney's instructions to the contrary, John visits Mehemet; there he discovers artifacts from Ananka's tomb, and angers Mehemet to the point where only the latter's Eastern sense of responsibility to one's guest prevents the high priest calling Kharis to action at once. On his departure, Mehemet releases Kharis, takes the Scroll and humbly commits them both to the care of their god. Then they set out to finish the task.

Gaining entry to the Banning mansion, Kharis is interrupted again by Isobel as he attempts to strangle John. Initially, the resemblance is blurred because Isobel is now gowned and coifed as a nineteenth century lady, and John has to gasp, "*Isobel ... your hair!*," whereupon she frees her tresses, and effecting an authoritative command, stops Kharis in his tracks. Mehemet orders Kharis to kill Isobel, an order he ignores with great effort. Mehemet, brandishing a knife, strides towards Isobel who faints away as Kharis intercepts him and breaks his back. Before help arrives, Kharis sweeps Isobel up and makes off with her—not to Mehemet's house, but to the swamp. He also has the Scroll, and with it, he can live again *and* revive Isobel to be his Ananka. Fortunately, he is thwarted by the humans, who rescue Isobel, shoot his mummy to pieces, and watch him sink with the Scroll still clutched in his hand to the bottom of the swamp.

After the sensational success of *Dracula*, Universal-International gave Hammer the rights to remake its horror cannon. The first three projects were to be *The Mummy*, *The Phantom of the Opera* (remade in 1962), and *The Invisible Man* (which was never done). It was one of the biggest American/British film deals ever, led by Al Daff for Universal and James Carreras for Hammer.

Jimmy Sangster had the task of scripting the new film. He saw, at some point, the Tyler-Chaney movies, "How else could one explain the same character names and plot elements," he told the authors in August 1993, but kindly thought about it in more detail for a meeting with the authors in December 1996. "The names are a kind of *homage* to the old films which I saw in a group. It wasn't a detailed study—more a kind of mood setting. I don't do a great deal of background research if it isn't in the *Encyclopedia Britannica*, I don't want to know. That's what you pay technical advisors for." He did, however, smile in appreciation when

Peter Cushing and Raymond Huntley attacked by Christopher Lee as *The Mummy* (Hammer/Universal, 1959).

the subtle shift in the plot was remarked upon — that in his film, Ananka is not reborn as Isobel and that neither Ananka or Isobel loved Kharis during their lifetimes. There is no trance-state in which Isobel is ruled by him, no stirring of an age-old memory; this is a *new* plot.

As the eponymous hero, Christopher Lee gives one of his most compelling horror performances ever. Kharis has enormous physical presence, combined with heart-breaking sensitivity conveyed by his expressive eyes and body mime; to have deprived Kharis of speech both removes any accusation

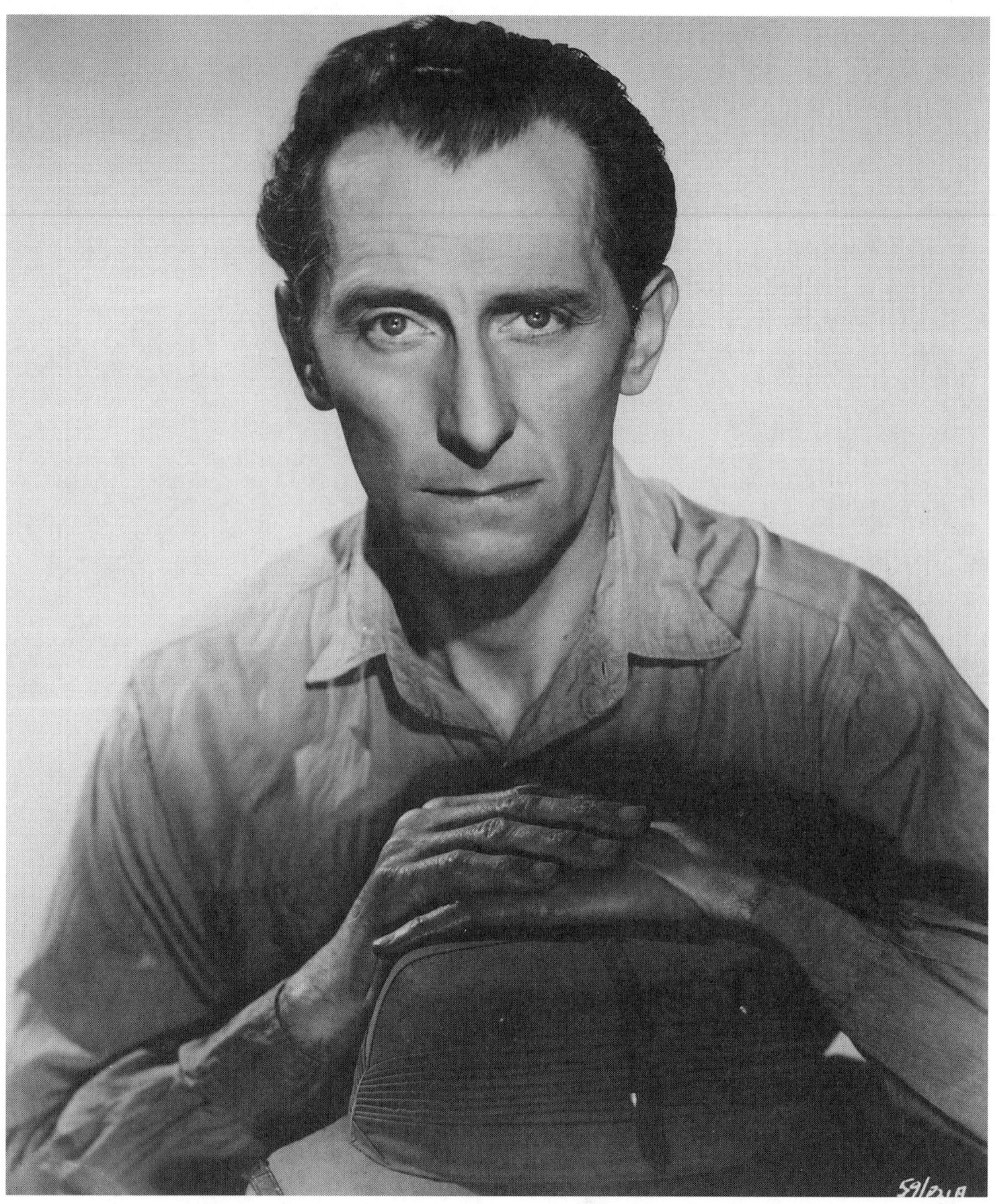

Peter Cushing as John Banning in *The Mummy* (Hammer/Universal, 1959).

of plagiarizing Karloff's mummy and strengthens the mummy's moments on screen. There are no misunderstandings about Kharis's thoughts and actions thanks to Lee's superb performance. "Christopher Lee's Kharis was statuesque, athletic and heartrending: three notable innovations" (*Hammer Horror* May 1995). However, the part helped to fix Lee in the minds of film producers as a horror star par excellence—a two edged sword. Later, Leslie Halliwell would comment, "Hammer's master of horror was constantly apologizing for his horror roles, hoping to find the great dramatic character he thought he deserved; but like Karloff before him, he had been typed by accepting the role of the Frankenstein monster, and when he played Dracula after that, there was only one way he could go; the same way. *The Mummy* was inevitable." (*The Dead That Walk,* 1986).

Peter Cushing matched the power of Lee's Mummy with his own performance as John Banning. The physicality of their meetings is a cinematic tour de force, and they have seldom been better paired in a movie. This casting, according to *The Daily Cinema* (February 27, 1959), was considered "a must" by Universal-International.

Cushing was Hammer's premier star, well known for his television and stage work in Great Britain and his numerous films all over the world. Volumes have been written about both actors, but it is true to say that, whenever they were paired in a movie, the audience could be sure of a first class night out. And with Hammer, making films was often a cooperative task, with everyone tossing ideas around as Peter Cushing remembered in his autobiography: "When I saw the posters advertising the film, I noticed that Christopher Lee ... had a large hole in his diaphragm with a beam of light passing through it, which was never referred to in the script, so I inquired how it got there. 'Oh,' said the publicity man, 'that's just to help sell the picture.' Oh, I thought — that's just not on. John Banning (my part) was attacked by Kharis, the mummy, so I asked Terry if I could grab a harpoon hanging on the wall of Banning's study and during the struggle for survival, drive it clear through my opponent's body. And that's what I did, thus giving some sort of logic to the illuminated gap depicted on the posters. Christopher was pleased, too— he said it made a nice change from stakes." (*Past Forgetting— Memoirs of the Hammer Years* 1988).

Eddie Powell, Christopher Lee's stunt double, remembers filming the climax of the film, sinking slowly into the swamp with the Scroll. "Funnily enough, they thought that was going to take a hell of a long time to do. I did it all in one take and Michael Carreras said, 'Whatever money you're paying him, double it!' I'd saved them so much time when they could be shooting other things, so it worked out very well" (*Hammer Horror* May, 1995).

The Mummy went into production on February 25, 1959, ending on April 16, at Bray Studios. Two weeks at Shepperton were used for the swamp scenes, involving the tank. Terence Fisher created the perfect adult fairy tale. He is reported as saying, "These pictures are a genuine cinema form. I have always strenuously tried to avoid being blatant in my pictures. Instead, whenever possible, I have used the camera to show things— especially nasty things— happening by implication" (*The Kinematograph Weekly,* March 26, #1959). Fisher's skill, together with his technical team, led to the film being described thusly in *The Aurum Film Encyclopedia,* Volume III, "Horror"): "Fisher's surrealist use of color, at its most unforgettable in the nightmarish scenes of the mummy's death in the swamps and in the opening sequences set in Ancient Egypt, together with his unnerving sense of camera position and cutting, give the movie a genuinely macabre poetry never achieved in mummy films before or since" (Hardy, 1958). Hammer films were being shot on the warm, saturated colors of Technicolor, and Fisher, with his team, created a distinctive style, which some critics disliked. "A pretty dull film, not helped by unimaginative sets or garish color" (Halliwell, 1986). Fisher himself explained to the authors (October 1974), "There are some occasions when *cinema verite* is useful, but when you are making *these* films, the studio settings, the colors, the lighting, they all create a new reality for the duration of the film, do you see? Personally, I prefer to create this reality ... I don't like the hand-held camera wobbling down the street and washed out natural colors."

As ever, Hammer saved money and stayed on schedule and under budget by

Yvonne Furneaux as Princess Ananka in *The Mummy* (Hammer/Universal, 1959).

revamping sets from *Yesterday's Enemy* and *The Man Who Could Cheat Death*. Bernard Robinson wryly described himself as, "The Marks and Spencer of the film world" but his sets are a perfect blend of economy and lushness. The Egyptian sets convey the period, aided by Andrew Low's advice, but they are not academically accurate, since that is not their purpose. Many a reader of hieroglyphs will point out the repeated phrasing round the set — necessitated by quick application via a stencil, or the fact that Ananka seems to have misappropriated some of Tutankhamen's belongings since his name is on them; or that tomb paintings are found to be as fresh and beautiful upon reopening a tomb as the day they were painted. But Robinson knew that the images of the artifacts were in the back of his audiences' memory, creating the period and feel, and that the ruse of fading and flaking the paints would sharpen the feeling of centuries having passed, together with skeletons from sacrificed servants grouped where they fell. Andrew Low went on promotional tours with some of the artifacts round the cinema circuit.

When one considers the care taken with the objects—Margaret Robinson reduced to tears by Low for not having the correctly shaped noses on the ushabti figures, or the wrong shade of paint on the god-mask—it is astounding that management decided to leave the misnaming of the god alone. Many of those involved in the project protested, but management, in its wisdom, decided that the cinemagoing public would not notice. They did.

Roy Ashton's makeup and mask for the mummy were splendid, and the bandages that completed the image were worked to destruction by the most physical mummy the screen had ever seen; covered in slime, tramping through woods, jumping through broken windows, fighting, being shot and speared, and finally carrying the heroine through mucky water. Has a makeup ever suffered and survived so much? Compare the report of Jack Pierce creating Imhotep and the almost static, brief appearance of the mummified creature. Kharis was the most athletic mummy—the nearest ever to the *running* mummy of Conan Doyle's *Lot 249*.

Ashton's biggest problem came with his other mummy—the Princess Ananka. Yvonne Furneaux was a classic regal beauty, a point repeatedly stressed to her by management. Being mummified was not a problem. Being interred was—for a mummy's headdress is not flattering to a twentieth century eye. Furneaux kept pushing it up above her lovely forehead. Minions kept replacing it, to be told, "Michael says I must be beautiful." In the end, as the late Mr. Ashton gently explained to the authors (1979), "I waited until she was swathed in gravecloths and lay in the sarcophagus, then I bent down and said, 'Please excuse me' and rearranged the headdress properly. She wriggled a bit and glared, but she was too gracious to hold a grudge!"

The reviews were splendid. "Hammer Films have made the most distinguished of English horror films" (*The London Times*, September 28, 1959). "Spectacular. Gripping story, first rate characterization, star value" (*The Kinematograph Weekly*, August 13). "Well tried ingredients plus Egyptological know how" (*The Observer*, September 27). "The climax is properly frantic" (*The New York Herald Tribune*, December 17).

After the trade show on August 20 at the Hammer Theatre, *The Mummy* premiered at the London Pavilion. The huge exterior displays were recorded for posterity in *Gorgo* (1960). Over the first four days, *The Mummy* broke the records for a Universal-International/Rank picture, and when it hit the ABC circuit, it broke the previous year's record set by Hammer's *Dracula*. Not only Andrew Low, but members of the cast made personal appearances to promote the film and led Philip Gerard to note "the real reason for Hammer's success is because Jimmy Carreras and Tony Hinds are real showmen. These men have built for Hammer an enviable reputation ... by delivering a box office product which represents the best in its class." (*The Kinematograph Weekly*, September 3)

The Curse of the Mummy's Tomb (1964, Hammer-Swallow) Produced February 1964; Released October (U.K.), December (U.S.); 80 minutes; Technicolor, TechniScope

Credits: Director: Michael Carreras; Producer: Michael Carreras; Associate Producer: Bill Hill; Screenplay: Henry Younger (Michael Carreras), Alvin Rakoff; Director of Photography: Otto Heller; Production Designer: Bernard Robinson; Supervising Editor: James Needs; Editor: Eric Boyd-Perkins; Music: Carlo Martelli; Musical Supervisor: Philip Martell; Assistant Director: Bert Batt; Camera Operator: Bob Thompson; Sound Recordist: Claude Hitchcock; Sound Editor: James Groom; Continuity: Eileen Head; Makeup: Roy Ashton; Hairstylist: Tris Tilley; Wardrobe: Betty Adamson, John Briggs; Casting: David Booth; Technical Advisor: Andrew Low.

Cast: Terence Morgan (Adam Beauchamp), Fred Clark (Alexander King), Ronald Howard (John Bray), Jeanne Roland (Annette Dubois),

George Pastell (Hashmi Bey), Jack Gwillim (Sir Giles Dalrymple), John Paul (Inspector MacKenzie), Dickie Owen (The Mummy), Michael McStay (Ra-Antef), Jill Mae Meridith (Jenny), Vernon Smythe (Jessop), Michael Ripper (Night watchman), Jimmy Gardner (First Workman), Harold Goodwin (Second Workman), Marianne Stone (Landlady), Bernard Rebel (Professor Dubois)

Egypt 1900; Professor Dubois (Bernard Rebel) is mutilated and murdered by desert tribesman for daring to excavate the tomb of RaAntef. His financial backer, Alexander King (Fred Clark), an enthusiastic but boorish American showman, plans to take the mummy on tour at ten cents a ticket, recouping his money while satisfying the public hunger for spectacle and knowledge. Sir Giles Dalrymple (Jack Gwillim) is the academic head of the dig and is publicly disgraced and banned from ever digging in Egypt again because he cannot dissuade King from his plan. Annette Dubois (Jeanne Roland), daughter of the murdered professor, and her fiancé John Bray (Ronald Howard) are helpless to stop King, but stay on his team in deference to Sir Giles' wishes.

Hashmi Bey (George Pastell) accompanies the party to England, hoping yet to secure the mummy for the Egyptian Museum. All reflect on the discovery as they return by luxury liner. Sir Giles is drinking heavily, Annette and John are in love and London is getting ever nearer.

During the evening Sir Giles and John are attacked in Dalrymple's cabin; the assailant then tries to hurt Annette, but is

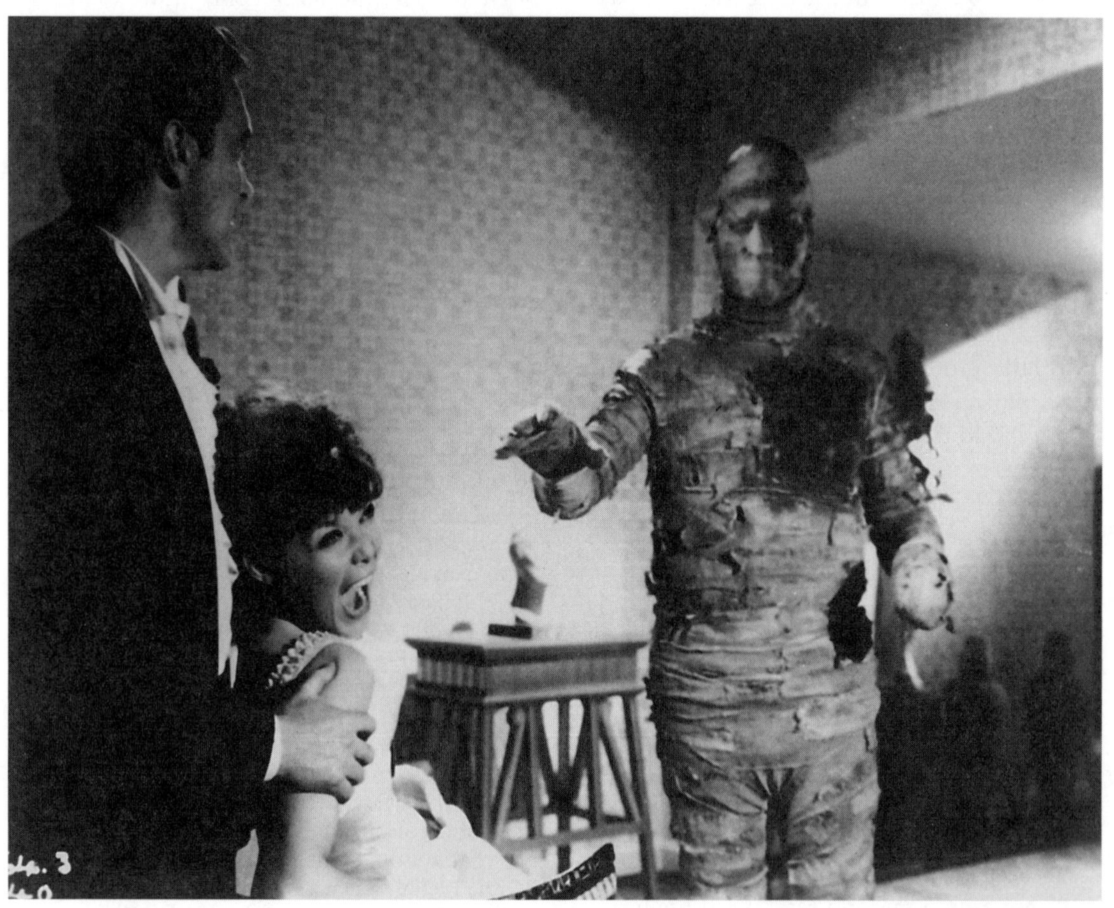

Terence Morgan and Jeanne Roland menaced by Dickie Owen in ***The Curse of the Mummy's Tomb*** (Hammer/Columbia, 1964).

intercepted and thrown overboard by the mysterious Adam Beauchamp (Terence Morgan). Beauchamp is interested in Annette and RaAntef, appearing to be a rich amateur archaeologist with a comfortable home, which he immediately puts at their disposal.

King has elaborate plans to present the mummy to the Press. Annette delights in explaining some of the beautiful friezes on the life of RaAntef (Michael McStay) and his brother Be, sons of Ramesses VIII. Ra was a seeker of wisdom and truth, Be a lover of life and the pursuits of the flesh. Ra sought spiritual grace in the desert and was venerated by nomads who made him their king and gave him an medallion of great power. Be sent assassins to his brother, with orders to bring his ring as proof of his death. The assassins killed Ra and hacked off his hand. Ramesses cursed Be for all eternity when he discovered the crime. Beauchamp by now is nearly incoherent with rage but asks about the medallion — had the excavators found it in the tomb? Annette denies its discovery and is a little disturbed by Beauchamp's attitude of "So much for your facts!" At a rehearsal they all see the mummy of RaAntef (Dickie Owen), as King opens the case.

At Beauchamp's home, he and Annette are becoming romantically involved. When John returns from setting up the exhibition, they have been embracing; Annette opens her bag and John sees a medallion. When asked, Annette replies that it was a gift from her father, though John insists it is from the tomb. Beauchamp, holding it reverently, disagrees with him. John declares that Sir Giles will be the final judge, and Annette and Beauchamp do not detain him. At Dalrymple's home, the great archaeologist tries to be helpful but is already drunk. John is curt with him and is left to study Sir Giles's books to authenticate the medallion. During his studies, he is struck from behind and the medallion stolen.

The press conference goes ahead with much ballyhoo. The coffin, however, is empty. King is concerned about his property, but more put out with the injured John insisting that something supernatural has happened to the mummy. He sends John home and decides to walk back to his hotel. He has two encounters on the way; he kindly pays a hooker to go home and have a good night's sleep, and he comes face to face with a revived RaAntef, who kills him by hurling him down the river steps.

Sir Giles, finding a note of the glyphs on the medallion, thinks that John has mistakenly translated them, but on further study is astounded. Simultaneously, the mummy arrives and crushes Dalrymple's skull with a small statuette from his desk.

John, convinced of the mummy's revival, searches Hashmi's lodgings, only to be caught in the act and the two join forces. They persuade the police to lay a trap for the mummy, manage to capture it briefly, and then watch helplessly as Hashmi, distressed by the sacrilege, apologizes to RaAntef and allows himself to be executed.

While they are laying the trap, Beauchamp has persuaded Annette to go away with him. She literally writes a "dear John" for Bray, asking him to forgive her. As she prepares to leave with Beauchamp, RaAntef appears and attacks Beauchamp; she screams, deflecting the mummy from his task as he comes to look at her. Annette faints clean away, but the arrival of Bray and the police make her betray her love for Beauchamp. Bray, however, cannot understand why the mummy attacked Beauchamp.

Later, Beauchamp takes her to his cellar where he has a private museum. The artifacts are those of a pharaoh, and he claims they are his. He says that he is Ramesses' son Be, and that the Pharaoh's curse for the murder had been eternal life — only to be ended by the hand of RaAntef. Beauchamp hangs the medallion around her neck and makes her reanimate the mummy. "While the hand of my brother yet lives, I must use it." His plan is to have RaAntef kill Annette as the last desecrator of the tomb, and lift the curse

George Pastell pays the ultimate price under the foot of Dickie Owen in *The Curse of the Mummy's Tomb* (Hammer/Columbia, 1964).

by killing him. He then plans to spend eternity in the afterlife with Annette. But they are interrupted by the arrival of Bray and the police.

Beauchamp, dragging Annette and followed by RaAntef, escape to the sewers. A metal door sealing them from the pursuers chops off Beauchamp's hand.

Explaining his plan to Annette, he is surprised that she is afraid to die. He orders the mummy to kill her, but it will not. Beauchamp tries to do the job himself, but is stopped by the mummy who kills him. He then tears the medallion from Annette's throat and walks away to pull the roof down on himself and his brother, as John, arrives to rescue her.

Sadly, Michael Carreras as producer, director, and writer (aka Henry Younger) could not weave the magic of Fisher and Sangster in *The Mummy* five years earlier.

Opinions differ as to the outcome. Some like the use of wide screen; others comment that "They (Hammer) ought to have realized after *Dracula Prince Of Darkness* (1966) that CinemaScope is the wrong shape for horror: it limits the possibilities for shock editing and for shadowy suspense" (Halliwell, 1986).

Carreras had, according to Denis Meikle's excellent book *A History of Horrors — The Rise and Fall of the House of Hammer* (1996), "renewed his reluctant association with Hammer by agreeing to direct, produce, a*nd* write another *Mummy* ... to provide a backup feature for *The Gorgon* (1963)" and that " the restrictions imposed by a budget of £103,000 ... gave *The Curse of the Mummy's Tomb* a certain disposable air, and not simply because of Dickie Owen's patched-up mummy suit."

To also save money—not for continuity of genre—the Reizenstein original score was revived. In truth, it reminds one more of Biblical epics than Ancient Egypt, but seemed appropriate at the time. Plus there were no major stars to pull the public either. Terence Morgan was best known in Britain for his role as Sir Francis Drake in a TV series and on film as the sadistic stepfather in *The Scamp* (1957), and Jeanne Roland, already renamed from her own Jean Rollins, was dubbed by the beautiful tones of she whom Hammer fans call *the universal voice* whose lyrical vocals grace many a Hammer—and competitors'—film.

Production started on February 24, 1964, and finished on May 8. The trade show was August 19 and the film was released as second feature to *The Gorgon* on October 18. On the whole, reviewers felt there was nothing new. "Eerie but routine shocker thrills. But, hand it to Hammer, they've got this kind of scary hokum down to a grisly art" (*The Daily Cinema*, August 21, 1964).

Carreras had intended to provide a comic-book, tongue-in-cheek revival of old Hammer, and had made an enjoyable film, but one which is but a pallid shadow of the company's first, and greatest, entry into the genre.

The Mummy's Shroud (1966, Hammer–7 Arts) Produced September 1966; Released June 1967 (U.K.); 84 minutes (U.K.) 90 minutes (U.S.); Technicolor (U.K.), DeLux Color (U.S.)

Credits: Director: John Gilling; Producer: Anthony Nelson-Keys; Screenplay: John Gilling (based on a story by John Elder); Director of Photography: Arthur Grant; Production Design: Bernard Robinson; Art Director: Don Mingaye; Supervising Editor: James Needs; Editor: Chris Barnes; Music: Don Banks; Musical Supervisor: Philip Martell; Production Manager: Ed Harper; Special Effects: Bowie Films Ltd.; Sound Editor: Roy Hyde; Sound Recordist: Ken Rawkins; Camera Operator: Moray Grant; Continuity: Eileen Head; Makeup: George Partleton; Mummy Costume: Rosemary Burrows; Hairstylist: Frieda Steiger; Assistant Director: Bluey Hill; Wardrobe Mistress: Molly Arbuthnot; Wardrobe Master: Larry Steward; Casting: Irene Lamb

Cast: John Phillips (Stanley Preston), Andre Morell (Sir Basil Walden), David Buck (Paul Preston), Elizabeth Sellars (Barbara Preston), Maggie Kimberly (Claire), Michael Ripper (Longbarrow), Tim Barrett (Harry), Roger Delgado (Hasmid), Catherine Lacey (Haiti), Eddie Powell (Prem, the Mummy), Dickie Owen (Prem in flashback), Richard Warner (Inspector Barrani), Bruno Barnabe (Pharaoh), Toni Gilpin (Pharaoh's Wife), Toolsie Persaud (Kah-to-Bey), Andrea Malandrinos (Curator)

An Ancient Egyptian prologue; Pharaoh (Bruno Barnabe) celebrates the birth of his son and heir, as his wife (Toni Gilpin) dies in childbirth. Concentrating on his son's upbringing, he fails to notice the rise to power of a rival for the throne. Matters come to a head when the rebels break into the palace and slaughter Pharaoh, but not before he has entrusted young Prince Kah-to-Bey (Toolsie Persaud) to the care of Chief Slave Prem (Dickie Owen). Prem escapes with the boy and a small band of followers to the desert where they all die, one by one. As the young prince dies, he entrusts Prem with his seal of office, and Prem in turn buries the prince as properly as circumstance will allow, carving a stela to record the act in the desert rocks. Kah-to-Bey has no great treasure, but he is laid to rest beneath a sacred shroud. Prem himself is later buried as a pharaoh because he wears the seal.

Now it is 1920. An archaeological team, led by Sir Basil Walden (Andre Morell) is lost in the same desert, searching for Kah-to-Bey's tomb. Party members Claire deSangre (Maggie Kimberley), a language expert, Harry Newton (Tim Barrett), a photographer and Paul Preston (David Buck), an archaeologist, sit out a sandstorm whilst deciding whether to continue their search. Claire, something

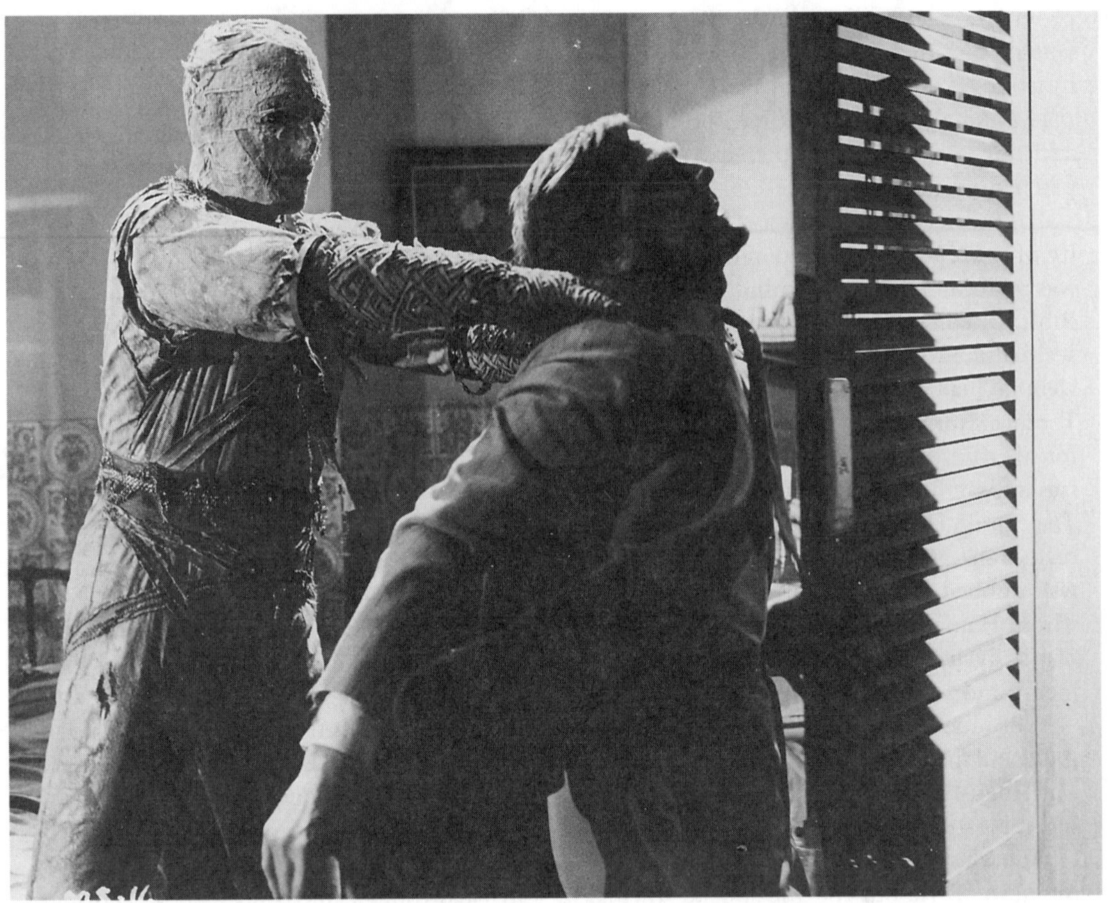

Eddie Powell's costume in *The Mummy's Shroud* (Hammer/20th Century–Fox) was based on a specimen in the British Museum.

of a psychic, is sure they will find the tomb but fears an unknown danger that will come afterwards, that not all the party will survive.

As the sandstorm ceases they find themselves at the rock where Prem carved his memorial. Reinvigorated, they rush to find the tomb only to be scared witless momentarily by the screeching arrival of the self-appointed Guardian of the Tomb. Hasmid Ali (Roger Delgado) warns of a curse on tomb desecrators but he is ignored. Sir Basil, attempting to read an inscription, is bitten by a snake.

Stanley Preston (John Phillips), the boorish financier who has bankrolled the expedition, arrives in Egypt with his long-suffering wife Barbara to mount a rescue mission. He is clearly more concerned with the cash than the fate of the archaeologists, and is amazed that Walden could have got lost at all. However, his superego trips him up during a press conference arranged by his obsequious aide, Mr. Longbarrow (Michael Ripper), when his wife suggests, in reply to a journalist's inquiry, that he will personally lead one of the rescue teams, and he cannot be seen to back out.

Preston Sr.'s rescue party arrives shortly after Sir Basil is hurt. The discovery of the tomb being paramount, they press on with excavating while Stanley stays safely out of danger of snakebite or hard work, dictating spurious memoirs of the rescue and dig to Longbarrow. When the burial chamber is opened, they all enter with varying degrees of excitement and interest. Stanley wants the publicity and kudos of the discovery — Sir Basil wants everyone to appreciate the finer points of the burial. Uncovering the sand-dried body of Kah-to-Bey with gentle hands, Sir Basil asks Claire to translate the words on the shroud for his patron. Claire demurs—she is afraid of the power of the words.

Back in town, the finds are exhibited in the Restoration House, where all of Walden's finds are checked and catalogued. The celebration of reuniting Kah-to-Bey with faithful Prem is dimmed by Walden's collapse and the party's shock on hearing that instead of being hospitalized he has been committed to an asylum. Angrily, Paul accuses his father of jealousy towards Sir Basil and his discovery.

Hasmid Ali, using the shroud, revives the mummy of Prem to wreak vengeance on the desecrators. Sir Basil, escaping from the asylum, finds temporary shelter with a mad old woman, Haiti (Catherine Lacey), who tells him that he will soon be dead. Sir Basil sees a reflection in her crystal ball, and before the image fully registers in his mind, Prem has crushed his skull.

The body is discovered by the museum cleaner; no one seems to have noticed that the shroud no longer covers Kah-to-Bey. Harry Newton remembers seeing a huge shadow on the previous evening but scoffs at Claire's conviction that something supernatural is happening. He gives her negatives of the shroud to study and returns to his darkroom only to be attacked by Prem, who is unstoppable. Harry dies, and the darkroom is destroyed.

Preston Sr. by now is rattled; he instructs Longbarrow to make travel arrangements to return to England. Paul and Claire both refuse to leave. Longbarrow is thrilled that he may go too, but cannot lie to Inspector Barrani (Richard Warner) who has

Maggie Kimberly, Eddie Powell, Andre Morell, and David Buck gaze at *The Mummy's Shroud* (Hammer/20th Century–Fox, 1967).

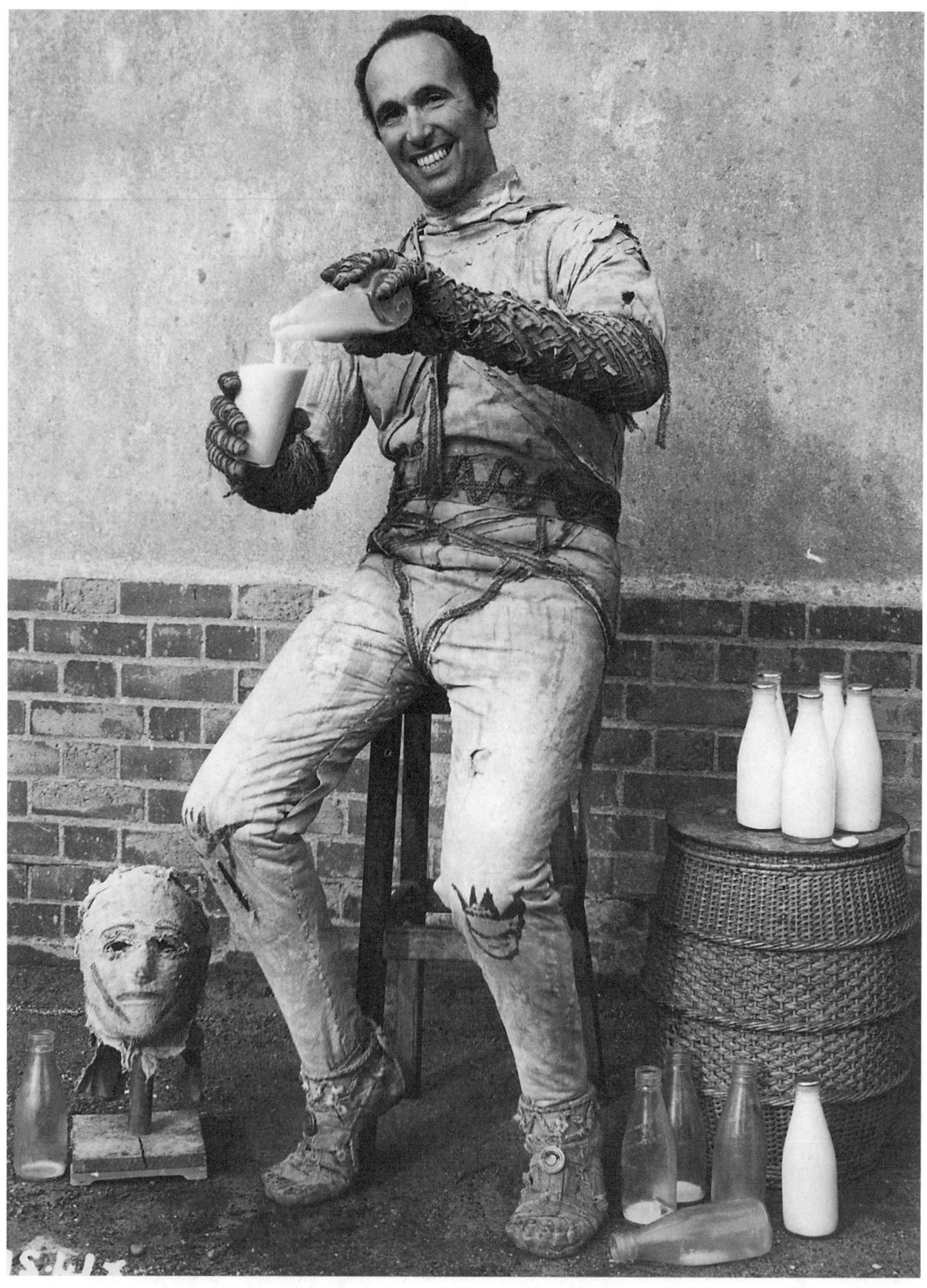

Eddie Powell keeps up his strength with milk, not tana leaves, for ***The Mummy's Shroud*** (Hammer/20th Century–Fox, 1967).

expressly forbidden them to leave. Preston Sr. insists that Longbarrow makes further arrangements, but this time only for his employer, and covertly at that. Longbarrow, anxious to please, breaks his glasses in his haste to go to the docks and so only sees Prem as a blur when the mummy comes to kill him, wrapping him in the mosquito nets before hurling him to his death.

Preston Sr., abandoning his wife, who is deliciously unconcerned for her safety as she did not enter the tomb, sets out for the docks; he is intercepted by Hasmid Ali who feigns assistance, and is promptly murdered by Prem. Inspector Barrani now decides that it might be wise to let the rest of the party leave but neither Paul or Claire will go. Claire keeps an appointment with Haiti who tells her how to rescue those who are left, using the words with the power to destroy, which are on the shroud.

Claire dutifully approaches Prem and begins the ritual—but Hasmid Ali revives the mummy, orders it to destroy her, and cackles that the power to destroy and command rests with whomever *holds* the shroud, whilst speaking. At that moment Barrani shoots him in the back, Paul grabs the shroud, and runs to Claire's side, supporting her during the recitation. Prem stops abruptly, sags to the ground and pitifully crumbles his own skull as his mummy falls apart. Claire gently recovers Kah-to-Bey with the shroud, passing by the pile of dust and rags.

The Mummy's Shroud, Hammer's third excursion into Egypt, had a slightly better budget than its predecessor at £134,049. John Gilling, veteran of many a Gothic horror, was to both script and direct the film from a story outline by Tony Hinds, who was writing as John Elder. Originally, it seems, both Andrew Low and Franz Reizenstein were to join the team but were replaced by Don Mingaye and Don Banks, respectively.

It was the last Hammer film to be shot at Bray. Shooting began September 12 and ran six weeks, ending October 21. One day was allocated for the desert scenes—a quarry at Wapsey's Wood near Gerrards Cross. Everything else, barring a couple of stock shots, was built at the studio.

Les Bowie worked his usual economic magic for the effects, recreating the Restoration House on a raised floor so that Ian Scoones could lay underneath and put his hands through, into the wrappings, to crumble Prem's head. The finished scene is both original and evokes some sympathy for the mummy, still carrying out his Pharaoh's commands after so many centuries. Scoones says that Les and he tried all sorts of materials to get the right effect, from acid to poppadoms ... in the end we used Fuller's Earth mixed with paint dust on a wax head" (*Hammer Horror*, May 1995).

The casting of the film was interesting too. Andre Morrell as the elegant Sir Basil was a well known and respected actor from films and television, and a previous Hammer hero in *The Hound of the Baskervilles* and *The Plague of the Zombies*. His younger counterpart was first to be John Richardson, changed at the eleventh hour to David Buck, the late husband of Hammer's Maddie Smith. Buck had a large fan following due to his television series *Tales of Mystery and Imagination*.

John Phillips, a well-known character actor from British television and from films like *Village of the Damned* and *Torture Garden*, completed the main male characters. But it is Michael Ripper in his support role as Longbarrow who steals the film. Ripper, much loved by Hammer fans and acknowledged by Christopher Lee at the Hammer retrospective at London's Barbican Centre in August 1996 as "the best known Hammer face," received a standing ovation from the invited audience at that very special evening to which the authors were immensely proud to have been invited.

Prem, in retrospect, was Dickie Owen, who had previously worn the bandages as RaAntef in *Curse of the Mummy's Tomb*, but the bandaged one on this occasion was Eddie

Powell, Christopher Lee's stunt double, who wryly commented that he accepted after he believed Lee had turned it down as yet another mime job. "Generally, I do a film *because* there is no dialogue!" And more seriously, "The design of that costume was copied from a museum, so all the markings were very authentic. The mask was open at the back and every time they put it on they had to glue it down" (*Hammer Horror*, May 1995). When Harry Newton threw acid on Prem, the fumes permeated the mask and wrappings and Powell had to run for his life to pull them off and get his breath back, and the sharp-eyed will see him bandaged but not masked during the climax. Roger Delgado, always the villainous foreigner, played his role with manic delight and completed the team.

On the distaff side, the casting was good. Elizabeth Sellars, a serene beauty, had been in the first film shot at Bray by Hammer—*Cloudburst*—and now she would grace their last. Catherine Lacey was an eminent British actress who had worked for Hitchcock, Michael Powell and Orson Welles, and she produced a tour de force as the crazed Haiti that had universal critical praise. The last and least effective lady was Maggie Kimberley, probably more known for the publicity shots for the movie than for the film itself. Those poor souls who went to see a half dressed blonde threatened by a rampaging mummy were in for a disappointment.

After a May 3rd trade show, the film premiered at the New Victoria and went on to general release on June 18. Rarely has a film united the critics; this one did—they hated it. "It takes up, somewhat crudely, the old theme of the curse of the tomb" (*The Daily Telegraph*, May 19). "Hopeless, grade B British mummy item that drags out again all the trite and tired nonsense" (*Castle of Frankenstein* 12). "Stilted rehash of the old avenging mummy routine, brightened from time to time by Catherine Lacey as a toothless hag cackling imprecations into her crystal ball (in a salon more redolent of the Earls' Court Road than mysterious Egypt). The rest of the cast huff and puff over their moribund lines, and the plot contains no surprises" (*Monthly Film Bulletin*, June).

A damning, private report prepared by McCarthy of Whitfield Street, London W1 for Warner-Pathé, the distributors, commented, "This is a rather run-of-the-mill would-be thriller about the tombs of the ancient Pharaohs. It is, in fact, devoid of any novel ideas and the spectacle of stalking and murdering people has had its day in this field of entertainment. Only in the last scene when the mummy crumbles to dust does it reveal that ingenuity which is so vital to this class of film."

Not fleshy promo-photos, or absurd advertising—"Beware the beat of the cloth wrapped feet!"—could save it, and yet Ripper's Longbarrow stays with you long after the final credits. The final word must be Gilling's, "I wasn't very proud of *The Mummy's Shroud*. In fact, I think it was one of my worst!" (*Little Shoppe of Horrors* Richard Klemensen)

Blood from the Mummy's Tomb (1971, Hammer-EMI) Produced January 1971; Released October (U.K.), May 1972 (U.S.); 94 minutes; Technicolor

Credits: Director: Seth Holt (completed by Michael Carreras); Producer: Howard Brandy; Screenplay: Christopher Wicking (based on Bram Stoker's novel); Director of Photography: Arthur Grant; Production Design: Scott MacGregor; Music: Tristam Cary, Musical Supervisor: Philip Martell; Editor: Peter Weatherley; Sound Editor: Roy Hyde; Continuity: Betty Harley; Makeup: Eddie Knight; Wardrobe: Rosemary Burrows; Wardrobe Mistress: Diane Jones; Assistant Director: Derek Whitehurst; Hairdresser: Ivy Emmerton; Special Effects: Michael Collins; Sound Recordist: Tony Lumkin; Sound Camera: Tony Dawe, Dennis Whitlock; Production Supervisor: Roy Skeggs; Production Manager: Christopher Neame

Cast: Andrew Keir (Fuchs), Valerie Leon (Margaret/Tera), James Villiers (Corbeck), Hugh Burden (Dandridge), George Coulouris (Berigan), Mark Edwards (Tod Browning), Rosalie Crutchley (Helen Dickerson), Aubrey Morris (Dr. Putnam), James Coussins (Older Male Nurse),

Valerie Leon in Hammer's 1971 ***Blood from the Mummy's Tomb*** is a long way from Boris Karloff and easily the movies' best looking Mummy.

David Jackson (Younger Male Nurse), Tamara Ustinov (Veronica), David Markham (Dr. Burgess), Joan Young (Mrs. Caporal), Graham James (Youth in Museum), Jonathan Burn (Saturnine Young Man), Penelope Holt, Angela Ginders (Nurses), Tex Fuller (Patient), Madina Luis, Omar Amoodi, Abdul Kader, Ahmed Osman, Oscar Charles, Soltan Lalani, Saad Ghazi (Priests)

Ancient Egypt; the beautiful Queen Tera (Valerie Leon) is feared by her priesthood due to her mastery of supernatural power. Severing her right hand, on which she wears her talisman, a giant ruby containing a representation of the Plough constellation, they feel they have curbed her power forever. Her hand, thrown to the jackals, has a life of its own and avenges the desecration. Tera waits.

In modern times, Professor Fuchs (Andrew Keir), leading a British team, rediscovers the tomb. All identifying hieroglyphs have been erased by the priests and they are gratified, on opening her mummy case, to find her name inscribed on her ring. The discovery of a perfect body in regal attire, surrounded by occult artifacts has different effects on each member of the party, and they are all stunned at the severed hand found on the floor by the sarcophagus.

Thousands of miles away, Fuchs's wife dies giving birth to their daughter Margaret at the very moment of their finding the Queen, whose dead wrist bleeds.

Twenty-one years pass; it is Margaret Fuch's birthday and she has grown into a regal beauty, the image of the ancient Queen. To celebrate, Margaret (Valerie Leon) is gifted with Queen Tera's talisman by her father, and from that moment a change begins. Her boyfriend, Tod Browning (Mark Edwards), is fascinated by the ring—convinced it belongs to Tera. Professor Fuchs has, in all the years, published no account of his discovery or of the contents of the tomb. Tod's friend Dandridge (Hugh Burden), another member of the original team, recognizes both the ring and—he believes—the owner, when Tod takes her to visit the museum.

Margaret has nightmares where she speaks in the ancient tongue, and feels compelled to return home in the middle of the night. She is further unsettled when she sees her father's cellar-study for the first time, for he has recreated Tera's tomb, and the ancient beauty lies in her golden casket waiting for ... who knows? As her father lies unconscious, Margaret meets Corbeck (James Villiers), another of the original archaeologists, but one who is keen to use Tera's skill and power for his own ends. It seems that both he and Fuchs wish to see her desire for resurrection achieved, but Fuchs fears her power and wishes to control the ritual. Corbeck prefers to "go with the flow" and let Tera control the outcome—provided he can rule with her.

Margaret, infused with the spirit of Tera, undertakes to collect all the occult artifacts that the archaeologists had so assiduously divided amongst themselves to limit Tera's power. Berigan (George Coulouris) is relieved of a sacred snake from the asylum that has been his home since the expedition, and killed by the telekinetic power of the Queen. Dandridge, too, loses his life and the jawbone of the jackal he was guarding. With each death, the ragged wrist of Tera's mummy bleeds. Corbeck feels in no danger since he has joyously relinquished the Scroll of Life, which was his burden, but Tod becomes obstructive and Tera's spirit disposes of him.

By now, Dr. Putnum (Aubrey Morris) fears Margaret, recognizing her more and more as Tera and not the little girl whose birth he attended. For him, the fear comes too late, and Tera kills him too. Corbeck finds Fuchs trying to dispose of the body and suavely takes over. Margaret has gone to retrieve the last artifact—a statue of the cat goddess Bast from Helen Dickerson (Rosalie Crutchley) who had eschewed Egyptology for astrology after the discovery of Tera's tomb. Corbeck arrives at Dickerson's home just after Tera's vengeful attack and brings the near-fainting Margaret back home.

The ritual begins; Margaret/Tera heals the wounds she inflicted on her father and he begins to see her in a different light. The artifacts are placed on their marks. When the severed hand is replaced in the coffin, the limb mends itself. Corbeck begins to read the Scroll while Margaret and Fuchs grovel at the foot of Tera's coffin. Fuchs realizes that Margaret as a separate soul does not exist, and that, should the ritual be finished, she will die.

With an enormous final effort he plunges at the mummy; Tera's arm snakes up and she tears out his throat. Margaret drives a dagger deep into the mummy's breast unleashing psychic energy and gushing blood. The mummy fixes its grip on her as the house is destroyed around them.

Finally, in hospital, a bandaged form lies still. The nursing staff talk quietly about the traumatized patient is pulled from a collapsed house. The eyes open ... a frightened murmur in the throat — but who has survived? Margaret Fuchs or Tera, Queen of Egypt come again?

The history of this film is the stuff that movie legends are made of; within days of filming commencing, Peter Cushing, who was to play Fuchs, was called from the soundstage by an urgent message from his longtime secretary and friend Joyce Broughton. Helen, beloved wife of Cushing, has been rushed to hospital and died shortly after. Andrew Keir was quickly cast in his place; he brought a strength and authority to the role that is miraculous considering the speed with which he had to work. Christopher Wicking had produced a script based on the Bram Stoker novel, *The Jewel of Seven Stars*, cutting down the historical span of the story and the more sensational aspects such as Tera's seven-fingered hand. He had also shrunk the geography to interior sets, in the main, whilst keeping to the spirit of the novel by setting it in modern times as Stoker had written it.

Filming was a week from completion when director Seth Holt died suddenly, which was disastrous not only for the loss of a gifted filmmaker, but because Holt had not shared his vision or cutting plan of the film with anyone. Michael Carreras, who had just rejoined Hammer as managing director, had to rescue the project and try to make sense of what was already shot. Holt had had a fascination for the mummy genre. It is ready-made exotica implanted into modern times — ancient rituals imposing upon our modern understanding and defeating us.

"For it is rarely by skill or technical know-how, but usually by pure luck (or by the diversion of another cult, another religion, upon whose reliance the scientist has to sacrifice his rationality) that the heroes in such movies or stories free themselves or the heroine from mortal danger — or rather immortal danger. That is why there is so often within us this unconscious understanding that we — and the scientist-archaeologist on our behalf — should not tamper with things that are gone. It is a fact of superstition, but it still governs the way we think" (Hutchinson, 1983).

The cast were uniformly good, with Villiers' cynical Corbeck played exceptionally well. Opinions on the casting of the beautiful and statuesque Valerie Leon as Margaret/Tera are united. "The stand-out is Valerie Leon ... a statuesque beauty of unusual handsomeness. Leon was an early 1970s icon in TV advertising and bit part acting. This was one of the few opportunities she was given to shine, and she made the most of it" (Boot, 1996). "Leon is excellent in the dual role of mummy and daughter, making the scarcity of her appearances in fantasy films all the more regrettable" (Hardy, 1985).

Blood from the Mummy's Tomb overcame its real life tragedies and became recognized as one of Hammer's few good horrors. Filming ceased on February 20 and a trade show was held at Metro House on October 7 — a wait that perhaps echoes the decision to release it as a *second* feature because of "uncertainties over the final cut" (Meikle, 1996).

The critics seemed unusually gentle; most noted Holt's passing with regret and congratulated the company on the completed film. The film was shown on October 7 at the National Film Theatre on the South Bank as part of the British Film Institute's tribute to Hammer Films. This celebration, together with the Queen's Award to Industry bestowed on the company in 1968 for services to the economy, proved that Hammer Films—vilified by upmarket journalists and self-created arbiters of taste a decade before—was part of the British film scene, and a viable part at that.

"This is the real thing. It could well turn out to be a cult rave for more sophisticated devotees." (*Today's Cinema*, October 15). "Tremendous fun, skillful, and wonderfully energetic." (*The New York Times*, May 22, 1972). "*Blood from the Mummy's Tomb* is Holt's most distinctive work, and effortlessly the best of Hammer's recent attempts to develop the classic horror themes.... It's all as if Holt had superimposed the psychological-suspense methods of his thrillers onto the Gothic mechanics of the genre; the result (as in the work of all true pioneers) makes the genre seem like new" (Tony Rayns).

As the finale (to date) of Hammer's journey into the mysteries of Ancient Egypt, *Blood from the Mummy's Tomb* was a creditable offering and miles better as an end piece to a genre than Universal had managed with its declining series. Interestingly, it has been suggested that this movie is high on the list for the revived Hammer Film Productions company, under the helm of the Roy Skeggs dynasty, to be remade. The news item appeared in *Shivers* magazine as Hammer was being honored by a retrospective at the Barbican Centre in London, to mark "the most successful studio in the history of British Cinema ... now hailed as one of the most vital and exciting elements of post-war British cinema" (*The Daily Mirror*, 1996, August 2–29).

Jonny Quest—The Curse of Anubis (U.S., 1964, TV, Animation)

Jonny Quest was one of the top adventure heroes of sixties television, rivaling James West (*The Wild, Wild West*) and Napoleon Solo (*The Man from U.N.C.L.E.*). Jonny was a bit different from West and Solo in that he was around eleven years old and a cartoon character.

The show ran from September 1964 to September 1965 in prime time, then moved to Saturday morning, where it became a staple, running variously from 1967 to 1980. Jonny's father, Benton, was a scientist, and the lad joined him, bodyguard Race Bannon, Hadji (a young Indian boy), and pet dog Bandit on—you guessed it!—a series of incredible adventures. One involved a living mummy.

The head of the god Anubis is stolen from an Egyptian tomb, reactivating a huge mummy, which for centuries, has guarded the tomb. The thieves, quite rightly, fear a curse. Concerned that the theft could create problems in the Middle East, Dr. Quest becomes involved. The adventurers meet Amhad Kareem, a shady character on the fringes of archaeology, when he asks Dr. Quest to visit his desert encampment. When a scorpion—killed by Bannon's whip—nearly strikes them in their room, Kareem becomes a suspect.

Hadji and Jonny find the Anubis head in a nearby ruin, placed there by Kareem. He plans to use the Quest party as scapegoats in his plan to reunite the Arab nations. The villain unleashes poisonous snakes into the treasure chamber, but Jonny and Hadji escape. Dr. Quest and Race arrive and are captured at gunpoint by Kareem's goons, but the mask of Anubis falls on Bandit who, while running wildly, makes it seem alive. His henchmen gone, Kareem is killed by the Mummy who causes the chamber to collapse.

Jonny Quest was produced by William Hanna and Joseph Barbera, the team that brought you *Yogi Bear* and *Huckleberry Hound*.

The animation was a bit stiff—definitely sub-Disney—but the drawings were lifelike and well detailed. The Mummy resembled Christopher Lee in stature and was more effective than many live action attempts. For a cartoon mummy, this wasn't too badly done.

* * *

The Cat Creature (U.S., 1973, A Screen Gems Production for Columbia Pictures)

Credits: Producer: Douglas S. Cramer; Director of Photography: Charles Rosher; Teleplay: Robert Bloch; Story: Douglas S. Cramer, Wilford Lloyd Baumes, Robert Bloch; Director: Curtis Harrington; Associate to Producer: Wilford Lloyd Baumes; Associate Producer: Robert Anderson; Music: Leonard Rosenman; Art Director: Ross Bellah, Carey Odell; Film Editor: Stan Ford; Casting: Sally Powers; Set Decorators: Audrey Blasdel, John Franco; Makeup Supervision: Ben Lane; Special Effects: Roy Maples; Assistant Director: Robert Anderson; Casting Executive: Renee Valente; Music and Sound Effects: Sunset Editorial; Titles: Phill Norma; Cinefx/acmelab: Filmed at Burbank Studios for Douglas S. Cramer Productions

Cast: Meredith Baxter (Reena), David Hedison (Roger), Gale Sondergaard (Hesther Black), John Carradine (Hotel Clerk), Renee Jarrett (Sherry), Keye Luke (Thief), Kent Smith (Frank Lucas), Start Whitman (Lt. Marco), Peter Lorre, Jr. (Pawnbroker), Milton Parsons (Deputy Coroner), John Abbott (Dr. Reinhart), William Sims (Bert), Virgil Frye (Donovan)

Frank Lucas (Kent Smith) arrives at the dead of night to complete the inventory of a collection of objets d'arts belonging to a recently deceased collector. He is annoyed to find that the electricity has already been disconnected, but not wishing to waste time, conducts the rest of his work by flashlight. Unbeknownst to him, a thief is also in the house.

Lucas finds a special room stuffed with precious Egyptian antiquities. One in particular attracts him, a mummy case which he opens to find the mummy inside; and around its neck, on the *outside* of the wrappings, a heavy gold amulet of a cat's face with emerald eyes. As he fetches his recorder, the thief tiptoes from his hiding place and takes the amulet, making a beeline for the front door. Growling cat noises are heard, shadows play and a scream rings out.

The following day Roger (David Hedison) is called to the mansion as an historical expert requested by Lt. Marco (Stuart Whitman) who is investigating the murder of Frank Lucas. Roger is shown the mummy case that now has deep scratches on it as though some of the hieroglyphs have been cut out. He also tells Roger that animal hairs were found in the wounds on Lucas's body.

In downtown L.A., Hesther Black (Gale Sondergaard) runs a disreputable occult shop partly as a front for fencing stolen goods. She and Marco are old adversaries. Marco has played Roger the tape of Lucas's description of the amulet, and his subsequent death and the pair are now doing the rounds of known fences to see if the piece is being offered for sale. Hesther has an assistant, Sherry (Renee Jarrett), who is working to raise funds to buy a car and leave the city. The thief had earlier tried to persuade Hesther to buy the amulet, and when she refused, had run out of the shop leaving his case with the jewel behind. Hesther gives Sherry the case as she leaves for the weekend, and on the way she acquires another item—a lost, hungry, imperious black cat.

Back home, Sherry tries to make the cat comfortable, but finds it has blood on its whiskers; as it stares at her from its perch in the opened case, she walks entranced to the balcony and throws herself off.

At Hesther's shop, a young woman called Reena applies for the vacant position of shop assistant, begins work, and gets to meet Marco and Roger. Roger is much taken with her and finally gets to take her to dinner and begin a romance. Marco, meanwhile, is told by Hesther that she has seen the amulet, and gets a description of the thief. Wholesale slaughter breaks out as everyone who comes into contact with the amulet is killed—apparently by a huge cat. The pawnbroker who touched the amulet (Peter Lorre, Jr.) has his throat torn out and the thief is found dead in his hotel room, much to the amusement of the hotel clerk (John Carradine).

Roger is finding Reena a complete mystery; she is supposedly house-sitting for friends in a secluded villa overlooking the city. She appears to have no past, and is loathe to tell him anything about herself. Marco retrieves the amulet and Hesther is murdered by the phantom cat; the policeman set to watch her shop is also killed.

Roger takes the amulet to an expert who can read the hieroglyphs and learns that it was set about the mummy's neck to imprison it in the coffin. In ancient times the wearer had been a devotee of the goddess Bast—a devotee who killed and drank blood to attain immortality. The orthodox priesthood of Bast had caught and slaughtered all those who practiced this perversion, and had punished some with the living death. On the amulet is a warning not to remove it, or the wearer will walk and kill again says his colleague, Dr. Reinhart (John Abbott).

By now, Marco's policeman's nose tells him that Reena is the most likely suspect in the murders, but Roger asks for time to talk to her, and Marco agrees. Roger goes to the villa where all is in darkness. Reena is hysterically relieved to see him and complains that the neighborhood cats have been howling outside all day. When Roger looks, there are no cats. She asks him to run away with her and start a new life, but when he faces her with the truth of her murderous way of life she does not apologize. She explains that she needs to kill to live, and that she will share immortality with him. She describes the pleasure she feels in her new, young body and all the joys it can give her. And she tells him of the horrors of the crawling centuries in the mummy case, "unable to move, unable to feel, and yet conscious of every crawling second." When it is obvious he will not go with her willingly, she changes to the cat and begins to stalk him through the villa in the dark. The hunt nearly proves fatal for him and one last struggle gives him the opportunity to put the amulet around the cat's neck; it vanishes, to be replaced by Reena in her priestess garb, clutching the chain.

Reena cannot remove it, and blunders through the French windows, changing again to the cloth-wrapped mummy of the opening scenes. All the neighborhood cats converge on the mummy and tear it to shreds while ghostly voices intone the ancient rites. Marco and his officers arrive, but by now there are only departing moggies, a few scraps of bandage, a pile of dust, and a skull encircled by a heavy gold chain and amulet.

This TV movie is Robert Bloch at his best. Even the seventies fashions do not get in the way of a cracking good plot, and the suspense is cleverly built. The appearance of Sondergaard and Carradine is an additional bonus, and Sondergaard manages to be creepier than the Cat Creature, while elegant as a feline at the same time. Meredith Baxter comes into her own in the final scenes when she can drop the sweetie-pie image of the young woman for the persona of the scheming priestess. If you can find this movie on a late night run somewhere, it's well worth a look.

Worlds Beyond—Guardian of the Past (U.K., 1979, A pK Production, TV) Released c.1979; 25 minutes; Technicolor

Credits: Executive Producers; George Walker, Wilfred Aquilina; Co-Producers; Alan Radnor, Bob McIntosh; Series Devised and Produced: Alan Radnor; Director: Adrian Cooper; Associate Producer: Mark Cassidy; Title Music: Ian Stanley; Music: Darryl Ing; Production Supervisor: Ron Kackson; Assistant Director: Ken Baker; Location Manager: Rufus Andrews; Script Supervisor: Marjorie Lavelly; Sound Recordist: David Jones; Sound Editors: Jean Sheffield, Terry Poulton; Dubbing Mixer: Andy Nelson; Costumes: Janice Wild; Wardrobe Master: Terry Smith; Hairdresser: Jeanette Freeman; Makeup: Eddie Knight; Stunt Coordinator: Alan Stuart; Special Effects: Mirage; Casting: Marilyn Johnson; Production Design: Keith Wilson; Director of Photography: Ray Orton; Film Editor: Des Saunders; Titles and Opticals: GSE Ltd.

Cast: Paul Freeman (Richard Wentworth), Mary Tamm (Susan Wentworth), Terence Alexander (Jeremy), Terence Conder (David), Edita Brychta (Brigitta), Amanda Root (Julia), Hilary Mason (Mrs. Dobson), Michael Burns (William Purvis), Martin Fisk (Police Sergeant), Paddy Ryan (Mr. Purvis)

In England's stockbroker belt, Mr. Purvis (Paddy Ryan), master carpenter, is completing a display cabinet for Mr. and Mrs. Wentworth for an ancient bone fragment. As he finishes the task, a large plank of wood sails off a high shelf and slams, edgewise, into his back.

At home, Richard (Paul Freeman) and Susan (Mary Tamm) Wentworth are having dinner with David (Terence Conder) and Julia (Amanda Root), their young houseguests, and a visitor, Jeremy (Terence Alexander), a member of the Society for Psychical Research. They are discussing the Wentworths' recent visit to Egypt and how Susan had "acquired" the bone of an ancient princess for her collection while visiting a dig. There is some half serious talk of tomb curses and Jeremy is asked if the Society has any documented evidence of the existence of a curse in its archives.

During dinner William Purvis (Michael Burns) delivers the display cabinet. Richard thanks him, inquiring about his father's accident, only to learn that Mr. Purvis is permanently paralyzed. Richard is concerned that William has made a special effort to deliver the cabinet under the circumstances, but the young man is adamant that his family wanted it and its contents out of the house as fast as possible. The diners admire the cabinet and the bone — identified as a pelvic bone — as the young man rushes back to his van.

A storm is brewing as he drives away at speed. Down the windy lane from the house a shrouded figure waits, perfectly still in the gale, watching as the van crashes. The au pair, Brigitta, (Edita Brychta) sees the mummy outside the dining room window and screams; the men rush to investigate but see no one. Jeremy is persuaded to stay for the night, and as the women leave the men talking, they see a shadow upstairs, but Susan insists it must be the housekeeper getting Jeremy's room ready.

Jeremy meets the emergency services and the police as he starts his journey back to London next morning. Young Purvis is dead, having lain there all night with his pelvis smashed. "Yes of course," murmurs Jeremy, "It would be his back." Jeremy returns to the house to find the Wentworths breakfasting alone as David and Julia have gone fishing by the weir near the house. He tells them that he is convinced the bone has power, and that the Society has similar stories on file. Richard scoffs at the notion. They are astonished, however, to find it missing from the case.

In the kitchen Susan is holding the bone and appears to be in a trance. It takes two men to get her to loosen her hold on it. Meanwhile she has a vision of the pair by the weir, the wind rising suddenly as the mummy stands nearby, and David's fishing flies being blown into his face to slash his eyes. David is blinded, ending his promising career as a painter.

Richard is still skeptical, but Susan now regrets that she stole the bone from the dig while Jeremy offers to fly back to Luxor with it and have it reburied. Brigitta, in a trance, attempts to stab Richard during dinner; the bone is back in the box. All the group except Jeremy are mesmerized by chanting voices and throbbing drumbeats. One by one they leave the house in procession, walking towards the weir. Jeremy tries desperately to stop them but fails. He sees the mummy watching in the distance; then he rushes back to the cabinet, smashing the glass, unaware of the mummy right behind him.

He sprints through the grounds to see the procession on the edge of the weir, guarded by the mummy. Jeremy hurls the bone at the mummy, who vanishes. Wind and sounds cease, the group wakens, surprised at their surroundings. Jeremy looks relieved as they turn to go back to the house.

This British series was always screened in the depths of the night, and so never made a vast impression on the viewing public but was nevertheless a splendid collection of strange tales purportedly from the files of the real-life Society for Psychical Research. The same idea was later developed for American television, shot in color, and starred Shari Belafonte as one of the investigating scientists, making it much more attractive for TV viewers.

The Awakening (1980, Orion) Released Summer 1980 (Europe), September 1980 (U.S.); 102 minutes; Technicolor

Credits: Producers: Robert Solo, Andrew Scheinman, Martin Shafer; Director: Mike Newell; Screenplay: Allan Scott, Chris Bryant, Clive Exton (based on the novel *The Jewel of Seven Stars* by Bram Stoker); Camera: Jack Cardiff; Editor: Terry Rawlings; Music: Claude Bolling; Production Design: Michael Stringer; Art Director: Lionel Couch; Costume Design: Phyllis Dalton; Sound: Brian Simmons; Associate Producer: Harry Benn; Assistant Director: Neill Vine-Miller.

Cast: Charlton Heston (Matthew Corbeck), Susannah York (Jane Turner), Jill Townsend (Anne Corbeck), Stephanie Zimbalist (Margaret Corbeck), Patrick Drury (Paul Whittier), Bruce Myers (Dr. Khalid), Nadim Sawalha (Dr. El Sadek), Ian McDiarmid (Dr. Richter), Miriam Margoulies (Maternity Doctor)

Egypt, 1961: Matthew Corbeck (Charlton Heston), a British archaeologist, finds the secret tomb of Queen Kara. With Jane Turner (Susannah York) he enters the tomb just as his wife, Anne, (Jill Townsend) gives birth to their daughter, Margaret. The marriage soon disintegrates due to Corbeck's interest in both Kara and Jane, and Anne takes Margaret with her to New York.

Eighteen years later, Corbeck—now married to Jane—sends Margaret (Stephanie Zimbalist) an artifact from Kara's tomb as a birthday gift. She visits her father in England and is told the history of Kara, who, forced to marry her father, she mysteriously killed him. Kara's mummy is now in England.

Both Dr. Khalid (Bruce Myers) and Paul Whittier (Patrick Drury), Corbeck's assistant, do not think Kara should be in England. Khalid dies in an accident, and Paul, in love with Margaret, remains silent.

Corbeck and Margaret, who is fascinated by Egyptian occultism, go to Egypt and obtain Kara's internal organs ... and the Jewel of Seven Stars. The Jewel has the power to restore life. Jane attempts to destroy the organs and is killed in an "accident."

Margaret believes she is being possessed by Kara, and goes to Dr. Richter (Ian McDiarmid) for help; instead, she kills him.

Corbeck performs the occult ritual that will restore Kara but, finally realizing the danger to Margaret, stops the rites. When he tries to destroy her mummy, Kara causes a statue to fall on him. Kara now lives ... in Margaret's body.

A highly expensive attempt to bring Bram Stoker's *The Jewel of Seven Stars* to the screen, failed alarmingly despite an competent cast, good technical staff, and normally workmanlike writers. Shot in modern costume, in keeping with the spirit of the novel that was a contemporary occult thriller, *The Awakening* failed ever to convey the power of the long-dead psychic queen and otherworldliness of the plot. Stephanie Zimbalist did not have the skill the play the two roles with subtlety and Charlton Heston is agonizing as the Egyptologist who, supposedly brilliant, is the last to realize his daughter is the fount of all the mayhem.

Jack Cardiff puts his usual beautiful finish to the visual glories of the story but his talents are negated by the directorial style of Mike Newell, creating his first feature film and employing the jumpy, visually disjointed style that was prevalent at the time, especially in TV shows and British commercials. The violence in the movie is nasty rather than graphic, and fails to move the audience. After less than average reviews in Europe, Orion reportedly trimmed five minutes of original material and added new visual and sound effects before releasing the film in America. To no avail. Critical opinion on both sides of the Atlantic pivoted on the view

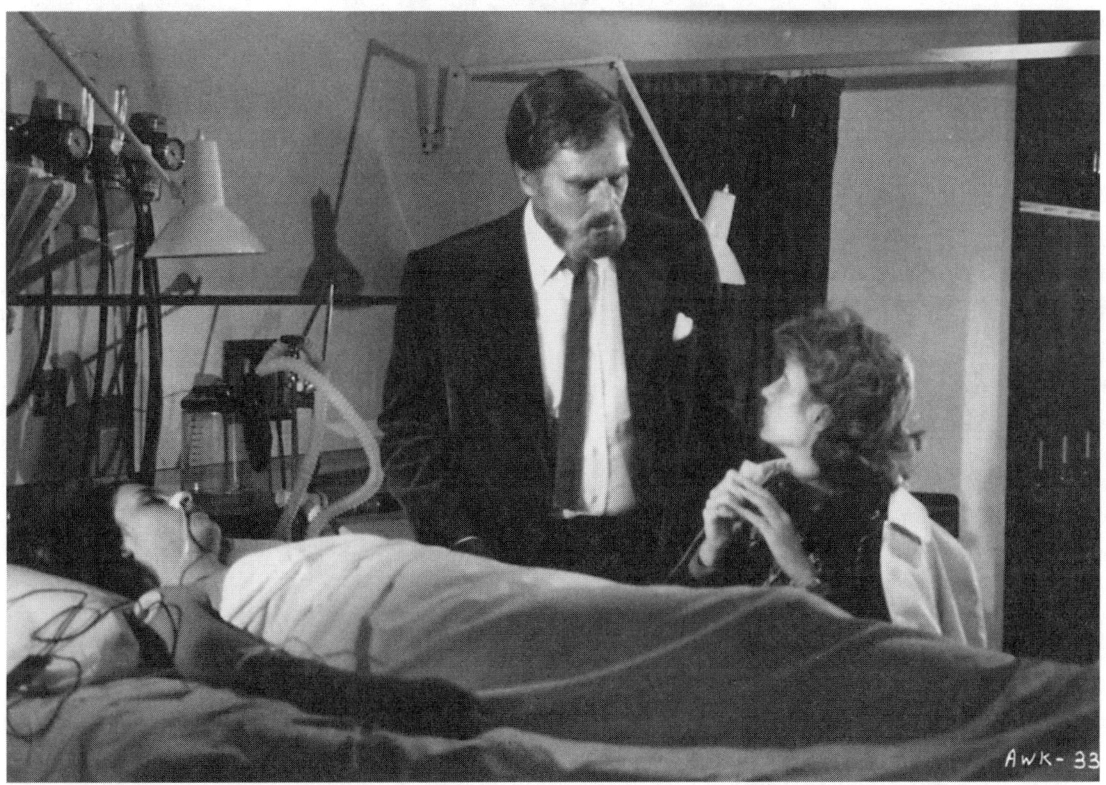

Stephene Zimbalist, Charlton Heston, and Jill Townsend await *The Awakening* (1980).

that *The Awakening* could have done with a longer sleep ... and that audiences had been induced to one. The authors, having seen the procedure of script-by-committee working well for other filmmakers, notably Hammer and Universal, are puzzled why the three gentlemen concerned created such a dull script from an interesting—albeit wordy—novel. Clive Exton in particular is known for well-paced, exciting scripting in his other numerous TV and film projects.

Dawn of the Mummy (U.S./Italy/Egypt, 1981, Goldfarb) Released 1981; Color

Credits: Director/Producer: Frank Agramo; Screenplay: Frank Agramo, Daria Price, Ronald Dobrin; Camera: Sergio Ribini

Cast: Brenda King, Barry Sattels, George Peck, John Salvo, Joan Levy, Diane Beatty

This American/Italian/Egyptian coproduction was, according to Bryan Senn and John Johnston's *Fantastic Cinema Subject Guide* (1992), pretty nasty, and, as such, was almost certainly a direct-to-video release. It was not reviewed by *Variety*, and no evidence of a theatrical release could be found.

A fashion photographer takes his models to an Egyptian tomb for a shoot and disturbs the Pharaoh's resting place. His guardian mummy comes to life and, with the help of the Pharaoh's zombie-like slaves, destroys the intruders and the locals. The nastiness includes cannibalism, making this (thankfully) the first mummy picture in which the tomb desecrators are eaten. And, hopefully, the last.

Timewalker (U.S., 1982, New World release of a Dimitri Villard Production in association with Wescom Productions) Released November 1982; 83 minutes; De Luxe Color

Credits: Director: Tom Kennedy; Producers: Dimitri Villard, Jason Williams; Executive Producer: Robert Shafter; Screenplay: Karen Levitt,

Tom Friedman; Director of Photography: Robbie Greenberg; Music: Richard Band; Sound: Mark Uland; Production Manager: Mark Allan; Stunts: Harry Wowchuk; Second Unit Director: Skip Schoolnik; Transformation Scene: NW Effects

Cast: Doug (Ben Murphy), Susy (Nina Axelrod), Peter (Kevin Brophy), Rossmore (James Karen), Parker (Robert Random), Dr. Melrose (Austin Stoker), Willoughby (Clint Young), Linda (Shari Belafonte-Harper), Dr. Hayworth (Antoinette Bower), Jeff (Jason Williams)

Opening shots of a journey through the Solar System, pinpointing Egypt with the compulsory shots of the Pyramids, Sphinx, Sakkara, Luxor, and Abu Simbel, in a matter of seconds, set the scene. An earthquake during a college expedition to Tutankhamen's tomb reveals a hidden chamber, a sarcophagus, and many twisted, agonized skeletons. A mystery!

America: Safe back on campus, the artifacts arrive and are unloaded with due ceremony, in the presence of Linda, the college deejay and photographer (Shari Belafonte—Harper in her film debut). Continuing to unpack and record his "find" the professor (Ben Murphy)—known as Doug to his students—asks his favorite student, Susy, (Nina Axelrod) to translate from the inner name plate of the sarcophagus. "*Ankh—Venharis*" quoth she, "*Noble Traveller.*" Opening the inner plate they find a mummy, reasonably preserved and coated in a dry green mold which they conjecture caused the disfigurement and deaths of the soldiers. A sample is collected for analysis.

Doug tells the students assembled that he has a papyrus, "the scroll of dedication" on which is recorded the discovery of the traveler by Tutankhamen's soldiers in the desert, the strangeness of the visitor, and the fact that Pharaoh himself came out to greet him. In embracing his visitor, Pharaoh had fallen sick and died, as had all who ministered to him. The only survivor had been the traveler, who had fallen into a kind of coma. As he speaks, a lab assistant arrives to x-ray the mummy and its coffin. The scroll is put into a glass jar to protect it until further examination is possible. The students leave since this is a safety-conscious college, although they wear rubber gloves to touch the mummy—no masks, just gloves!—and x-raying is a dangerous technique. Susy remains, as does the chief engineer, Parker, who is also Doug's friend. Three x-rays are taken before it is realized that the machine is at danger level, and zapping at ten times the required dose. Doug bundles the radiologist out and orders a quick return of the plates.

The plates are not what the professor ordered ... some are only just of satisfactory exposure, and one has some strange round marks on it, near the mummy's skull. The radiologist decides to shoot some more, clandestinely, whilst Susy and Doug pore over the papyrus. Peering at the mummy, there is no apparent reason for the marks, so he searches the sides of the sarcophagus and finds a hidden drawer. Inside is a pouch with strange crystalline gems and an object shaped like a ouija board planchette with lines and hollows inscribed thereon. He pockets the gems, replaces the board, closes the drawer, and takes the replacement plates. So eager is he not to be caught that he does not see a light begin to glow in the mummy's thorax after the x-ray. Back in his lab, he is pleased with the new plate but is almost caught by Parker, so he hides the old plate behind a transformer. Since he cannot subsequently retrieve it, he figures it's safe from authoritarian eyes and abandons it.

Doug shows Parker a diagram he found rolled in the scroll—it makes no sense to him and is on a material he cannot classify. The mummy meanwhile is revived; searching the drawer, the board is now covered with green goo. The light in its chest scintillates. Across town the radiographer is attempting to sell the gems, saying they are three thousand years old, but the jeweler replies that they are worthless; he must find another way to turn gems into greenbacks.

Campus politics run rife—the senior members of the faculty, and those who have been "passed over" by Doug insist on making the discovery public, despite dire warnings about the haste, the lack of investigative work, and the unknown mold. A media event is planned, and begins against Doug's advice. The students he puts to guard the mummy take their places, and one spots green goo dripping down the side of the sarcophagus. He dips his naked finger in it and screams as the stuff bites into his flesh. Chaos briefly ensues as he is hospitalized, but the event goes on ... revealing an empty mummy case!

The media relish the college's embarrassment; any mummy joke you can think of, they broadcast. The campus heirachy decide it is a student prank, and issue a warning to return the mummy. Doug also wants a warning issued about the fungus/mold, but has to arrange that himself, courtesy of the delightful deejay, whose studio is so cheap because it is right next door to the campus's nuclear reactor!

All this while the mummy has his own agenda, assembling pieces of equipment and cannibalizing oddments of electrics. The audience sees everything from his point of view via a green filter. In setting up his HQ, the mummy kills a security man and leaves a smudge of fungus on the door. The same fungus is discussed by Doug and the pathologist; it breaks down tissue and doubles itself every hour, provided it has enough nourishment—flesh! The student who had the blob of goo on his fingertip is now covered to his elbow and amputation seems the only way to save his life.

Back at the students' lodgings, normal things like a peeping tom are happening. The peeping tom is our old friend with the gems, and to apologize to his girlfriend, he gives her a gem which is now attached to a chain. "Where did you get this?" she breathes ecstatically. "I found it in an old box," murmurs Mr. Cool. He subsequently sells the rest of the gems to his buddies at fifty dollars a go, and they pass them on to young ladies whom they admire.

The mummy cruises the campus, looking for its property. As the light in its chest scintillates, the gemstones echo the pattern. It finds one gem with baby-sitter Ellen and her boyfriend Greg. Ellen goes to comfort the baby, only to be mugged by the mummy, who snatches her gem, pushing her away with its hand on her face. She is taken straight to hospital with dry green mold on her from the wrappings. Greg, aghast, describes the attacker, "horrible face ... mummy..." while Parker finds the laboratory wrecked.

Each time the mummy reacquires a gem and sets it in the board, it glows and the college electrical system goes haywire. As it works, the pathologist floods a sample of the dry mold with x-rays, and reactivates it. A frantic phone call to the hospital is too late—Ellen's face is eaten away as she is x-rayed as part of her post-attack treatment.

The students have a frat costume party. A student/mummy, Peter, upsets his friends by peeking at them necking on a bench. When the real mummy comes along, he's yelled at as a creep! He takes another gem from a student, killing him in the process. The police find more fragments of mummy wrapping.

Ben and Susy share their theory of an alien traveler. Sunlight through the window is projected through Susy's gem and throws a schematic on the wall; it reminds her of radio plans her brother had. "It matches the design on the diagram, so the crystals and the design must be connected," says Doug (well, he is a professor isn't he?). He suggests contacting NASA, too.

The mummy continues to cruise the campus; in the deserted library, Susy does some research for Doug. The mummy is drawn to her crystal, which responds to his proximity, and a chase through the campus ensues, ending in her falling from the roof and surviving! She is adamant that he did not seek to hurt her—he only wanted the gem. The spoiled x-ray is discovered, and the number of gems becomes known. The mummy reclaims another, having had the audience think that another coed will be victim in her shower.

Doug calls the deejay to bring her camera to the reactor; the campus heirarchy appear, convinced he has orchestrated the whole show, and Ankh-Venharis arrives with the last gems. The transfixed humans watch him complete the transmitter, reform as an alien being, and fade before their eyes. Doug smiles quietly. A new star glitters above.

For all its faults, this movie is an interesting variation on a theme, created rather like a comic strip with the action splicing from one scene to another. There are some delightful comic moments for light relief, and a fleeting, touching shot of the mummy under a full moon, studying the starfield. There is an abundant use of dark rooms and torch beams, way before *X Files*, setting the mood and a few genuinely scary moments. Its biggest fault is not finding its niche; is it comic strip, horror/thriller, student days remembered, or fantasy/sci-fi? For all that, it's well worth a look — and maybe it will titillate a new generation of screenwriters to the possibilities still hidden in Egyptian soil.

The Monster Squad (U.S., 1987, MGM) Released August 1987; 81 minutes; Metrocolor, Panavision

Credits: Director: Fred Dekker; Producer: Jonathan Zimbest; Screenplay: Shane Black, Fred Dekker; Executive Producers: Peter Hyams, Rob Cohen, Keith Barish; Director of Photography: Bradford May; Production Design: Albert Brenner; Editor: James Mitchell; Special Effects: Richard Edlund; Monster Makeup: Stan Winston; Music: Bruce Broughton; Production Manager: Neil A. Machlis; Art Director: David Haber; Set Design: Roland Hill, Harold Fuhrman

Cast: Andre Gower (Sean), Robby Kiger (Patrick), Stephen Macht (Del), Duncan Regehr (Count Dracula), Tom Noonan (Frankenstein), Brent Chalem (Horace), Ryan Lambert (Rudy), Ashley Bank (Phoebe), Michael Fasutino (Eugene), Mary Ellen Trainor (Emily), Leonardo Cimino (Scary German Guy), Jonathan Gries (Desperate Man), Stan Shaw (Detective Sapir), Lisa Fuller (Patrick's sister), Jason Hervey (E. J.), Adam Carl (Derek), Carl Thibault (Wolfman), Michael MacKay (Mummy), Tom Woodruff Jr. (Gillman), Jack Gwillim (Van Helsing)

Van Helsing (Jack Gwillim) and his band of "freedom fighters" mess up an opportunity to destroy Dracula (Duncan Regehr) and his dark forces forever. During the spoiled ritual, Van Helsing and his followers are sucked into a time vortex generated by a crystal amulet.

One hundred years later:

In modern America, it's an ordinary day. Sean (Andre Gower) and Patrick (Robby Kiger) are in trouble because their passion for monsters is interfering with their classwork. Horace (Brent Chalem) is being bullied by other boys because he is overweight, and is rescued by his cool friend Rudy (Ryan Lambert), whom he wants inducted into their Monster club by way of a thank you. Sean's little sister, Phoebe, (Ashley Bank) also wants in — but the boys aren't at all "p.c.," and Phoebe's peeved. They are all scared of an elderly German (Leonardo Cimino) who lives in seclusion in the street, but of nothing and no one else.

At home, Sean's Mom (Mary Ellen Trainor) and Dad (Stephen Macht) are having marriage problems because dad's a cop and always out. Mom tries to follow Sean's interests but gets the monsters mixed up — she has, however, bought him Van Helsing's diary at a garage sale (!), but it's in German, so they have to make a new friend to get a translation. Judging by the concentration camp tattoo on his arm, he knows all about monsters.

Meanwhile, Del, Sean's Dad, has a bad work shift; a priceless mummy has gone missing from the museum and a crazy prisoner (Jonathan Gries), who insists he's a werewolf, has been shot though the body and has disappeared on his way to the morgue. And the guy driving the van has had his throat ripped out. Like we said ... just another day.

Just to make life interesting, Count Dracula has appeared on American soil, bringing with him the corpse of the Frankenstein monster (Tom Noonan); they call on their local friends for help, so the mummy (Michael MacKay) and the gill man (Tom Woodruff Jr.) join the merry band along with the werewolf (Carl Thibault). The purpose of the trip is to find and destroy the amulet at its one vulnerable moment in time (a hundred year cycle) so that evil can reign forever.

The kids understand what is going on and create the Monster Squad. Little Eugene is personally plagued by the mummy in his closet, and by losing his candy bar to the gill man by the swamp, which just happens to be at the end of Sean's back yard where the club members meet in Sean's tree house. Eugene writes to the military for assistance. The others prepare for battle looking for a virgin who will repeat the ritual, and making Phoebe's new friend a member of the squad (did we say he's the Frankenstein creature? no? well, it's just another day....) An unsuccessful foray into Dracula's lair puts them in great danger, deprives them of Frankenstein's help, and furnishes them with the amulet. They are pursued by the mummy that manages to grab Phoebe and tries to pull her from the truck. Rudy finds a loose piece of mummy wrapping, winds it around an arrow, and shoots it into the trunk of a nearby tree. The mummy quickly unrolls to nothing but a skull skidding on the road to town.

The final battle is to take place in the town square. In a lucid moment, the werewolf has warned Del that Sean's life is in danger, and he and his sidekick are phased when they drive *through* Dracula's limo on the way to rescue the kids. Del and Emily, his wife, are equally flabbergasted when Dracula blows up the clubhouse, turns into a bat, and flies off.

Dracula **(Duncan Regehr),** ***The Mummy*** **(Michael MacKay), and** ***The Wolfman*** **(Carl Thibault) gang up in** ***The Monster Squad*** **(1987).**

Rudy kills the vampire maids and Horace blows the gill man away while Patrick's sister (Lisa Fuller), the town fox, recites the ritual that doesn't work because of a guy "who doesn't count!" Del and Sean battle the werewolf and the Count. Rudy finally dispatches the werewolf with silver bullets. Phoebe is enlisted as ritual virgin and begins to recite, coached by the elderly German. Dracula tries to hurt her, but is hauled away by Frankenstein. The ritual completed, the vortex reopens and begins to suck everything in. Dracula makes one last grab at Sean, who stakes him and is grabbed by a human rope clinging to the public benches. Van Helsing appears in the vortex grabbing Dracula, grinning, and giving the kids the thumbs-up sign. Phoebe doesn't want Frankenstein to go, but the vortex is too strong, so she throws him her soft toy as a keepsake. The vortex closes, all hell ceases, and the Army roll into the square looking for Eugene. Just another day...

The Monster Squad is a great romp from start to finish, going at a whirlwind pace, doing exactly what you think it's going to do, making you laugh, gasp, and say aah in all the right places. A kind of comedy rite of passage movie for all the family, it is the one movie the authors can think of where *all* the Universal-created monsters appear in one screenplay.

Regehr is a superb Dracula, menacing everyone in his path, and only having any regard for his old friend the Frankenstein monster. Allusions to old scripts come thick and fast and are welcomed by the audience with nostalgia and enjoyment. One of the authors particularly likes Horace socking Dracula in the face with a slice of pizza oozing garlic — and of course, the foot-dragging, slowly plodding mummy of the 40s B-movies. Michael MacKay is splendid in recreating the jerky movements and foot sliding, bandaged, skinny creature, imbuing it with just the right note of menace. Tom Noonan's Frankenstein has such love that you can feel Boris Karloff smiling down on him. Van Helsing may be familiar to Hammer fans as Sir Giles Dalrymple of *Curse of the Mummy's Tomb*, where he came to an equally sticky end.

The production values are splendid and the finished film is immensely enjoyable both in itself and for the memories it evokes of shades gone by.

Tales from the Darkside—The Movie (U.K., 1990, Paramount) Released 1990; 93 minutes; Technicolor

Credits: Director: John Harrison; Producer: Richard P. Rubinstein; Screenplay: Michael McDowell (*Lot 249* segment, based on Sir Arthur Conan Doyle's story), George Romero (*Cat from Hell* segment, based on Stephen King's story), Michael McDowell (*Lovers' Vow* segment); Director of Photography: Robert Draper; Editor: Harry B. Miller III; Production Design: Ruth Ammon; Art Director: Jocelyne Beaudon; Set Director: Jacqueline Jacobson; Costumes: Ida Gearon; Production Manager: Victoria Westhead; Special Makeup Effects: KNB EFX Group

Cast: Deborah Harry (Betty), Christian Slater (Andy), David Johansen (Halston), William Hickey (Drogan), James Remar (Preston), Rae Dawn Chong (Carola), Robert Klein (Wyatt), Steve Buscemi (Bellingham), Matthew Lawrence (Timmy), Robert Sedgewick (Lee), Julianne Moore (Susan), Michael Deak (Mummy)

In the segment *Lot 249*, Edward Bellingham (Steve Buscemi), a brilliant if creepy university student, has lost a prestigious scholarship to Lee (Robert Sedgewick), a fellow student. Lee's girlfriend, Susan (Julianne Moore), is the sister of Andy (Christian Slater), who lives on the floor above Bellingham. Lee and Andy have inherited wealth, but Bellingham must work to support his studies. He works in the museum library while Susan, after whom he lusts, works there on a voluntary basis.

To make matters worse, Susan has penned the thesis that won Lee the scholarship, and as an insurance policy she has anonymously accused Bellingham of the theft of a priceless artifact from the campus collection. Bellingham, busily unpacking a mummy he has bought and hopes to resell at a profit, is very bitter about the incident.

Unwrapping the mummy with Andy, Bellingham explains the ancient process to his ever greener costudent. Looking at the hideous unwrapped face, Bellingham demonstrates the removal of the brain via a metal hook through the nose; then he re-opens the body cavity incision and rummages about in the mummy's insides. As well as the usual packing, he finds an ancient document on vellum. Studying it, he denies to Andy that he can read it and Andy goes back to his own room.

Later he hears a chant, and turning down the TV hears Bellingham reciting the ritual. The lights fuse, and Andy is knocked over by someone rushing down the stairs. Bellingham and he follow the figure and find Susan, who has also been knocked over. She uses the time that Bellingham takes to get her a restorative brandy to hide the stolen artifact in his rooms.

Lee wakes in a beery haze to the sound of breaking glass. The mummy (Michael Deak), revived, is stalking around his apartment, rummaging in the closet and finding ... a metal coat hanger that it twists into a brain hook. Grabbing Lee by the throat, it shoves the hook into his living — but not for long! — brain, and leaves the body in a heap for Susan to find.

Susan, fetching in black, starts to tidy the flat, making rude comments about her lately departed love. The mummy appears behind her, catches her by the window as she tries to escape, and fillets her back with the same scissors she had used to stab it. It then stuffs the body cavity with flowers, winds a few bandages around it, and leaves it neatly in a chair where Andy finds it.

Meanwhile, the college authorities, on another tip-off, have found the artifact and Bellingham is ordered to leave. Andy, realizing what must have happened, appears in his room, ties him to a chair, and proceeds to destroy the mummy, finally burning the pieces in the fireplace. He then demands the document. Bellingham tries to resist but appears too afraid, and Andy destroys the rolled vellum. The next day, as Bellingham leaves, he says he'll keep in touch. Riding away in a taxi he is maniacally amused; Andy doesn't know a third dynasty manuscript from a piece of Roman porn!

Andy, comfortable in his college room once more, answers a knock on the door. Lee and Susan are there, rather the worse for wear, and crazy of course ... they chorus, "Bellingham sent us!"

This is a delicious send-up of Conan Doyle's *Lot 249*, played with spirit and fun by the cast. The mummy is a magnificent special effects/makeup job and reminds you of all the old Universal mummies rolled into one. Its feverish dispatch of Lee with the brain hook makes you laugh instead of shudder, and you cannot feel any sympathy for any of the rich kids. Bellingham, constantly on the verge of uncontrolled madness, is a joy too. Watching it, the authors had nostalgic feelings for the horror comics of their early teens.

The Mummy Lives! (Canada, 1993, Global) Released straight to video; 98 minutes; Color

Credits: Director: Gerry O'Hara; Line Producers: Allan Greenblatt, Chaim Shatir; Screenplay: Nelson Gidding; Photography: Ava Koren; Music: Dov Seltzer; Editor: Danny Shik; Production Designer: Kuli Sander; Associate Producer: Anita Hope; Executive Producers: Yoram Globus, Christopher Pearce; Producer: Harry Alan Towers; Assistant Director: Michael Engel; Camera Operator: Offer Inov; Stunts: Eric Norris; Sound: Shabtai Sariq; Costume: Laura Dinulescu; Makeup: Scott Wheeler, Min Over; Special Effects: Nanny Rozenshtein; Prosthetics: Michael Rapp

Cast: Tony Curtis (Azira/Dr. Mahassid); Leslie Hardy (Sandra/Kira); Greg Wrangler (Dr. Williams); Jack Cohen (Lord Masten); Muhamed Bakri (Alexstas); Mosko Alkelai (Kroll); Moshe Ivgi (Ali); Yosi Chiloach (Capt. Mahmood); Uri Garnel (Tomb Guard); Yigal Naor (Official); Eli Dankor (Museum Director); Yossi Graber (Judge); Charlie Buzaglo, Rafi Weinstock (Priests); Amos Lavie (Museum Guard)

Although these things are difficult to predict, it's very likely that *The Mummy Lives!* could be the last "traditional" mummy film. Not that it's bad enough to pull the plug on a character that's been a screen staple for sixty five years (the picture is not *that* terrible), but the film proves, if nothing else, that there's nothing new to say on the subject and that watching a rehash of decades–old clichés doesn't quite make it either.

Despite some wonderful sets, decent photography, and some honest to Amon-Ra location work, *The Mummy Lives!* isn't much better than *Abbott and Costello Meet The Mummy*— but it *is* funnier, due to Tony Curtis in the lead.

So— how *is* Tony Curtis as the Mummy? He's about as convincing as Boris Karloff would have been in *Some Like It Hot.* Not only does Curtis look absurd in his Egyptian robes— like a cross between Yassir Arafat and John Travolta — he does *nothing* to alter his urban American delivery ("Yondah lies de pyramid of my foddah"). Wearing costumes like poor Curtis is forced to wear is a gift (see Christopher Lee in Hammer's *The Mummy*) bestowed on few, and Tony doesn't have it.

After a credit sequence interspersed with a time-consuming trip through the Zodiac, *The Mummy Lives!* begins moving ... sort of.

Sandra (Leslie Hardy), an attractive but troubled young woman, arrives in Cairo just as a dig, led by millionaire Lord Maxton (Jack Cohen), is beginning in "nearby" Luxor — actually three hundred miles away. She is experiencing strange dreams of ancient Egypt, and why not? She's a reincarnation of Kia, a concubine of the god Zoth. Three thousand years before, Kia was "violated" by Azira (Tony Curtis), a high priest. For his crime he is sentenced to you know what. And you can guess who is about to unearth his tomb.

Hungry for success, Lord Maxton ignores both the authorities and a deadly curse and enters the tomb. Amidst the treasure they find the mummy of Azira, who strangles the guard and soon appears in human form as Dr. Mahassid, Egyptologist.

Meanwhile, Sandra has been experiencing terrifying dreams of Ancient Egypt. Under their spell Sandra smashes a mummy case at the Museum of Archaeology and pulls the hand off its inhabitant — actually *her* mummified hand, wearing Azira's ring — and is interviewed by hunky Dr. Williams (Greg Wrangler), a psychiatrist, who offers his help.

Oddly enough, they become romantically involved until Sandra comes under the power of Dr. Mahassid, who had a twofold plan — to resume his millennia-old affair with Kia, and annihilate the violators of his beloved Egypt. Sandra and Williams take off for Luxor to see the tomb despite Mahassid's condemnation of the dig. His confrontation with Lord Maxton, whom he had previously assisted, leads to him being banned from the site.

Dr. Mahassid apologizes to Lord Maxton and gives him a cat, which promptly claws Maxton's eyes. In the hospital, Maxton receives a fatal visit from Mahassid. As for Sandra/Kia, Mahassid plans to be reunited with his lost love on the "Night of the Embrace" when Jupiter and Mars are in configuration; and he will then sacrifice her to Zoth to regain his god's favor. Sandra confounds his plan by setting Mahassid ablaze.

The Mummy Lives! was a Yoram Globus/Harry Alan Towers production, which explains a lot. The picture just *might have* worked with a different actor — say Omar Sharif— if they wanted a former star in the lead. Curtis really has given good performances but has none of the ... whatever it takes ... to play a role like this. Karloff and Lee — yes; Curtis— no. He shines in one scene only, in which he berates Lord Maxton for robbing Egypt's treasures, but that's about it.

The film is not without its other faults including a cobra that rattles like a diamondback and a very confused Egyptian mythology. The movie was supposedly suggestive of Edgar Allan Poe's *Some Words with a Mummy* (well, they both have the word "Mummy" in the title!).

Hercules: The Legendary Journeys (Episode: "Mummy Dearest") (New Zealand, 1996, MCA Television) Released 1996

Credits: Coordinating Producer: Bernadette

Joyce; Coproducers: David Eick, Liz Friedman; Producer: Eric Gruendemann; Supervising Producer: Robert Bielak; Coexecutive Producer: John Schulian; Executive Producers: Sam Raimi, Robert Tapert; Series Creator: Christian Williams; Writer: Melissa Rosenberg; Director: Anson Williams; New Zealand Production: Chloe Smith; Unit Production Manager: Eric Gruendeman; First Assistant Director: Wayne Rose; Second Assistant Director: Claire Richardson; Director of Photography: John Mahaffie; Editor: Steve Polivka, ACE; Visual Effects Supervisor: Kevin O'Neill; Production Designer: Robert Gillies; Costume Designer: Ngila Dickson; New Zealand Casting: Diana Rowan; U.S. Casting: Betty Hymson-Ayce, CSA; Extras Casting Director: Tracy Hampton; Stunt Coordinator: Peter Bell; Second Unit Director: Chris Graves; Music: Joseph Lo Duca; Camera Operator: Peter McCaffrey; Gaffer: Brett James; Key Computer: Geoff Jameson; Wardrobe Design Assistant: Janis MacEwan; Visual Effects: Flat Earth; Digital Composite Supervisor: Kevin Kutchaver

Cast: Kevin Sorbo (Hercules), Galyn Gorg (Princess Anaket), Robert Trebor (Salmoneus), John Watson (Sokar), Mark Newnham (Mummy), Alan de Malmande (Phineus), Henry Valaso (Keb), David Still (Thief #1) Derek Ward (Thief #2), Jim Rawdon (Porter), Patrick Kuntze (Delivery Man), Gregor McLennan (Guard #1), Graham Lauder (Cecrops's Ghost)

Hercules (Kevin Sorbo), in Attica for the feast of the dead, is chosen by the imperious Princess Anaket (Galyn Gorg), attended by her chief slave Keb (Henry Valaso) and her entourage to find the mummy of her ancestor, stolen by thieves. Also searching for the mummy is Sokar (John Watson), who wants to use the power of the mummy to marry Anaket and take the Egyptian throne.

The mummy, meanwhile, has been bought by Salmoneus (Robert Trebor) to be the chief exhibit in his House of Horrors waxworks; having removed the mummy's golden ankh, the seat of its power, Salmoneus inadvertently frees it to go on a rampage round the city.

Hercules fights both the princess's unshakable belief in slavery, and the strength of the mummy, whose speed and agility perplexes them all.

"Where's the foot-dragging classic mummy we all know and love?" bemoans Salmoneus.

At the moment of greatest danger, Keb dies to protect his Princess. The mummy destroys Sokar and absorbs his power but is defeated by Hercules's quick action in turning it into a giant top and dunking it in boiling wax. Anaket frees the dying Keb and vows to return to Egypt and free all slaves. She tries to persuade Hercules to be her consort, but he declines the honor. Salmoneus decides to melt down his House of Horrors and make thousands of little G.I. Joe — Hercules figures to make his fortune. The remains of the mummy stir in the vat as the credits roll.

This delightful series from New Zealand has classicists tearing their hair out and everyone else roaring with approval. The gods are spoiled brats, Hercules has constant trouble with his jealous stepmother, Hera the Queen of the Gods, fights injustice like Superman with almost equal powers, avoids pneumatic ladies with a deft touch, and apart from being a touch ingenuous at times, is an altogether great role model.

The "hip" dialogue and rampantly anachronistic machinery, together with the many visual jokes, make it a fun experience to watch. In this episode, the mummy was superbly created by the makeup, wardrobe, and effects team. As Kevin Sorbo recalls, "I still think that this was one of the best jobs the boys from WETA, that's the special effects company down in Wellington, did with the mummy. I mean, it looked great on TV, but in person I think it scared the hell out of me! ... this thing was spooky-looking ... *The episode was just perfect for Halloween*" (Weisbrot, 19980). Additionally, the references to the mummy movies we all know and love only made it more delicious. The creative team includes remarks in their credits, too, to extend the fun. Recently, a many tentacled baby monster called Obi, was the star, and the end credits noted "In deference to baby Obi, no calamari were served to cast or crew during the making of this film."

At the end of *Mummy Dearest*, the credits noted "Any similarity between our Mummy and the foot-dragging classic we all know and love is purely intentional."

And from the wriggling fingers in the last shot ... we think he'll be back!

Under Wraps (U.S., 1997, RHI Entertainment-Disney) Released 1997; approx. 95 minutes; Color

Credits: Writer: Don Rhymer; Director: Greg Beeman; Casting: Julie Taylor, CSA; Unit Production Manager: Bernie Caulfield; First Assistant Director: Richard W. Abramitis; Second Assistant Director: Sharon Gerland; Stunt Coordinator: Leon Delaney; Set Decorator: Caitlin Blue; Property Master: Eric Holst; Costume: Jacqueline Aronson; Makeup: Cheri Montesanto-Medcalf; Hairstylist: Ann Montesanto; Mummy created by KNB Efx Group Inc.; Title Design: Nina Saxon Film Design; Visual Effects: Flash Film Works; Music: David Michael Froth; Production Design: Mario Caso; Director of Photography: Mark Gray; Executive Producers: Don Rhymer, Mireille Soria, Tracey Thompson; Producer: Bernadette Caulfield

Cast: Adam Wylie (Marshall); Mario Yedidia (Gilbert); Clara Byart (Amy); Ken Campbell (Bruce); Corrine Bohrer (Amy's Mom); Penny Peyeer (Gilbert's Mom); Ed Lauter (Kubat); Bill Fagerbakke (Mummy/Ted); Atim Udoffia (ER Nurse); Greg Watanabe (Doctor); Linda Gehringer (Connie); Kenneth John (Principal); Reuben Grundy (Cop); Anni Long (Jane); Christine Patterson (Female Mummy); Joshua Dennis (Leonard); Ryan Schofield (Todd); Nakia Burrise (Page); Velina Brown (Mother in Park); Robert Bailey, Jr. (Boy in Park); Louis Landman (Kubat's goon); Sean McFarland (Goon at window); Lance Brady (Art Dealer); Wilma Bonet (Desk nurse)

On the eve of Halloween, monster-loving Marshall (Adam Wylie), his geeky best friend Gilbert (Mario Yedidia), and Amy (Clara Byart) inadvertently reanimate a mummy hidden in the cellar of their late *bete noir*, Mr. Kubat (Ed Lauter), when they go to examine the "weird stuff" Amy's Mom (Corinne Bohrer) has been commissioned to sell to pay his IRS debts. The children adopt the mummy (Bill Fagerbakke) and christen him Harold, teaching him English, clothing him in thrift store gear, and trying to keep him out of trouble. Harold enjoys learning about life in 90s America and sympathizes with Marshall over the latter's Mom's apparent new love. Marshall is coping with his parents' divorce, and missing his dad.

The children have two big problems; it becomes apparent that Harold must be recoffined before the end of Halloween on pain of losing his soul, and Mr. Kubat is far from dead and wants his property back. With the help of their slightly older friend Bruce (Ken Campbell), they rescue Harold and his coffin, help to capture Mr. Kubat and his ring of thieves, and return Harold to the museum in time for him to bid his queen, an exhibit, a fond farewell before resting for eternity.

These processes enable Marshall to mature enough to put away his monsters and to urge his Mom (Linda Gehringer) to marry her boyfriend.

This Disney Channel movie is great fun. The young cast fills their roles with a believable innocence, teetering as they are on the edge of adolescence. The grown-ups are a plausible background. The mummy, made by KNB Effects (who went straight from this movie to providing the deadly mummy in *Talos, the Mummy*), is a wonderfully cuddly, baggy creature that reminds one of the mummy in *Abbott and Costello Meet the Mummy*. The boys at KNB seem to be specializing in mummies lately; they did *Under Wraps*, then *Talos the Mummy*, and then went on to Stephen Sommers's *The Mummy*. As Howard Berger—the B in KNB—quipped, "You could say KNB are mummy's boys at the moment!"

Buffy and the Inca Mummy Girl (U.S., 1997, Fox TV-Mutant Enemy) Released October 1997 (U.S.), April 1998 (U.K.); 45 minutes; Color

Credits: Creator/Executive Producer: Joss Wheadon; Writers; Matt Kiene, Joe Reinkemeyer; Director: Ellen S. Pressman; Unit Production Manager: Gary Law; 1st Asst. Director: Robert D. Nellans; 2nd Asst. Director: Randy La Follette; Story: Christopher Beck; Theme: Nerf Herder; Director of Photography: Michael Gershman; Production

Designer: Carey Meyer; Editor: Regis B. Kimble; Casting: Marcia Schulman, CSA; Costume Design: Cynthia Bergstrom; Production Sound Mixer: Maury Harris, CAS; Art Director: Stephanie J. Gordon; Set Director: David Koneff; Prop Master: Ken Wilson; Camera Operator: Russ McElhatton; Hairstylist: Jeri Baker; Makeup: John Mcldonado; Special Makeup Effects: John Vulich; Vampire Designs: Burnam Studios; Visual Effects: Pop; Producers: Mutant Enemy Inc., Kuzui Enterprises, Sundollar Television

Cast: Sarah Michelle Gellar (Buffy), Alyson Hannigan (Willow), Nicholas Brendon (Xander), David Boreanaz (Angel), Anthony Stewart Head (Giles), Jason Hall (Devon), Charisma Carpenter (Cordelia), Ara Celi (Ampata), Kristine Sutherland (Joyce Summers), Hendrik Rosvall (Sven), Joey Crawford (Rodney), Danny Strong (Jonathan), Kristin Winniaki (Gwen), Gil Birmingham (Peruvian Man) Samuel Jacob (Peruvian Boy).

Buffy (Sarah Michelle Gellar) is irritated by having to host Ampata (Ara Celi), an exchange student, despite Xander (Nicholas Brendon) and Willow (Alyson Hannigan) lending a hand so that the Slayer can do her thing unimpeded. There is an added complication when Xander falls in love with Ampata. Cordelia (Charisma Carpenter) thinks she has the worst deal since her visitor, Sven (Hendrik Rosvall), cannot speak English and doesn't share her interests. Xander's new love is a revived Inca mummy that requires frequent blood letting to keep her youthful looks; she is the Chosen One of her people, sacrificed 500 years before and held in her tomb by a sacred seal, and a guard. When Willow's boyfriend Rodney (Joey Crawford) attempted to steal the seal, it was broken as Ampata drained him and was freed to murder Buffy's real visitor — a boy.

Giles and the gang piece the clues while Ampata murders fresh victims. She also draws Buffy's sympathy by talking about her lonely, loveless life — a thing the Slayer can empathize with in no small way.

At the school dance, Ampata begins to drain Xander but cannot continue because she has come to love him. Buffy, Giles, and Willow go to Xander's rescue by the mummy's sarcophagus. Momentarily winded, Buffy cannot prevent the mummy from grabbing Willow. "Just let me have this one," she pleads to Xander. "It's never gonna happen," is his reply, but he offers himself to Ampata instead, just as Buffy stakes her. She dies in his arms. It will be a long time before Xander's life is back to normal.

This episode is a good example of the show's format generating interesting variations on old plot ideas, using the school as a background. The TV series has an edge that the movie, which spawned it, lacks, plus sharp and witty scripts, and characters interesting enough to keep the viewer watching. The special makeups are effective and not overdone. A nice addition to a mummy collector's list!

Bram Stoker's Legend of the Mummy (U.S., 1997, Goldbar Entertainment Unapix Films) Released 1997 (video); 96 minutes; Color: Fotokem Fototronics

Credits: Writer/Director: Jeffrey Obrow; Producers: Harel Goldstein, Bill Barnett; Executive Producers: Robert Barnes, Jeffrey Obrow; Story Adaptation: Jeffrey Obrow, Lars Hauglie, John Penny (based on the novel *Jewel of Seven Stars*); Line Producer: Gina Fortunato; Coproducer: Tad Driscoll; Director of Photography: Antonio Soriano; Editor: Gary Meyers; Music: Rick Cox; Production Design: Kan Larson; Costume Design: Caroline Marx; Casting: Rosemary Welden; Special Effects Makeup: Chad Wahsam, Chris Fording; Stunt Coordinator: Eddie Perez; Stunt Performers: Ted Barba, John Barrett, Frank Lloyd, Debbie Carrington, Mark Orrison, Jennifer Caputo; Unapix Executive: Alicia Reily; Assistant Art Director: Amy Perry; Set Decorator: Bryce Holthousen; Sculptor/Scenic Artist: J. R. McGarnty; Sculptor/Prop Master: Rick Smith; Muralist: David Rau; Queen Tera's Sapphire: Ken Lauer Bevelling; Key Makeup: Sandy Williams; Key Hair: Gary Particone; Makeup Artist: Stacey L. Smith; Costume Supervisor: Ric Spencer; Costume: Nicci Stevens; Special Effects: Ultimate Effects: John Hartigan, Paul Sokol; Post Production Supervisor/Visual Effects Supervisor: Eric Valente; Sand Pit Bugs: Ray Pettitt; Titles and Opticals: T&T Optical Effects; CGI Transformation: E Film

Cast: Louis Gossett Jr. (Corbeck), Amy Locane (Margaret Trelawney), Eric Lutes (Robert Wyatt), Mark Lindsay-Chapman (Daw), Lloyd Bochner

(Abel Trelawney), Mary Jo Catlett (Mrs. Grant), Aubrey Morris (Dr. Winchester), Laura Otis (Lily), Julian Stone (Jimmy), Richard Karn (Brice Renard), Portia Doubleday (Young Margaret), Rachel Naples (Queen Tera), Donald Monat (Hutchins), Kelly Perine (Keene), Kahlil Sabbagh (Bedouin Guide), Victoria Tennant (Mary), Stayce Allison (Woman), Cher Summers (Operator), Tico Wells (Young Corbeck), John Rixy Moor (Young Trelawney)

In present-day Marin County, California, wealthy Egyptologist Abel Trelawney (Lloyd Bochner) has received the final piece of a stela that will enable him to restore the long-dead Queen Tera (Rachel Naples) to life, the culmination of his life's work. Trelawney has amended the Queen's plans, however, by destroying the mummies of her court, intending to replace them with himself and his friends. His daughter Margaret (Amy Locane), recently returned from her father's imposed exile, calls on Robert Wyatt (Eric Lutes) to help her when Trelawney's unconscious and lacerated body is found in his study.

Daws (Mark Lindsey-Chapman), the security chief, suspects everyone. Mrs. Grant (Mary Jo Catlett), the faithful housekeeper, believes the artifacts that fill the house are dangerous to her beloved employer, and her daughter Lily (Laura Otis) just wants to escape the strange house for the bright lights of the city.

Wyatt's friend Brice (Richard Karn) is entranced by Trelawney's discoveries and the secrecy surrounding the tomb's contents. People in the household begin to die as Tera's power grows, and Margaret becomes more imperious as the days pass.

Wyatt finds Corbeck (Louis Gossett Jr.) in an asylum, a self-committed patient who has been terrified by the implications of the work he and Trelawney have done over the decades in pursuit of Tera's dream of reincarnation. When he hears that Margaret is at the mansion, he knows there is only one course of action — the ritual to restore the queen.

Trelawney, Daws, Wyatt, Margaret Corbeck, and the doctor (Aubrey Morris) carry all the queen's belongings to her reconstructed tomb in the grounds. Unwrapping the queen, Corbeck places the great ruby in her seven-fingered hand as the final preparation for her rebirth. Margaret ensures that only she, Corbeck, and Wyatt are present as the ritual begins. Wyatt panics and tries to stop the ceremony, but Corbeck renders him insensate. Margaret becomes the conduit for Tera's rebirth, and Corbeck's reward is death.

A short while later, a recovered Trelawney accepts the jewel of seven stars from his daughter as she leaves for her wedding with Wyatt. After an exhausting consummation of the marriage, Wyatt becomes aware of the changes in Margaret and stares in horror at his lacerated back, knowing as he sees the scratches grouped in sevens that his wife is Tera.

This latest attempt to film Stoker's *Jewel of Seven Stars* has a lot to commend it although it appears to have gone straight to video. Alan Frank, writing in *The Star*, gave it seven out of ten. It has several delightful touches; filmed in a modern setting as Stoker wrote in a modern (to him) setting, it updates the letters of Margaret and her father to a message on an answerphone and instructions on a dictaphone. It also comes to grips with the original dark ending to the novel where Tera triumphs. The plethora of mummies is a little confusing, even after Corbeck's explanation about Tera's court. The flashbacks are nicely done, and brief to the point of subliminality with commendable effort on the artifacts, etc. The seven-fingered hand of Tera is well constructed too. There is also the neat touch of Aubrey Morris again playing the Trelawneys' doctor as he did in Hammer's *Blood From The Mummy's Tomb*. We find ourselves in disagreement over this opus; one of us loves the homage to the novel and the near-perfect rendering of it on film, while the other longed for less talk and more action. Gossett Jr. heads a solid cast, although Lutes, known mostly for *Caroline in the City*, seemed slightly out of place at first, and Victoria Tennant is sadly underused.

Mummies Alive!—The Legend Begins (U.S., 1998, Buena Vista Home Entertainment-DIC Productions) Released 1998; approx. 60 minute; Color animation

Credits: Executive Producers: Andy Heyward, Ivan Reitman, Mike Maliani, Robby London, Daniel Goldberg, Joe Medjuck; Producer/Director: Seth Kearsley; Story: Mark Edens; Teleplay: Steve Cuden, Len Uhley, Ted A. Pedersen, Francis Moss; Story Editors: Eric Lewald, Julia Lewald, Michael Edens; Coexecutive Producer: Janice Sonski; Development Consultant: Phil Harnage; Post Production Executive: Stacey Gallishaw; Production Supervisor: Emily Wensel assisted by Tracy Hansen; Assoc. Producer: Margaret M. Dean; Assoc. Producer Post Production: Christy Buskirk; Production Coordinators: Kimberly Smith, Lisa Atlas, Judy Reilly, Zoe Seals; Casting/Voice Direction: Marsha Goodman, Shirley McGregor Ford; Talent Coordinators: Brenda Frank Gail Fabrey; Script Coordinator: Lori Anderson assisted by William A. Ruiz; Script Assistants: Patrick Boylan, Michael Walsh; Director of Research: Renee Toporzysch; Research Assistant: Jay Bryant; Music Supervisor: Karyn Ulman; *Mummies Alive* Theme and Cues: Raw; Music: John Campbell; Music Assistants: Delfino Hernandez, Tanya D. Davis; Main Title Animation: Mook Animation; 3-D Computer Animation: Yarrow Cherey; Author: Louis Gassin

Cast: Graeme Kingston, Scott McNeil, Pauline Newstone, Gerald Plunkett, Cree Summer, Bill Switzer, Dale Wilson

Egypt in 1525 B.C.: The evil sorcerer, Scarab, kills the pharaoh's son and his four warrior bodyguards, led by the heroic Jakal. To punish his son's murderer, the pharaoh buries Scarab alive and curses him to endure fifty lifetimes buried in Egypt's sands. But in 1928, Scarab's tomb is located by archaeologists and opened, releasing the villain on an unsuspecting world.

Coming forward to modern-day San Francisco, we find the 3500 year old Scarab disguised as the world's richest man. When Jakal and the guard come back to life as the powerful armored mummies, they are still sworn to protect their boy pharaoh from the evil sorcerer — even in the spirit world.

Jakal must face the agony of his reincarnated brother and teenage nephew joining forces with the evil Scarab to annihilate the mummies and destroy the world. However, might and justice prevail eventually after the usual thrills and fights, leaving the mummies to find a new cause — their own TV series, of course!

Mummies Alive! is as good a way as any to pass a wet Saturday morning if you are babysitting, and a fairly plodding, odyssey-type movie that explains the origins of TV's Armored Mummies. Well, you did want to know where they came from — didn't you? Slightly less effort than reading a comic book, it is certainly noisier, but no more complex. Having said that, it was fun!

The Curse of Tittikhamon—A Play in the Stage Series: Movies That Never Got Made (1998, Armstrong Arts— stage production)

Credits: Screenplay: Michael Armstrong; Director: Allen Stone; Producer: Krisztina Vaszko; Songs: Danny Beckermann, Max Early; Music: Mark Hartley; Choreography: Stuart Vaughan; Production Design: Krystyna Loboda Iwaniec; Sound Design: Matthew Diss; Director of Lighting: Julian McCready

Cast: Keanu Cruise; Dustin Schwarzenegger; Demi Bonham-Carter; Dolly Pitt; Uma Paltrow; Quentin Van Damme; Whoopi Streisand; McCauley Di Caprio; Godzilla; and Michael Armstong as Babe Bette

As you can tell from the "cast," this was an event rather than a serious piece of theatre! Michael Armstrong needs no introduction — director of *Mark of the Devil, The Haunted House of Horror*, and writer of *The House of Long Shadows*. He gave his fans a once-in-a-lifetime opportunity to see his never-filmed 1978 screenplay *The Curse of Tittikhamon* at London's New End Theatre July 7–August 2, 1998. Presented as a World Premiere play in a series entitled "Movies That Never Got Made" with a celebrity charity gala on July 19 in aid of CRUSAID, it was written as a send-up of mummy movies with a Mel Brooksish style of humor galloping through it. Director Allen Stone reinvented Armstrong's concept as a live radio broadcast, with seven actors playing all forty characters, a pianist scoring the piece as it goes along, and a harassed sound effects man trying to keep up with all the spoof horror-thriller elements. Armstrong, with his usual enthusiasm, described this latest project as "the Goon Show Meets The Reduced Shakespeare Company meets The Curse of the Mummy's Tomb. And it's a musical too!"

Sadly, the expected transfer to the West End did not take place, but a grand time was had by all audiences during this limited run.

Talos the Mummy (1998, Carousel, Luxembourg) Released 1998; 115 minutes; Color by Deluxe

Muraglia/Sladek productions in association with 7th Voyage, Imperial Entertainment Group and KNB EFX Group, Inc. A Carousel Picture Company Production.

Credits: Script: John Esposito (from a screenplay by Russell Mulcahy and Keith Williams); Coproducers: Russell Mulcahy, Lance Reynolds; Associate Producers: Howard Berger, Sterling Belefont; Production Manager: Meinir Stoutt; First Asst. Director: David Daniels; Second Asst. Director: Iseult Frere; Produced in assoc. with Brimstone Entertainment; Coexecutive Producers: Scott Vandiver, Phil Botana; Produced in association with Telepool; Costume: Cynthia Dumont; Makeup Design: David Myers: Art Directors: Peter Powis, Simon Bowles; Script Supervisor: Sheila McNaught; Location Manager: Pascal Charlier; Camera Operator/Stedicam Operator: Alessandro Bolognesi; Second Camera Operator: Peter Field; Casting (Luxembourg): Lynx Productions: Set Dressing: Manu Demoulling; Wardrobe Master: Tiny Nicholls; Costumes Supplier: Angels & Bermans, London; Hair Stylist: Vivia Nowak; "Wadjet Eye" by Mark Brazier Jones; Sound and Editorial Services: Signet Soundelux Studios, ADR Recording London, dB Post Limited London; Special Makeup Effects: KNB EFX Group Inc.; Visual Effects: Flash Film Works, Black Box Digital Inc., Voodoo Arts: Historical Research: Tatanka Film Research, Ron Sladek; Music: "Mummy Groove" by Jim Vincent, courtesy of Planet Void Music; Color/Prints: Deluxe Labs on Kodak. Produced in association with The Pharaohs Company Ltd.; Production Executives: Tom Reeve, Jeff White; World Distribution: Buena Vista Film Sales.

Cast: Jason Scott Lee (Detective Riley); Louise Lombard (Samantha Turkel); Sean Pertwee (Bradley Cortese); Lysette Anthony (Dr. Claire Mulrooney); Michael Lerner (Professor Marcus); Jack Davenport (Detective Bartone); Honor Blackman (Captain Shea); Christopher Lee (Sir Richard Turkel); Shelley Duval (Edith Butros), Gerard Butler (Burke); Joe Polito (Parsons); Ronan Vibert (Young); Bill Treacher (Stuart); Elizabeth Power (Elizabeth); Cyril Nri (Forensics); Roger Morrissey (The Mummy); Edward Tudor Pole (Blind Man); Craig Stuart (Nahil); Anthony Beselle, Jamie Treacher (Museum Guards); Ann Overstall (Olga); Enzo (Prince Talos); Waris (Princess Nefriama); Alex Torino (Nizwar); David Sterne (Morris); David Henry (Coroner); Les Woodhall (Paperman); Tim Hope-Frost (Bus driver); Mike West (Police Guard); Nicholas Hume (Nizwar's friend); Alison Bullivent (Maid); Cairan Mulhern (Nervous student); Luke De Lacey (Wisecracking student); Herve Sogne, Valerie Schiel (Stand-ins); Diane Wiersma, Annemiek Boomstra, Ronald Schuwbier (Stunts).

In 1948, Sir Richard Turkel (Christopher Lee), leading an archaeological dig in the Valley of the Kings, searching for the High Priest Maya, finds a doorway. He knows on reading the hieroglyphs around the doorway that they have found something infinitely more dangerous, but he cannot persuade his companions to leave the tomb sealed. Having meticulously completed his dig log, and having undertaken other precautions, he is present as the door is breached. A miasma engulfs the party, who fall, desiccating, as they try to escape. In a supreme final effort, although his body is in pieces, Turkel triggers the explosion that will reseal the tomb for another fifty years.

In 1998, the Berkley Expedition are to reopen the tomb. A member of the team is Samantha Turkel (Louise Lombard), Sir Richard's granddaughter, who is perturbed by his log of the previous dig. The problem is, was he crazy or not before he blew up the previous party? With great care, they enter Talos's tomb and find it like none other. The sarcophagus is suspended in a deadly spiked cavern that looks as though it was designed to keep something in rather than stopping tomb robbers. Desiccated, impaled corpses litter the floor, and the walls and roof are covered with glyphs and schematics of the skies. Samantha's fiancé dies as he throws her a Wadjet Eye protective amulet that hangs from one of the spikes. Nevertheless, the contents of the tomb are brought to the British Museum for the Millennium Exhibition.

The display of finds is impressive—Talos's rough-hewn sarcophagus is displayed open with the tattered remains of his wrappings inside. There is no body. As a heavenly conjunction of planets—held by some as the beginning of Armageddon—swings into place, the display is destroyed, the wrappings go missing, and people begin to turn up dead. One victim has eyes missing, another lungs, a third his liver. All the victims are from different parts of the world, and the British police—with Captain Shea (Honor Blackman) at the head—are baffled as is their American counterpart, Riley, (Jason Scott Lee) on loan from the detectives at the U.S. Embassy. Riley is the quintessential skeptic who takes an age to believe that what is going on here is not your ordinary serial killer. While he is becoming a believer, he is also falling in love with Sam.

Using data collected by Cortese (Sean Pertwee), Riley discovers that Talos is regaining various parts of his body that were entrusted to his followers before Pharaoh Amenhotep's guards could kill him. Talos is also Pharaoh's son-in-law, a one-time banished Greek sorcerer who became trusted and loved by the royal family. The Princess Nefriama, who loved and married him, was keeper of his heart—literally.

Cortese, using the help of Edith Butros, a psychic (Shelley Duvall), tries to prevent Talos from achieving his goal, but only succeeds in being arrested for the murders.

When Sam is taken by the mummy wrappings, animated by the spirit of Talos, the remaining members of the dig, Professor Marcus (Michael Lerner) and Dr. Claire Mulrooney (Lysette Anthony), join forces with the psychic to rescue her using necromancy and the body of the lately dead Cortese.

As the planets swing into alignment, the four chase through a ruined building site as Talos reassembles himself. He takes first Marcus and then Mulrooney and fights Riley for the life of Sam. Since both Riley and Sam believe she is Nefriama come again, they think they have won as Riley reluctantly kills her. But *Riley* is the descendant, as Talos shows him as he rips out Riley's heart and places it in his own chest whilst Mulrooney watches in adoration. Her last act of sacrifice to her new god is to offer herself as the serial killer to the police, who (finally) arrive, leaving Prince Talos to live again in Riley's image.

Filmed in the Grand Duchy of Luxembourg under the Audiovisual Certificate Program, *Talos the Mummy* was awaited with keen anticipation. Mulcahy's film wins the stakes for the most creative new look at the genre. "When you see this pile of rags, I want you to get the chills," Mulcahy predicted. The inclusion of Christopher Lee as the archaeologist, Sir Richard Turkel, was one of Mulcahy's cherished dreams, Hammer's Mummy being his all-time favorite film. When Mr. Lee walked onto the set, an awed lull came over the cast and crew, much to Lee's amusement. It looked like an offering to be savored by the public as well as its creator. "When Christopher Lee brought all those words to life in the 1948 flashbacks, I became so emotional I nearly broke down. It's a total dream come true... I've made a neo-Hammer mummy film starring my absolute idol, Christopher Lee, and I've cut him in half in what will be a showstopping death scene. It really doesn't get any better than this," Mulcahy rejoiced.

After much ballyhoo, instead of going head-to-head with Universal's new *The Mummy*, it went straight to video rental to coincide with the theatre opening of its rival. In the U.K. it achieved a higher certification—15 to the 12 awarded to the big-screen opposition, but virtually all reviewers were disappointed. For example, *Starburst* #251 says: "...begins on a promising note, with a classic pre-credit sequence but it's downhill from there, as Mulcahy's Hammer homage slowly unravels into a predictable and pointless shlocker. The film isn't helped by its frequently laughable special effects, or by Mulcahy's atypically restrained direction ... watchable but never wonderful." Tom Weaver, noted author, commented to the authors, "Tony Timpone somehow saw Talos the Mummy (120+ minutes) and said it was fair; what I saw was just the U.S. version, 80-something minutes and retitled *Tale of the Mummy* and I'd say it's fair minus."

Christopher Lee is splendid in his cameo as the tortured archaeologist, exuding a quiet dignity that makes the audience wish he had not vanished before the credits roll. In an homage to Lee's mummy, at one point we have Talos punctured by a shotgun, and the lights from the hallway shining through the hole in his midriff, just like the poster of the Hammer opus. Jason Scott Lee looks a touch bemused as the hero, while Anthony, Lerner, and Pertwee are wasted. Lombard, Treacher, and Power are better known for their various TV series, which seemed of more interest to the tabloid reviewers than the content of the movie.

Sadly, the special effects let the film down — mummy wrappings looking like animated scotch tape rather than linen, and wounds that look as though they were pasted in by CGI. While audiences are eager to "suspend disbelief," in the words of Terence Fisher, rather obvious effects do much to detract from that suspension. The *idea* behind the plot was interesting and innovative. What a pity finances obviously scuppered the end result. Filmed in thirty-seven days in September 1997, it was no mean feat for an idea for a movie conceived at Christmas 1995, as Mulcahy recovered from a skiing accident. He and his partners obviously put a great deal of work into this film, but if you don't have $80 million these days, it shows.

The Mummy (U.S., 1998, Universal) An Alphaville Production, A Stephen Sommers Film; 120 minutes; Color

Credits: Director and Screenplay: Stephen Sommers; Screenplay: Stephen Sommers; Screen Story: Stephen Sommers, Lloyd Fonvielle, Kevin Jarre; Producers: James Jacks, Sean Daniel; Director of Photography: Adrian Biddle, BCS; Production Designer: Allan Cameron; Film Editor: Bob Ducsay; Executive Producer: Kevin Jarre; Coproducer: Patricia Carr; First Assistant: Cliff Lanning; 2nd Unit Director: Greg Michael; Post Production Supervisor: Doreen A. Dixon; Special Effects Supervisor: Chris Corbould; Live Action Creature Effects Supervisor: Nick Dudman; Egyptology Consultant: Dr. Stuart Smith; Camera Operator: David Worley; Art Directors: Tony Reading, Giles Masters, Clifford Robinson, Peter Russell; Key Makeup Artist: Aileen Seaton; Key Hairdresser: Tricia Cameron; Visual Effects Supervisor: John Andrew Berton Jr.; Visual Effects Producer: Jennifer Bell; ILM Character Design Supervisor: Jeff Mann; ILM Animation Supervisor: Daniel Jeanette; ILM Visual Effects Producer: Tom Kennedy; Film Editor: Kelly Matsumoto; Sound Design/Re-recording Mixer: Leslie Shatz; Costume Design: John Bloomfield; Stunt Coordinator: Simon Crane

Cast: Brendan Fraser (Rick O'Connell); Rachel Weisz (Evelyn); John Hannah (Jonathan); Kevin O'Connor (Beni); Arnold Vosloo (Imhotep); Jonathan Hyde (Egyptologist); Oded Fehr (Ardeth Bey); Omid Djalili (Warden); Erick Avari (Curator); Aharon Ipale (Pharaoh Seti); Patricia Velasquez (Anck Su Namun); Carl Chase (Hook); Stephen Dunham (Henderson); Corey Johnson (Daniels); Tuc Watkins (Burns); Bernard Fox (Winston Havelock); Mohammed Afifi (Hangman); Abder Rahim El Aadili (Camel trader); Simon Crane (Stunt Coordinator); Jake Arnott, Mason Bell, Isobel Brook, Chequer, Porl Smith, James Traheme Burton, Ian Warner (Mummy Performers)

In Thebes, capital city of Seti I (Aharon Ipale), the Pharaoh's mistress Anck Su Namun (Patricia Velasquez) is caught by her master, betraying him with Imhotep (Arnold Vosloo), High Priest, aided and abetted by Imhotep's priests who stand guard. Doomed, the lovers attack their master and Anck Su Namun kills him as his guards break through the door. She insists that Imhotep escapes as he will be the only one capable of resurrecting her, and she kills herself as the guards lunge forward, spitting, "My body is no longer his temple."

Arnold Vosloo as Imhotep, in what restarted the series, *The Mummy* (Universal, 1998).

Anck Su Namun is properly mummified, but Imhotep steals her body and flies with it to Hamunaptra, City of the Dead, to enact the ritual from the Book of the Dead that will restore her to life. But he is discovered and mummified alive with flesh-eating scarab beetles— a punishment so dire it had never been used before. Should the mummy ever rise from the Hom-Dai curse, a terrible fate would befall the world, "I would arise a walking disease, a plague upon mankind, an unholy flesh eater with the strength of the ages, power over the sands, and the glory of invincibility. I would be an unstoppable infection upon this world. The Apocalypse ... The End." To prevent this, Pharaoh's guard, the Medjai, were to guard his burial place for all time to prevent anyone releasing him. And so the centuries passed.

In 1925, Foreign Legionnaire, Rick O'Connell (Brendan Fraser), his pal Beni (Kevin O'Connor), and their troop are held down under enemy fire at Hamunaptra. No longer the great city we once saw, it is now ruined and desolate. The Tuaregs are determined to wipe them from the planet and another group overlooks the battle — the Medjai, still patiently on duty. When the Tuaregs are rousted by some strange force, O'Connell survives. Some of the Medjai want to finish him off, but their leader Ardeth Bey (Oded Fehr) merely says, "The desert will kill him." But it doesn't — and he knows where he has been, as well as having kept a strange box that he found in the city as a souvenir.

In Cairo, clumsy librarian Evelyn Carnahan (Rachel Weisz) is cataloguing and, inadvertently, wrecking the book collection at the Cairo Museum of Antiquities. Burning to be a real Egyptologist, but overlooked by all, including her charming but less than honest brother Jonathan (John Hannah), she is told in no uncertain terms by the curator (Erick Avari) that her tenure is down to her dearly loved and respected late parents, and not her own — not inconsiderable — accomplishments. Jonathan brings the long-suffering Evelyn a box with strange hieroglyphs, which she manages to undo. The papyrus inside also depicts a map to the fabled City of the Dead, but the curator "accidentally" destroys it. The problem remains that the former owner of the box, who knows the way to Hamunaptra, is about to be executed and must be rescued so that they can find the city. Jonathan dreams of treasures, Evelyn of validation for her craft, and both of fame and fortune. The warden (Omid Djalili) dreams of riches and allows them to buy the freedom of the bemused O'Connell in the nick of time. O'Connell, sure he is about to die, startles Evelyn with a kiss. She is even more startled — and enchanted — when he arrives at the docks the following morning shaved, washed, trimmed, and extremely full of himself.

Journeying upriver, the party meets a group of American archaeologists bound for the same spot, led by Beni. During a quiet moment, Evelyn and O'Connell exchange information about Hamunaptra, and she is surprised that he is so well informed, for a treasure hunter. During the night, both parties are attacked by Hook (Carl Chase) and his men; the boat is destroyed, all their belongings, apart from the puzzle box rescued by Jonathan, are lost in the Nile, and the race is on to get to the city. O'Connell's group buys camels from a trader who also provides Evelyn with nomad clothes.

Both groups dash to Hamunaptra as the sun rises and find the eerie city in the crater of an extinct volcano. Great statues rise from the sand, ruins abound, and the doorways to the depths of the city are stuffed with sand. Evelyn collects the ancient mirrors so that they can have light when they find their way in. Arguments ensue about who digs where and our doughty band find themselves under a statue, where Evelyn feels they should find what they are looking for — the golden Book of Amun Ra. They find Imhotep's sarcophagus instead and discover that the puzzle box, when unlocked, makes the perfect key to unlock the mummy case. The Americans,

Brendan Fraser and Rachel Weisz prepare to face *The Mummy* (1999).

meantime, narrowly escape death by acid courtesy of an ancient booby trap, and the Warden, scavenging for gemstones, liberates a scarab beetle that burrows into his head and makes him kill himself. Jonathan suggests that Hamunaptra is cursed, but no one will listen. The following day they open the mummy case; the condition of the mummy is shocking, and the inside of the lid is torn with the occupant's frantic attempts to escape, and the bloody inscription, "Death is only the beginning."

The Americans have found a chest in the base of an Anubis statue — its translated contents warn them of a cursed undead; the rest of the Egyptian workforce run off when they hear it and even Beni is scared. The Americans feel, however, that they have the last laugh; they have beautiful canopic jars and a strange book while our heroes only have a rotting corpse. Evelyn, stung, tells them of Imhotep's importance, how he was mummified, and how, should he be resurrected, he would bring down the ten plagues of Egypt on the world. The group starts to talk about this before settling down for the night. Later, Evelyn borrows the strange book and begins to read aloud from it as Imhotep's mummy eyes open. The Egyptologist (Jonathan Hyde) awakens as she reads and screams at her not to say the words, but it is too late. Locusts invade the campsite and send them running into the underground temple for safety, where they are met by waves of chittering scarabs. Taking cover, Evelyn is parted from the rest of the group.

Burns (Tuc Watkins), separated from the other Americans, loses his glasses and thinks he has found a fellow countryman. Sadly, he has met Imhotep, who takes his eyes. Without Burns's glasses, he mistakes Evelyn for Anck Su Namun; when he tries to speak to her, it is evident that he has taken Burns's tongue as well. Fortunately, they others arrive and O'Connell blasts the mummy with an elephant gun. Escaping, they run into the Medjai, led by Ardeth Bey, who tells them exactly what they are up against. Beni, still trapped in the city, meets Imhotep, and by accident stumbles on a language — Hebrew — that Imhotep understands. To save his life, he becomes Imhotep's servant.

O'Connell, having got his party back to Cairo, suggests leaving. Evelyn wants to stay and fight. The Americans are also planning to leave, but Burns is revisited by Imhotep and Beni. Imhotep absorbs Burns to aid his regeneration. Outside, the natives are wailing because the plague of blood has arrived. O'Connell realizes that this means the mummy has followed them, and they face him, powerless. The regeneration has produced a muscular corpse, and O'Connell's shooting of it has no effect. Evelyn's cat, however, repels the mummy, who vanishes in a swirling sandstorm.

As Evelyn and the survivors discuss the tragedy with Ardeth Bey and the curator, the sun goes into eclipse. Leaving Evelyn safely locked in her room, Jonathan and O'Connell go in search of the Egyptologist, but find Beni, who is looking for the Book of the Dead. Beni warns that Imhotep wants the Book and Evelyn so that he can resurrect Anck Su Namun. Outside, Imhotep catches the Egyptologist and regains another canopic jar. He unleashes the plague of flies with a hideous scream. He regenerates some more when he captures and kills Henderson (Stephen Dunham), and oozes into Evelyn's room as a stream of sand.

O'Connell and Jonathan burst in as a rotting Imhotep kisses a horrified Evelyn. O'Connell uses the cat to drive the mummy away again and Imhotep once more becomes the sandstorm. As our heroes are driving to the museum, Imhotep unleashes boils and sores on the population and turns the crowd into zombies chanting his name. Evelyn is busy attempting to translate hieroglyphs that will tell her the whereabouts of the Book of Amun Ra. Discovering that it is in the base of the statue of Horus back at Hamunaptra, they attempt to leave the city, but are caught by the mob. Imhotep uses the final American survivor to complete his regeneration.

Imhotep (Arnold Vosloo) takes to the street in *The Mummy* (1999).

Trapped, Evelyn agrees to go with Imhotep to save the others but he betrays her, and they only survive by the noble death of the curator.

To get to Hamunaptra quickly they need the services of a World War I air ace, Winston Havelock (Bernard Fox). Ardeth Bey and Jonathan, strapped to the wings, with O'Connell as copilot, Havelock races across the desert. Imhotep sends a raging sandstorm to kill them but is distracted by Evelyn. Our heroes escape except for Havelock, who dies the hero's death he had always craved. The men search for the Horus statue as Evelyn is forced underground by Imhotep.

Jonathan is rescued by O'Connell cutting a burrowing scarab out of his flesh; it tries to return and O'Connell blasts it to kingdom come. Imhotep has resumed the ritual he began three thousand years before. Beni is loading treasures onto a camel, but keeps coming back for more. Using Anck Su Namun's desiccated organs, Imhotep frees his mummified priests and the undead guards of the temple to destroy the humans. Nothing, it seems, can stop them. In the nick of time they find the golden book and blow a hole in the wall with their remaining stick of dynamite to escape. Evelyn, chained to the altar, watches the ritual helplessly. The mummy of Anck Su Namun comes to life beside her, and Imhotep prepares to stab Evelyn's heart to complete the restoration of his love. Jonathan bursts in with the Book of Amun Ra, unable to open it because Imhotep has the key. He is not as practiced as Evelyn at hieroglyphs either, and has trouble translating whilst also avoiding Imhotep and the priests. Whilst he creates this diversion, O'Connell frees Evelyn. A battle ensues for control of the mummified Soldiers-of-Death, Jonathan barely winning. O'Connell tries to evade the onslaught and Evelyn is pursued by a murderous Anck Su Namun, who means to use the sacrificial knife on her to complete the ritual. The moment it seems Imhotep has won, Jonathan completes the translation and the soldiers tear Anck Su Namun's mummy apart. Imhotep, mad with rage and grief, grabs the book from Jonathan and appears unperturbed by O'Connell slicing off his arm. Repairing himself, he does not notice that Jonathan has stolen back the key that he and his sister use to open the book, whilst O'Connell takes a beating.

Finding the passage she needs, Evelyn calls up a vortex; from it comes Anubis in a golden chariot. He takes Imhotep's soul away, leaving the priest vulnerable at last. Evelyn tells O'Connell the now mortal Imhotep can be killed. O'Connell impales him on a sword and the body falls into the seething bog that surrounds the altar. As he sinks, he says something in the ancient tongue. Evelyn translates, "Death ... is only the beginning." In Seti's treasure room, Beni accidentally trips the switch that will cause the city to sink into the sands. Beni is trapped with the treasure, the darkness, and the sounds of thousands of approaching scarab beetles. The others escape, with Jonathan bewailing their losses. In the saddle bags of the camel, though, is the gleam of gold.

Lauded as one of the Summer blockbusters, *The Mummy* had an almost simultaneous release on both side of the Atlantic. Originally publicized as a remake of the Karloff movie, it was reintroduced as "inspired by" the classic in the press. Having cost some $80 million, it drew similar reviews in Europe and the U.S.

"*The Mummy* veers alarmingly from kiddie horror to lowest-common-denominator comedy with such breathtaking crassness that the chopping and changing tone becomes the scariest thing about it.... Frankly, Hammer did this sort of thing a lot better and far less expensively" (Alan Jones, *Starburst* #251).

"Ms. Namun makes an unforgettable entrance barely wearing what looks like one of Cher's old Oscar frocks," wrote Jim Byerley for *HBO Film Review*. "It may be the most expensive mummy movie ever ... but as directed by Stephen Sommer, *The Mummy* ... is far from the most memorable." While

Roger Ebert of the *Chicago Sun Times* wrote, "There is hardly a thing I can say in its favor, except that I was cheered by nearly every minute of it." Walter Addiego in the *San Francisco Examiner* notes the film has "Indiana Jones pretensions.... An ancient Hollywood curse says that old movies with marketable titles are forever doomed to be remade as mediocre, wannabe blockbusters ... tired as a two-day-old sandwich ... looks derivative."

Andrew O'Hehir in *Salon* magazine remarked, "Despite his studly physique Brendan Fraser isn't enough of an action hero to keep *The Mummy* from unraveling ... if you prefer movies where it seems like somebody involved might have given a crap, skip it." *Time Magazine*'s Richard Schickel called it, "hopelessly overwrought and deeply dopey." Author Bob Madison, on the other hand, commented, "Don't believe the bad press.... The only problem with *The Mummy* is that it is not violent enough for contemporary horror films and too innocent for action pictures. It is also funny without ever descending into camp and incredibly stylish ... a true delight."

Perhaps these views actually diagnose the problem — the film tries to be too many things to too wide an audience. From a personal point of view, both the authors enjoyed it immensely as a blockbuster movie and spectacle. Neither of us found it as fulfilling as the movie we had been led to believe from all the shooting publicity we were going to see. A remake of the Karloff original would have been bearable — we know so much more about Ancient Egypt than the audiences of the thirties did; the color and the technical effects would lend themselves to a sumptuous remake. *No one* in the original movie intentionally made us laugh — indeed it is only the slightly outdated acting methods that draw a smile now. The story is as powerful as ever; one's emotions are brought into play by the implacable creature who has waited so long for his heart's desire that he will allow nothing to stop him. We believe the reason there were so many howls of derision or anger was that people were expecting the millennium to end with a proper horror movie centered on a mummy.

The splendid cast, headed by Brendan Fraser, John Hannah, and Rachel Weisz turned in gutsy performances. Undoubtedly, there will be more Rick O'Connell movies; he played the young American with all the charm, wit, and style of Errol Flynn in *The Adventures of Robin Hood*. John Hannah, better known in Britain as a dramatic actor, showed remarkable comic timing and talent. Ms. Weisz's Evelyn was a perfect *Boys' Own Paper* heroine, and very easy on the eyes. But the finished product did not draw one back to the cinema again and again, as we had hoped. It did, however, make a vast amount of money, making a sequel inevitable if not necessarily required viewing.

All the talents of ILM, beautifully detailed sets and artifacts, wonderful locations, terrific costumes and the best technical support imaginable should have given us a movie to be enthralled by as well as entertained. And why go to the trouble of an Egyptology consultant when he's not allowed to stop the voice-over intoning "Thebes!" just as the camera has panned past the pyramids and sphinx (several hundred miles apart, no less!) or having *five* canopic jars when every history student from high school upwards can tell you there are only ever four, or having books with covers and pages ... and so on. Dr. Stuart Smith must be so chagrined.

Our "mole" in the Egyptology Department of The British Museum tells us that the department members took in this movie on a group outing. Reportedly they spent the time muttering to each other over the mistranslated subtitles and the mistakes in the archaeology — but had a good time, for all that!

The Eternal (1999, Trimark Pictures Inc.)

Released on video 2000 High Fliers Video Distribution Ltd.; 91 minutes; Color

Credits: Written and Directed: Michael Almereyda; Casting: Billy Hopkins, Suzanne Smith, Kerry Barden, Jennifer McNamara; Music Supervisor: Barry Cole for Clear Music; Music: Simon Fisher Turner; Costume Designer: Prudence Moriarty; Production Designer: Ginger Tougas; Film Editors: Steve Hamilton, Tracy Granger; Director of Photography: Jim Denault; Coproducers: Jay Polstein, Amy Hobby; Executive Producer: Laurie Parker; Producers: Mark Amin, David L. Bushell. Featuring "Johnnywas" performed by Stiff Little Fingers

Cast: Alison Elliott (Nora); Jared Harris (Jim); Christopher Walken (Uncle); Lois Smith (Mrs. Ferriter); Karl Geary (Nora's son)

In this film the mummy is a Druid witch whose body has been preserved in an Irish peat bog. Alison (*The Spitfire Grill*) Elliott is Nora, an alcoholic New Yorker who returns to her native land with her husband Jim (Jared Harris) and son to stay with her grandmother and her Uncle Bill (Christopher Walken). Her uncle just happens to have the bog-mummy in his basement, and the witch uses Nora to try to regain her life and power. In a clever twist on the usual plot—heroine as the reincarnated lost love of the mummy—the heroine *is* the reincarnated mummy. *The Eternal* uses its moody Irish setting to slowly build into a bloody film with one good Nora and one bad Nora roaming round the family mansion's dark and echoing corridors. Almereyda seems to have reinvented the mummy movie with the same zest with which he reworked vampirism in the stylish *Nadja*. Sadly, it went straight to video, though it is thought that the version released is cut down from the previews shown. A lot of the plot seems to have stayed in Almereyda's mind—or ended up on the cutting floor—and the result is a disjointed opus that is quite hard to follow. Hitchcock once made the point that a puzzled or questioning audience was not fulfilling its role, *viz.*, emoting. This is definitely a case in point.

The All New Adventures of Laurel and Hardy: For Love or Mummy (1999)

Two actors who bear a passing resemblance to the great comic duo play their nephews in this horror spoof. Its only purpose appears to be to prove that remaking *Psycho* was not the world's worst idea, but it does achieve three remarkable feats. One: It offends the vast army of Laurel and Hardy fans. Two: It offends horror movie aficianados. Three: It achieves the death of the revival of the mummy movie in the same year it began! This abomination went straight to satellite and cable TV, where it passes a wet afternoon when nothing else is on.

Bram Stoker's Legend of the Mummy 2 (2000, Rapid Heart Pictures) Third Millennium Distribution Ltd.; 85 minutes; Color

Credits: Screenplay: Matthew Jason Walsh; Story: Matthew Jason Walsh, David Decoteau ; Coproduced: Michael Catland; Produced: David Silberg, Sam Irwin, David Decoteau ; Directed: David Decoteau; Casting: Robert McDonald CSA, Perry Billington CSA; Music Composed and Conducted: Jared Depasquale; Studio Design: Chris M. Jacobson; Costume Designer: Edward Reno Hibbs; Special Character Makeup Effects Designed and Produced: Christopher Bergshneider, Jeffrey S. Farley

Cast: Jeff Peterson, Trent Latia, Ariana Albright, Russell Richardson, Michelle Erikson, Brenda Blondell, Michael Lutz, Christopher Cullen

Six archaeology students are spending the summer at an isolated compound with their college professor. Together they are working on an exciting discovery: an ancient mummy that has been found in a ruined temple. Little do they realize that the mummy was the evil servant of an ancient rain god and that one of their group has the power to bring it back to life to wreak it's master's deadly revenge. After the silent curse of centuries, the creature plans to unleash its evil power.

Someone had a bad idea after watching *Bram Stoker's Legend of the Mummy* (which was not a bad film): a sequel! Except that it bears no resemblance to the plot of the first offering and the makers probably meant "Too" and not "2." A group of annoying, oversexed airheads masquerading as archaeology students are systematically put to death by the shambling bandaged one, and after half an hour you are rooting for *him*! As per the formula, the virgin who does not succumb to the blandishments of her male co-eds holds the key to their (depleted) survival. As a spoof it might have been mildly amusing, but these film-makers meant it.

The Mummy Returns (2001, Alphaville Films (US) Imhotep Productions UIP) 130 minutes (U.K.); 129 minutes (U.S.); Color: DeLuxe Sound mix: DTS/Dolby Digital/ SDDS; Cert: 12 (U.K.); PG: 13 (U.S.)

Credits: Written and Directed: Stephen Sommers; Produced: Sean Daniel; Exec. Producers: Bob Ducsay, Don Zepfel; Original Music: Alan Silvestri; Cinematography: Adrian Biddle; Film Editing: Bob Ducsay, Kelly Matsumoto; Casting: Joanne Colbert, Kate Dowd; Production Designer: Allan Cameron; Art Directors: Giles Masters, Tony Reading; Costume Design: John Bloomfield; Makeup: Tricia Cameron (key hair), Nick Dudman (special makeup effects), Alison Seaton (key makeup); Production Supervisor: Jo Burn; 2nd unit Director Cliff Lanning; Art Dept. Coordinator: Chloe Barbier; Sound Design: Leslie Shatz; Sound Editor: Valerie Davidson; Music Editors: John & Sienna Finklea; Sound Effects Editor: Jon Olive; Special Effects Supervisor: Neil Corbould; Animatronic Model Design: Chris Barton; Live action creature effects supervisor: Nich Dudman; Visual Effects Supervisor: John Berton; Industrial Light and Magic Staff: Ann McColgan, Aaron Muszalski, Seth Rosenthal, Megan Upcraft et al.; Stunt Dept. Coordinator: Greg Campbell; Stunt Coordinator: Steve Dent; Jeweller: Martin Adams; Production Coordinator: Judy Britten; Director of Photography: Harvey Harrison; Film Editor: Kevin Holt; Supervising Armourer: Richard Hooper

Cast: Brendan Fraser (Rick O'Connell); Rachel Weisz (Evelyn Carnahan O'Connell/Princess Nefertiri); John Hannah (Jonathan Carnahan); Arnold Vosloo (High Priest Imhotep); Oded Fehr (Ardeth Bey); Patricia Velasquez (Meela/Anck Su Namun); Freddie Boath (Alex O'Connell); Alun Armstrong (Curator); Dwayne 'the Rock' Johnson (the Scorpion King); Adewale Akinnuoye-Agbaje (Loch-Nah); Shaun Parker (Izzy); Bruce Byron (Red); Joe Dixon (Jacques); Tom Fisher (Spivey); Aharon Ipale (Pharaoh Seti I); Quill Roberts (Shafek); Donna Air (showgirl); Trevor Lovell (Mountain of Flesh)

In pre–Dynastic Egypt, a great warrior, the Scorpion King (Dwayne 'the Rock' Johnson) trades his soul to Anubis for an invincible army following a crushing defeat. To save his new acolyte, Anubis creates the oasis of Ahm Shere in the desert as a power base for the new army and its grave when he consigns the Scorpion King to languish in the bowels of the Pyramid of Gold awaiting release in some distant future.

In 1933, Rick O'Connell (Brendan Fraser) is again in Egypt with his wife Evelyn (Rachel Weisz) and their son Alex (Freddie Boath). Alex is both braver than his father and cleverer than his mother but as mischievous as any young boy left to his own devices on a dig in a ruined temple. Rick and Evie are excavating the lower reaches of the temple when Evie experiences another in a series of waking dreams she has been having about life at the court of Seti I. Because of the dreams she knows how old doors are unlocked, and she finds a casket bearing the insignia of the Scorpion King which contains the Bracelet of Anubis. The removal of the casket precipitates the flooding of the corridors, and the O'Connells only just make it out in time. They do not know that Alex has been repelling marauders while they have been busy, and none of them are aware that Meela (Patricia Velasquez), the curator (Alan Armstrong) and Lock-Nah (Adewale Akinnuoye-Agbaje) have recovered the resin-coated corpse of Imhotep (Arnold Vosloo) from Hamunaptra. Only Ardeth Bey (Oded Fehr), faithful leader of the Medjai, is ever watchful. He hears that the O'Connells have the bracelet and are on their way home to London, whence the other party must go if they are to steal the artifact and resurrect the Mummy.

Home in England, the O'Connells are not yet unpacked when Evie tries to persuade

Rick to go in search of Ahm Shere and the Army of Anubis. Resorting to smooch tactics to get her way with her besotted spouse, she doesn't notice Alex fiddling around with the casket, finding the bracelet and slipping it on. On contact with his arm it acts like a projector and shows him the way to the oasis and the Pyramid of Gold, but fearing parental retribution, he doesn't tell his parents what has happened. Shortly after, the house is attacked and the villains flee with the casket and a sceptre that Jonathan regards as his own. Surprisingly, Ardeth Bey arrives to help during the attack. As the party recovers, Ardeth Bey tells Rick that his son, now ruefully showing the grown-ups the bracelet, has seven days to reach the Pyramid of Gold or die. Seeking answers at the British Museum, the O'Connells leave Alex with his uncle in the car while they break in with Ardeth Bey. Inside Evie is captured and prepared by Meela as the reviving sacrifice for Imhotep. Meela appears to have a hatred of Evie that defies explanation. During the revival ceremony, Rick rescues Evie and Imhotep is left desiccated and depleted but powerful enough to send his minions after them. The O'Connell party is chased all over London in a double-decker bus, pursued by mummies who unfortunately capture Alex. Ardeth Bey comforts his friends with the knowledge that Imhotep cannot hurt Alex while he wears the bracelet.

To Egypt where Rick calls in a favor from his old buddy Izzy (Shawn Parker) who has a hot air balloon with a boat as its basket. The party set off in pursuit of Alex and Imhotep who are traveling by train. Clever Alex is terrified by Imhotep's growing power as he consumes the lives of his helpers. Meela is revealed as the reincarnation of Anck Su Namun, as much in love with the power of Imhotep as she was when she died for him after Seti's murder. And now we see why the guards came when they did: They were called by the Princess Nefertiri, daughter of Pharaoh and keeper of the Bracelet of Anubis, reincarnated as Evie O'Connell. Even Rick has some part to play from the ancient tale as Bey finds a Medjai tattoo on O'Connell's forearm. The nearer to Ahm Shere they get, the stronger Evie's memories of the past become.

As Imhotep gets stronger, Alex plots to escape, and when it proves impossible, he leaves a trail for his parents to follow. Despite all the obstacles Imhotep puts in their path, he cannot stop the O'Connells from recovering Alex and getting him into the Pyramid of Gold in the nick of time on the seventh day, although he manages to sever the link the Medjai have with Ardeth Bey as they track the Mummy across Egypt. Having helped rescue Alex, Bey rejoins the Medjai to fight the Army of Anubis. The Medjai are outnumbered and painfully human against a hellish force that seems to have no end. Astonishingly, they beat the vanguard of the Army, but then they see the bulk of the force approaching from afar and prepare to die fighting.

In the pyramid, Rick is relieved to have saved Alex's life only to be heartbroken by the death of Evie. As he goes to wreak vengeance on Imhotep and Anck Su Namun, he realizes that there is a greater threat: The Scorpion King is not a legend but lives as a monster. Imhotep is enraged that the gods strip him of his powers to fight his hideous opponent. Rick just wants them all dead as he sees no reason to go on without Evie. In the precincts, however, Alex is hypothesizing with his uncle about the possible power of the book Imhotep has brought to Ahm Shere, and Jonathan recognizes it at once. Using it, Alex recalls the soul of his mother, with a little help from his uncle.

Inside, the battle is not going well. As he fights, Rick realizes that the only weapon that will kill the Scorpion king is the sceptre that they lost at the beginning of their journey—a sceptre that can become a magic lance. Through many tribulations, he finally grabs it and hurls it at the monster's heart. It falls, as does the Army battling the Medjai, who get covered in dust from the crumbling corpses of their enemies.

The revived Evie (now fully aware of her royal status) and Anck Su Namun engage in battle as they had done centuries before, and Evie prevails. As she does, the edifice begins to crumble and all must flee. Imhotep falls into a fiery trench, begging his love to rescue him. She, however, flees the destruction and leaves him to his fate. With a sigh, he releases his grip on the crumbling edge of the trench and plummets. Anck Su Namun is trapped in the falling rubble. Jonathan, Evie, Rick and Alex climb the pyramid as the oasis is sucked beneath the sands, and they are rescued in the nick of time by Izzy. Jonathan almost loses his life by grabbing the diamond tip of the pyramid, but they are all safe in the flying-boat and the world is once more a safe place in which to live. Evie, holding her husband close, asks, "Shall I tell you what Heaven's like?" to which he replies, "Later!"

Colossal pre-release publicity heralded the arrival of *The Mummy Returns*. The reprise of the star cast was trumpeted, the even-better-than-first-time-round computer wizardry was lauded, and Stephen Somers was oft quoted as saying with delight, "If you liked the first one I'm just going to blow your socks off with this!" So it is surprising that the release of the film was damned with faint praise. Erik Childress said, "Not as deep and dark as the Indiana Jones trilogy, but still slightly entertaining" in an Internet review. Bob Bloom of the Journal and Courier, Lafayette, thought, "The Mummy's Return is the desperate comedian who machine guns joke after joke because he needs a fix of laughter like a junkie needs his fix of heroin. *The Mummy Returns* is a fast-food movie, you view it, are entertained and leave. It leaves no lasting impression. Nothing profound. Nothing deep." Brian Webster in the *Apollo Review Guide* commented, "Lovers of the original will probably like this CGI-laden spectacle too. This isn't enjoyable ... because it's contrived, over-blown and does nothing with the characters. To call *The Mummy Returns* phony is kind of like calling *The Poseidon Adventure* wet but it's still a point worth making." Issue 122 of *Heat* magazine in the U.K. responded with, "The whole gang from the 1999 blockbuster is back, except this time with more villains, more action and a whole lot more CGI. A bit of a mess—but an entertaining one, as the monster box-office attests." And *Empire* (June 2001) says, "Somers now has his chance in the spotlight; and as long as he keeps the pace at whip-cracking speed and the tone light, it looks like the Mummy's return will be a resoundingly triumphant one."

Certainly there is something for everyone. Weisz and the model-turned-actress Velasquez are easy on the eye in ancient bikinis, fighting in a hypnotic blend of several martial arts, and indeed worked immensely hard to do most of the fights themselves. The lovers of CGI effects have a veritable feast—the return of Imhotep's fighting mummies, the new pygmy mummies of Ahm Shere pulling victims down into the long grass for all the world like Jurassic Park II, the flying boat reminiscent of Baron Munchausen ... one could go on. There are, of course, delightful touches: the *homage* to Universal's greatest Mummy movie in the sequences where Evie and Meela revive memories of the past; the moment where Alex takes the same steps as his uncle had in *Mummy* I in deciphering the glyphs; the appearance of sinister Nubian Lock-Nah as an agent of Imhotep, again as in the Karloff movie. The most moving sequence in the film is Oded Fehr's face as he prepares to face the invincible army and certain death, which brings a chill to the soul. Entertaining though this film undoubtedly is, however, it is too derivative. All the links with past movies provide a counterpoint to the film and its theme of eternal cycles. And fans of Elizabeth Peters find the married, tactile O'Connors and their clever son just too much like her wonderful Emersons and their precocious son Ramses. Somers has produced a terrific summer-break movie, spending twice the budget of his first opus. It is gorgeous on the eye, engaging (however briefly) on the mind and worth a couple of hours of anyone's time, but in the last analysis, it doesn't touch your heart. So many people worked so hard, so many fields of the movie industry poured themselves into this effort, but you come away wanting more. Initially, the plan was to keep the action in London. Dear old University College became the British Museum just as it did in *The Awakening* many years before — the cranes were up outside the real one to build the Great Court and would have been too difficult to disguise. But the urge to go for the spectacle won out, and we ended up with a soulless movie despite all the effort. What a pity.

Some final thoughts on the mummy on film: The great majority of mummy movie fans would be thrilled if *someone* would put their creative talents into a real, heart stopping, serious horror movie featuring a mummy. The money-holders appear to believe we are too sophisticated, too fixated on CGI effects, and too blockbuster focused to appreciate a *proper* mummy movie. Please believe us, we are not!

Dare we hope, as the trade papers tell us, that 2002 will see *Belphegor, The Phantom of the Louvre* starring Julie Christie and Sophie Marceau? According to *Film Review* #606 (June 2001), "Based on a cult French TV series from the Sixties, Belphegor traces the haunting of the Louvre by a tormented Egyptian spirit. Marceau will play Belphegor and Christie is Glenda Spencer, an Egyptologist brought in to investigate a mummy newly discovered in the depths of the world's biggest museum." And if this doesn't come off ... will somebody out there do Anne Rice's *Mummy*. Please?

III

The Mummy in Novels, Short Stories and Children's Books

The study of Ancient Egypt, its people, and their customs and beliefs, is part of many countries' history curricula. The revelation of the lives of ancient folks is thrilling, maddening, and often shocking to those of the twenty-first century, considering the ancient world's focus on empire building and its racist attitudes. The actual practice of Egyptology, however, is a vibrant, ongoing science, adding immeasurably to the current knowledge base and understanding of a whole raft of disciplines.

So, too, is the New Age interest in and study of ancient beliefs and practices. Alongside these two defined lines, a peripheral literature has evolved—the mummy story, whose history is longer than the average reader might think. Herodotus retells the story of Khaemwaset, eleventh son of Ramesses the Great in the 19th Dynasty, and his encounter with sentient mummies. A hundred years before the discovery of Tutankhamun there were stories about mummies, some inspired by ancient tales, but most probably generated by the explorers who had filled the exhibition cases of Western museums. William Bayle Bernard wrote a farce that remained popular throughout the 1830s and 40s called *The Mummy; or, the Liquor of Life!* But the earliest is probably Jane Webb's three-volume story, *The Mummy; A Tale of the Twenty Second Century*, appearing in 1827. While mostly a somewhat whimsical tale about the technological developments of the future and the place of women and their liberation in that time, it has some powerful moments when the heroes enter a pyramid and watch the resurrection of the pharaonic mummy.

In 1832, the *New York Evening Mirror* published an anonymous piece about galvanic resuscitation entitled *Letter from a Revived Mummy*, which is thought to have inspired Edgar Allan Poe. In 1840, Theophile Gautier set the genre off with *Le Pied de Momie* (in English, *The Mummy's Foot*; also known as *Princess Hermonthis*). This story, incidentally, provided the idea for one of the earliest mummy movies, exmagician Walter Booth's *The Haunted Curiosity Shop* in 1902. Gautier also wrote, and is more famous for, *Le Roman de la Momie* (*The Romance of the Mummy*), published in 1857. The prologue

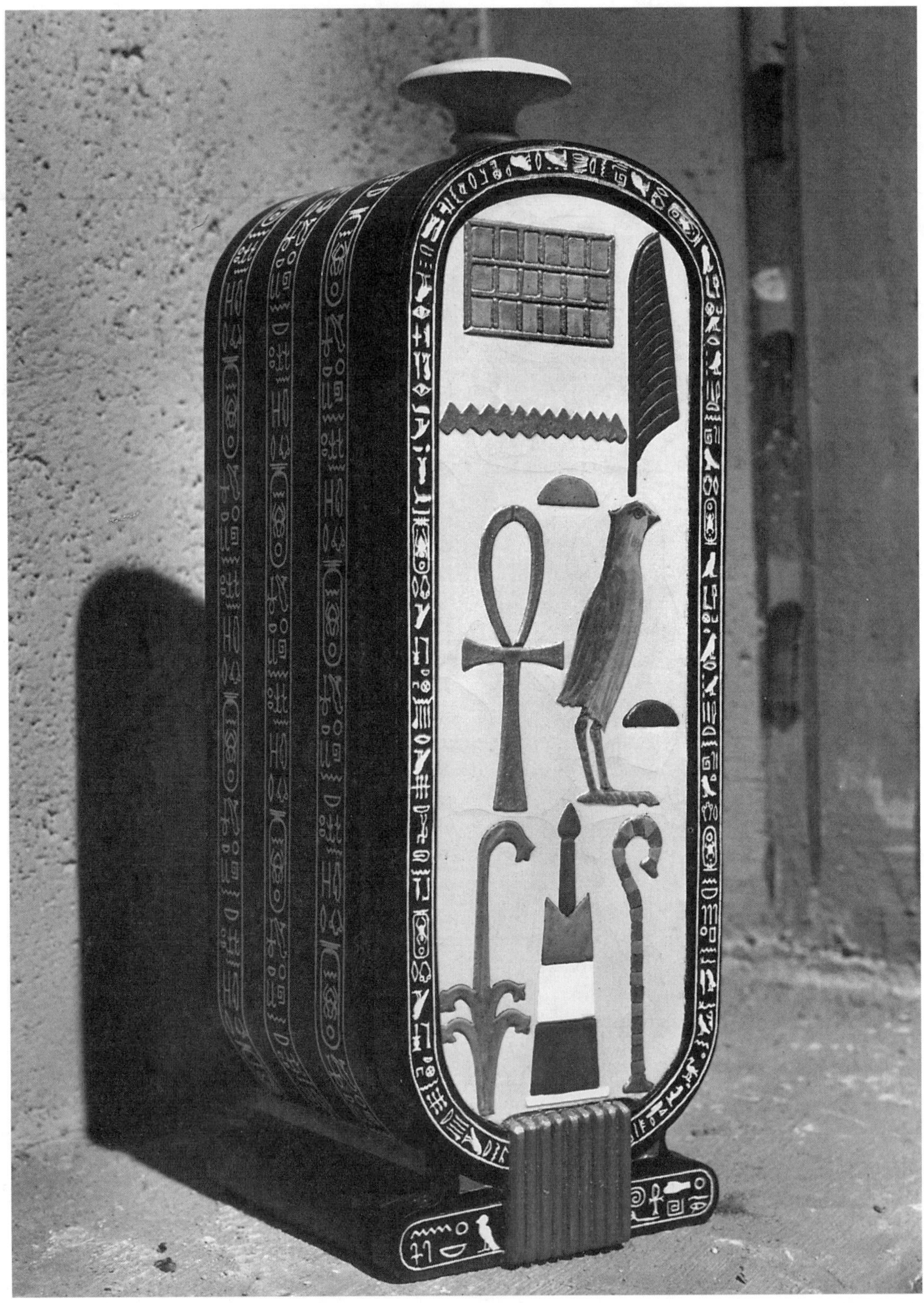

The Scroll of Life for *The Mummy* (Hammer/Universal, 1959).

is so uncannily like the real discovery of Tutankhamun's tomb sixty five years later that, as Christopher Frayling puts it, "It goes some way to explaining why Carter's finds were treated by the public as an exotic mix of fact and fantasy" (Frayling, 1992).

Then Poe took up his satirical pen in 1845 to scribe *Some Words With a Mummy,* and so begins the collection of mummy stories through the decades to the present day.

Khaemwaset and the Mummies (Anon., 19th Dynasty Ancient Egypt, Retold by Herodotus)

Ramesses the Great, during the course of his exceptionally long reign, married many times and had a vast harem of concubines. In his endeavors to establish his dynasty, which was comparatively new when he ascended the throne, he fathered 198 sons and 106 daughters. Because he attained great age, many of his sons went to judgment before him and were the reason for one of the most fascinating tombs in the Valley of the Kings—KV5—currently being excavated by Kent Weeks and his team.

Khaemwaset was the eleventh son born to Ramesses. He was intelligent and perceptive—acknowledged as possibly the most gifted of Pharaoh's offspring. In furtherance of his gifts, Pharaoh appointed him High Priest of Ptah in Memphis. Working in the temple, the young prince did not disappoint his father's hopes, and grew in stature, knowledge, and talent, developing all the while an insatiable thirst for knowledge that occasionally led him astray and an understandable arrogance in his own worth. Yet he was also a kind and thoughtful man.

As the years passed, Ramesses chose a bride for his son, and her gentle nature provided the counterpoint to his avid scholarship. The arrival of children, much loved by parents and grandparents alike, also added to Khaemwaset's joys. Only one goal remained for the prince whose knowledge of the world, of the gods, of nature, and of the magic arts had won him admiration and respect throughout the kingdom; he burned to have occult knowledge and to attain the powers of the gods.

Most of Khaemwaset's time was spent in study in the library of the temple, which contained the accumulated knowledge of the kingdom. In an ancient scroll, cracked and virtually illegible, Khaemwaset found a clue that could help him achieve his final goal. He read of a magician called Neferkaptah who owned a spell book whose power was so potent that the mysteries of the universe obeyed his will. To his surprise, Khaemwaset read that Neferkaptah was a prince, son of a long forgotten Pharaoh whose wife, Ahwere, had been chosen by his father and who had borne a son, Mer-ib, who had been mooted as a future Pharaoh because his own father loved learning too much and did not crave earthly power. Khaemwaset had found a mirror soul.

On reading further, the young prince discovered that Neferkaptah had also trawled the ancient wisdom to find the power of the gods; that one day he had been so engrossed in his studies that he had forgotten his holy obligations to Thoth, in whose temple he served. Towards dusk on that fateful day, Neferkaptah had heard someone laughing behind him and had found a very old but vigorous looking man in the shadows. The man had mocked his studies and revealed that he knew the resting place of the Book of Thoth, whereby all things could be ruled. Neferkaptah agreed, after bargaining, to finance the preparations for, and burial of the old man and the setting up of an endowment for mortuary priests in exchange for the location of the book.

With Pharaoh's permission, Neferkaptah set out for Koptos with his wife and son to acquire the book, and after many trials, he held it in his hand. He read the contents and became godlike in his knowledge and power and immediately shared the book with his wife and son, who also changed. But by then Thoth knew that his book had been stolen, and he exacted a terrible vengeance. When

Ecclesiastical Chair and Stool. ***The Curse of the Mummy's Tomb*** (Hammer/Columbia, 1964).

Pharaoh arrived at Koptos he found all three members of his family dead and had them entombed with the book and a solemn warning never to disturb it again.

Having read the history, Khaemwaset worked feverishly to discover the location of the tomb. It took many months before he was successful, and then he called on his half-brother Anhureru to help him. Leaving their families, the brothers secretly left on their adventure. They found the tomb, and after three days of hard work, they were able to enter it.

They were surprised to find the burial chamber flooded with a radiance that came from the book which lay on a dais between the two largest sarcophagi; but as Khaemwaset reached to take it, the lids slid back and the mummies sat up. Anhureru was petrified, though Khaemwaset kept himself under control. Neferkaptah spoke, "Rash intruders, who are you that dares to disturb the eternal rest of Neferkaptah and his kin?"* (Dee, 1998). When Khaemwaset asserted that as a son of the king he had godly blood in his veins and that his patron was the god Ptah, the mummies just laughed at him. Neferkaptah succinctly told the prince what he was about to do and questioned his wisdom and judgment in the matter. Khaemwaset replied that he had had intelligence enough to learn of the scroll, and to find the location of the tomb and that he felt it pointed to his fitness to own the Book of Thoth and the wisdom and knowledge it contained. Neferkaptah warned, "I gave my earthly life for the magic of the scroll. Its power destroyed my mortal being, and those of my wife and child. Do you think that we would part with it so easily?" But Khaemwaset insisted that he should take the book, and so they decided to play a game of senet to choose who should keep the book. "The sorry cadavers of Neferkaptah's wife and child gathered the board and pieces with many a creak and groan from their rotting joints, setting the game between them. Thus was semblance given of a game between life and death." This suited the young prince who was an acknowledged master of the game — but he soon discovered that so was his opponent! Losing the game, he asked to change the rules to a series of games to be played until one player cried off. As he agreed, Neferkaptah won the first game and struck Khaemwaset with the gaming board. The young prince found himself unable to move, ankle deep in the sandy floor while Ahwere and Mer-ib reset the board for the next game.

Neferkaptah won the next game and again struck Khaemwaset, who sank up to his knee joints in the sand. As the mummies set up the board again Khaemwaset called to his brother to go to Pharaoh for help. Brave Anhureru ran to his father, obtained an amulet to rescue his brother with and entered the tomb again to find only the head and right hand of his brother above the sand! As the scarab amulet encircled his head, the sandy floor pushed him out and Khaemwaset was able to grab the scroll. He plunged it under his clothes, extinguishing its light, and followed the shouts of his brother to safety. The voice of Neferkaptah followed him, "Foolish mortals, the book which you hold will bring nought but grief and misery to you and all your kin. I prophesy that you will bring it into the tomb of your own free will."

The princes returned to Memphis, but Khaemwaset was filled with nameless dread. Questioned by Pharaoh, he admitted that he had not read the scroll. Pharaoh suggested that he humbly return it, and the prince promised to think on the matter and pray for guidance.

A few days later, he encountered a beautiful woman in the grounds of the temple and became so overcome with lust that he forgot everything else in his life. The lady, Tabibu, was the daughter of a priest of Bast, and invited the young prince to her home where his passion could be subsided. Khaemwaset

**Quoted material in this story is taken from Jonathan Dee,* Chronicles of Ancient Egypt *(Collins and Brown, 1998).*

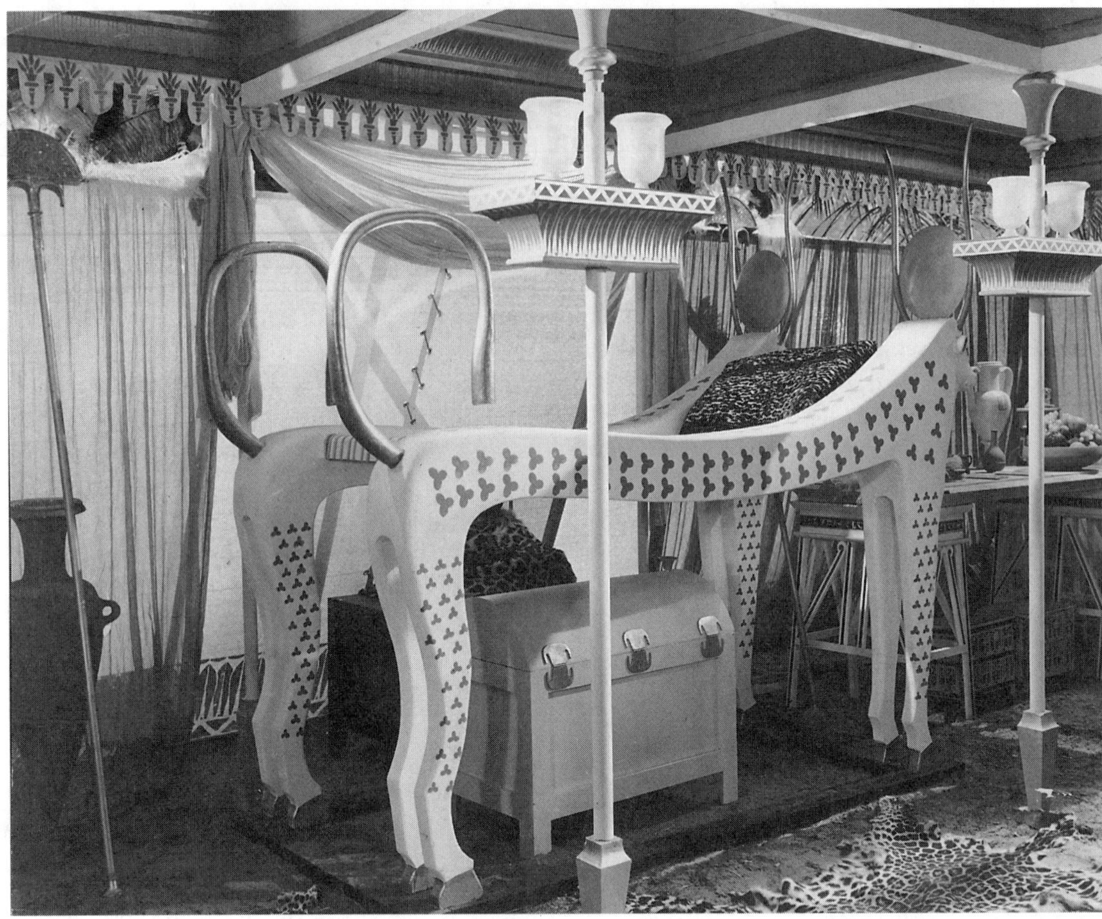

"Artifacts" from ***The Curse of the Mummy's Tomb*** **(Hammer/Columbia, 1964).**

shared his intentions with Anhureru, who was appalled by what his brother was about to do, but he could not change Khaemwaset's mind. However, when the prince arrived at Tabibu's house, she expected him to make her an official concubine and endow her with all his worldly goods. He agreed, and the documents were drawn up. Still she prevaricated — his brother and children had arrived and wished to see him. Tabibu persuaded Khaemwaset to prevail on his brother and the children to hand over all their wealth and property too, which he also did. But before she would bed him, her final demand was the death of his brother and children in case they should prove a danger to her. Stupid Khaemwaset agreed once more and ordered the executions, but as he tumbled into the bed-chamber his head swam and he found himself naked, travel-stained, and sweating on the open desert floor with the Book of Thoth near his hand. To his surprise, Pharaoh was there, too, and demanded an explanation.

Khaemwaset miserably confessed that he had given all his wealth to Tabibu, that of his brother and children too, and that worst of all, he had had them killed so that he could fulfill his passion. Pharaoh wryly replied that everyone was well and happy and awaiting Khaemwaset's return to Memphis. Khaemwaset's sense of shame now overcame his joy — all Pharaoh's men knew how stupid he had been. But Pharaoh called for clothes for the naked prince and sensibly suggested the he should return the scroll to the tomb immediately. Joyful that it had all been a dream, Khaemwaset again entered the tomb, surprised to find no evidence of any disturbance. Even so, he greeted his long-dead hosts warmly, and reverently replaced the scroll, asking forgiveness before bidding them farewell. As he walked to his father's chariot a huge sandstorm blew up, covering the entrance for all time. And in the sound of the wind, Neferkaptah had the last word, "Count yourself fortunate young prince that no further harm ensued from your theft of a book that is the property of the gods themselves."

Herodotus recorded many of the ancient stories of Egypt in his writings of his travels. Indeed, the Magic Book is the basis for hundreds of tales throughout the history of storytelling. Not surprising then that it should reemerge centuries later as one of the main "props" of stories of walking mummies. Hollywood was never backward in adopting good stories— especially when they were out of copyright!

The Mummy (by Jane Webb, 1827)

It is the intention of the authors to give the reader a flavor of examples of mummy stories that have been researched for the fiction part of this book. While the normal format would be flavor first, comment after, the sheer volume of Jane Webb's work precludes this approach.

Jane Webb was still a teenager when she wrote her book *The Mummy! A Tale of the Twenty-second Century*, which was published in 1827. At nineteen, penniless at the death of her father, and of genteel upbringing where the acquisition of a profession was a difficult task, she set out to emulate her contemporaries Ann Radcliffe, Mary Shelley, and Elizabeth Inchbold by writing a blockbuster novel.

There are three volumes of the tale — a potpourri of chills, thrills, romance, heroism, pseudoscience, and occultism together with a little scientific prophecy revolving around the premise of the revitalization of the mummy of Pharaoh Cheops, in 2126. If you have the stamina, the three volumes are an interesting read despite turgid prose, wooden characters, and unbelievable plot twists because of the ingenuous picture of a future feminist England. Apart from Cheops, the main characters are Dr. Entwerfen, a "clownish genius," manservant Gregory, and the gallant hero Edric.

This happy band make their way to Egypt where they determine to revive the body of Cheops to prove the efficiency of the Doctor's electrical reanimation machine. Having achieved their aim, Cheops makes off with their hot air balloon and they have to give chase. Cheops makes for England where he becomes involved in a challenge for the throne. Some six hundred pages later, he returns to Egypt and his pyramid, leaving England once more safe in the hands of a benevolent female monarch, providing a happy ending.

Everett Bleiler, a historian of early science fiction, has described the book as "a strange stew." In *The Arkham Sampler* (Spring 1949) Bleiler wrote, "It is the strange remnants of Frankenstein rehashed, where man is again earnestly adjured not to meddle scientifically with things beyond his power, where the mummy of Cheops, revived by unholy science, serves as does the monster in Frankenstein as an active albatross, throttling the dabbler." Jane Webb deserves to be better known today — all literary history records of her is that she married an admirer of her book — John Claudius Loudon — and devoted the rest of her life to writing books on gardening. Copies of her novel were very, very rare, until recently republished.

Edric and the Doctor, guided by Samuel, an elderly Arab guide, have penetrated the depths of Cheops's pyramid, and now stand by the side of his immense sarcophagus, surrounded by the air-dried mummified remains of his slaves and the mummy case of his confidant and prime minister.

> The doctor removed the lid, and shuddered as the crimson tinge of the everlasting lamp fell upon the hideous and distorted features thus suddenly exhibited to view. This sepulchral

> light, indeed, added unspeakable horror to the scene, and its peculiar glare threw such a wild and demoniac expression on the dark lines and ghastly lineaments of the mummies, that even the doctor felt his spirits depressed, and a supernatural dread creep over his mind as he gazed upon them.

Shaking off the feeling, they examine the tomb and the sarcophagus in detail. They cannot understand much of the details of the tomb but feel threatened. Nothing loathe, they look at the long-dead king.

> They both uttered an involuntary cry of astonishment, as the striking features of the mummy met their eyes ... calm, vindictive and concentrated hatred.... Awful, indeed, was the gloom that sat upon that brow, and bitter the sardonic smile that curled those haughty lips. All was perfect as though life still animated the form before them, and it had only reclined there to seek a short repose. The dark eyebrows, the thick raven hair which hung upon the forehead, and the snow-white teeth seen through the half-open lips, forbade the idea of death; whilst the fiend-like expression of the features made Edric shudder, as he recollected the purpose that brought him to the tomb, and he trembled at the thought of awakening such a fearful being from the torpor of the grave to all the renewed energies of life.

The Doctor is suddenly unsure and suggests they leave, but Edric grasps the equipment and begins to set up the machine.

> Innumerable folds of red and white linen, disposed alternately, swathed the gigantic limbs of the royal mummy; and upon his breast lay a piece of metal, shining like silver, and stamped with the figure of a winged globe. Edric attempted to remove this, but recoiled with horror, when he found it bend beneath his fingers with an unnatural softness; whilst, as the flickering light of the lamp fell upon the face of the mummy, he fancied its stern features relaxed into a ghastly laugh of scornful mockery.... [Edric] stood immovable, and gazing intently on the mummy, whose eyes had opened with the shock, and were now fixed on those of Edric, shining with supernatural luster.... The mummy's eyes still pursued him with their ghastly brightness; they seemed to possess the fabled fascination of those of the rattle-snake, and though he shrank from their gaze, they still glared horribly upon him.

But worse is yet to come. "Edric saw the mummy stretch out its withered hand, as though to seize him. He saw it rise gradually — he heard the dry, bony fingers rattle as it drew them forth — he felt its tremendous grip — human nature could bear no more — his senses were rapidly deserting him."

The everlasting lamps fail and all plunges to darkness. Edric faints clean away. Later, he is revived by the Doctor and they both hurry to escape the tomb. Having gained the blessed air and sunshine of the outdoors, they find that the mummy has stolen their balloon and escaped, watched in horror by Gregory the manservant. "The dried distorted features of the mummy looked yet more hideous than before, when animated by human passions, and his deep hollow voice, speaking in a language he [Gregory] did not understand, fell heavily upon his ear, like the groans of fiends."

We shall pursue him no longer...

The Mummy's Foot (by Theophile Gautier, 1840)

A young man enters a Paris curio shop, as is his custom, and after refusing the offer of swords, knives and other weaponry, decides on a marble foot — at least it looks like marble. Actually, explains the aged, odious dealer, it is a mummy's foot.

The young man buys the foot of Princess Hermonthis for five louis, to use as a paperweight. Inordinately proud of his purchase, he strides through the streets of Paris. "I considered," he muses, "as beneath contempt all those who did not possess as I did so notoriously Egyptian a paperweight, and it appeared to me that the proper business in the life of a sensible man was to have a mummy's foot on his writing table."

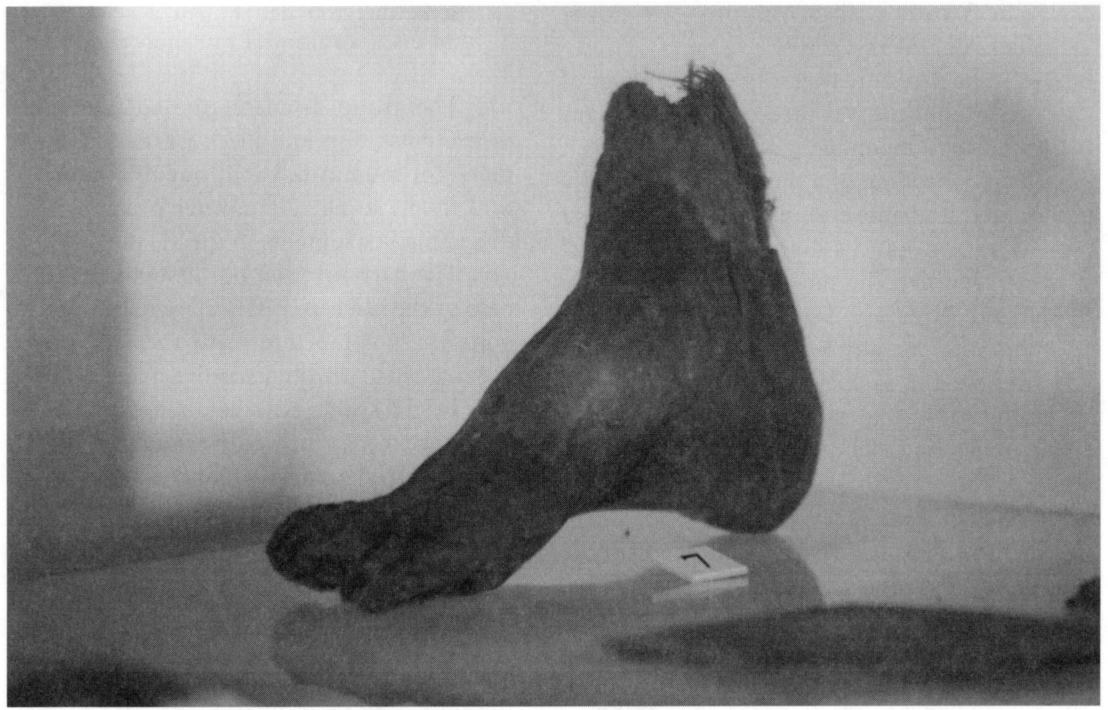

Gruesome souvenir of a nineteenth century trip to Egypt. (Courtesy Colin Cowie 1998).

He falls into a deep sleep and an even deeper dream. The foot, "instead of remaining quiet — as behooved a foot which had been embalmed for four thousand years — commenced to act in a nervous manner; contracted itself and leaped over the papers like a startled frog." The princess enters his rooms, hopping on one leg since she lacks a foot. She is beautiful, and round her neck is a beautiful green clay figure. She reaches for her foot which is hopping about the desk, and, at the young man's bidding, reattaches it.

Deeply grateful, she invites him to visit her father and other pharaohs in a huge temple. They do, and he asks the princess's father for her hand in marriage, since he has so kindly returned her foot. It is, however, the disparity of their ages that upsets Pharaoh and makes him refuse. "If you were even only two thousand years old," replied the ancient King, "I would willingly give you the Princess; but the disproportion is too great; and, besides, we must give our daughters husbands who will last well; you do not know how to preserve yourselves any longer, even those who died only fifteen centuries ago are already no more than a handful of dust; — behold! my flesh is solid as basalt." Pharaoh then shakes the young man's hand to prove his point.

The young man is awakened by a friend shaking him hard. As he passes his desk, the foot is gone. In its place is a green clay figure.

One writer who took up the theme of the mummy was Theophile Gautier (1811–72) with a story whose title is more chilling than its subject matter. This delightfully whimsical tale is both charming and interesting as the genesis of a slowly developing subgenre. The ending is pure Hollywood! The fantastic story is merely a dream — or is it, for a tangible piece of evidence exists to prove otherwise. Film fans will recall the coin from *Miracle in the Rain*, or the scarf in *Portrait of Jenny*, proving that well-known Old Testament edict, "There is nothing new under the sun."

Some Words with a Mummy (by Edgar Allan Poe, 1845)

The narrator, after a splendid supper of Welsh rabbit, is wakened from sleep by his friend Dr. Ponnonner, who invites him to an official unrolling of a mummy—an eagerly awaited academic evening out, at the time of Poe's story—at his home at eleven o'clock that evening. The museum has apparently blessed the occasion since they had a pair of mummies recently brought in from Egypt. The narrator, unable to resist, arrives at his friend's house to find the mummy already stretched on the dining table.

The mummy's unrolling proceeds; first it is taken from its oblong box. "The material was at first supposed to be the wood of the sycamore ... but upon cutting into it, we found it to be pasteboard, or, more properly, papier-mâché, composed of papyrus." The paintings and hieroglyphs are noted with interest, and one of the party, Mr. Gliddon, translates its name for the group—"Allamistakeo."

They have difficulty in getting to the second case without damaging it, but finally succeed in freeing a coffin-shaped case, much smaller than the first. It appears discolored by the resins that filled the space between the two containers.

They have more success with the second; the third case is tightly inside it and "highly aromatic" with the perfume of cedar. Finally they come to the mummy. Instead of layers of bandages, they find the body encased in a sheath of papyrus covered with plaster, thickly gilded and painted. A wonderful collar of cylindrical glass beads in a pattern of gods encircles the neck of this form, its twin around the mummy's waist.

> Stripping off the papyrus, we found the flesh in excellent preservation, with no perceptible odor. The color was reddish. The skin was hard, smooth and glossy. The teeth and hair were in good condition. The eyes (it seemed) had been removed, and glass ones substituted, which were very beautiful and wonderfully life-like, with the exception of somewhat too determined a stare. The fingers and nails were brilliantly gilded.

The group discusses the color of the skin and its cause, and check for the expected marks of mummification, but they cannot find them, so Dr. Ponnonner prepares his dissecting instruments to invade the body.

The narrator then points out the lateness of the hour and they all agree to postpone the postmortem until the following evening since it would require many hours. One bright spark, however, suggests that a galvanic experiment would not take so long. The electrodes are prepared, and the mummy is prodded until suitable contact is made.

> Morally and physically—figuratively and literally—was the effect electric. In the first place, the corpse opened its eye, and winked very rapidly for several minutes, as does Mr. Barnes in the pantomime; in the second place, it sneezed; in the third, it sat up on end; in the fourth, it shook its fist in Dr. Ponnonner's face; in the fifth, turning on Messieurs Gliddon and Buckingham, it addressed them, in very capital Egyptian.

The long-suffering mummy takes them all to task; he is not surprised at the doctor's behavior, but *is* surprised—and mortified—that they had a hand in it, when he supposed them his friends. "What am I to suppose by your permitting Tom, Dick and Harry to strip me of my coffins, and my clothes, in this wretchedly cold climate? In what light (to come to the point) am I to regard your aiding and abetting that miserable little villain, Doctor Ponnonner, in pulling me by the nose?"

The mummy, trembling from the cold, is immediately cared for by the group who offer an odd assortment of clothes, cigars, wine, and a seat by the fire before they fall into a lengthy conversation with the honored "guest."

The resulting conversation between the mummy and the scientists points up the superiority of Ancient Egyptian civilization over that of nineteenth century America, although it becomes clear during their discussions that this is not a de facto mummy. Allamistakeo, in a cataleptic fit, had been prepared for burial by friends.

> "I repeat that the leading principle of embalmment consisted, with us, in the immediate arresting, and holding in perpetual abeyance, all the animal functions subjected to the process. To be brief, in whatever condition the individual was, at the period of embalmment, in that condition he remained. Now, as it is my good fortune to be of the blood of the Scarabaeus, I was embalmed alive, as you see me at present."

Poe's story is not horrifying or thrilling — indeed it was intended to amuse its readers in satirical form. It has his usual melancholy feel, and touches on his own particular horror, the possibility of being buried alive. It also gives him the opportunity to comment on the development of his own society during the discussion on comparative civilizations. The description of the unrolling is so precise that Poe either read extensively around the subject or had himself been present at such an occasion. His only other reference to mummification came in *Ligeia* where the antihero has his Egyptian first wife, the lady Ligeia, buried according to ancient practices and then horrifies his contemporaries as he repeats the process on his second English wife, the lady Rowena. In a drug-sated period of mourning, he hears something approach his room; he has truly loved Rowena after being nearly destroyed by the passing of Ligeia. He had even offered his soul for the return of his first wife before marrying the golden-haired English beauty. A bandaged form enters his room, and before he swoons away, begins to unwind the wrappings around its head. Madness comes as he sees, not the golden tresses of Rowena, but the raven-hued locks of the lady Ligeia.

Lot 249 (by Sir Arthur Conan Doyle, 1890)

At Oxford, in 1884, medical student Abercrombie Smith shares a turret wing with Edward Bellingham and Monkhouse Lee, each having their own room. Smith is warned by his friend Hastie to steer clear of Bellingham. "There's something damnable about him, something reptilian. My gorge always rises to him." He is a man of strange interests.

Bellingham is engaged to Lee's sister Eveline, whom Hastie fancies, and initially Smith puts his friend's distaste down to jealousy. But, after learning more he is not sure. The previous year Bellingham pushed an old woman to the ground because she stood in his way, and was punished by a beating from Long Norton, which ended the matter.

One night, Smith's studies are interrupted by a scream — Bellingham's. Rushing down to his room, Smith is accompanied by Lee. Smith is stunned to see that Bellingham's room is filled with Egyptian antiquities ... including a 6'7" mummy. Smith brings Bellingham out of his faint, advising him to "drop these little midnight games with mummies."

"I wonder," Bellingham replies, "whether you would be as cool as I am if you had seen —"

The mummy is nameless, Bellingham having purchased it at an auction as Lot 249. It is a horror. "The features, though horribly discolored, were perfect, and two little nut-like eyes still lurked in the depths of the black hollow sockets. The blotched skin was drawn tightly from bone to bone, and a tangled wrap of black, coarse hair fell over the ears. Two thin teeth, like those of a rat, overlay the shriveled lower lip."

Against his better judgment, Smith begins a minor association with Bellingham — and soon experiences an odd event. He hears movements in Bellingham's room when the occupant is out. Suspecting that Bellingham has a woman, Smith keeps silent.

Sometime later, Long Norton is attacked. "But who—," asks Smith. "Ah, that's the rub!" says Hastie. "Norton swears that it was not human. He was nearly strangled by two arms as strong and thin as steel bands."

Smith overhears a row between Bellingham and Lee over Eveline; soon afterwards Lee is nearly drowned. Smith inquires how he fell in; "I was standing by the bank and something from behind picked me up like a feather and hurled me in."

Smith, on visiting Bellingham's rooms, is astonished to find the mummy out of its case and missing, but back in place moments later. Suspecting the worst, Smith confronts Bellingham. "You'll find that your filthy Egyptian tricks won't answer in England!"

Smith is nearly attacked while out walking. "This horror was bounding like a tiger ... blazing eyes and stringy arms outthrown."

Smith goes to Bellingham's rooms with a revolver, a watch and a large knife. "You must cut it up and burn it," he orders. Bellingham realizes that Smith will shoot him unless he complies, and so he sets to and hacks the mummy to bits, casting the pieces into the fire. "A thick, fat smoke oozed out from the fire, and a heavy smell of burned resin and singed hair filled the air. In a quarter of an hour a few charred and brittle sticks were all that was left of Lot 249."

The mummy now destroyed, Bellingham leaves Oxford, and vanishes in the Sudan.

Sir Arthur Conan Doyle wrote two mummy stories during the 1890s that reflect his lifelong interest in things occult. Of the two, *Lot 249*, is the most animated, though perhaps less interesting. Later, Doyle was to admit that the revival of the mummy has been somewhat vague, and that it was rather static at the times it was not used by Bellingham for vicious purposes.

Most importantly though, in those brief moments when the mummy becomes Bellingham's weapon, its animal strength and power shine from the pages; it is a formidable opponent of mortal man and the archetype of the avenging mummy that would become part of movie lore in decades to come.

The Ring of Thoth (by Sir Arthur Conan Doyle, 1890)

John Vansittart Smith, a respected English Egyptologist, visits the Louvre museum in Paris to enjoy the unparalleled collection of antiquities enshrined there. His interest, however, lights on an attendant rather than the artifacts. "The regular statuesque features, broad brow, well-rounded chin, and dusky complexion were the exact counterpart of the innumerable statues, mummy-cases, and pictures which adorned the walls of the apartment.... Smith, fixing his eyes upon the fellow's skin, was conscious of a sudden impression that there was something inhuman and preternatural about its appearance."

He curtly guides Smith to the Memphis collection and does not reply when Smith rhetorically asks if he is Egyptian. Smith goes to his studies and forgets his impressions of the attendant. He works assiduously, and eventually falls asleep, unnoticed, in a corner. The bells of Notre Dame, chiming midnight, rouse him and stir a delicious amusement as to his predicament — locked in with all the treasures he loves! He is not alone, however, as a gleam from a lamp shines out further down the gallery. The light is slowly coming towards him, pausing here and there, but getting ever nearer. Smith fears burglars, and snuggles further into his corner, hoping not to be discovered. "The figure was wrapped in shadow, but the light fell full upon the strange, eager face. There was no mistaking the metallic, glistening eyes and the cadaverous skin. It was the attendant with whom he had conversed."

Smith's first impulse to reveal himself and ask to be shown out is quickly replaced by the stealthy movements of the attendant who was obviously not carrying out ordinary duties. The attendant proceeds to unlock a case and liberate its mummy, putting it gently on the ground. He then unwraps it — and Smith realizes from the sounds and smells that the mummy had not been previously disturbed. Curiosity overcoming caution, Smith moves nearer to watch as the wrappings fall back to reveal "a cascade of long, black, glossy tresses ... a low, white forehead, with a pair of delicately arched eyebrows ... a pair of bright, deeply fringed eyes, and a straight well-cut nose ... a sweet, full, sensitive mouth, and a beautifully curved chin." Smith is startled into a murmur, but is unnoticed by the attendant who cradles the mummy in his arms, grieving for many moments before suddenly smiling and whispering in an ancient tongue, then springing up to rifle through a nearby case of jewels. He appears to be testing the rings from the case with a strange liquid.

Most are cast aside until "a massive ring with a large crystal set in it, he seized and eagerly tested with the contents of the jar. Instantly, he uttered a cry of joy, and threw his arms out in a wild gesture that upset the pot and set the liquid streaming across the floor to the very feet of the Englishman."

Confronting each other, Smith explains his presence while the attendant confesses that he would have murdered Smith had he found him just a few minutes earlier. As it is, Smith is warned not to interfere on pain of death, but the Egyptologist merely asks to be shown out. When the attendant asks his name, he recognizes it as one famed in Egyptology but "Your knowledge of the subject is contemptible." While Smith is spluttering in shock, the attendant adds "Yet it is superior to that of many who make even greater pretensions." Smith realizes that the man is speaking from firsthand knowledge of the life of ancient times, but before he can ask the thousands of questions forming in his mind, he sees that the mummy is deteriorating and her beauty already destroyed. Taking the catastrophe as a sign, the attendant decides to share his story with Smith, who may do whatever he considers necessary with it.

He explains that he is called Sosra, and that he is a trained mystic as well as a physician. During his studies he had found an elixir which conferred a greatly enhanced life span on those who used it, fighting age, disease, and the effects of violence on the body. Sosra, having taken his elixir, had fallen in love with the governor's daughter who, untreated, fell ill of the plague and died. Though grieving, he could not follow her into the afterlife. The girl's other faithful lover, Parmes Priest of Thoth, was also protected by his friend's elixir, but he had found an antidote and, sure that his friend would not stumble on the secret, had eradicated the "blessing" of the elixir and joined his beloved in eternity. Before his death he had hidden the antidote in his ring. Sosra had therefore spent four centuries frantically searching for the ring, only to discover that Parmes had buried it with his love. Having traced the mummy to Paris, he had taken the job of attendant at the Louvre. Now he planned to take the antidote and finally join the one he loved.

Sosra escorts Smith to the door leading to the Rue de Rivoli and bids him goodnight, closing the door firmly. Smith returns to London, pondering the strange tale and finds an epilogue in his copy of the *Times*; a strange discovery had been made by the cleaners opening the Louvre Museum: "...one of the attendants lying dead upon the floor with his arms around one of the mummies. So close was his embrace that it was only with the utmost difficulty that they were separated." It was noted that the man was eccentric and of uncertain habits, and that he had died of some long-standing heart disease, it was assumed, in the act of robbing the museum.

The Ring of Thoth introduced the theme of love across the centuries for the first time into mummy literature, and in Sosra, the concept of an articulate and erudite member of an ancient society. There is so much of *The Ring of Thoth* in Universal's first mummy film starring Boris Karloff that it is strange that Conan Doyle's contribution is not acknowledged. This second offering from Doyle is more thoughtful, more mystic, and more detailed than *Lot 249* but lacks its power. Between the two plots, Doyle appears to have invented most of the movie mummy lore for some time to come.

The last word must be Sir Arthur's— on hearing of the tragic death of Lord Carnarvon, he was interviewed on his views of "the mummy's curse" during a trans-Atlantic journey to America on the *Queen Mary*. It was thirty years since he had written Sosra's story, and by now he was a confirmed spiritualist and perhaps not *entirely* compos mentis. He said, "An evil elemental may have caused Lord Carnarvon's fatal illness. One does not know what elementals existed in those days, nor what their power might be. The Egyptians knew a great deal more about those things than we do." Could be a quote from a script, couldn't it?

Iras: A Mystery (by "Theo Douglas" [Mrs. H. D. Everett], 1896)

An Egyptologist unwraps the ancient mummy of the beautiful Iras who subsequently wakens from suspended animation. They fall in love and marry, but Iras is gradually degraded to her original mummy state as seven magic pendants are removed from her necklace by a series of accidents.

The Romance of the Golden Star (by George Griffith, 1897)

Set in the land of the Incas by author George Griffith, a leading science fiction writer of his day, the romance unusually features a Peruvian mummy in a series of adventures.

Pharos the Egyptian (by Guy Boothby, 1898)

A long and intricate novel, *Pharos the Egyptian* features an immortal Egyptian visiting London. Originally it was a serial in *Windsor Magazine*, July to December 1988, before being released as a book the following year. Old Pharos is the living entity of a 3,000-year old mummy of Ptahmes the Magician, who had served the Pharaoh of the Exodus.

The Jewel of Seven Stars (by Bram Stoker, 1903)

Malcolm Ross, a young but respected lawyer, has recently met and fallen in love with a youthful regal beauty named Margaret Trelawny. He fervently hopes that she reciprocates his feelings, and has offered his friendship and help to her during an idyllic afternoon on the river.

During this outing, Margaret has confided that she has only lately come to live with her father, Egyptologist Abel Trelawny, in his great house in London. The house is more museum than home, except for Margaret's private apartments, and Margaret is in awe of her father though she loves him greatly. Her birth had cost her mother's life, and her parents had been deeply in love, and Margaret feels responsible for his mourning.

Soon after this meeting, Margaret sends for Ross in the middle of the night. Though the summons is grave, Ross is thrilled to be able to help and be calmly reassuring to the young woman who has found the inert figure of her father, bloodstained, in front of a safe in his bedroom. Not having other friends, Margaret has taken up Ross's promise of help, and he moves into the guest room at her request.

During Abel Trelawny's coma, Ross learns many things. He becomes acquainted with the Trelawny lawyer who astonishes them with instructions that antedate the coma as to the conduct of the household while it lasts. Margaret leans on Ross's relations with Scotland Yard and his calm logic as her father undergoes another invisible assault.

The young couple become acquainted with Corbeck, Trelawny's seeker of artifacts, and through him learn of the ancient queen whose tomb and longed-for resurrection are the passions of his friend and patron.

This ancient queen had been feared by her priesthood, and her wise father had had her instructed in all manner of occult sciences during her education. She had conducted many experiments, including a lengthy sojourn in the tomb, and had prepared for her death, burial and subsequent resurrection with enormous care, relying on her talisman, a giant ruby, within whose depths sparkled the constellation of the Plough, called the Jewel of Seven Stars. This jewel had been carved into a scarab of great beauty, and had words of power inscribed upon its surfaces; it was paramount in the ritual to give her new life. According to legend, it had been found in a meteorite that had struck the earth at the moment of her birth — the remaining fragment having been carved into a mysterious coffer that appeared unopenable.

The ancient sorceress had identified with the jewel because she had been born with seven fingers on her right hand. Seven became her special number, and the North, as symbolized in the Plough, the venue for a new life, free of a malicious and scheming priesthood. Only they had finally defeated her — hacking her name from the front of her burial place, and cursing any who disturbed the now Nameless One. She became the subject of legend and the centuries passed.

A Dutch seventeenth century traveler found her tomb.

> Within the sarcophagus was a body, manifestly of a woman, swathed with many wrappings of linen, as is usual with all mummies. From certain embroiderings thereon, I gathered she was of high rank. Across the breast was one hand, unwrapped.... But this hand was strange to see, for it was the real hand of her who lay enwrapped there; the arm projecting from the cerements being of flesh, seemingly made as like marble in the process of embalming. Arm and hand were of dusky white, being of the hue of ivory that hath lain long in air. The skin and nails were complete and whole, as though the body had been placed for burial overnight.

Touching the hand, the traveler found the skin pliable, and on moving it, discovered the great ruby beneath. His Arab helpers had tried to open the coffer but had failed, and it had then occurred to the traveler that they might kill him and sell the treasure from the tomb. Although the canopic jars had only contained oil, and few portable treasures were apparent. One of the Arabs had broken off the hand to use as an amulet, and its ragged wrist was stained as if with blood. The man had died shortly after, giving the hand a ready–made legend. During a following night, all the Arabs had perished, while the traveler slept safe, holding the jewel.

Trelawny and Corbeck had later found the tomb the traveler wrote about. A strange trance had held them three days in the tomb, during which time Margaret was born. Having taken the mummy and artifacts from the tomb, the two were distraught to find their collection gone, but found that the mummy was back in its burial pit when they retraced their steps. After this expedition, Trelawny commissioned Corbeck to find all the missing artifacts, and planned the Great Experiment.

As well as the history of Tera, for such was the name of the ancient queen, Ross has to come to terms with Margaret's changing moods. Sometimes she is so aloof that his heart aches, sometimes she is the sweet girl he fell in love with, and always she is the focus of Tera's power. Corbeck, having been robbed of a set of lamps that are vital for the Great Experiment of Tera's rebirth, is delighted when Margaret finds them in a drawer in her room. When Trelawny awakes, he is gratified at Margaret's choice of confidant, and agreeable to Ross's courtship of his daughter. He insists that Margaret should show Ross her birthmark — a ragged red line around her wrist, with little droplets of skin-like blood splatters.

Margaret seems to have a telepathic link with the queen and is able to give noble explanations in answer to any fears the party has about Tera's intentions. As the time for the ritual draws near, the party decamps to Trelawny's Cornish hideaway with its underground cavern that he has equipped to facilitate the experiment. All unnecessary persons are sent away and the countdown begins. The cavern is redressed as Tera's burial chamber.

Margaret sadly agrees to her father's insistence on the destruction of Tera's mummified familiar, an object loathed by her own huge pet cat, Silvio. The cat mummy is unwrapped and burned so that it cannot be a danger to them. Margaret has a premonition that the queen's spirit will inhabit her old body for the duration of the night, thus ensuring the party's safety and her nonintervention in the experiment. She hopes this will allay their fears. Trelawny then begins to unwrap the queen to his daughter's horror and indignation. As the task is nearly complete Trelawny looks up at his daughter. "Do not be uneasy, dear! See! there is nothing to harm you. The queen has on a robe.—Ay, and a royal robe, too!"

But Tera is not dressed in the glorious gown, nor the jeweled girdle that lies with it. These are clothes for the new life, not grave garments. Margaret is sure they are bridal clothes, and in the instant she says so, Trelawny lifts them from the naked body of the queen and they all stare at her perfection. "And yet the white wonder of that beautiful form was something to dream of. It was not like death at all; it was like a statue carved in ivory by the hand of a Praxiteles."

They are all astounded by the queen's likeness to Margaret—particularly Ross who notes that Tera is wearing an identical jewel in her hair to the one Margaret wore on the night they had met. Trelawny gasps, "It looks as if you were dead, my child!"

Margaret spends the remaining daylight hours preparing Tera for the experiment, dressing her in the gown and gems, and brushing her hair. Ross finds her transformation heartbreaking; with every hour she becomes paler and more withdrawn.

The newly dressed mummy is laid in its sarcophagus in the cavern, reunited with the severed hand at last. Under the hand is the Jewel of Seven Stars. Ross has the task of turning on the electric lights when needed, so his post is away from the others who hover around the queen. The ancient lamps are lit, and their special light opens the coffer and releases a pungent colored gas contained therein. The gas seems drawn to the body which begins to glow in response. Ross wishes he was with the others to see what is illuminating their faces with wonder and glory.

> I saw something white rising up from the open sarcophagus. Something which appeared to my tortured eyes to be filmy, like a white mist. In the heart of this mist, which was cloudy and opaque like an opal, was something like a hand holding a fiery jewel flaming with many lights. As the fierce glow of the Coffer met this new living light, the green vapor floating between them seemed like a cascade of brilliant points—a miracle of light!

But just then the mood changes; the storm outside blows open the shutters and the wind practically extinguishes the lamps. Black smoke now pours from the Coffer, the lamps are dimmed. Ross sticks to his post, but longs to go to Margaret as the smoke thickens and he loses sight of the group around the sarcophagus. He sees a movement of something white, but getting no response from Trelawny he tries to turn on the electric light, which fails. Groping his way across the cavern he stumbles on a body he believes to be Margaret and carries it through pitch dark to the house. "It may have been that hope lightened my task; but as I went the weight that I bore seemed to grow less as I ascended from the cavern."

He lays the body in the hall and goes in search of candles that will illumine his way back to his beloved. But she is not there. Only the queen's bridal gown, the girdle of gems around its folds, and the Jewel of Seven Stars where the heart should be lay there. Ross rushes back to the cavern with two candles and is horrified to find them "where they all stood. They had sunk down on the floor, and were gazing upward with fixed eyes of unspeakable terror. Margaret had put her hands before her face, but the glassy stare of her eyes through the fingers was more terrible than an open glare." Doing what he can, it becomes obvious that nothing will help and the solitary survivor concludes, "It was merciful that I was spared the pain of hoping."

When the novel was reprinted in 1912, the ending had changed to: Ross, during the experiment, waits at his post by the lightswitch. As the light from the lamps fades, he asks whether he should turn on the light, and Trelawny replies in the affirmative. Even with the lights he can only see Margaret's dress dimly in the smoke and makes for her side. He makes sure that she is alright and suggests opening the shutters to disperse the smoke, as she replies sleepily, "They will be all right. They won't get any harm." The cavern and its contents are covered in a sooty substance, the sheet that had covered Tera is thrown back but there is no sign of the queen. Margaret reports,

> Until the smoke grew too dense I kept my eyes on the couch, but there was no change. Then, when all grew so dark that I could not see, I thought I heard a movement close to me.... I thought it might be the queen waking, so I put down poor Silvio ... But all we could find was a sort of ridge of impalpable dust, which gave out a strange dead odor. On the couch lay the jewel of the disc and plumes which the queen had worn in her hair, and the Star Jewel which had words to command the gods.

In the Autumn, records Ross, he married Margaret who wore the queen's bridal gown, jeweled girdle and the disc and plumes in her hair. "On her breast, set in a ring of gold made like a twisted lotus stalk, she wore the strange Jewel of Seven Stars.... At the marriage the sunlight streaming through the chancel windows fell on it, and it seemed to glow like a living thing." Ross is blissfully happy with his restored Margaret who seems to embody all the greatest gifts of the ancient queen. When Malcolm Ross expresses his sadness that the Queen did not live again as she had hoped his loving wife replies, "Do not grieve for her! ... She dreamed her dream; and that is all any of us can ask!"

The reissue of the book in 1912 changed the ending and deleted chapter XVI, "Powers—Old and New." It remains unclear whether Stoker made these changes in the text prior to his death or whether his publishers did with his wife's tacit permission. Whatever the truth, it is amazing that so small a change has so marked an effect on the overall feel of the novel.

Bram Stoker—better known for the archvillain Count Dracula—had a large circle of interesting and influential friends and acquaintances, moving as he did in the aristocratic and artistic circles of his day. Though burdened with work as Sir Henry Irving's devoted business manager, he found time during his infrequent holidays to assiduously research the background details of his novel projects. In *The Jewel of Seven Stars* his research encompassed not just the current findings of Egyptology, and in particular a fascinating female pharaoh now called Hatshepsut, but all kinds of scientific and pseudoscientific experiments of his day. He was acquainted with Sir Flinders Petrie, Sir Ernest Wallis Budge, and Sir Arthur Conan Doyle, and had know Oscar Wilde and his father, Sir William, for some time. Wilde Sr. was a rabid amateur Egyptologist and a friend to many eminent scholars in the field.

Along with the historical background, Stoker played with many occult themes. Some scholars are sure that Stoker was himself a member of the Amen-Ra Temple of the Hermetic Order of the Golden Dawn, but there appears to be no firm evidence to show he was an initiate. He was, however, fascinated with spiritualism and psychical research, and toyed with the themes in his Gothic novels, and he corresponded with the President of the Society for Psychical Research, Sir Oliver Lodge.

The book begins as a mystery-thriller; who is the attacker in a locked room? It is set in modern London—a ruse often used by movie makers, and for the same reasons of economy and reality—and in two great houses. While littered with Egyptiana, it is curt about Egypt itself. The academics and amateur historians admired the glories of Ancient Egypt, and delighted in cataloguing, restoring, reassembling, and classifying the scattered remains of the ruined civilization in the safety of Europe and America, far away from the indigenous inhabitants and their supposed degeneracy. They felt the Empire of Ancient Egypt was a kind of way station in the rise of reason, but its scientific advances seemed to pivot on mysticism and the occult rather than scientific knowledge.

The story is traced entirely through Malcolm Ross's eyes and he acts as the devil's advocate, balancing the Judaeo-Christian ethic of his day with the seductive mysticism of Tera, the growing schizophrenia of Margaret, and the almost evangelistic zeal of her father to use the Old Magic. Two long flashbacks give us the *historical* background to the story that we need if we are to take sides in this cosmic battle. Margaret becomes a kind of psychic filter paper, straining the worst — i.e., most liberated — of Tera's longings through her own sweet and noble Christian nature. Volumes could be written about "The Role of Woman in Stoker Novels," although we do not propose to study it in depth in this book. Margaret/Tera, virgin/libertine, woman-on-a-pedestal-to-be-protected-and-worshipped/woman-seducer-to-be-resisted — Stoker's personal life and history guided his pen as he wrote about women. The apparent multiple personalities of Margaret, the use of light as a catalyst in the experiment, the hoped for reincarnation of the queen, the reverence for science as a means to bring it about — all these facets of the story are echoes of the concepts animating the minds of Stoker and his contemporaries. They stood on the threshold of an explosion of science, technology, exploration, discovery, *and* understanding (they believed) of the past. Plus, they were sure that their society was the brightest and the best and assured of their place in it.

An American reviewer wrote, "It would be impossible to say what one really does think of Mr. Bram Stoker's *The Jewel of Seven Stars*. It is one of those books that challenge the opinion by their very interest." (*New York Times Saturday Review of Books* 5, March 1904). "A truly thrilling tale" wrote another (*Times Literary Supplement*, 6 November 1903). Agreeably received by most critics, the mystery Stoker had penned seemed to provoke in its readers a sense of unease that lingered; reprinting it ten years later the *publisher* insisted on a happy ending to replace the original sharp, tragic finale. Opinions on the text still remain mixed; it is a puzzle, resisting interpretation. Carol A. Senf describes it as "the most difficult to categorize" of all his works. (The Critical Response to Bram Stoker, 1993).

Small wonder then, that there have been few attempts to bring it to the screen. Hammer in 1971, in their normal economic style, and Anglo-American in 1980 with a much larger budget, real location filming, and Charlton Heston as the Egyptologist. Of the two, Hammer wins in providing a supernatural thriller with occasional chilling moments. Both are faithful to Stoker in that the action is presented in a modern time frame. The Anglo-American offering, entitled *The Awakening*, was not so kindly received by critics "At 105 minutes, the longest horror film on record and almost certainly the dullest except when it is being actively unpleasant.... Charlton Heston is the archaeologist taking much longer than the audience to realize whose spirit is killing his colleagues and whose daughter the evil is working through ... at least three critics concluded their remarks with the suggestion that the project had really needed more sleep before being awakened" (Halliwell, 1986).

The best rendering of the novel to the screen — the television screen — was also in 1970 in an episode of the series *Mystery and Imagination* called *The Curse of the Mummy*. Screened on February 23, it has never, to the authors' knowledge, been seen again, but like the novel, it lingers in the minds of those who saw it. Isobel Black and Patrick Mower led the

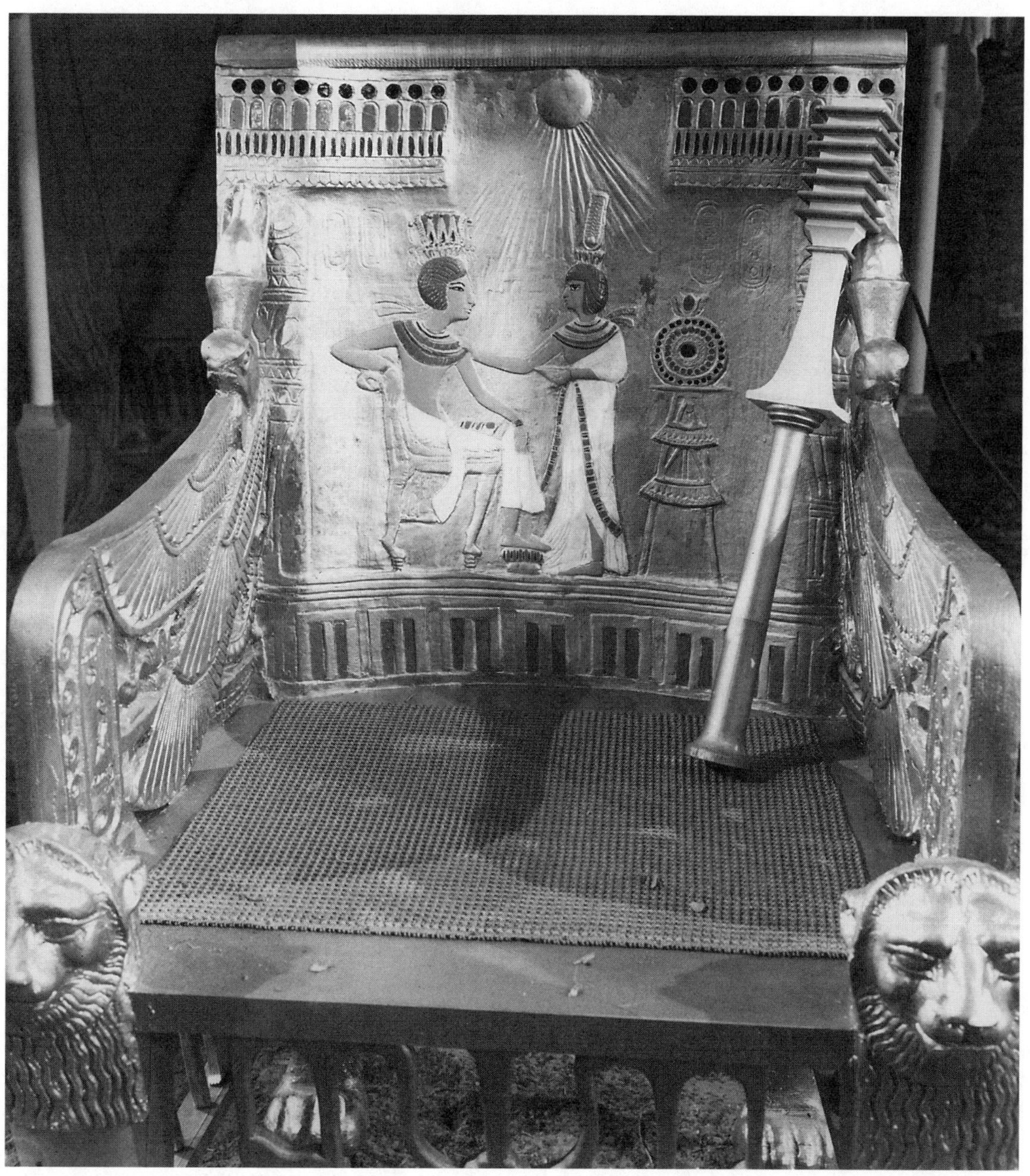

The mummy's chair from *The Curse of the Mummy's Tomb* (Hammer/Columbia, 1964).

cast, and John Russell Taylor provided the script. The piece was set in Victorian England and was the most faithful transfer of the novel to date, with the original ending. Isobel Black played Margaret/Tera with a splendidly haunted look. It is believed that the piece was filmed on video and the tapes wiped years ago, though Jonathan Alwyn, the series producer, believes that there must have been a telecine print for overseas sales where the technical equipment was incompatible with the British system. When sharing his thoughts on the series with *Shivers* magazine, Alwyn wryly commented that the series' reputation "will remain secure the more it remains a figment of mystery and imagination."

The Mummy and Miss Nitocris; A Phantasy of the Fourth Dimension (by George Griffith, 1906)

Two ancient Egyptians and Princess Nitocris are reincarnated in contemporary Britain.

The Mummy Moves (by Mary Gaunt, 1910)

A somewhat turgid piece; Mary Gaunt was a real-life explorer whose nonfiction accounts of her travels in China, Turkestan, West Africa, and Siberia knocked spots off her attempts at fictional adventure.

Edwardian Mummy Short Stories

Mummy short stories were de rigueur in Edwardian times. Among the more memorable were "The Mysterious Mummy" by A. Sarsfield Ward, who later renamed himself Sax Rohmer, which appeared in *Pearson's Weekly Christmas Extra*, 26 November 1903; "The Mummy of Thompson-Pratt" by C. J. Cutliffe-Hyne, appearing in *Atoms of Empire*, 1904; Clive Pemberton's "The Bulb" from *The Weird o' It* in 1906; and the great Algernon Blackwood's "Nemesis of Fire" from *John Silence* in 1908. Finding any of these pieces of pulp fiction has proved either very difficult or financially unviable during the researching of this book. The authors offer the titles in hopes that more interested readers will join the search!

The Eye of Osiris (by R. Austin Freeman, 1911)

The tale begins with a newspaper report of a vanished Egyptologist, one John Bellingham, whose disappearance is noted by John Thorndyke, a lecturer in Medical Jurisprudence "or Forensic Medicine, as it is sometimes described." He draws the attention of his students to the newspaper and suggests that they will find it a rewarding subject to file for future reference as the clues, as reported in detail in the paper, are most intriguing. Since his students know his skill in the field, and admire the methods he employs in his work, they all troop off after lectures to buy copies of the paper. Thorndyke's fascination rests on the vexed question of survivorship.

> The gentleman who has disappeared, Mr. John Bellingham, is a man well known in archaeological circles. He is recently returned from Egypt, bringing with him a very fine collection of antiquities—some of which, by the way, he has presented to the British Museum, where they are now on view—and having made this presentation, he appears to have gone to Paris on business. I may mention that the gift consisted of a very fine mummy and a complete set of tomb furniture. The latter, however, had not arrived from Egypt at the time when the missing man left for Paris, but the mummy was inspected on the fourteenth of October at Mr. Bellingham's house by Dr. Norbury of the British Museum, in the presence of the donor and his solicitor, and the latter was authorized to hand over the complete collection to the British Museum authorities when the tomb furniture arrived; which he has since done.

Mr. Bellingham was reported to have returned on November 23 and gone directly to Charing Cross, where he made a trip to Eltham to visit a cousin, Mr. Hurst. Since that gentleman had not returned from town, Mr. Bellingham was made comfortable in the lounge by the housemaid. He intended to write letters until Mr. Hurst returned. However, when Mr. Hurst came home there was no one in the lounge and he was so disturbed by the strange events that he left for London immediately to find Mr. Bellingham's solicitor. That gentleman, Mr. Jellicoe, was also alarmed and together they journeyed to Woodford to the home of Mr. Godfrey Bellingham, the missing man's only brother. The staff at G. Bellingham's house believed him to be absent, but directed the visitors to the library, which was in an annex separate from the house, where they could expect to find Miss Bellingham, Mr. Godfrey's daughter. In the library, both Miss Bellingham and her father, who had come in by the back gate, listened to the strange tale and maintained

Mummy case of Artemidorus, incorporating an encaustic portrait of the deceased. Roman period, early 2nd century A.D. (Courtesy of the British Museum, ©British Museum.) The British Museum is featured in the story "The Eye of Osiris."

that they had not seen John. Walking back to the main house, Mr. Jellicoe noticed an object in the grass: "They all recognized it as a scarab which Mr. John Bellingham had been accustomed to wear suspended from his watch chain. There was no mistaking it. It was a very fine scarab of the eighteenth dynasty fashioned in lapis lazuli and engraved with the cartouche of Amenhotep III" The discovery only added to the mystery that deepened when, upon inquiries, Mr. John Bellingham's case was discovered at Charing Cross in the Left Luggage Office. It had been deposited just after the arrival of the Continental Express, and it led to the conclusion that John Bellingham had gone directly to Eltham. He had not been seen since.

A very full description of John Bellingham had been printed by the papers including the fact that he had an old Pott's disease fracture on the left ankle, a linear, longitudinal scar on each knee from surgery, and a vermilion tattoo on his chest of the Eye of Osiris. "There certainly ought to be no difficulty in identifying the body. But we hope it will not come to that," Thorndyke tells his students.

The tale then skips some two years, and the author finally reveals himself as one Paul Berkeley, recently qualified as a physician and currently filling in for an old friend. As part of his brief, he is visiting a patient at home in Nevill's Court. He is surprised and delighted when the Court appears to be a tranquil haven off the busy alleys of London, and the house somewhat idyllic with its lovely old garden. A family servant, Miss Oman, takes him to a room to await his patient, where he inadvertently overhears two men quarreling. The whole house is absolutely impoverished but scrupulously clean, Berkeley notes. In an attempt to dampen his hearing by clapping his hands over his ears, Berkeley looks rather foolish to the grave young woman who comes to fetch him to meet her father.

The elderly gentleman is unwell because of an accident with a hansom cab a short while before, which has undermined his confidence, and the argument previously overheard has not helped. Berkeley likes the man and wishes to help in any way he can. Listening to the tale his patient tells, Berkeley recognizes him as Godfrey Bellingham and understands some of the causes of his illness. The night before his brother had disappeared, he was an independently wealthy man with prospects and a dearly loved brother. The following day he was bankrupt, for all intents and purposes, and bewildered by the mystery of his brother's disappearance. Berkeley tells him of Thorndyke's interest when Bellingham begins to explain the legal complications of his brother's vanishing. Painfully conscious of his inability to pay professional fees, he demurs the offer of consulting Thorndyke, so Berkeley offers himself as a substitute confidant.

Shortly thereafter, Berkeley happens to meet Thorndyke and an old student friend, Jervis, who now works as Thorndyke's assistant. Over drinks, Berkeley mentions the Bellinghams' problems to his old mentor. Thorndyke recollects the details with amazing accuracy. He promises an unofficial opinion on the case if it will help Mr. Bellingham. Thorndyke has a theory about the case, arrived at from the clues in the newspaper, but he will not share it as he prefers the others to reach their own conclusions. Only one comment from Thorndyke distresses Berkeley as they go over the clues. "The girl must have been in it if her father was" for young Dr. Berkeley has fallen quietly — and swiftly — in love with Miss Bellingham.

Godfrey Bellingham willingly enlarges on his family's past to satisfy Berkeley's interest; John Bellingham's crazy will has caused much trouble. He had desired to be buried with his ancestors in St. George's cemetery near the family home in Queen Square, or one of the burial places appertaining to his native parish. This he used as a condition of inheritance. If John was not buried where he designated, the whole inheritance would go instead to Hurst. And Hurst was pushing for a legal declaration of John Bellingham's death. Mr. Jellicoe, the solicitor, Mr. Hurst, and Godfrey Bellingham were all listed as executors of the will, so the complications increase at every turn. Hurst, realizing Godfrey's financial difficulties, has offered to make him an annuity from the legacy, but for all time, even if John Bellingham is subsequently found. If Godfrey accepts, he and his daughter will lose any claim on the estate, and he will not do it. Berkeley obtains permission to recount all this to Thorndyke on the strict understanding that Bellingham is not soliciting an unpaid-for service. Leaving the house, he discovers that Miss Bellingham makes some money by doing historical research for various authors.

Bringing Thorndyke and Jervis up to date, Bereley unwittingly reveals his interest in Ruth Bellingham. Thorndyke is more interested in the dreaded will, and asks his young friend to obtain a copy if possible. On his way to the surgery, Berkeley buys a paper with the headline "Horrible Discovery In A Watercress Bed At Sidcup!" which turns out to be a report of fragments of a dismembered body being found during a routine clearing of watercress beds. The bones of a left hand minus its third finger had been found, the complete arm including the shoulder blade and collar bone. The pathologist in charge maintained that the bones had been in the water over a year since there was no soft tissue left and that the missing finger had been amputated. The land where they were found belonged to John Bellingham. The description of the bones and their locality has Berkeley worrying that they were the missing Egyptologist's remains.

Deciding to discuss his thoughts with Thorndyke, Berkeley must first perform surgery, where he is surprised to find Miss Bellingham, who has had an accident and injured her hand quite severely. She is particularly distressed because she has some research to do on the Tell-el-Amarna letters of the heretic pharaoh, born Amenhotep IV, and subsequently renamed Akhenaten. Berkeley immediately puts his skill at shorthand at her disposal and they agree to work together in the British Museum so that she can complete her task. The more they work, the more Berkeley falls in love, and she with him too. One afternoon they meet Mr. Jellicoe in the museum and he goes with them to see John Bellingham's bequest. Mr. Jellicoe also has a passion for Egyptology, and he specializes in scarabs. Whilst talking about her uncle, Ruth says that he always wore a scarab ring on the third finger of his left hand, a perfect copy of a ring belonging to Queen Ti, the mother of the heretic pharaoh. So perfect was the copy that the one in her possession was too large for her to wear safely, while he uncle had had to force his on and was unable thereafter to take it off. She promises a copy of her uncle's will and shows Berkeley the facade of the house at Queen Square, not far from the museum.

Thorndyke is fascinated by the complications of the will, and sure that Hurst will move to have Bellingham declared dead. He persuades Berkeley to arrange a supper party for Godfrey and Ruth Bellingham to which he and Jervis are to be invited and they devise a way of helping Mr. Bellingham that he will not be able to refuse. Berkeley continues to help Ruth research the Armarnan letters, and during one of their trips to the museum she insists on introducing him to her very dear friend. Berkeley burns with jealousy until confronted by the mummy of Artemidorus; the mummy has served as Ruth's confidant and confessor during her lonely youth. But on leaving the idyll of the museum, they see the headline "More Mementoes of Murdered Man" on the placards. Ruth tells Berkeley that Miss Osman keeps her up-to-date on the gory details and that she privately believes the remains to be those of her uncle John.

Mr. Jellicoe checks the state of Godfrey Bellingham's health and his domestic habits with Berkeley before calling on a matter of business. Mr. Jellicoe perplexes Berkeley, but seems the model of propriety in the matter of the Bellingham estate. Hurst, having pushed the matter, there will be a hearing to declare John Bellingham legally dead. The supper party is successfully concluded with Thorndyke taking the case, but using another solicitor as front man. Mr. Bellingham's interests safeguarded, they await developments.

A few days later, Berkeley is pressed into attending an inquest on the unknown bones, and the notes he makes are used carefully by Thorndyke to brief the solicitor, who is, ostensibly, acting for Godfrey Bellingham at the hearing in the probate court. The court finds that there is insufficient evidence to suppose that John Bellingham is dead and refuses the petition. Finding himself alone with Ruth at the museum, Berkeley declares his feelings and is mortified when she turns away and leaves him. It takes him some while — and a gracious note, with her copy of the Osiris ring as a parting gift — to realize that Ruth is trying to protect him from being associated with a possible murderess! While he stumbles miserably through his daily chores, the papers once again reveal a new clue "The Missing Finger"; a set of finger bones and a ring had been recovered from a well in the garden of the house the Bellinghams had lived in until John's untimely disappearance.

Berkeley is distraught, but comforted by the fact that Thorndyke remains placid as ever; Miss Bellingham is puzzled about the lack of police activity and their failure to arrest her in the face of such circumstantial evidence.

> She said quietly, "It is useless to delude ourselves. Every known fact points to the certainty that it is his body. John Bellingham is dead; there can be no doubt of that. And to everyone except his unknown murderer and one or two of my own loyal friends, it must seem that his death lies at my door. I realized from the beginning that the suspicion lay between George Hurst and me; and the finding of the ring fixes it definitely on me...." The quiet conviction of her tone left me for awhile speechless with horror and despair. Then I recalled Thorndyke's calm, even confident, attitude, and I hastened to remind her of it.

Arriving at Thorndyke's for a conference, Ruth and Berkeley find a note pinned to the door saying that he is conducting an experiment at the British Museum with Dr. Norbury and that they are to join him there as soon as possible. Let into the museum after hours, they pick their way through gloomy galleries to Dr. Norbury's laboratory. It transpires that Thorndyke is x-raying a mummy under Norbury's interested gaze. They all watch in rapt attention as the huge sheet of photographic paper is developed, the image emerging eerily before their eyes. The image shows that some of the mummy's teeth are filled and that it has a tattoo on its chest — the Eye of Osiris! Metallic objects on the knees register well too. Dr. Norbury expresses his sadness that John Bellingham was not there to share their discovery of the strange properties of his gift. "And then Thorndyke, in his quiet, impassive way, said 'John Bellingham is here Doctor Norbury. This is John Bellingham.'" Dr. Norbury is astonished, maintaining that the mummy was on view in the Museum for three weeks before Bellingham's famous disappearance. "'Not so,' said Thorndyke, 'John Bellingham was last seen by you and Mr. Jellicoe on the fourteenth of October, more than three weeks before the mummy left Queen Square. After that date he was never seen alive or dead by any person who knew him and could identify him'."

Thorndyke suggests that Mr. Jellicoe can perhaps explain how Bellingham's body came to be in the cartonnage case, and how the remains of Sebek-hotep, who should be there, had been scattered about to put the authorities off the scent. Finding the body in the British Museum had ironically complied with John Bellingham's will and made Godfrey the chief heir and executor as well as lifting the shadow of murder from the family! Ruth can now listen to Berkeley's restated protestations of love, and return them. Having taken Ruth home, Berkeley returns to Thorndyke and the two, joined by Jervis, go to call on Mr. Jellicoe. At his door they are joined by Inspector Badger of the CID and let in only after agreeing to hear Mr. Jellicoe out before he is formally arrested.

Jellicoe offers them sherry, which they decline, and he congratulates Thorndyke on his powers of detection. He confirms all the steps Thorndyke lists as clues towards his assumption that Jellicoe is responsible for Bellingham's body being in the museum. It transpires that Jellicoe had loaned Hurst a large sum at the same time the strange will had been drawn up by John Bellingham. Since Hurst saw no way of inheriting the legacy under normal circumstances, he had happily signed his interest in the legacy, for a nominal sum, to Mr. Jellicoe in exchange for the loan.

On the evening that Dr. Norbury had inspected the real mummy, shortly after the Norbury's departure, Bellingham had died accidentally, leaving Jellicoe with a corpse, and the temptation to inherit a great deal of money and a priceless scarab collection. He had decided to do a rough mummification process on John Bellingham and substitute him for the gift to the museum. The time was propitious, for the rest of the gift was still en route from Egypt; Jellicoe had time to mummify Bellingham and place him in the cartonnage case, resealing it with bitumen. The new mummy and the real artifacts could then be sent to the museum where they would be safely locked away in full public gaze. The time available also enabled to Jellicoe to lay the false trails to Eltham and Woodford, and to deposit the scarab in the garden.

Jellicoe, however, provided too many clues from then on. The bones were too perfect; no marks of dismembering were found, which suggested that the skeleton had fallen apart rather than being chopped up. No bones that would have categorically identified Bellingham were found. No adipocere was found on the bones, which further strengthened Thorndyke's suspicion that the bones did not belong to Bellingham. Mr. Jellicoe, to support the theory that the bones were Bellingham's, had deposited the finger bones and ring in the well and overplayed his hand, so to speak.

As the last of the clues are verified, Jellicoe falls dead by his own hand, perhaps anticipating the verdict of the court.

This novel was included in a collection of six detective novels assembled by Mr. S. S. Van Dine for the publishers Charles Scribner's Sons, where it was published in 1928 as part of *The S. S. Van Dine Detective Library.* It is this copy that the authors discovered in a secondhand bookshop in Royal Tunbridge Wells, England, whilst researching the fiction section of their book. Sue Cowie, in particular, was fascinated by it for its setting has changed very little since it was written, and Artemidorus is still smiling gently at passersby from his case in the British Museum. Indeed, as this is being written, he is appearing on a poster advertising the special exhibition of the British Museum's Roman Mummies for the Summer of 1997! The only point at which she disagrees with the taste of the heroine in the novel is that her own particular friend at the British Museum is one Sennenmut, whom she visits on every trip to that glorious place. Surprisingly, this novel is one of the few to feature a mummy where it does not climb out of its case and go on a rampage, but its existence is the pivot of the plot. It is fun to read and work out for oneself who the villain of the piece is—this is not one of those maddening whodunnits where the reader is deprived of clues supposedly in the detective's possession. If it has a drawback, it rests in the quaint though beautiful writing and long descriptive passages, reminding one of the contemporary literary forms. Indeed, the republished *The Jewel of Seven Stars* came out at the same time, and the burgeoning science of Egyptology was inspiring many to study the treasures that were being accrued by the world's great museums in much greater detail.

The Mummy (by Ricardo Stephens, 1912)

Beginning in much the same vein as *The Jewel of Seven Stars*, an accursed mummy is brought to England to be studied in London. There it triggers a series of murders. The denouement, however, reveals the killer to be a mad professor; there is no supernatural element in what is essentially a thriller-mystery. Popular enough in its day to be reissued in the 20s, it eventually sank into oblivion.

"The Valley of the Sorceress" (by Sax Rohmer, from the collection Tales of Secret Egypt, 1918)

Neville, Assistant Inspector of Antiquities, has had correspondence from his friend and colleague Condor, an archaeologist, working among the ruins of Deir-el-Bahari. Both Neville and Condor are interested in the long-dead Queen Hatasu, whose monuments grace Deir-el-Bahari, and Condor is convinced that he can clear up the mystery that seems to center on the queen.

> For him, as for me, there was a strange fascination about those defaced walls and roughly obliterated inscriptions. That the queen under whom Egyptian Art came to the apogee of perfection should thus have been treated by her successors; that no perfect figure of the wise, famous and beautiful Hatasu should have been spared to prosperity; that her very cartouche should have been ruthlessly removed from every inscription upon which it appeared, presented to Condor's mind a problem only second in interest to the immortal riddle of Gizeh."

Neville's own view is that the queen practiced the Black Arts, and he had published a monograph entitled "Hatasu, The Sorceress" on the subject, opining that she had died as a misuse of her power, and that her successors' revulsion at her practices resulted in her excision from all official records, denying her a rightful place in the afterlife.

Condor had gone to excavate at Deir-el-Bahari expecting to "find there the mummies of Hatasu — and another; the latter, a certain Sen-Mut, who appears in the inscriptions of the reign as an architect high in the queen's favor." Interestingly, as a codicil to his letter, Condor had written that a beautiful Arab girl had appeared from nowhere, begging his help and protection.

No news had come for nearly a month when Condor wrote again — this time on the eve of a momentous discovery—confiding that his native workforce had all deserted him. The Arab girl was gone, too. Be that as it may, he intended to finish his excavations, even if it had to be done single-handedly.

His third and last letter had been even stranger. He had borrowed a digging party from the British archaeological camp downriver, and they had just resumed work when the Arab girl reappeared, begging him on pain of his life and her own to take her down the Nile to Dendera. As he finished his letter to his friend, he was wrestling with the propriety of allowing her to travel alone, or accompanying her and thereby stopping the work.

Neville contemplated traveling to Luxor to see Condor and the girl, but before he could leave, he heard that Condor was in the hospital at Cairo. He had been bitten by a rabid cat, and died before Neville could get to see him. "I never saw him before the end, but they told me that his howls were horribly like those of a cat. His eyes changed in some way, too, I understand and, with his fingers all contracted, he tried to scratch everyone and everything within reach. They had to strap the poor beggar down, and even then he tore the sheets into ribbons."

Neville reports that he decided to finish the excavation and their work. He made the trip to Deir-el-Bahari and, utilizing all Condor's plans, notes, etc., he approached the dig—finding to his astonishment that the shaft was once again full of sand and debris! He was told that Condor was so eager to finish the work that he would often work on alone at day's end by lamplight; on the night he was bitten he had been working in the shaft when, it was supposed, the rabid cat had fallen into the pit and attacked him in terror.

But there was no explanation of the refilling of the shaft. Settling into camp, Neville went to bed and slept well, anticipating the work to come.

In the early hours he was wakened by a cacophony of dog howls from the nearby village — and an uneasy feeling. "In short, I fancied that the thing which had alarmed or enraged the dogs was passing from the village through the Holy Valley, upward to the Temple, upward to the plateau, and was approaching *me*."

Suddenly, his tent flap was raised and he found himself staring at an Arab girl! He grabbed her wrists, and shone a light in her face, dispelling the sensation that her eyes were glowing like a great cat's. And at once she began to plead for his protection. "I — Edward Neville, archaeologist, most prosy and matter-of-fact man in Cairo ... *knew* that this nomad who had burst into my tent, upon whom I had set eyes for the first time scarce three minutes before, held me enthralled; and yet, with her wondrous eyes upon me, I could summon up no resentment, and could offer but poor resistance." Neville managed to resist her pleas, and offered her a disguise and money to escape the locality, remarking that he believed she was the same girl who had appeared to his friend, Condor. She reacted with contempt and swept out of the tent; when Neville followed seconds later, no one was to be seen.

The excavations now proceeded well; the shaft was being cleared quickly, and Neville calculated that four days' work would bring him to the spot where Condor had stopped. Condor's notes opined six days' digging through limestone after that, to penetrate a passage that communicated to Hatasu's tomb.

During the night, Neville was wakened by the village dogs— and that uneasy feeling again. This time he saw feline eyes glowing in the dark, and shot at them, believing some wild cat had strayed into camp from the desert. The following night was uneventful, despite the mutterings of the native workmen prior to retiring; when Neville was awakened by Hassan, his headman, he was told of something strange that had occurred. Going to the dig, he was amazed to find the shaft completely refilled and his workers gone.

Neville and Hassan decided to redig the shaft themselves, and set to work with a vengeance. Sleeping the sleep of the exhausted, Neville dreamed of encircling cats eyes and howling feline voices all night, but found on waking that the day was well advanced. Seeking Hassan, he found no one, only a shaft filled to the brim and a note in Arabic "Fly, Neville Effendi! This is a haunted place!"

As Neville continued the dig — alone — he became aware how neatly his actions were matching those of the late Condor. He finally decided that he would go in search of another crew the following day and settled down for an uneasy night. A ring of cats eyes surrounded him in the darkness— a ring with just one gap. Leaping through the gap, he had found himself outside his tent. The ring regrouped, and now the gap was in the direction of the shaft. On reaching the shaft, he noted with dread that the ring had closed around him and was getting nearer and nearer. A voice had spoken in his head, ordering compliance, or the certainty of sharing Condor's fate. And he had heard another voice — his own — laughing.

On waking the following morning, he found himself on the edge of the desert plateau, bloodied and bruised, aching in every muscle. And the shaft "was reclosed to the top." Sax Rohmer, pseudonym of Arthur Ward meaning "freelance" supposedly in Anglo-Saxon, is best known nowadays for the thirteen novels he wrote about the archcriminal Fu Manchu. At the time of the discovery of Tutankhamun's tomb, though, he was equally well-known for his mystery stories set in the world of Egyptian archaeology — *The Sins of Severac Bablon* (1914), *The Brood of the Witch Queen* (1918), *Tales of Secret Egypt* (1918), and *The Green Eyes of Bast* (1920). He also wrote a nonfiction work entitled *The Romance of Sorcery* (1914) whose focal point was Egyptian magic. His most prized possession was said to be a copy of the Egyptian *Book of the Dead* that was a gift from British music hall comedian George Robey. Rohmer and his wife had honeymooned in Egypt in 1913; they were fortunate to have as their guide on part of their visit,

Rex Engelbach, who was Curator of the Cairo Museum and an assistant of Flinders Petrie, who was called "the father of Egyptology" by his contemporaries. Rohmer *borrowed* Petrie's name for one of his regular characters in the Fu Manchu stories. He was particularly impressed by Engelbach and subsequently wrote of him, "Popular conception of a working Egyptologist is grotesquely wide of the mark. We must substitute a tough specimen of humanity with leather lungs and hardy frame, his skin baked by the sun to a dark copper color; grain, nerve and muscle ready for any emergency. An absentminded, flabby Egyptologist would be lucky if he lasted three months." A loose adaptation of this tale played at the Q Theatre in London in 1928 — part of the Tut mania cash in.

Twenties and Thirties Mummies

The discovery of Tutankhamun led to a plethora of writers taking up their pens to take advantage of the *curse of the pharaohs* and other such rot. We offer a list of the more memorable in the same spirit as our previous Edwardian list.

The Palgrave Mummy by Florence M. Pettee (1929); *The Mummy Case* by Dermot Morrah (1933); *The Mummy's Curse* by Thomas S. King (1933), and *The Mummy's Hand* by Mrs. Coulson Kernahan (1933).

Weird Tales, a U.S. serial publication, contains many bizarre and thrilling mummy stories, some of which we review in more detail below.

"Imprisoned with the Pharaohs" (by Harry Houdini, ghosted by H. P. Lovecraft from Weird Tales May/June, 1924)

Harry Houdini, on vacation with his wife in Egypt, is traveling incognito, but professional pride forces him to reveal his identity while on board a Nile cruiser. Consequently, he is thereafter recognized and harassed by his fellow travelers and some of the natives, too.

The Houdinis are disappointed in the mainly European feel of Cairo, and long to share a more *Arabian Nights* atmosphere that they had come to Egypt, armed with their Baedeker guidebook, to find.

They foolishly engage a guide in the native quarter, unaware that it would be safer to have their hotel — the legendary Shepheard's — arrange one. "The man, a shaven, peculiarly hollow voice and relatively cleanly fellow, who looked like a pharaoh and called himself Abdul Reis el Drogman, appeared to have much power over others of his kind" (Houdini, 1924). As the evening draws on, the party is gratified to feel that they are at last experiencing what they came to Egypt for.

> The red sun sank low ... poised on the world's rim like that ancient god of Heliopolis — Re-Harakhte, the Horizon-Sun — we saw silhouetted against its vermeil holocaust the black outlines of the Pyramids of Gizeh — the palaeogean tombs there were hoary with a thousand years when Tut-Ankh-Amen mounted his golden throne in distant Thebes. We knew we were done with Saracen Cairo, and that we must taste the deeper mysteries of primal Egypt — the black Kem of Re and Amen, Isis and Osiris....

Since the rest of his party is exhausted, Houdini elects to go on a nocturnal tour with his native guide — alone. During the tour, Abdul Reis has a set-to with another guide and the matter is resolved by an agreement to a boxing match on the flattened top of the Great Pyramid at midnight — an established custom amongst the natives, it seems. Each duelist assembles his own team of seconds for the fray, and Houdini is delighted to be asked to be a second. They then spend the rest of the late evening in all the lowest dives assembling Abdul's team of seconds. A long donkey ride brings Houdini's group to the plateau after the departure of the last tourists. The boxing match is brief, and he is pleased when Abdul seems to have won, but then events begin to shift.

> I myself seemed to be more a center of notice than the antagonists; and from my

> smattering of Arabic, I judged that they were discussing my professional performances ... in a manner which indicated not only a surprising knowledge of me, but a distinct hostility and skepticism concerning my feats of escape. It gradually dawned on me that the elder magic of Egypt did not depart without leaving traces, and that fragments of a strange secret lore and priestly cult practices have survived surreptitiously amongst the fellaheen to such an extent that the prowess of a strange hahwi or magician is resented and disputed. I thought of how much my hollow-voiced guide Abdul Reis looked like an old Egyptian priest or pharaoh or smiling sphinx ... and wondered.

He does not wonder long, for they grab him, blindfold and bind him, and carry him away, disorienting him in the process; he feels sand beneath his bound limbs and then is suspended from a rope, through a rough hole, down a long channel whose flinty sides grate into his flesh, and finally he dangles through an unfathomable abyss to land on a rock floor. Terrified and exhausted, he momentarily loses consciousness after mentally registering the smell of the cavern in which he is now imprisoned: "A creeping odor of damp and staleness curiously unlike anything I had ever smelled before, and having faint overtones of spice and incense that lent an element of mockery." He is sure that they have dropped him into the pit under the sphinx to test his powers as an escapologist under the hardest conditions they can arrange. In his unconscious state he dreams of a huge, yellow, hairy-clawed paw reaching out to engulf him. On waking, he decides it is the spirit of Egypt, that has subtly drawn him over the preceding weeks to this test and that the spirit is older by far than even the history of that ancient land, and dangerous to body and soul. He dreams of ancient rituals, strange gods and priests, and processions. "And behind it all I saw the ineffable malignity of primordial necromancy, black and amorphous, and fumbling greedily after me in the darkness to choke out the spirit that had dared to mock it by emulation."

In his dream, Abdul Reis is identified as Khephren, who raised the second pyramid and carved the features of the sphinx to resemble his own; and as he wakes he determines to get out as speedily as possible. First, he has to rid himself of blindfold and bindings. Still attached to the rope that lowered him, he knows that if he moves his tormentors will know he has survived, but try as he may, he cannot stop the movement of the rope. It suddenly begins to fall on him in hideous great loops. He realizes how *much* rope there must be and struggles under the growing weight and mass of it, succumbing again to oblivion.

Gaining his wits once more, the burden of the rope is gone. Oblivion has brought more nightmares— he has dreamed of long-dead mummies, of rituals, of the processes to preserve the body for all eternity, the passing of centuries as the dead wait, and other things. "It was to have been a glorious rebirth — but not all souls were approved, nor were all tombs inviolate, so that certain grotesque mistakes and fiendish abnormalities were to be looked for. Even today the Arabs murmur of unsanctified convocations and unwholesome worship in forgotten nether abysses, which only winged invisible kas and soulless mummies may visit and return unscathed." He remembers old tales of hideous composite mummies, part human, part animal, and of Khephren who leads the unholy host as their high priest with his ghoul-queen at his side, and a question he had idly asked himself in the glories of sunlight springs unbidden to his mind. "What huge and loathesome abnormality was the sphinx originally carved to represent?"

Mentally checking himself in preparation for escape, he is startled to be more slashed and blood-caked than his descent should warrant, and he wonders at the cause and what has stopped its continuing. Drawing on his courage and resource, he escapes the bonds the Arabs have placed on him — to find it so dark that he might still have been blindfold. Undeterred, he sets off following a foul airflow across the limitless dark space. Eventually, he realizes that this is not the path to freedom; as he continues in the hope of finding a way out, he plummets down a huge staircase and knocks himself out.

Coming round yet again, he rallies himself with wry the thought that his lapses into unconsciousness are like the changes of scenes in a crude cinema melodrama, and while doing so bumps into what he comprehends is a gigantic column. Crawling onward interminably, he encounters more columns and then hears the sound of an unholy procession approaching. The worshippers in the procession are carrying torches, and though there are legions, the blackness is barely penetrated, so vast is this subterranean temple. The very sound they make is so terrifying that Houdini is determined not to look at them, and turning away, his soul is shriveled by the mere sight of their shadows! The shadows, sounds, and smells tax his sanity—every so often he peeps to see if they have all passed—only to slam his eyes shut again. But a great shout forces them open, and he sees the adherents hurling sacrificial gifts to the yawning maw of the rock, led in worship by the sneering Khephren and his queen, "beautiful Queen Nicotris whom I saw in profile for a moment, noting that the right half of her face was eaten away by rats or other ghouls." He realizes that the god they worship is actually present in the abyss, and it may be the Unknown One who was worshipped before the Egyptian gods were known.

Deciding that this is the perfect time to escape, while the worshippers are too rapt to notice him, he makes for the huge stairs. Halfway up, the shout comes again and he is drawn to watch. Something was emerging from the gap.

> It was as large, perhaps, as a good-sized hippopotamus, but very curiously shaped. It seemed to have no neck, but five separate shaggy heads springing in a row from a roughly cylindrical trunk.... Out of these heads darted curiously rigid tentacles which seized ravenously on the excessively great quantities of unmentionable food placed before the aperture.... Its locomotion was so inexplicable that I stared in fascination, wishing it would emerge farther from the cavernous lair beneath me.

And as it does, the full horror breaks on Houdini and he makes a final dash for freedom and sanity. The morning sun finds him on the sands before the Great Sphinx. He had seen "the five-headed monster—and that of which it is the merest forepaw....

In retrospect, he concludes it was all a dream or a hallucination brought about by his abduction and the rigors of his escape. At least, he wants to believe it was—for if not, does that hideous thing not still exist so close to the footsteps of happy tourists??

This delicious piece of Arkhamia in absentia was penned by Howard Phillips Lovecraft, ghosting for Harry Houdini, escapologist extraordinaire but no literary genius, commissioned by the editor of *Weird Tales*.

Houdini had entertained the editor with a tale of his abduction and ordeal in escaping "an ancient subterranean temple at Gizeh," which may or may not have been based on fact, for he was a great showman. The editor, recognizing a terrific yarn, asked Lovecraft to "put this into a vivid narrative form" Not surprisingly, it turned out to be Lovecraft's greatest commercial success to that point in his career, and as a consequence, he was offered the editorship of *Weird Tales* magazine.

Lovecraft seems to have emulated Stoker in the matter of this story; the premise appears to have been suggested by part of Sax Rohmer's *Brood of the Witch Queen*, and the background details certainly come from the Baedeker *Guide to Egypt and the Sudan*. For all that, the resulting tale is pure Lovecraft.

Interestingly, Houdini was not only known as showman-escapologist, but also an avid debunker of fake spiritualist mediums. In the mid–1920s, most of his newspaper coverage was for this pursuit. He is thought to have been a true believer, which is why he hunted down the fakes so fanatically; he arranged with his widow to contact her on the first anniversary of his death as his final investigation into the possibility of communicating with the dead. One of the observers at the — sadly — unsuccessful event was Sir Arthur Conan Doyle. Sir Arthur was perhaps more gullible than Harry, and they had crossed swords on the subject many times during Doyle's 1923 lecture tour of the United States.

The peculiarly Lovecraftian horror of ancient hateful gods has not permeated the movie world much, but it lives on in the world of the comic — or graphic — novel, animating the mummies of those stories. Mayhap in these days of the Computer Generated Image, Lovecraftian mummies might be a viable concern, but the authors sincerely hope that this facet of the genre stays where it plays best — in the minds of the avid readers.

A Visitor from Egypt (by Frank Belknap Long, from *Popular Fiction* [1930] and Arkham House [1946])

A strikingly dressed man enters a New England museum, his face obscured by a scarf. After presenting his card to the curator he is warmly welcomed. Sir Richard is an acknowledged expert on Egyptian religion.

"Are the pre-dynastic remains from Luxor on exhibition?" he asks. "Are the bones tinted?" Bones were often painted red or blue in an attempt to preserve the remains and, as Sir Richard bitterly notes, to cheat Osiris of his prize. He states that the god must have been offended at this attempt to circumvent his power over death as laid down in The Book Of The Dead.

"I believe the Book of the Dead, as we know it, was a forgery," Sir Richard explains to the aghast curator, "Parts of it are undoubtedly predynastic, but I believe that the Judgment of the Dead, which defines the judicial prerogatives of Osiris, was inserted by some meddling priests as late as the historical period.... Osiris does not judge. He takes. He is the Dark God." And he treasures what belongs to him — the bones are, to Sir Richard, blasphemous.

The topic changes to a book of fiction the curator is reading called The Transfiguration Of Osiris. Sir Richard believes gods can become pure flame at will. "'It would be dreadful,' continued Sir Richard, 'if the god had no control over his transfiguration; if the change occurred frequently and unexpectedly; if he shared, as it were, the ghastly fate of Dr. Jekyll and Mr. Hyde.'"

Having explained earlier that the scarf covers an injury sustained aboard ship, Sir Richard suddenly demands water — a constant need caused by the accident. He shuffles off to the basement lavatory. Cries of "Fire!" are raised by the staff, and the curator rushes to Sir Richard's aid. He emerges from the flames hissing, "Fool! You have sinned irretrievably!"

He makes his way to the Antiquities Room where he discards his clothing.

> ...only his back was visible. But it was not an ordinary back. In a lucid, unemotional moment, Mr. Buzzby would have called it a nasty, malignant back, but in juxtaposition to the crown that topped it there was no Aryan polysyllable suggestive enough to describe it. For the crown was very tall and ponderous with jewels and unspeakably luminous, and it accentuated the vileness of the back. It was a green back. Sapless was the word that ran through Mr. Buzzby's mind as he stood and stared at it. It was wrinkled, too, horribly wrinkled, all criss-crossed with centuried grooves.

The poor curator tries to be inconspicuous, but the creature is aware of him; it silently glides towards him, clutching in its hideously thin arms a collection of painted bones from the broken cases.

The creature cackles as it advances on the terrified man, whose reason leaves him pleading and supplicating, gibbering and crawling along the floor. "But the figure, when it got to him, merely stooped and breathed on him. Three times it breathed on his ashen face and one could almost see the face shrivel and blacken beneath its warm breath." It then glides away with its prize, unseen by the rest of the shaff. It is never seen again.

Later, as the coroner examines the body of the curator, he notes, "the conclusion was unavoidable that the curator had been dead for a long, long time."

Many readers enjoyed this addition to the mummy canon. Many others remarked upon the beginning being reminiscent of H. G. Wells's *The Invisible Man*, others that it has elements of M. R. James's *The Tractate Middoth*. It is, however, powerful enough to frighten the reader despite being somewhat muddled in construction. It also added the concept of a vengeful being with supernatural powers to mummy lore. At this point it appears that screenwriters suddenly became aware of the existence of this treasure trove of mummy stories and began to transfer most of the elements contained therein to treatments and screenplays.

The Nameless Mummy (by Arlton Eadie, 1932)

Peter Venn is forty, a life-long bachelor, and curator of the Helmstone Museum. His special — and only — joy is showing visitors through the Egyptian section. Tonight he has closed the museum early to unpack a new shipment of artifacts, including a mummy case with no external identification.

After removing the coating of the ages, Venn reads an inscription in Latin — "*Kingdoms, honors, riches are frail and fickle things — and wonders.*"

His reverie is interrupted by the appearance of a mysteriously beautiful woman, who rouses Venn's interest — and more. Her imperious manner soon puts him off, but he is strangely unable to ask her to leave. Venn's interest increases when she reads from a papyrus the writings of the Thirteenth Dynasty.

She orders Venn to return to the Museum later that evening and, despite himself, he complies. Together they open the mummy case. Inside is the perfectly preserved body of a Roman soldier — and a name plate. It is the mummy of Mark Antony. The woman at Venn's side is Cleopatra.

She explains that she drank blood flowing from the statue of Isis, which gave her immortality. The antidote, should she wish it, is a green powder contained in a ring. Cleopatra faked her suicide to evade capture, substituting a loyal servant, but her lover Antony was not in on the ruse and fell on his sword.

Cleopatra now longed for death, but the ring was on Antony's finger and his tomb hidden. Before Venn can react, Cleopatra seizes the ring and joins Antony in death.

Monkeys (by E.F. Benson, 1933)

Dr. Hugh Morris, a respected London surgeon, is given to occasional vivisection if he feels the end is justified. While dining with his friend Jack Madden, they discuss the latter's impending trip to excavate a tomb at Luxor. Dr. Morris, a workaholic, declines Madden's invitation to join him.

They see a small animal in the yard — in great pain. Using the opportunity afforded by the animal, Morris plans a previously untried operation for the morning.

Later, Madden receives a telegram in Egypt from Dr. Morris, who will soon be joining him. Upon his arrival he tells a strange tale. After clamping the monkey's vertebrae with a metal band, Dr. Morris had observed the animal constantly till its death two days later. When performing surgery the next day, he had had a frightening hallucination — a monkey sitting on his patient's chest. His own physician advised immediate rest.

While recuperating, Dr. Morris watches the excavation of the mummy of A-pen-aron, whose tomb is guarded by images of a large ape — and a curse. Madden, through superstition and respect, always reinters mummies after taking their treasures. Dr. Morris is stunned to see, as she is unwrapped, that spinal surgery similar to his own experiment on the monkey was successfully performed 3500 years before.

Before returning to London, Dr. Morris removes the vertebrae to prove his theory to colleagues. On the trip home he is haunted by images of monkeys. His friend Madden is unaware of the stolen vertebrae.

At his London home Dr. Morris shows the vertebrae to his servant and retires. The man is awakened by screams and sees his master being mutilated by a huge ape. When Madden learns what his friend has done, he returns to Luxor and reinters A-pen-aron, whose missing vertebrae has mysteriously been replaced.

A Mummy's Hand That Came To Life (by Cheiro, from *Real Life Stories*, 1934)

Cheiro, a world famous palmist and mystic, writes "I relate a strange but true story of a mummy's hand that after some thousands of years showed remarkable signs of coming back to life...."

He had spent eighteen months working in the kings' tombs with Professor von Heller, making wax impressions of the hieroglyphs on the walls. During that time, the men were looked after by an elderly Arab.

As Cheiro prepared to leave for England, the old Arab asked for a private interview and during it gave him "*something wrapped up in one of those bandages that are found bound round the limbs of mummies ... the right hand of a mummy in a magnificent state of preservation. I stared back in astonishment— it was a long beautifully shaped hand, evidently of a woman. The nails were perfect in shape, even the gold-leaf that the ancient Egyptians used instead of the red paint that ladies employ today was as good as when it had first been put on.*"

The hand had been severed from the wrist and mummified by some strange process which made it seem as though it was carved from a piece of hard, dark wood. And on the first finger shone an ancient gold ring inscribed with hieroglyphs. The old Arab explained that the hand belonged to the seventh daughter of the heretic Pharaoh, Atennaten; Princess Makitaten had remained faithful to her father's creed when her brother-in-law, Tut-Ankh-Amen, had restored the Old Gods. The princess had raised an army and attacked the new monarch, dying in the battle. Vengeful priests had hacked off her sword arm and mummified the hand to put it on display as a warning to others. The hand had been passed down through the old Arab's family with its legend, and now it was being given to Cheiro, for he was the chosen one who would care for it.

"The curse that was placed on that hand has not yet been fulfilled. Listen carefully for you are the one selected to carry out its purpose." As Cheiro listened, the old man told him that his return to London would not herald a happy, settled period of his life as he had planned. There would be no home and no rest; he would find that his wealth was forfeit and that to survive he would have to turn to the teaching of occult studies. It was to be his fate to take the most despised of these sciences—palmistry—and make it universally respected. Because of his new profession, he would meet royalty and important world figures, and become famous.

> It is true, her mummy found a resting place by the tomb of her father, King Atennaten, and will some day be brought to light. The part of the curse unfulfilled is that her right hand would sooner or later be carried and exhibited in all the principal countries of the earth and would find no rest until after the end of a great war, when the lost tomb of her brother-in-law, the King Tut-Ankh-Amen, would be discovered.

At the end of the great war, on the eve of the discovery of the pharaoh's tomb, the hand would seek to escape from Cheiro's care and the ka imprisoned in it would seek reunification with the princess. Until then, the hand would be his talisman, and he would protect it. And he swore an oath to do so.

It seemed that the hand protected him through the years; foiling a robbery, preventing a near-fatal elevator accident, and warding off terrorist bands during a brief spell when Cheiro and his wife lived in Ireland during The Troubles. As the couple prepared to move to London, strange events occurred.

Cheiro discovered that the hand, which had always been hard, had become flaccid and appeared to be bleeding. "Have you ever heard of a mummy's hand, or any part of a mummy showing signs of bleeding after having been embalmed for over three thousand years?" he asked a chemist friend who checked it out and tried to restore it to its former condition by any means possible. The report confirmed that it was human blood coming from the hand, and in desperation the chemist soaked it in pitch and shellac to restore its rigidity.

Some while later, when all the contents of the house had been moved save for their personal belongings and the hand, that ancient relic softened and bled again ... this time beginning to melt in the process. Cheiro was loathe to pack it up in such condition and was considering what to do when a band of thieves broke into the house. They grabbed the hand, greedy for the ring, but ran screaming at the sight of its blood. Once again it had protected them.

A few nights later, Cheiro and his wife agreed that they should cremate the hand as it was unfit for further journeys. While they waited for the fire to heat up, they walked in the grounds of the house, talking about Thebes and the land of Egypt they both knew so well. Recalling the old Arab's words about the hand trying to get free, they returned to their sad task. His wife suggested an ancient prayer she kept remembering, before the burning, and as the words ended, he reverently confined the hand to flames. The flames turned white and brilliant, and the house filled with the perfume of spices—and outside the door the wind rose dramatically and the doors blew open. Something began to take shape in the doorway and move into the house:

"...the form of a woman, with head, shoulders and body down to the hips, clearly outlined and every moment growing clearer. It was a very beautiful and remarkable face that finally looked toward us. Nobility, grandeur and pride of race seemed marked in every line, while the eyes—no words of mine can describe them. Large, deep-set, lustrous eyes that shone with a radiance of their own." The woman was dressed in ancient royal robes, with jewels to befit a princess. She moved to the fireplace, seemed to bend slightly and then faced the astonished couple with "both hands clasped together as if in a moment of ecstasy." The figure glided to the doors and vanished, leaving them totally unable to speak. As dawn broke, they reverently gathered the burnt bones, agreeing to reinter them in Egypt at the earliest possible opportunity. The princess's ring, thereafter, was Cheiro's most precious possession.

On arriving in London after a terrifying journey, the papers were full of the discovery of Tut-Ankh-Amen's tomb. The date of the find—a day after they had cremated the princess's hand—was coincidence was so unsettling that they had discussed it with several friends when they heard that Carnarvon was going to Egypt for the official opening of the tomb.

Discussing the news by the fire late one evening, Cheiro's wife was finishing a sketch she had been working on of the spirit princess while he was writing. The lights dimmed, and again they were in the presence of the long-dead lady. Raising her right hand, she pointed at his pad and he wrote unconsciously. When the vision faded and the lights returned, he read the message—for Lord Carnarvon. "It was to the effect that on his arrival at the tomb of Tut-Ankh-Amen he was not to allow any of the relics found in it to be removed or taken away. The ending of the message was 'that if he disobeyed the warning he would suffer an injury while in the tomb — a sickness from which he would never recover, and that death would claim him in Egypt.'"

Cheiro sent the message to the Earl, who read it and remarked upon it to his friends. He was, however, not about to be put off the project. Cheiro records the known facts— the Earl disobeyed, was stung by an insect, contracted blood poisoning, and died.

Cheiro, also known as Count Louis Hamon, was the best known and most respected palmist of his day. He wrote many books on the subject and had the kind of client list that read like a worldwide *Who's Who*. His name is often used as a spirit name by today's clairvoyants and mystics but no one has ever achieved his status.

He would have known the Earl of Carnarvon and his wife Lady Almina, who was reportedly as interested in Cheiro's pursuits as any of her social circle. He would also have known Aleister Crowley, the infamous practitioner of the Black Arts. Both Carnarvons also had "readings" from a psychic called Velma, and she wrote in detail about a reading she had done for the Earl shortly before he left for the last trip he made to Egypt. She maintains that she warned him about a grave peril she saw in the lines on his hand, and that they had sought further confirmation in a crystal reading that frightened and awed her. In recounting it to the Earl, she again warned him to stop the dig on pain of death. He had considered for awhile the possibility of ancient power being still active in the Valley, but concluded with a shrug of his shoulders and a smile, "But what an adventure! A challenge to the psychic powers of the ages, Velma! What a challenge!" And not long after ... he died ("Velma," *My Mysteries and My Story* 1929).

The Eyes of the Mummy (by Robert Bloch, from *Weird Tales* [1938] and Arkham House [1945])

An unscrupulous young man, fascinated by magic and the mysteries of ancient Egypt, is drawn into a society of occultists in New Orleans. There, one of the party was killed under supernatural circumstances while examining the mummy of a priest of Sebek. The young man swears to avoid any contact with the black arts of Egypt...

Years later, he again meets Professor Weildan, who had smuggled the mummy into America. Lured by the promise of wealth — and perhaps more — he agrees to accompany Weildan to Egypt. There they will exhume another Sebek priest — and his fabulous jewelry.

The expedition begins badly: Weildan kills his Egyptian informant when the man holds out for more money. They find the tomb easily — too easily — and begin to inspect the mummy case. By reading the inscription they learn that the priest had his eyes torn out ... while still alive.

When the case is opened, they discover why; the eyes have been replaced by magic jewels. As the young man stares into them he is hypnotized by their occult power, and an horrific change occurs. "Good God!" he shrieks, "I'm in the mummy's body!" The priest, in human form, walks off. The young man, with rotting fingers, pulls the jewels from their sockets, ending the obscene body exchange. He finds Weildan on the tomb floor, dead from a stroke.

Outside the tent, the young man examines the jewels, assuming they have no power when removed from the mummy. He is wrong — the exchange is repeated. Trapped in the mummy's body, disintegrating in the air, the young man dies while typing a warning.

Beetles (by Robert Bloch, 1938)

The Narrator tells the tale of his longtime friend, Arthur Hartley, and the tragedy that befell him on his return from a dig in Egypt. Hartley, once a jolly, brilliant, gregarious fellow, shuns his friends and acquaintances and resigns his post at the institute. He has become a haunted shadow of his former self and everyone but the narrator accepts the changes, though they all comment on the situation with concern.

Visiting Hartley at home proves to be quite a problem, but having gained entry to the apartment with Hartley's grudging agreement, the narrator notices few changes, save for Hartley's use of incense before a figurine of Horus. "Thick gray spirals of smoke arose in the approved style of exotic fiction, and I smelt the pungent tang of strong incense. That was the first puzzler ... incense was definitely alien to the Arthur Hartley I knew. 'Clears away the smell,' he remarked."

Through Hartley's apparent ravings, his friend learns that he lives in dread of scarab beetles, which he believes are hunting him down in response to a curse that he has brought upon himself. Sunlight or pure flame keeps them at bay but they teem in the shadows and follow him everywhere. When they had met in the hallway of the apartment, he had been clutching a large brown parcel which is shown to contain industrial strength insecticide that Hartley fervently hopes "may defeat the powers of Evil." Laughing hollowly, he explains that he used to laugh at curses and the like. "...curses on old pottery and battered statues never seemed important to me. But Egyptology—that's different. It's human bodies, there. Mummified but still human."

It transpires that his last dig had been successful. They had found pottery, furniture, bas-reliefs and mummies—mummies that Hartley believed were cursed. An action of his had led to the curse being activated—a curse that he had read on a mummy case but disregarded. During the voyage home, he had begun to be haunted by the presence of thousands of scarab beetles and his only recourse on his return was to resign his post and become a recluse, lest his actions endanger his friends.

Urged by his friend to explain why the Curse of Scarabaeus should strike him, Hartley confesses. "I stole a mummy ... the mummy of a temple virgin. I must have been crazy to do it; something happens to you under that sun. There was gold in the case, and jewels, and ornaments. And there was the Curse, written. I got them—both." Initially, Hartley had believed that the Curse was to be forever haunted by the beetles and deprived of human comfort thereby, but he had lately come to believe that their objective was to kill him for his sin. He told his friend the stolen mummy would be proof of his sanity, should anyone try to have him committed and also proof of the manner of his passing should he die. His terror is so real that his friend almost believes in the creatures himself before he floods the room in light and reveals—nothing.

Going swiftly to his friend, Dr. Sherman, the narrator arranges that the two of them should visit Hartley later that night. Hartley will be institutionalized and cured of his delusions, overwrought as he is by guilt at his crime, but they have to use the narrator's skeleton key to gain admission when Hartley does not answer the door.

The smell in the apartment is composed of incense, insecticide, and some other musty odor. They find Hartley dead in bed and Sherman goes for help, instructing his shocked friend to touch nothing. Alone with his thoughts, the recognition of the strange odor breaks into his conscious mind—beetles! But there is no evidence of their method of entry to the house. Searching the second bedroom, the Narrator finds the stolen mummy case, slightly ajar. Inspecting the mummy, he discovers just a husk with a large hole in the abdomen from which beetles were crawling. Running to the death scene, he searches Hartley's body for wounds, but there are none. The body is, however, far too light for a man of Hartley's build. Hartley had told him that the beetles swarmed over him every night and that he feared to sleep in case they killed him.

> As I gazed at him now, he seemed empty of more than life. I peered into the ravaged face more closely, and then I shuddered. For the cords on his neck moved convulsively, his chest seemed to rise and fall, his head fell sideways onto the pillow. He lived—or something inside him did! ... I knew how

> Hartley had died, and what had killed him; knew the secret of the Scarab Curse and why the beetles crawled out of the mummy to seek his bed.... Just as I fainted, I saw Arthur Hartley's dead lips part, allowing a rustling swarm of black Scarabaeus beetles to pour out across the pillow.

Robert Bloch's two contributions to the subgenre of mummy short stories appeared in *Weird Tales* eight months apart—*The Eyes of the Mummy* in April and *Beetles* in December of 1938. We shall probably never know why he had a sudden passion for mummy mysteries; but his *Beetles* must have subconsciously eaten into his readers' long-term memory, reemerging perhaps as the dreaded curse in Universal's *The Mummy* (1998) as an even larger teaming hoard, but still hell-bent on protecting holy things.

The Vengeance of AI (by August Derleth and Mark Schorer, Better Publications Inc., 1939)

Peter Harris leaves London for Cairo to meet his fiancee, Margaret Levering, who has gone to investigate her father's death. Lord Warrender, an Egyptologist, was killed when a colossal statue of Ai, the Moon Goddess, crashed down on him.

Harris, once in Cairo, meets Ernest Lumsden—a friend of Warrender—and his associate, Sheik Al-Jubal. They explain that Warrender, after making certain that the huge statue was firmly anchored to its base, attempted to remove a golden amulet from its neck. After the "accident" the monstrous statue was found mysteriously back in place. Even worse, Margaret believes that her father is, even yet, the victim of a horrific curse; his spirit, she thinks, is condemned to run from tomb to tomb, guarding the mummies on each night of the full moon. She refuses to return to London until the curse is broken or revealed to be untrue. Since two witnesses to her father's "accident" have died mysteriously, Margaret dismisses the latter possibility.

The party leaves Cairo for the Valley of the Moon and the Tomb of Ai, hoping *not* to encounter Lord Warrender's spirit. They make camp, and later, with Harris and Margaret watching, Lumsden trains a searchlight on the tomb. With the added light of the full moon, the scene is almost blinding. Lumsden circles the area with the light and they see ... nothing.

Margaret resolves to return to London. But Lumsden tells Harris a chilling secret—Warrender *was* there. Lumsden purposely obscured him from Margaret with the blinding light. After telling Harris to guard Margaret in her tent, Lumsden and Al-Jubal form an occult circle and break the ancient curse. "It's not easy to break a curse," Lumsden says cryptically," and sometimes there is a penalty."

In London Harris receives a telegram from Lumsden—Al-Jubal was found dead, near the tomb. Harris' subsequent letter to Lumsden is returned, marked "Cannot Be Found."

The Man in Crescent Terrace (by Seabury Quinn, *Weird Tales*, 1946)

Drs. Jules De Grandin and Samuel Trowbridge encounter a bleeding. terrified, and screaming young woman while out walking. They hail a cab and take her to Trowbridge's house for treatment.

Edina Laurace claims to have seen a sloppily dressed man being chased by a mummy "...tall, almost six feet, and bone thin ... the color of a tan shoe and entirely unclothed. It ran in a peculiar way, like a marionette moved by unseen wires." After stabbing the man, it slashed her shoulder as she ran from Crescent Terrace. "Its lips were like tanned leather and I could see the jagged line of its teeth."

The doctors report the incident to Det. Lt. Costello, who, had earlier that evening, investigated a stabbing on Crescent Terrace. Louis Westbrook, a low-level informant, was found ripped to pieces. Dr. De Grandin states that he was killed by a mummy.

The trio observe the residents of the small street and close in on one Grafton Loftus, who served in Egypt with the British Army in World War I. Scotland Yard informs them that Loftus has been associated with diabolic cults ... and possibly human sacrifices. An eye witness claimed to have seen a mummy raised from the dead.

They approach Loftus's house and are attacked by the mummy, which is incinerated by De Grandin's cigarette lighter. When confronted, Loftus sneeringly states that no judge–jury would believe their story. De Grandin agrees, and pushes him down a staircase, breaking the sorcerer's neck.

From the late 1940s until the late 1980s, mummy stories were largely relegated to the pages of comics—or graphic novels, if you prefer the term—where they generally revealed themselves to be stranded or imprisoned aliens or alien robots (oh for a new plot!). With the exception of Stan Lee's series *The Living Mummy* where the eponymous hero had been a live Egyptian once, the rest are great and gaudy to look at but have no substance ... and the authors should know ... we read dozens of the darned things in researching this book. Well, that's our excuse anyway.

Mummies in this dormant period punctuated many a film, TV series, and book as subplots, but never as the leading character. Many fictional characters *encountered* mummies: Herman Munster, patriarch of *The Munsters*; the crew of the Nautilus in *Voyage to the Bottom of the Sea*; Ilya Kuryakin in a movie spin-off of *The Man From UNCLE* entitled *One Spy Too Many*; the eponymous sleuth-priest of *The Father Dowling Mysteries*, Dr. Who (on TV, video, *and* novelization of the script) in *The Pyramids of Mars*; the Hardy Boys in *The Mummy Case*; Kolchak in *The Night Stalker*; *The Outer Limits*; the infant members of *The Monster Squad*; Sherlock Holmes in Spielberg's *Young Sherlock Holmes*; Wilbur Smith in *River God* and *The Seventh Seal*; the group of friends in *Scooby-doo, Power Rangers*, and other protectors of the galaxy; Poirot in TV's *Hercule Poirot Investigates*; Ayesha in H. Rider Haggard's *She*; the parents of the Crypt Keeper in *Tales from the Crypt*; Judge Dredd; Swamp Thing; Sam Beckett et al. from *Quantum Leap*.

Deserving of a special mention is Elizabeth Peters—in real life Egyptologist Barbara Mertz, author of many a fascinating serious tome—for creating the Victorian sleuth and Egyptologist Amelia Peabody and her eccentric family, who clatter around Egypt at the dawn of real archaeology, always involved with murder, intrigue, and antiquities smuggling. One can only imagine with envy the intellectual fun Mertz gets by letting her ingenious imagination dance with her considerable knowledge of the background to create such scrumptious stories!

The Long Night of the Grave (by Charles L. Grant, 1986)

Set in turn of the century fictional Oxrun Station, Connecticut: The killer mummy is rarely glimpsed in this eerily atmospheric book and is referred to as "Blackshadow."

Cities of the Dead (by Michael Paine, 1988)

Believed by many to be the finest mummy novel since Stoker's opus, it is set in 1903–04. Taking the form of a diary kept by Howard Carter, it marvelously invokes the atmosphere of Cairo and the lives of the people working there. The focus is Carter's discovery of a horrifying child mummy who appears to have been embalmed whilst still alive; the miasma of mysticism and magic makes for a potent read.

The Mummy—Or Ramses the Damned (by Anne Rice, Chatto and Windus, 1989)

Lawrence Stratford, retired head of Stratford Shipping, has given his life to his passion—the study of Ancient Egypt, as an active excavator. He has found an astounding tomb, which offers him an infinite number of puzzles. The puzzles excite him, but frighten his faithful friend and helper, Samir.

Inscriptions identify the owner of the tomb as Ramses the Damned and describe him as "Once Ramses the Great of Upper and Lower Egypt; Slayer of the Hittites, Builder of Temples; Beloved of the People; and immortal guardian of the kings and queens of Egypt throughout time. In the year of the death of the Great Queen Cleopatra, as Egypt becomes a Roman province, I commit myself to eternal darkness; beware, all those who would let the rays of the sun pass this door."

Both Lawrence and Samir believe Ramses the Great's mummy to be in the Cairo Museum, but further study leads Lawrence to begin to understand this may not be so. The tomb contains treasures that are ancient in concept, but executed in Roman times, other than the ring worn by the mummy, which appears to be ancient indeed. Contained in the tomb are papyri that Lawrence translates, telling how Ramses, crazed by grief at the death of his love, Cleopatra, had hidden the cursed elixir that gave him immortality amongst the queen's poisons— and Lawrence finds the jars. Writings in hieroglyphs, Greek, and Latin, all appear to be by the same hand — and yet how??

While Lawrence ponders the puzzle and longs to be alone with his discovery, his sleazy nephew Henry, sole and disappointing male heir to the Stratford millions, wants to interrupt him. Henry, whose father Randolph had taken on control of the family business when Lawrence retired, has embezzled vast sums to cover his debts. Henry hopes Lawrence's discovery will make him careless of the papers that he needs to sign to cover the fraud. But Lawrence refuses and is angry when Henry meddles with the artifacts, pointing out the dangers of the poisons.

All the while, Lawrence is desperately missing the one presence that would share and understand his emotions— his daughter Julie. Sunshine has crept into the tomb, illuminating the mummy, and Lawrence fancies it is different than when he first discovered it. Henry persuades Lawrence to drink the coffee that Samir has brought, but not before he has added one of Cleopatra's poisons. Lawrence dies, staring at the mummy. Henry forges the signatures he requires and believes he has got away with both fraud and murder.

In Edwardian London, Elliott, Earl of Rutherford, almost crippled with arthritis, rejoices in the fact that his son and heir, Alex, hopes to marry Julie Stratford. She will grace their title and bloodline, and her millions will help the cash-strapped aristocrats. Julie, however, is not ready for the marriage and wonders if she ever will be, although she acknowledges that it would be a brilliant match, socially, and Alex would die to make her happy.

Her uncle Rudolph and the Earl both encourage the match. News of her father's death gives her breathing space on the marriage and she makes two important decisions. First, she intends to bring the treasures of Ramses, including the mummy, to London to exhibit as her father would have done, and second, she intends to take her place on the board of the firm, taking a fully active part in its affairs. The exhibition in her home is successful, and nearly everyone speaks to the mummy, which has a presence they do not understand. Julie, having read her father's notes, now understands something of Ramses' strange history and is fascinated by him.

Henry moves into Julie's house to chaperone her, and feels uncomfortable as the exhibition is laid out. He finds her as intransigent as her father in the matter of signing papers without reading them, and Henry finds himself in a horrific deja vu reality as he poisons Julie's coffee. As Julie is to drink it, she freezes— the mummy is coming towards her, reaching out and grabbing Henry, who flees the house shrieking.

Julie watches spellbound as the mummy crawls into the early morning sunlight of the conservatory; the light restores it to vibrant good health.

> Then it rose on its knees with quiet grace and reached down into the fountain with its

> bandaged hands, scooping up the sparkling water to its lips. It drank and drank the water, with deep sighing gulps. Then it stopped and turned towards her, wiping away more of the thick ashen layer of linen from its face. A man looking at her! A blue-eyed man with intelligence looking at her!

As Julie battles with her mixed emotions, the mummy, mimicking Henry's voice perfectly, shows her how Henry killed her father and tried to kill her. The shocks are coming thick and fast, and as her maid screams at the scene she sees on entering the room, Julie at last faints. Regaining consciousness, Julie finds the mummy waiting patiently.

> And there was the mummy, standing right there. Nothing about it imagined. Not the dark lock of hair fallen down on his smooth broad forehead. Or his deep shadowy blue eyes. He had torn loose more of the rotted stuff that covered him. He was bare to the waist, a god, it seemed at the moment. Especially with that smile. That warm and embracing smile.

As Julie acknowledges to herself that this is the most beautiful man she has ever seen, the forces of law and order, brought about by Henry, begin to batter the door. Truly her father's daughter, Julie drags Ramses to her father's room, indicates the bath and clothes, and tells him to stay. Then she begins to deal with her unwanted visitors but Ramses joins them in a dressing gown, still wearing his scarab ring; Julie introduces him as Mr. Ramsey — a friend of her father's just arrived from Egypt. Her visitors leave, but her uncle is unhappy that she is unchaperoned. Henry flatly refuses to go back.

Having eaten and drunk, Ramses goes about learning English in his own fashion, as Latin is somewhat inconvenient, and Julie not fluent enough to tell him all he wants to know. He does not need sustenance, other than the sun, but he enjoys the pleasure of eating and drinking. He does not need sleep, and during the hours of darkness he either consolidates the things he has learned during the day, or listens to music, or reads. Soon he is as articulate as any of Julie's circle. Julie conceives a plan of education for him, to span the centuries he has slept and to take her mind off the growing attraction she has for him. Ramses decides that he will kill Henry for he is king, court, and justice in his world. Julie will not let him, and he bows to her wishes.

While Julie and Ramses explore the city, Elliott shares with Samir the secret of the revived Pharaoh. Coming home, they find Samir waiting. Samir is devastated when Ramses tells him, in the ancient tongue, that Julie is safe with him because he loves her. While Julie sleeps, Ramses visits Samir in his office at the museum, and is shown around the antiquities. Samir and Ramses agree that it would be safer to take Julie to Egypt since Ramses longs to go. Julie's relations and the Rutherfords decide to go too, so she is cursed with Henry's presence. Ramses nearly reveals himself at the first dinner on board ship, and from then on dines privately with Julie. Henry proceeds to drink himself into insensibility to cope with the fear. Before the journey, Ramses has brewed more of the elixir, and carries it concealed about him.

Egypt! Ramses is desperate to find his Alexandria, but only fragments exist. Henry decamps to his mistress's house and the rest of the party are glad that he is gone. Ramses finds his memories unbearable, and they leave Alexandria for Upper Egypt and his monuments. At Abu Simbel, Julie and Ramses become lovers and Ramses experiments with a mummified hand, which he revives with the elixir — and then they return to Cairo.

On a visit to the museum, Ramses comes across an unknown, damaged mummy, but recognizes the great love of his life with no difficulty. The sight of it crushes him. Later, Elliott follows Ramses back to the museum and realizes that the pharaoh intends to revive Cleopatra. But it is not like his own revival. Elliott observes with growing horror:

> The light shone in its huge staring eyes, the eyelids eaten away, the hair thickening and writhing as it grew sleeker and blacker and tumbled down longer over the bony shoulders. But dear God, what were the patches of white all over it? They were the bones of the thing, the bare bones where the flesh had been torn away, perhaps centuries ago! Bare bone showing in the left leg, bare bone in the right foot, bare bones in the fingers struggling to reach Ramsey.

Elliott understands the revenant is not whole — and mad — and in pain. As the museum guards grab Ramses, Elliott follows Cleopatra, having retrieved the remaining drops of the elixir. In Latin, he explains he is a friend, and will take her to safety.

Cleopatra kills a serving woman as Elliott takes her to Henry's mistress's home.

Ramses breaks out of prison, leaving Julie and Alex to cope with the authorities. Cleopatra is shot by Henry, who then realizes what she is. She snaps his neck easily, and his mistress arranges to dispose of the body — bribed by Elliott — and to care for Cleopatra. Ironically, Henry becomes a tourist artifact — mummified and sold as an antiquity! Becoming Cleopatra's lover, Elliott realizes he must get more elixir to finish her healing process. He has to find Ramses, who will decide what next to do. Cleopatra has difficulty in remembering who she is, and delights in killing.

Elliott leaves Cleopatra in the safe house with instructions to remain, but she goes out to explore in her confused way, stealing and murdering her way across Cairo. Ramses confesses all to Julie, but she makes him understand that it is not Cleopatra who has returned — just a copy; the soul is gone and only a thing remains. Ramses had not died, he is truly immortal; Cleopatra is just a mad automaton.

Elliott offers Ramses Cleopatra in exchange for the elixir. Fortunately, Ramses follows him to the hiding place, as Cleopatra attempts to kill her rescuer. Rescuing Elliott, Ramses forces the healing fluid into her mouth and completely heals the body. Making love to her, he realizes the mind is not healed though the flesh is.

Elliott is pleased to blame all the deaths and robberies on the missing Henry Stratford, and gets the authorities to relinquish all the confiscated passports so that they may leave Cairo. It only remains for the party to attend the opera before their departure. Cleopatra, having escaped from Ramses, is also preparing; she steals clothes for the opera ball and kills the shop assistant. Then she meets and seduces Alex. At the opera, Cleopatra tries to revenge herself on Ramses by killing Julie, whom Alex has told her about. She is pleased that Ramses has not given Julie the elixir — unaware that Julie has refused the offer — and that Julie can die. Fortunately, she is disturbed in the act, and by the time Ramses understands what has happened, she has vanished with Alex. Elliott understands the cruel game Cleopatra is playing with them; she will be at the ball following the opera. The confrontation is electric, but she escapes once more with Alex, motoring across the desert pursued by Ramses. The chase ends as Cleopatra's car is struck by a train and explodes. Alex is thrown clear — she, apparently, is destroyed.

Julie and Alex prepare to leave for London. She still refuses the elixir. Despite everything, Elliott still wishes to have it, to Ramses' distress. Later that day he finds that Ramses has granted his request. On the ship going to England, Julie decides to kill herself from the loneliness of being parted from her love, but he is there and saves her, persuading her to join him in immortality and everlasting love.

In Egypt, a young doctor ministers to a patient he is told has been taken, badly burned, from a train wreck, but as he sees her in the sunshine, he thinks the information must be wrong because she is so beautiful...

Anne Rice is better known for her vampire chronicles, but *The Mummy* is a splendid work. The character of Ramses is finely drawn and the tale is woven with a dream-like quality. "A fresh and powerful imagination — she makes us believe everything she sees" (*New York Times Book Review*). "Her voluptuous prose draws readers into an erotic landscape where the sensual delights are dark-edged, terrifying and utterly compelling" (*The Village Voice*).

The plot uses the theme she explores so well; the interplay of the immortal and their living brethren. Born in New Orleans in 1941, Anne Rice spent many years in San Francisco before returning to the city of her birth. Her first vampire novel, written to cope with the pain of losing a child in terrible circumstances, brought her to literary prominence. Those who wondered if she was a one-novel author were disabused of the notion by the appearance of more vampire tales, a novel about Italian castrati set in the eighteenth century, and a series of witch tales.

The Mummy remains for the time being a monolith on the subject, but the open end hopefully suggests other encounters with the characters. And the successful transfer of *Interview With a Vampire* to film has also led to the announcement that *The Mummy* will be filmed in the not too distant future: reportedly (*Entertainment Weekly*, May 31, 1991), Rice Struck a $3 million deal with 20th Century–Fox, and James Cameron has been slated to direct. Details may change, of course, but this is one project that the authors look forward to seeing upon completion. For the time being, speculation about the film makes a wonderful after dinner conversation. Who will be cast as the Mummy — certainly not any of the diminutive screen stars of today; Ramses *has* to be six feet plus— and gorgeous to look at too— or movies will not match the spell of the novel.

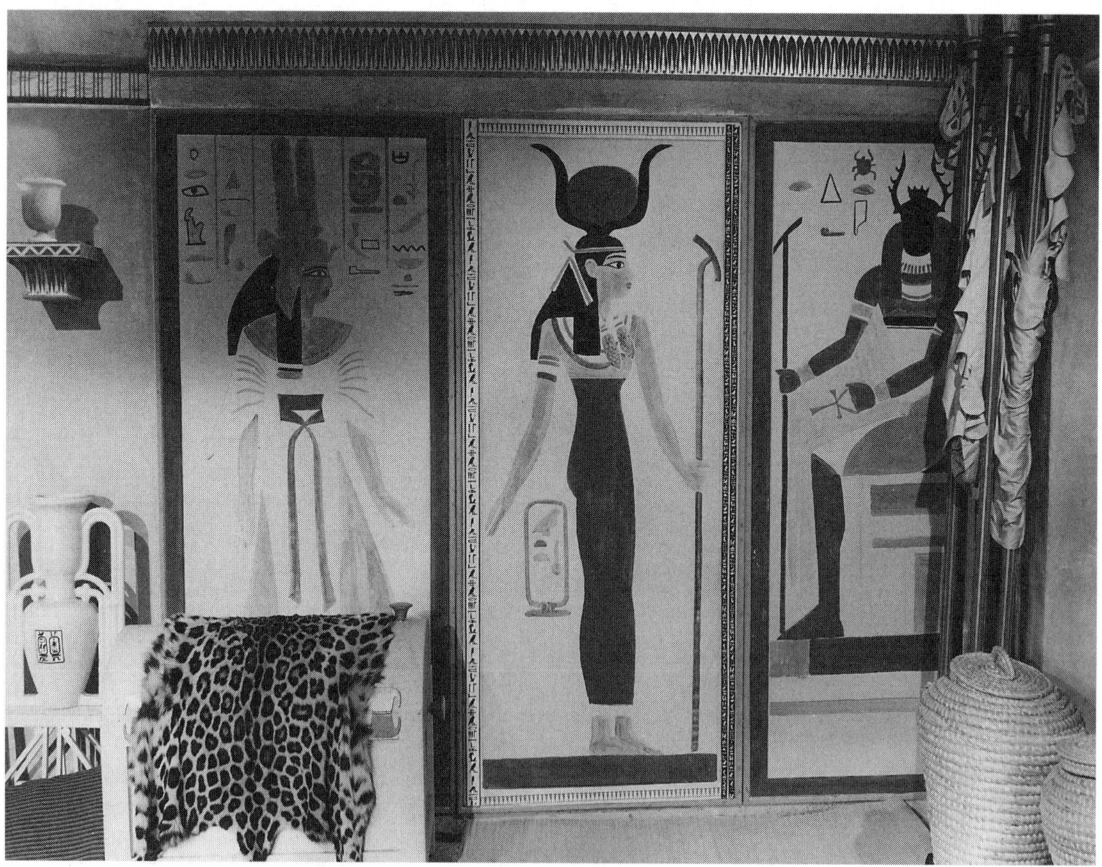

Inside the tomb in *The Curse of the Mummy's Tomb* (Hammer/Columbia, 1969).

That kind of presupposes someone new and fresh to the movie scene — and an instant star of the actor lucky enough to be cast — for it must be one of the biggest movies of its year. The fun comes from casting *the rest* of the players!

* * *

Children's Literature

Some time ago, educational research in the United States and Great Britain reached a somewhat disturbing conclusion; reading standards of young people were under close scrutiny and appeared to be slowly declining despite enormous efforts by educationalists and the vast majority of parents, supported vociferously by politicians of all persuasions. Coupled with a detailed study of their other leisure pursuits, the researchers concluded that television, sports, and electronic games were depleting the time youngsters spent reading.

A more detailed study of preferred reading materials showed another startling fact — that a majority of boys who elected to read, chose predominantly factual materials in support of their other interests and seldom indulged in fiction. As a result, it was felt their creative language faculties were being eroded along with their other reading skills. These conclusions led to a determined effort to provide reading materials that would woo young male readers into those previously unknown regions of print, and a new section of fiction emerged — exciting, chilling fantasy — the B movie of the print world! And to date, the ruse seems to be working well. Not only are boys turning to these stories, but girls are enjoying them too and both sexes are rediscovering the fun and escape to be found between the covers of that *"video made of paper,"* as one eight-year-old boy described a book (in conversation with author Sue Cowie).

Perhaps we can share some of the *genre* as pertains to our overall subject.

There's a Pharaoh In Our Bath! (by Jeremy Strong, illustrated by Nick Sharratt. Puffin Books, 1997)

In the town museum, Professor Jelly and Mr. Grimstone, head of the Ancient Egyptian collection, are preparing to disturb the mummy of one Sennapod, Pharaoh of the "Four-fifths Dynasty" who is reputed to have been buried with a map to his fabulous treasure. Jelly is disturbed by the Curse of Anubis that he reads on the sarcophagus, but Grimstone only cares for the treasure and eggs him on. The mummy is uncovered and begins to move before the greedy pair can unwrap him. They faint with fright and he wanders, hungry, into the night.

Enter the first of many cats which take a fond liking to the mummy, and make him feel a little less lost in this rainy, cold world to which he has woken. Enter, too, kind Tony Lightspeed, seller of ice cream, whose van is parked near the museum. Sennapod collapses with hunger and stress, so naturally Tony takes him home to his wife and children. (Well — wouldn't you?) The children, Ben and Carrie, are not surprised as their Dad is always playing knight errant: their mother is somewhat put out by their smelly guest but willing, as always, to help.

Sennapod initially is displeased with the Lightspeeds' lack of deference, but Mrs. Lightspeed's cheese sandwiches and solicitous care, together with the affection of Rustbucket, the family cat, and the children's kindness in making his royal regalia (from cardboard and felt tip pens) begin to mellow the Ancient One. He tells them that someone must have opened his coffin and read the curse; he explains that he was mummified by a new process where his intestines were not removed, neither was his brain, and the group concluded that persons unknown are after the treasure.

Meanwhile, Sennapod's royal cat Crusher of Worms — known to his royal master as Tiddles — has also awoken and given the two grave robbers the idea for a cruel plan to make the pharaoh give up the treasure map. Jelly discovers from ingenuous Mr. Lightspeed that Sennapod is staying with the family and the next shock is the arrival of a hieroglyphic ransom note — the map for the cat.

The Lightspeeds, Rustbucket, and Sennapod dash to the museum acquiring an army of cats en route. Mr. and Mrs. Lightspeed are soon captured, bound in old mummy wrappings, and imprisoned in mummy cases. The children don masks and pretend to be Egyptian gods to rescue their friend, ably assisted by the cats. A short battle ensues, the villains are routed, and all those endangered are rescued. Sennapod has his beloved cat, the police have the crooks, and the Lightspeeds have a new friend — the location of whose treasure remains a secret.

There's a Pharoah was voted seven out of ten in a straw poll of eight to ten year olds as a good story with plenty of excitement. Their principal, who also read it alongside them, was entertained and surprised at the amount of accurate Egyptology enshrined in the tale. The author, Jeremy Strong, who used to work in a bakery putting jam into 3,000 doughnuts per night, loves writing stories because it's "the only time you alone have complete control and can make anything happen." His stated ambition is to make his readers laugh.

The Goosebumps series of books whose motto on each volume reads " Reader beware — you're in for a scare!" are firm favorites with young readers. The formula contains a young hero/heroine with whom the reader identifies as the narrator, a good value system by which the majority of characters operate, and glorious— but ultimately defeated — baddies. Two volumes in the series currently have a place in our study.

The Curse of the Mummy's Tomb (by R.L. Stine, Scholastic Publications, 1994)

In *Curse*, the hero, Gabe, arrives in Egypt with his parents to visit his uncle Ben Hassad, a famous archaeologist. Both sets of Ben's grandparents were Egyptian and they had emigrated to America in the 1930s, so Ben is thrilled to be visiting the roots of his family and anxious to visit his uncle at the pyramids. His parents think it is unlikely to be allowed and Gabe, disappointed, turns to thoughts of food, drink and TV in disgust.

On arriving at the hotel, Gabe's parents are called away, having arranged that his uncle will take care of him. Gabe thinks that is fine, although it means he will have to suffer the company of his older (just) cousin Sari, whose intelligence, street-cred, and independence are almost unbearable.

Alone in the hotel, Gabe studies his lucky charm, a mummified child's hand called "the Summoner." It fails to comfort him as the door slowly opens to reveal — a mummy! Gabe gets ready to scream ... but the mummy laughs and so does Sari as she stands behind her Dad, the practical joking Egyptologist.

Gabe and Sari are tolerated by the team working in the pyramid as long as they do not get in the way. Uncle Ben believes he has found a burial room in Khufu's pyramid and the children hope to be allowed to be present when it is opened. In the meantime, they are taken to the dig where Gabe manages to get left behind whilst doing up his trainers.

Alone, he comes upon a sarcophagus and is brave enough to open it, only to be shocked to find Sari inside, laughing at him. Just then an extremely angry Ben finds them, cutting short their visit in fury. Well, what parent doesn't react in anger when first learning that their pride and joy has effectively put life and limb on the line? Sari diverts her father's ire by telling him how she had just scared the socks off Gabe and they all return to the hotel.

The following day the children are somewhat at a loss for something to do. Uncle Ben decides that they will tour the Cairo Museum whilst he attends a business meeting there, but as Gabe and Sari argue over breakfast cereals, the plans are changed. Two of Uncle Ben's workers have fallen mysteriously ill and have been hospitalized. He tells the children to remain in the hotel while he visits the hospital. After his departure, however, the two decide that it would be acceptable to go to the museum alone and set out on foot, having been told that they are a mere two streets away.

Initially they are delighted with the museum, with the mummies and the statues. Sari is surprised that the ancients appeared to be much smaller than she. Gabe goes into lurid detail — as only young boys can! — on how a mummy was prepared and turns Sari's stomach with his loving description. While Sari is trying to regain her equilibrium and retain her breakfast, Ahmed, one of her father's trusted workers, enters the room. He looks so angry and threatening that they decide to leave and rush to escape, only to find that he has them cornered.

Ahmed crossly asserts that Sari's Father has sent him to fetch them and they feel rather foolish for having run away, but when he insists that they travel the short distance in his car, they begin to have misgivings again. Caught in traffic, they use the pause to escape the car but become lost as they duck and dive through the streets to evade Ahmed. Finally jumping into a taxi, Sari asks the driver to take them to the hotel, only to hear him laugh and point to the other side of the street — they have found their way back quite accidentally.

Shortly after their return, a dazed Uncle Ben comes in, too preoccupied to listen to Sari's tale about Ahmed. His workers have been scared speechless by something they have seen in the tomb and he cannot explain it. Sari's words finally penetrate his worries, but he assures the pair that Ahmed's credentials are impeccable and that they are being silly. But when he decides that he must return to the pyramid, Sari insists that she and Gabe must go, too, as they are too fearful to remain in the hotel without him.

Arriving at the pyramid, Uncle Ben repeats the safety lecture and makes sure each child has the proper equipment to go down into the tunnels. Gabe checks the mummy hand in his pocket for luck while Sari looks down on his superstitious behavior. As he bends to tie up his trainer lace, Gabe is left behind in the tunnel and finds himself all alone in the darkness!

Walking quickly through the tunnels, anxiously seeking his relatives, Gabe is horrified to find the floor cracking beneath him — and then it suddenly breaks and down he falls. His torch reveals a hand — an arm — and then a body. A mummy. "Eyeless, mouthless, the bandaged face seemed to stare back at me, tense and ready, as if waiting for me to make the first move." The air in the room is foul, but as Gabe shines his torch around he realizes that he is in a chamber crammed with mummies and with the paraphernalia to create mummies. Moving carefully to explore the room, he comes upon an ancient but still sticky tar pit. The gravity of his plight suddenly hits home together with the conviction that something is not quite right ... some of the mummies are distinctly odd. Gabe grabs for his safety bleeper only to find that it has been smashed during his fall, and he is unable to call for help.

The smell, the darkness, the crunch of insects underfoot, and the realization of his peril push Gabe into panic. Waving his flashlight wildly, he realizes that it is not the floor that is moving but hordes of scorpions scurrying across it. Then hands suddenly pull him free of his tormentors — Sari's hands — followed by Sari's lecture on people who get lost and wander off when they were told not to. Gabe is almost too grateful for the rescue to object about the lecture — almost. She maintains that her father is really angry but Gabe insists that his uncle's anger will pass when he sees the mummy preparation chamber that his fall has uncovered.

Sari, for once, is impressed but puzzled about some of the mummies that are standing up against the wall. Everything her father has taught her about mummies feeds her conviction that these particular specimens are not quite right. Using her safety bleeper to summon her father, she and Gabe are aghast when Ahmed comes into the chamber instead.

Ahmed says that he had tried to warn the archaeologist about the curse, but that Ben would never listen. He says that they have violated the Sacred Preparation Chamber of the Priestess Khala who had decreed four thousand years before that unbelievers should never enter it on pain of death. Ahmed proudly tells how he has terrified the workforce but that his ploys have not made Ben abandon the dig. He therefore stands ready to carry out the Curse of the Priestess. The children suddenly understand why some of the mummies are strange — they are new mummies, victims of Khala's curse, mummified whilst still alive!

As Ahmed is quietly telling them that they sealed their fate by playing in the priestess's sarcophagus on the first day of their visit, a rope descends through the hole made by Gabe's fall, and down the rope comes Sari's father, surprised to find Ahmed also present. It takes a little while for him to understand what great danger they are all in, but he tries to talk to Ahmed in the hope of protecting the children. Ahmed, however, will not listen and simply adds that the archaeologist is now also doomed for having entered the room, deftly knocking him out as he speaks.

It is left to Gabe to try and protect Sari as Ahmed ignites the tar pit to prepare for their burials. To keep them out of his way, he shoves the pair into a huge mummy case beside the one where he had already deposited the unconscious Egyptologist. Sari is concerned about her father's ability to breathe inside the case — blanking out their imminent deaths. Sari's confession that she is afraid is a surprise to Gabe who tells her that he is too frightened to be frightened! They try to plan a way out but are scared witless by something moving inside the case with them.

Fortunately it's Uncle Ben who has managed to wriggle free and come to find them but their escape from the chamber remains the ultimate challenge.

As they make their way to the escape tunnel Ahmed returns. He has decided not to mummify them but to boil them in the tar pit instead. And he expects them to jump into the pit willingly. Gabe, aghast, hauls the mummy hand — the Summoner — from his pocket and holds it aloft.

> I can't explain what was going through my mind. I was so terrified, so overwhelmed with fear, that I was thinking a hundred things at once. Maybe I thought the mummy hand would distract Ahmed. Or interest him. Or confuse him. Or frighten him. Maybe I was just stalling for time. Or maybe I was unconsciously remembering the legend behind the hand that the kid at the garage sale had told me. The legend of why it was called the Summoner...

Initially, however, nothing happens. Then Ahmed screams that it is the hand of the priestess herself — at least that is what Gabe thinks he hears because at the same moment all the ancient mummies in the chamber begin to move towards them. Ahmed stares in disbelief — he throws his burning torch at the advancing army but the flames do not stop them. One ancient picks Ahmed up to fling him into the tar pit. The group is effectively rescued by the ancient ones! Ahmed struggles from the mummies' grasp and bolts down the escape tunnel. Gabe checks the Summoner, still clutched in his hand and when he looks up again at his cousin and uncle they are staring in disbelief at the mummies who are quietly at rest again in their original places. Uncle Ben's litany is *"We're okay. We're okay."* He's a scientist after all and is having trouble taking all the events in. He does shake Gabe's hand and formally thank him for his help though.

Over a celebration breakfast in the hotel the next morning, Uncle Ben is still finding the recent happenings difficult to accept but he urges Gabe to take great care of his talisman. Gabe, intent on scaring Sari, pretends to call up the ancient ones again and they both freeze as the door slowly opens.

Gabe's parents have come to take him back!

Going at a cracking pace, this story has a cliff-hanger at the end of every chapter and the young readers who sampled it thought it was a great idea to encourage them to read further! Reading like a literary version of a movie serial of the fifties, it held everyone's attention and interest, and even encouraged some of the class to attempt their own (much gorier!) versions of the original premise.

Return of the Mummy (by R.L. Stine, Scholastic Publications, 1995)

In *Return*, Gabe is back! One year older and alone he is on the plane to Cairo to visit his famous uncle, Egyptologist Ben Hassad. As the plane prepares to land, Gabe reflects gloomily that his cousin Sari will also probably be around.

The purpose of Gabe's visit is for him to share in the moment when his uncle opens the burial chamber that he has located in the pyramid, and Gabe finds the prospect thrilling — even worth having to cope with his thirteen year old cousin who, according to Gabe, is so competitive that she can make eating breakfast into a contest! However, he carries his talisman, the mummy hand named the Summoner, which always feels warm and comforting, so he's ready for anything. But as the plane descends, Gabe touches it for luck — and it is ice-cold!

Sari and Uncle Ben collect Gabe from the airport; Gabe gloomily reflects that Sari has not changed a bit but suddenly feels guilty about his ambivalence — after all, Sari has to go to boarding school because her mother died when she was a baby and her father is away working for a great deal of the time. Gabe realizes with chagrin that his lot is definitely the better one.

Traveling out into the desert, Gabe discovers that his new home is a canvas tent beside the pyramids. As they are all catching up on family gossip, Gabe and Sari get a fright as a walking mummy grabs at Uncle Ben, but then it laughs. The archaeologist gleefully tells the pair that the mummy is his friend John who is an actor doing a commercial for a new stickier bandage! The grown ups are still laughing at their gag as Sari tries to pass off her terror by maintaining that she was in on the joke. To make amends, Gabe is given a pendant of a scarab beetle set in amber — a gift that he loves and examines carefully as Uncle Ben goes off to get them cold drinks.

Later that night Gabe cannot sleep. He imagines that the scarab in the pendant is moving and tickling him, and then tries to calm down and get some sleep. Over breakfast they discuss the tomb. Uncle Ben believes he has found a cousin of Tut, one Prince Khor-Ra. Sari speculates on the possibility of jewels and other treasures but her father reminds her that most tombs were robbed before archaeologists ever found them. She also quietly apologizes to Gabe, confiding that she is worried about her father and the effect an empty tomb might have on his dreams. As they go to enter the pyramid, a voice calls out to them to stop.

The very beautiful young woman tells them that she is a reporter who has permission to cover the dig. Somewhat put out, Ben agrees that she can observe, but not publish without his agreement, and can take no photos. Smiling, she agrees, introduces herself as Nila Rahmad, and enters the pyramid with the rest of the party. Nila, it emerges, has a pendant like Gabe's but hers is empty. Much better than wearing a dead bug round one's neck, according to Sari.

Once again, Gabe gets lost in the tunnels— his attention had wandered while he listened to his uncle trying to impress the reporter, speculating about adults and crushes. Only this time he falls through a wall, landing in a mass of spiders that crawl all over him. And we all know what Gabe thinks of insects.... In panic he thinks he sees a snake coming down towards him, but it is, of course, a rope lowered by Ben, who rescues him. Checking on his talisman for fear it has been crushed by his fall, Gabe is surprised when Nila asks if it is the Summoner. She tells him that she has studied a great deal but as Ben and she discuss its authenticity, the hand stretches and curls in Gabe's palm and he wonders if it is an omen.

Finally the day arrives; Sari is excited about jewels, Gabe just hopes the mummy is intact. Nila is soothingly full of admiration for Ben who allows her to photograph the breaking of the tomb seal for posterity. The opening is rudely interrupted by Omar Fielding, Ben's partner, who maintains that he had found a curse left by the prince and wants to delay the dig. Ben, ever the scientist, casts aside the fears, offers the workforce the chance to leave, which they decline, and opens the tomb. He does, however, joke that he will go in first and if he doesn't come back they can tell Fielding that he was right! Somehow they all tumble in together — but the tomb is bare!

Gabe waits for his Uncle's disappointment but Ben is already pressing on past this false chamber to the real one behind it. He cannot open the door except for a small crack and they settle down to wait. Neither can he resist teasing the children by telling them that he has made a big mistake — and as their hearts sink he begins to laugh and tell them that the tomb is bigger and more important than he had thought. There are the jewels Sari dreamed of, and more importantly, Prince Khor-Ru in his mummy case, intact. Fielding arrives with a police guard to protect the contents and then rushes away to publicize the find. The rest, content, have dinner under the stars. Nila congratulates Ben, and Sari asks her father about the superstitions for bringing a mummy to life. Indulgent in his joy at the find, Ben tells Sari the six words that are supposed to have the power to revive the dead. They also laugh about reanimating Khor-Ru for Nila to get a picture and a scoop.

When Ben and Nila have gone, Sari asks Gabe if he thinks her father and Nila are attracted to each other, but Gabe is more interested in trying out the incantation to revive the mummy — just to scare Sari. He imagines all the movies he has seen and carries out the ritual before a nonplused Sari but they both jump in fright when something comes!

But the something is Fielding, returned from his errand. He is looking for Ben whom he apparently forces to go with him to the chamber. When Fielding emerges alone, the children are sure that he has hurt Ben. They search all over the dig but cannot find him. In the chamber they discover Ben in Khor-Ru's mummy case to their horror. Then they wonder where the mummy is if Ben is in its case — and turn to find it slowly advancing on them. "The mummy blocked our path to the doorway. Moving stiffly, awkwardly, the ancient corpse dragged itself closer.... Its bandaged feet scraped over the floor sending up dark clouds of dust as it moved heavily towards us. A sour smell rose over the room. The smell of a four-thousand-year-old corpse coming back to life." As Gabe reaches for the Summoner for protection he is horrified to find it gone. He persuades Sari that they must outrun the mummy and summon help for her father. Nila arrives but not to rescue them. She has the mummy hand and is angry about their interference. She calls the mummy to her. "Come to me, my brother!"

Nila is the sister of Khor-Ru and has waited all the centuries to rescue him from the tomb. She says that the power of the Summoner, together with the ritual, made the resurrection possible. Then she orders the mummy to destroy the children. The mummy begins to obey but then lurches past the children to grab its sister's throat. "*Let me rest in peace.*" Gabe tries to stop the mummy's attack on Nila but is thrown off. His pendant is torn off and smashed — and as it is destroyed so Nila wails. Her soul has been protected as the scarab in the amber but now she is dying. Her body goes to dust and all that remains is a scarab beetle scuttling away from her clothes.

When Uncle Ben regains consciousness, all is as it was. The children try to explain but he tells them that he saw Nila carry out the ritual and revive her brother. He says that both he and Fielding had become suspicious of her when she let slip some facts about the ritual over dinner, facts that they hadn't passed on. He explained that, far from forcing him into the tomb, Fielding was taking him in pursuit of Nila. They were too late to stop her and she knocked him out as Fielding ran for help. He came to his senses just in time to see her turn into the beetle.

At that moment Fielding arrives with reinforcements, but they decide to tell him that Nila had escaped. Gabe is again the hero—he has saved the day and Sari must listen to his crowing. She does comment though on the fact that she expects the beetle to be after him for revenge. Gabe goes happily to bed at the end of his adventure, laughing at his cousin. And is bitten by a beetle!

This adventure of Gabe and Sari was the favorite of the two books among the ten and eleven year olds who read it. The plot is a bit meatier than *Curse*, and the readers felt they knew the main characters as friends at the start of the story. As a follow-up, the classroom curtains were closed, the lights turned off, and on a dark November afternoon, by candlelight, their Principal read them Howard Carter's account of the opening of Tutankhamun's tomb!

Ladybird Horror Classics — The Mummy (Ladybird Books Ltd., 1985)

Part of the series of classic horror stories abridged for young persons, *The Mummy* tells a simplified version of *Lot 249* by Sir Arthur Conan Doyle with wonderfully evocative illustrations. It retains the flavor of Doyle and most ten and eleven year olds who read it thought it was quite difficult, though they liked the plot. Some students recognized the story from a segment of a compilation horror movie that they had seen on TV — a movie whose rating should have precluded them from watching!

Mummies Alive! Official Annual (1998)

For those of us who like to keep up with our TV heroes in print, *Mummies Alive!* is nicely produced A4 hardback with colorful, dynamic graphics. The book contains a reprise of the genesis of the mummies, two complete stories, some quizzes, and a Who's Who of the characters to refresh your memory or clue you in if you happened to miss the movie or the pilot.

In the first story the archvillain Scarab, still disguised as the world's richest man, archaeologist Harris Stone, attempts to trap the reborn pharaoh — now 12 year old San Franciscan Presley Carnovan — by setting up an exhibition of his previous incarnation's belongings in the museum where Presley's mother works.

Presley feels drawn to the artifacts and hides in his own sarcophagus when attacked by Scarab's assistants, the Shabtis. Hearing his cries for help, his guardians, the armored mummies, invoke their spirit selves and break out of their sarcophagi to protect him.

Presley finds it harder to believe that he is Pharaoh reborn than that his new friends just happen to be 3500 years old. They introduce themselves and their various talents. One, surprisingly, is a girl (Surprising? Her name's Nefer, which means 'beautiful' in Egyptian!! I thought this series listed researchers in the credits. Oh well...). They are smuggled home by Presley, whose mother is fortunately nearly always at work, otherwise she would probably notice four large mummies and a mummified cat around her house. Scarab tries several dastardly plots to draw Presley and his guardians into the open. All involve exciting fights and the good guys always win — eventually. Presley's dad, by the way, came from Memphis— only not the one the mummies know and love!

In the second story, Scarab is getting desperate as his last lifetime (he had fifty) is ebbing away. To achieve immortality he must kill Presley and take his life force, and to achieve this end he calls the spirit of Geb from the next dimension through the Gate of the West, which just happens to run parallel with the Golden Gate. The spectral gate opens at sundown each day, allowing all manner of evil things through if the portents are right.

Geb is very powerful, bringing on an earthquake with his arrival. The Mummies know it is he, but Presley is very patient explaining about earthquakes, tectonic plates, and epicenters— it just so happens that they are *all* right. Geb, however, is very short on brain power and believes Scarab when he says that Rapses/Presley has called him to the world. Presley understands that, unless he goes to the gate, Geb will destroy the city and perhaps the world during an upcoming solar eclipse. The Mummies gather all their strength to fight Geb and Scarab. Scarab captures Presley and makes him recite an incantation for the transfer of souls as the eclipse begins. But the eclipse brings the dusk, the gate opens, and Geb arrives angrily. Presley saucily asks Scarab to admit that *he* called Geb, and Scarab happily brags about it as the huge creature rises in the water behind him. Geb drags Scarab through the gate, inadvertently rescuing Presley and the Mummies in the process. But Scarab will be back…

Children from seven to ten have reported enjoying this book enormously. They particularly like the Who's Who and have said it would help them to write their own stories on the central theme. It is, of course, a formula — format and Ancient Egypt.

Conclusion

Our dalliance with Mummies almost over—we ask, what next? The millennium has changed but the fascination with mummies goes on unchecked. A look through the TV guide will offer you world-class Egyptologists in your own home, keeping you up-to-date with the latest finds, digs, and theories. Go into any large museum shop and you can happily go home with videos to study to your heart's content. Your hard earned cash will, through your purchases, help in the upkeep of the museums and finance their future work. Or you can log on to the Net and be even more quickly updated. with Rosalie David's Manchester Mummy Project or Kent Weeks's work on KV5.

The sheer hard work comes home very powerfully when you can participate like this. One's old image of the Egyptologists neatly turned out and politely inquiring "Can you see anything? Yes—wonderful things!" is refocused to Weeks inching his way through tiny tunnels in the cement-hard debris of KV5 so as not to disturb the stratigraphy, with pads on knees and elbows to protect against the sharp limestone shards, hardhats because the roof is known to be unsafe, and flashlights because the electricity supply cannot reach that far yet.

> At this point, my feet were atop the debris in chamber 3, my stomach fifty centimeters lower, beneath the top of the door. My head was twisted painfully into the tiny space between the fill and the ceiling of the next chamber, sharp stones cut at my cheek, and fine silts turned to mud on my sweat-covered face. I was bent backwards nearly in a U-shape. My back scraped the lintel, my elbows the sides of the door. My hair caught in the many fine cracks in the ceiling. As I tried to move through farther, I got stuck. My feet and hands could find no purchase, and I couldn't crawl either forward or back. My flashlight was fading, the air was hot and humid, the silence total. Catharine had vanished into a side chamber, and Mohammed was somewhere behind me. For the first time in my life I was hit with an attack of claustrophobia [Weeks, 1998].

Alongside the serious works, is a proliferation of the slightly "kookier" stratum including mysterious, older, forgotten races such as the architects of Ancient Egyptian society, prophecies hidden in jewelry in Tut's tomb, and the "matching" of historical Egyptians with Old Testament heroes to name a few.

And our old friend—the Curse—still trundles merrily along. In *The Express* newspaper, February 15, 1999 a report by Nic Fleming begins: "When Peter Aldridge started seeing jewel-shaped blue lights in his

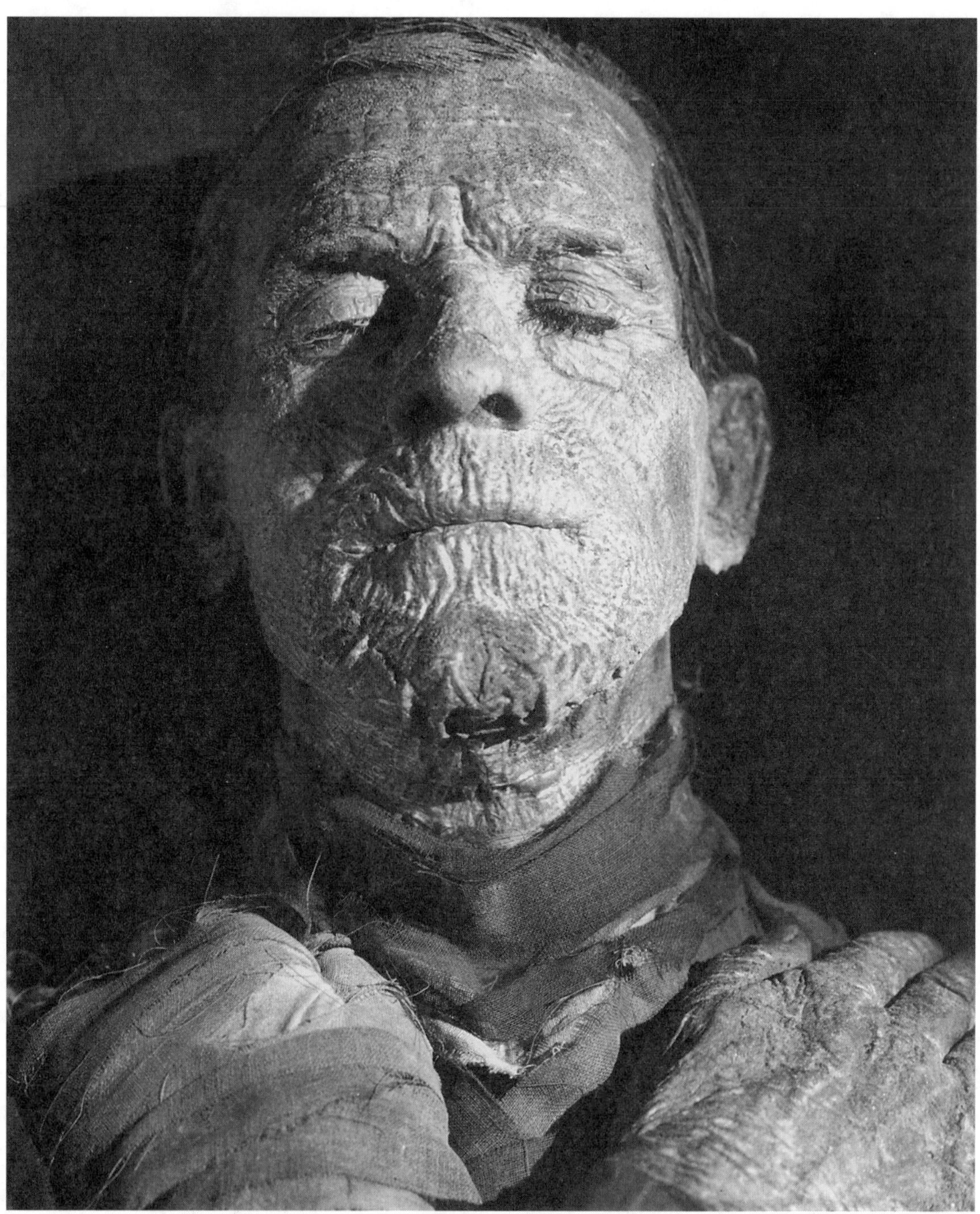

Boris Karloff in Jack Pierce's masterful makeup in *The Mummy* (Universal, 1932).

garden, his wife told him he might be going crazy. Now he's merely terrified after being told they appear above the final resting place of a cursed ancient Egyptian Mummy." The house, Low Hall, in Scalby, North Yorkshire, now belonging to the National Union of Mineworkers who use it as a rest home for retired members, was once the home of chocolate tycoon Joseph Rowntree whose son John brought the mummy home from a trip to Egypt in 1904. Having displayed it in his library on his return, John died — at 37 — and his relatives, who felt he had been the victim of a curse, buried the mummy in the garden. John's daughter, 98 year old Jean, says the mummy was the only thing in her childhood to cause her mortal fear. Mr. Aldridge refuses to dig up the mummy for fear of falling foul of the curse!

Meanwhile in *The Times* on February 18, 1999, Lord Porchester, heir to the present Earl of Carnarvon, talks about the Curse as a promo for a TV program about to be aired in which he retraces his great-grandfather's footsteps just weeks before his wedding. He is emphatic that he does not believe in the Curse and asserts "*As for great-grandfather he was just careless. He got a mosquito bite but, being the typical laid-back Englishman, he refused treatment — even iodine.... He just thought he was going to get better!*" Porchester's grandfather was a believer and locked up all the antiquities in the house; when the present Earl discovered them they were put on display at Highclere. Lord Porchester, on seeing the piece of blue jewelry thought it had been made in Taiwan though in reality it was 3000 years old!

And at the British Museum, where the Egyptian Galleries have been renewed to celebrate the Millennium, they still get inquiries about "the mummy on the Titanic." Part of its mummy *case* is on display as they patiently explain, because the mummy went down with the rest of the cargo but as dear Tania Watkins — who also patiently deals with authors! — remarks wryly," If it gets one more person to come to the museum and then hopefully come back again...it's worth it!"

Appendix: Chronological List of Mummy Films

Year	Title	Country of Origin
1900	*The Mummy*	(France)
1901	*The Haunted Curiosity Shop*	(U.S.)
1909	*The Mummy of King Ramsees*	(France)
1911	*The Mummy*	(U.K.)
1912	*The Vengeance of Egypt*	(France)
1913	*The Egyptian Mummy*	(U.S.)
1914	*The Egyptian Mummy*	(U.S.)
1915	*The Avenging Hand*	(U.K.)
1918	*Die Augen der Mumie Ma*	(Germany)
1919	*The Beetle*	(U.K.)
1926	*Mummy Love*	(U.S.)
1932	*The Mummy*	(U.S.)
1936	*Kalkoot*	(India)
	Mummy's Boys	(U.S.)
1939	*We Want Our Mummy*	(U.S.)
1940	*The Mummy's Hand*	(U.S.)
1942	*The Mummy's Tomb*	(U.S.)
1944	*The Mummy's Curse*	(U.S.)
1945	*The Mummy's Ghost*	(U.S.)
1948	*Mummy's Dummies*	(U.S.)
1949	*The Mummy's Foot*	(U.S.)
	G Men vs. the Black Dragon	(U.S.)
1953	*Haram Alek*	(Egypt)

Year	Title	Country of Origin
1955	*Abbott and Costello Meet the Mummy*	(U.S.)
1957	*The Pharaoh's Curse*	(U.S.)
	La Momia	(Mexico)
	La Momia Contra el Robot Humano	(Mexico)
1958	*Isabel, a Dream*	(Italy)
	Curse of the Faceless Man	(U.S.)
1959	*The Mummy*	(U.K.)
	La Maldición de la Momia	(Mexico)
1963	*Kiss Me Quick*	(U.S.)
1964	*Curse of the Mummy's Tomb*	(U.K.)
	Las Luch Adoras contra la Momia	(Mexico)
	Face of the Screaming Werewolf	(Mexico/U.S.)
1965	*Orgy of the Dead*	(U.S.)
1967	*The Mummy and the Curse of the Jackals* (not released?)	(U.S.)
1970	*Assignment Terror*	(U.S.)
	El Hombre que Vinó del Ummo	(Mexico)
	Santo y Blue Demon Contra los Monstruos	(Mexico)
1971	*Santo en la Vengenza de la Momia*	(Mexico)
	Blood from the Mummy's Tomb	(U.K.)
1972	*La Momias de Guanajuato*	(Mexico)
	El Castillo de las Momias de Guanajuto	(Mexico)
	Lips of Blood	(France)
1973	*La Venganza de la Momia*	(Mexico)
1980	*The Awakening*	(U.S.)
1981	*Dawn of the Mummy*	(U.S./Italy)
	The National Mummy	(Spain)
1982	*Timewalker*	(U.S.)
1987	*The Monster Squad*	(U.S.)
1988	*Waxwork*	(U.S.)
1990	*Tales from the Darkside*	(U.S.)
1993	*The Mummy Lives*	(U.S.)
1996	*Mummy Dearest*	(U.S./New Zealand)
1997	*Under Wraps*	(U.S.)
	Buffy and the Inca Mummy	(U.S.)
	Bram Stoker's Legend of the Mummy	(U.S.)
1998	*Mummies Alive!— The Legend Begins*	(U.S.)
	Talos the Mummy	(U.K.)
	The Mummy	(U.S.)
	The Eternal aka *Trance*	(U.S.)
	The All New Adventures of Laurel and Hardy: For Love or Mummy	(U.S.)
1999	*Bram Stoker's Legend of the Mummy 2*	(U.S.)
2001	*The Mummy Returns*	(U.S.)

Selected Bibliography

Adams, Barbara. *Egyptian Mummies.* Shire Publications, 1984.

Andrews, Nigel. *Horror Films.* Admiral Books, 1986.

Aylesworth, Thomas G. *Monster and Horror Movies.* Bison Books, 1986.

Bonaparte, Napoleon. *Description de l'Egypte.* Benedikt Taschen, 1994 edition.

Boot, Andy. *Fragments of Fear.* Creation Books, 1996.

Brier, Bob. *Egyptian Mummies: Unraveling the Secrets of an Ancient Art.* Michael O'Mara Books, 1996.

_____. *The Encyclopedia of Mummies.* Facts on File Inc., 1998.

Brunas, John, Michael Brunas, and Tom Weaver. *Universal Horrors.* McFarland, 1988.

Budge, Ernest A. Wallis. *The Mummy: Funeral Rites and Customs in Ancient Egypt.* Senate Publications, Studio Editions, 1995.

Carter, Howard. *The Tomb of Tutankhamen.* Sphere Books, 1972.

Cone, Polly (ed.). *Wonderful Things: The Discovery of Tutankhamun's Tomb.* Metropolitan Museum of Art, 1976.

Cushing, Peter. *Past Forgetting: Memoirs of the Hammer Years.* Weidenfeld and Nicolson, 1988.

David, Rosalie (ed.). *Mystery of the Mummies: The Story of the Manchester University Investigation.* Book Club Associates, 1978.

_____, and E. Tapp (eds.). *The Mummy's Tale.* Michael O'Mara Books, 1992.

Dee, Jonathan. *Chronicles of Ancient Egypt.* Collins and Brown, 1998.

Del Vecchio, Deborah, and Tom Johnson. *Peter Cushing: The Gentle Man of Horror.* McFarland, 1992.

Dudnand, Francoise, and Roger Lichtenberg. *Mummies: A Journey Through Eternity.* Thames and Hudson, 1994.

El Mahdy, Christine. *Mummies, Myth and Magic in Ancient Egypt.* Thames and Hudson, 1989.

Everson, William K. *Classics of the Horror Film.* Citadel Press, 1974.

Frank, Alan. *Horror Films.* Hamlyn Publishing Group, 1977.

_____. *Horror Movies.* Octopus Books, 1974.

_____. *Monsters and Vampires.* Octopus Books, 1976.

Frayling, Christopher. *The Face of Tutankhamun.* Faber and Faber, 1992.

Gardner Wilkinson, Sir J. *The Ancient Egyptians: Their Life and Customs* (Omnibus ed.). Studio Editions, 1988.

Gifford, Denis. *A Pictorial History of Horror Movies.* Hamlyn Publishing Group, 1973.

Halliwell, Leslie. *The Dead That Walk.* Grafton Books, 1986.

Hamilton-Patterson, James, and Carol Andrews. *Mummies: Death and Life in Ancient Egypt.* William Collins Sons and Co., 1978.

Hardy, Phil (ed.). *The Aurum Film Encyclopedia,* Vol. III: "Horror." Aurum Press, 1985.

Hobson, Christine. *Exploring the World of the Pharaohs.* Thames and Hudson, 1987.

Hutchinson, Tom, and Roy Pickard. *Horrors: A History of Horror Movies.* Hamlyn, 1983.

James, T. G. H. *Howard Carter: The Path to Tutankhamun.* Kegan Paul International, 1992.

Johnson, Tom, and Deborah Del Vecchio. *Hammer Films: An Exhaustive Filmography.* McFarland, 1996.

Ladybird Horror Classics: The Mummy. Ladybird, 1985.

McCarty, John. *The Modern Horror Film*. Citadel Press, 1990.

Meikle, Denis. *A History of Horrors: The Rise and Fall of the House of Hammer*. Scarecrow Press, 1996.

Miller, Mark A. *Christopher Lee and Peter Cushing and Horror Cinema*. McFarland, 1995.

Moore, Darrell. *The Best, Worst and Most Unusual Horror Films*. Publications International, 1983.

Mummies Alive! The Official Annual. Grandreams, 1998.

Norman, Bruce. *Footsteps: Nine Archaeological Journeys of Romance and Discovery*. BBC Books, 1987.

Partridge, Robert B. *Faces of Pharaohs: Royal Mummies and Coffins from Ancient Thebes*. Rubicon Press, 1994.

Perl, Lila. *Mummies, Tombs and Treasure: Secrets of Ancient Egypt*. Hodder and Stoughton, 1988.

Pirie, David. *A Heritage of Horror: The English Gothic Cinema, 1946–1972*. Gordon Fraser, 1973.

Reeves, Nicholas, and John H. Taylor. *Howard Carter Before Tutankhamun*. British Museum Press, 1992.

Reeves, Nicholas, and Richard H. Wilkinson. *The Complete Valley of the Kings: Tombs and Treasures of Egypt's Greatest Pharaohs*. Thames and Hudson, 1996.

Romer, John. *Ancient Lives: The Story of the Pharaohs' Tombmakers*. Weidenfeld and Nicolson, 1984.

_____. *Romer's Egypt: A New Light on the Civilization of Ancient Egypt*. Michael Joseph, 1982.

Shaw, Ian, and Paul Nicholson. *British Museum Dictionary of Ancient Egypt*. British Museum Press, 1995.

Spencer, A. J. *Death in Ancient Egypt*. Penguin Books, 1982.

Steedman, Scott. *Pockets: Ancient Egypt*. A Dorling Kindersley Book, 1995.

Stine, R. L. *Goosebumps: The Curse of the Mummy's Tomb*. Scholastic, 1994.

_____. *Goosebumps: Return of the Mummy*. Scholastic, 1994.

Strong, Jeremy. *There's a Pharaoh in Our Bath!* Puffin Books, 1997.

Taylor, John H. *Unwrapping a Mummy*. British Museum Press, 1995.

Tyldesley, Joyce. *Hatchepsut the Female Pharaoh*. Viking, 1996.

Weeks, Kent R. *The Lost Tomb: The Greatest Discovery at the Valley of the Kings Since Tutankhamun*. Weidenfeld and Nicolson, 1998.

Weisbrot, Robert. *Hercules: The Legendary Journeys: The Official Companion*. Doubleday, 1998.

White, J. E. Manchip. *Ancient Egypt, Its Culture and History*. Constable and Co., 1970.

Various editions of *KMT: A Modern Journal of Ancient Egypt*. KMT Communications.

Various editions of *Egyptian Archaeology: The Bulletin of the Egypt Exploration Society*. Egyptian Exploration Society.

Magazines

Little Shoppe of Horrors. Edited and published by Richard Klemensen.

The Horror Elite. Edited and published by Cowie/Manning.

Dark Terrors. Edited and published by Mike Murphy.

Shivers. Published by Visual Imagination Ltd.

Monsters from the Vault. Published by Monsters from the Vault Inc.

Hammer Horror. Published by Marvel Comics UK Ltd.

Midnight Marquee. Edited and published by Gary and Sue Svehla.

The House of Hammer. Published by Top Sellers Ltd.

Halls of Horror. Published by Top Sellers Ltd.

Starburst. Published by Visual Imagination.

Index

Numbers in *italics* represent photographs.